MOZART

MOZART

AN INTRODUCTION TO
THE MUSIC, THE MAN, AND THE MYTHS

ROYE E. WATES

AMADEUS PRESS
AN IMPRINT OF HAL LEONARD CORPORATION

Published in 2010 by Amadeus Press
An Imprint of Hal Leonard Corporation
7777 West Bluemound Road
Milwaukee, WI 53213

Trade Book Division Editorial Offices
33 Plymouth St., Montclair, NJ 07042

Illustration credits: p. 6: Bildarchiv Preussischer Kulturbesitz/Art Resource, NY; p. 12: Drawing (ca. 1777), Erich Lessing/Art Resource, NY; p. 19 (left): Painting (1819) by Barbara Krafft, Erich Lessing/Art Resource, NY; p. 19 (right): Painting (1789) by Joseph Lange, Alinari/Art Resource, NY; p. 22 (left): Painting (ca. 1770) by Peter Anton Lorenzoni or F. J. Degle, Erich Lessing/Art Resource, NY; p. 22 (right): Erich Lessing/Art Resource, NY; p. 25: Painting (1763) by Louis Carrogis Carmontelle, Erich Lessing/Art Resource, NY; p. 26 (left): Scala/Art Resource, NY; p. 26 (right): Erich Lessing/Art Resource, NY; p. 30: Bildarchiv Preussischer Kulturbesitz/Art Resource, NY; p. 33: Painting (1798) by Hans Hansen, Erich Lessing/Art Resource, NY; p. 35: Erich Lessing/Art Resource, NY; p. 37: Courtesy of Anne K. Austin; p. 39: Etching (1799) by Francisco de Goya y Lucientes, © The Trustees of the British Museum/Art Resource, NY; p. 42: Painting (1769) by Pompeo Batoni, Erich Lessing/Art Resource, NY; p. 67: Painting (1777) by Saverio della Rosa, Erich Lessing/Art Resource, NY; p. 70: Courtesy of Anne K. Austin; p. 72: Photo by Hermann Buresch, Bildarchiv Preussischer Kulturbesitz/Art Resource, NY; p. 89: Painting (ca. 1780) by Johann Michael Greiter, Erich Lessing/Art Resource, NY; p. 95: Etching (1782) by Johann Baptist Klauber after Johann Franz van der Schlichten, Bildarchiv Preussischer Kulturbesitz/Art Resource, NY; p. 100: Engraving (1776) by J. E. Nilson. Photo by Gjon Mill/Time Life Pictures/Getty Images; p. 123: Painting by Josef Ziegler, Erich Lessing/Art Resource, NY; p. 124: Engraving by Carl Philipp Schallhas, © Wien Museum; p. 140: Photo by Popperfoto/Getty Images; p. 144: Erich Lessing/Art Resource, NY; pp. 182–183: © The British Library Board. Zweig 63, ff. 0v-1; p. 187: Courtesy of Anne K. Austin; p. 208: Painting (ca. 1784) attributed to Ignaz Unterberger, Erich Lessing/Art Resource, NY; p. 231: Erich Lessing/Art Resource, NY; p. 235: JAKUB SUKUP/AFP/Getty Images; p. 295: Courtesy of Anne K. Austin; p. 299: Courtesy of Anne K. Austin.

Printed in the United States of America

Book design by Michael Kellner

Library of Congress Cataloging-in-Publication Data
Wates, Roye E.
  Mozart : an introduction to the music, the man, and the myths / Roye E. Wates.
    p. cm.
  Includes bibliographical references and index.
  ISBN 978-1-57467-189-6
  1. Mozart, Wolfgang Amadeus, 1756-1791. 2. Composers—Austria—Biography. I. Title.
  ML410.M9W27 2010
  780.92--dc22
  [B]
                                    2010032288

www.amadeuspress.com

CONTENTS

ILLUSTRATIONS

PREFACE

Mozart: An Introduction to the Music, the Man, and the Myths is for lovers of music who may know relatively little about either Mozart or classical music, but who are curious about both and eager to learn more. While the book makes no pretense at completeness—some subjects are treated cursorily, others not at all—by the end of it, I believe that you will be able to listen knowledgeably to all the chief forms of classical music, having acquired this skill through guided listening to twenty of Mozart's compositions; and that you will know more about him as both man and musician than many professional musicians do.

The shape of the book is largely chronological, interweaving history with biography and musical analysis geared to the nonmusician. Chapter 1 sketches basic cultural and biographical background, in the process opening up the shockingly large number of myths and legends that becloud our understanding of Mozart. As you'll quickly discover, he was a quite complex and fascinating man. Chapter 2 describes his childhood as a musical prodigy, touring Europe's major cities and courts from the time he was six.

Our study of his music begins in chapter 3, with explanations of characteristic musical designs used in instrumental works of his time— variation form, minuet form, rondo form, sonata form—each illustrated with examples from his compositions. Chapters 4, 5, and 6 trace his life and music through the three major periods of his adulthood: his futile journey to Mannheim and Paris in search of a job; his painful return to Salzburg; and his final decade in Vienna, where he died, quite suddenly, at thirty-five. By the end of chapter 6 we will have explored examples of his work in every major genre of that era: opera, concerto, symphony, chamber music, and church music. Chapter 7 chronicles his last year, ending with a discussion of the causes of his death and the manner of his burial. Chapter 8 outlines principal themes dramatized in that brilliant though largely fictitious movie *Amadeus*.

The book concludes with Excerpts of "Letters from the Childhood Tours," "Important People in Mozart's Life," "Building a Portfolio of Recordings," "What Should I Listen to Next?," "Notes for Musical Beginners," a glossary of musical terms, and an annotated bibliography.

Musical terms are defined and explained as the need for them arises in particular contexts, in addition to their definitions in the glossary of musical terms and often in "Notes for Musical Beginners" as well. Except where otherwise noted, all translations are my own.

I am deeply grateful to the friends, colleagues, and students who have helped to make this book much better than it would otherwise be. The distinguished writer and critic John J. Clayton has blessed me with friendship and support for decades, sharing his sensitive appreciation of music and offering his peerless editorial judgment on matters great and small. My Viennese Mozart friend Bruce Cooper Clarke not only cast a keen eye over initial drafts of this book and provided a great many criticisms and suggestions, but also went to superhuman lengths to locate a crucial illustration. Volkmar Braunbehrens, whose *Mozart in Vienna 1781–1791* is my favorite Mozart biography, offered warm appraisals of early drafts while also graciously pointing out historical errors; since that time, he has shared with me several extremely informative unpublished talks and essays. Richard Dyer, Dorothy Jones, Kathryn Libin, Stephanie Nelson, the late Craig Smith, and Jane Stevens read portions of the manuscript and recommended important additions or revisions. Conductor Susan Davenny Wyner and Mozart expert Dexter Edge have each given the final manuscript a detailed and thorough reading and offered a host of invaluable corrections and suggestions. William Lautzenheiser worked tirelessly to help prepare the book's first draft several years ago. Amy Feather, a radiant singer of Mozart's arias who is also a graphic designer, improved the layout of the second draft, and Anne K. Austin has given her time and considerable talents to shaping more recent ones, including the creation of illustrations for this publication. I am grateful for the editorial assistance of Abby Love Smith during the summer of 2008 and for expert editing by my Mozart colleague Elizabeth Seitz in 2009. Thanks also to the Boston University Music Library and its superb and warmly helpful head librarian, Holly Mockovak; to the staff of CAS Computing Services at Boston University and its director, Brian Anderson; to Frances Whistler and David Jones for their wise and generous counsel on matters related to publication; to my ever-helpful and hard-working office assistant, Kyle Sauer; and to the boundless creativity of my literary agent, Nancy Rosenfeld.

Amadeus Press has been a joy to work with throughout the many months of preparing the manuscript for publication. My warmest thanks to John Cerullo, publisher; Carol Flannery, editorial director; Jessica Burr, editor for this book; and Iris Bass, copy editor. The book has benefited in countless ways from their unfailing helpfulness, resourcefulness, and, above all, their patience.

Finally, a special word of gratitude to the scores of current and former students and adult auditors in my nonmajor Mozart class at Boston University, who each year have shared their reactions to successive drafts of the book. My hope is that this present version has taken the fullest possible advantage of these and all other suggestions; to whatever extent it has failed to do so, I offer my embarrassed apologies.

R. E. W.
Boston, May 2010

1

SEARCHING FOR MOZART

WHY THIS BOOK? SOURCES, MYTHS, AND A MOVIE

Why write a book such as this one, when there are already so many Mozart biographies on the market? For the simple reason that, while there are excellent studies of individual aspects or periods of Mozart's life and of certain works or groups of works, what we do not have—incredible as this may sound—is a reliable biography for people who are not already fairly familiar with his life, his music, and the cultural milieu of the eighteenth century, and who perhaps also don't know how to read music.[1] The lack of such a book seems strange when you consider these three factors:

- Mozart is extremely well known and has been for more than two centuries.
- His music is not only published and recorded, but played all over the world and instantly accessible on the Internet.
- There is vast primary documentation about him, including, above all, more than a thousand letters, hundreds of them written by Mozart himself.

So why isn't there such a book? The reasons are both numerous and complex, and the question deserves to be answered point by point.

Mozart Is Extremely Well Known

There is no other composer of the distant past about whom we know so many facts, and none with whom the average person is so familiar. Many people who know very little about classical music have seen *Amadeus*—either Peter Shaffer's play or the Milos Forman–Peter Shaffer movie, both of which are

---

1. See the annotated bibliography at the end of this book for comments on books about Mozart in English.

brilliant despite their staggering factual inaccuracies. (I separate the two because they differ in many respects. In this book, reference will always be to the film, because it is far more widely known than the stage play.) Most of us have grown up with associations of one sort or another about Mozart, acquired from a variety of sources—the movies, childhood music lessons, listening to CDs, going to concerts, or perhaps a parent who drummed his music into your head whether you liked it or not. Although some of these ideas we carry around with us may be based on historical fact, others form some gauzy part of our inherited Mozart mythology, buried deep within our collective memory and therefore exerting all the more impact on our adult experiences. The power of ingrained stereotypes is quite remarkable, as we know, until they are uprooted by facts.

In the following list of phrases frequently used to describe Mozart, which ones do you regard as dubious?

Mozart was (it is said):

1. emotionally abused by his stern, overbearing father
2. a wizard at the piano
3. a child-man, enormously talented but hopelessly immature
4. a genius who never revised his works because they were error-free
5. married to a wife, Constanze, who was utterly unworthy of him
6. persecuted by a public unable to appreciate him
7. commissioned to write the Requiem by "a mysterious stranger, dressed all in gray" (as the man has traditionally been described)
8. so terrified by this man, and so ill, that he thought he was composing the Requiem for himself
9. buried in a pauper's grave

More about this list later. All nine items will be discussed somewhere in this book.

It is interesting meanwhile to note a curious difference between Beethoven and Mozart.[2] Although there is also a flourishing Beethoven mythology, it emerged from people's impressions of his *music*—works so powerful, so intense that people imagined only a musical giant could have written them. They were referring to his path-breaking symphonies,

---

2. I borrow the idea of this comparison from the unpublished essay by Volkmar Braun-behrens, "Aus der Ferne oder aus der Nähe betrachtet: Das Problem der Biographik bei Mozart" [Whether Seen from Near or from Far: Problems in Mozart Biography], n.d.; ca. 2001, 7–8. Hollywood also made a movie about Beethoven, but *Immortal Beloved* is so dreadful a piece of work and so insulting to the composer that it's best forgotten.

particularly the third (known as the "Eroica" [heroic] because it was originally planned as a salute to Napoleon); the fifth; and above all, the ninth, which shattered precedent most notably by incorporating vocal soloists and chorus in its final movement to celebrate the joy (*Freude*) of human brotherhood. Added to these were the late piano sonatas and string quartets, works that seemed to explode traditional forms and plumb new depths of expression. The *Missa Solemnis* (Solemn Mass) also broke with tradition, to such an extent that the work was—and still is—unusable as part of a Catholic worship service.

Beethoven also worked hard to advertise himself, greatly assisted in his latter years by his first biographer, Anton Schindler, who simply fabricated portions of what became the Beethoven myth. In contrast, Mozart did relatively little self-promoting, he did so less effectively, and he had no Schindler. Furthermore, in his case it was not his music, but his *life* that spawned the tales. Turning him into a mythical figure began almost as soon as his body was in the ground. During the nineteenth century, over five hundred works about him were published in Germany alone. *Amadeus,* let it be known, contains scarcely any new ideas but mostly recycles notions (i.e., myths) that first saw print as far back as 1803 (Shaffer was no doubt unaware that he had been upstaged).[3] *Amadeus* is simply another in the long line of fictional and semifictional re-creations of this composer's life. People can't resist playing around with it; they are still at it today. This is how we grow up with large doses of mythology in our heads. This is the case not only for musical amateurs but for highly trained professional musicians as well, particularly—though unfortunately not exclusively—if their specialty doesn't happen to be Mozart.[4]

For example, were you able to separate the nine descriptions of Mozart into fact and fiction? Only number two, that Mozart was a wizard at the piano, is unreservedly true. Actually, statements like these are encountered so frequently, even in widely used and highly respected music-history textbooks, that if you missed all or most of them, don't worry; you are in excellent company. The other day I read in one such book that Mozart "was buried in a pauper's grave." This error doesn't invalidate the whole book, of course; but it does mean that thousands of undergraduate music majors will now keep this element of the Mozart myth rolling along to the next

---

3. The nineteenth-century book that most anticipates the movie is I. F. Arnold's *Mozarts Geist* (Erfurt, 1803).

4. A gifted young conductor once raved to me about a notoriously inaccurate Mozart biography. "We know the facts already, so it's great to have such a fine *interpretation* of them." A conductor who leads concerts of Mozart's music all over the world said on the radio in 2006, "We all know that he died penniless."

generation. The business about a pauper's grave was proven false nearly fifty years ago and the facts have been stated and restated many times; but for some reason, we don't seem to want to let this myth go. This is probably what accounts for the fact that of all Mozart's music, the work most often performed and recorded is the Requiem.[5] *Yet he himself wrote only a small portion of it;* the rest was composed by others after his death.

Full disclosure: I, too, grew up with a fantasy-Mozart in my head. What has surprised me is that replacing it with something closer to reality has not been a painful process at all, but a delightful one. It is exciting to meet a man far more complex and unpredictable—more of a genuine human being— than the 2-D figure I began with. As you and I work our way through this book, I expect the same thing will happen to you.

Mozart's Music Is Easily Available for Study

This statement can be broken down into five parts. As you will see, "easily available" is a bit of an exaggeration.

1. He wrote around 650 to 700 compositions

I'm guessing at the total number because we actually lack a comprehensive list of his works. Here are three other facts that not many people are aware of:

- Only about 25 percent of his works were published during his lifetime.
- Another 10 percent are sketches, fragments, or works left incomplete for reasons that in some cases are known, in other cases unknown.
- A third group consists of revisions of various compositions.

Contrary to legend, then, Mozart *worked,* a fact he emphasized to people who viewed him as some sort of musical automaton. He studied other composers' scores, he attended their concerts, he made music and talked music constantly; then, when he sat down to write his own compositions, he sometimes sketched ideas beforehand. He also left some works unfinished and never went back to them. True, many of his compositions have come down to us in manuscripts that reveal few if any signs of effort; still, he did not just pick up his pen and scribble down masterpiece after masterpiece. Nobody does that, not even Mozart.

The largest group of revised compositions are the operas. In the

---

5. Braunbehrens, "Aus der Ferne," 9.

eighteenth century you tailored your opera to the orchestra and singers employed by the particular theater in the particular city where the opera was to be staged. When the opera moved to another city to be performed by a different orchestra and a different cast for a different audience, certain sections might need to be rewritten. Thus there are no definitive editions of some eighteenth-century operas.[6] This didn't bother anyone; it was just the way things worked.

2. The standard critical edition of Mozart's works is the NMA

The NMA is the *Neue Mozart-Ausgabe*, or *New Mozart Edition*. The goal of this multivolume publication is to provide us with all of Mozart's music, each composition accompanied by a scholarly introduction and commentary. The NMA, however, remains incomplete—inevitably so, since new compositions do occasionally crop up. You'll find its tall red volumes, with Mozart's signature on the covers, in major libraries throughout the world. The entire contents of the NMA are also available online from the International Mozart Foundation in Salzburg, Austria—free!—at dme .mozarteum.at.

3. Mozart's works are arranged chronologically by "Köchel" (K) numbers

This can get a bit confusing, and I hope my summary doesn't make it more so.

Köchel catalogs of Mozart's works

In 1862, Ludwig Köchel undertook the Herculean task of dating all the works of Mozart and arranging them in chronological order (K. 1, K. 2, etc.[7]). However, as soon as he published his giant catalog, Köchel began to find, not only mistakes, but also a host of previously unknown compositions—discoveries that necessitated a *second* edition of his catalog, which was published by Paul von Waldersee after Köchel's death.

In 1936, a third edition came out. This was a total revamping, with wholesale renumbering, by the Mozart scholar Alfred Einstein (Albert's cousin). Next came catalogs four and five, which were actually reprints of the third edition. Köchel six (1964) was the work of Franz Giegling, Gerd Sievers, and Alexander Weinmann; seven (1965) and eight (1983) were

---

6. Operas were also customarily translated into other languages; Mozart's Italian operas generally appeared in German or French soon after their premieres. No composer complained about this, because it enabled audiences to understand the words and thus respond directly to the music. Modern-day objections to English-language opera in the United States would have been regarded by Mozart and his contemporaries as strange.

7. These numbers are sometimes written as KV, which stands for *Köchel-Verzeichnis*, German for "Köchel Catalog."

Ludwig Köchel

reprints of their edition. All of these publications are known as "Köchel" catalogs despite their quite significant differences.

Meanwhile, since the 1970s scholars have employed paper and handwriting analysis as important new ways of dating Mozart's manuscripts. After identifying the handwriting (either Mozart's or that of music copyists he employed), the type and size of paper used, and its watermarks, experts then join their findings to other sources of documentation, enabling them to date compositions with considerable accuracy.[8] The result has been to shift the chronological position of some "early" works to "late" and vice versa, requiring scholars to juggle supposedly rock-solid chains of events. We have also been able to identify some works as not by Mozart and unearthed manuscripts long thought to have disappeared. Since the Iron Curtain fell

8. The distinguished pioneer of this field was the late Alan Tyson, followed by Wolfgang Plath. Their work has been continued by the American scholar Dexter Edge, an expert on Mozart's Viennese period (1781–1791), and by Ulrich Konrad's work on Mozart's surviving sketches and fragments.

in 1989, compositions previously regarded as lost, including whole acts of operas, have resurfaced.

All these developments have wreaked havoc with Köchel numbers. For example, if (hypothetically) K. 323 and K. 324 already exist, but you locate a composition that chronologically has to be sandwiched between them, what number do you give it? The solution has been to add lowercase letters, creating (hypothetically) K. 323a. We now have a few K numbers that reach to lowercase *g* and beyond. A similar problem involves works whose chronological order within the catalog must be corrected—say (again hypothetically), if K. 323 really should be K. 480, but there is already a K. 480. This results in slashes, sometimes more than one of them, if the work has been reordered more than once. A notorious example, and there are others, is K. 182/166c/173dA.

The "New Köchel"

A whole "New Köchel" began in the mid-1990s and is currently under the direction of the International Mozart Foundation in Salzburg. This New Köchel, or NK, may be the last catalog to appear in printed form. Future editions will probably be online, making them available for instant (if, of course, always debatable) revision. Until the NK comes out, we have K6, as it's known (originally published in 1964, reprinted in 1965 and 1983), which is not up to date by any means.

4. Recordings

Here, too, all is not so simple. Aside from good vs. bad performances—a huge issue, here swept under the rug!—a sharp line can be drawn between recordings on "original" vs. "modern" instruments. I've placed both terms in quotation marks because *original* actually doesn't mean original eighteenth-century instruments, usually, but *reproductions* of them (or rebuilt old ones), whereas so-called modern instruments are manufactured more or less as they were in the *nineteenth century*. This makes both *original* and *modern* relative terms. Still, the distinction is important because the sound is utterly different, as you can hear whenever you compare performances, whether live or recorded.

My own preference, generally speaking, is for recordings on "original" instruments *provided that the performance is good,* because I like to experience something close to the sounds Mozart heard in his own ear. Fortunately, however, performers and conductors employing "modern" instruments are increasingly influenced by performances on "original" instruments, so that the gulf between them grows ever narrower. At the same time, there are so many "original" performances available that the chances of locating a good one are excellent. One important caveat, however, is acoustical space. In a large auditorium such as Boston's Symphony Hall, which seats two thousand, eighteenth-century instruments sound anemic. Concerts in Mozart's time would have taken place in someone's (large) house, a rented space, or, for operas, in something on the scale of a Broadway theater. A good venue for such music is a hall seating around eight hundred to one thousand. This whole situation began to change radically in the nineteenth century with the gradual decline of the patronage system; when that ended, you had to generate huge box-office receipts to keep a musical organization financially afloat, and this meant, over the course of the nineteenth century, larger halls, louder instruments, and bigger orchestras.

5. Background Music
For the most part, the Mozart we hear as background music is acoustical wallpaper: tinkle-tinkle Mozart, fed to us in bite-size excerpts sliced out of larger compositions, their darker, more disturbing moments withheld from our innocent ears. This musical caricature greets us everywhere—in upscale boutiques, in the dentist's chair, on telephone "hold" at prestigious corporations, and endlessly, it seems, in commercials on radio and TV.[9] We're not allowed to hear whole works, because they might include sections containing more threatening music; usually it's little blips—maddeningly, the same ones over and over again. With occasional exceptions, denser, more probing works are banished from our airwaves. The effect is to persuade us that Mozart's music is dimple-sweet, and that the composer himself never grew up and got serious, but remained a child-man.

There Is Vast Primary Documentation about Him, Above All, Letters
In German: These, along with detailed scholarly commentary, occupy seven volumes in the German edition and run from 1755 (the year before Wolfgang was born) to 1857 (when his last surviving son penned his last letters).[10]

In English: The standard English translation, by Emily Anderson, contains far fewer letters, a great many of which have been cut, and in such a way that you can't tell what is missing or how much. Anderson also

---

9. A few years ago, Saabs were hawked on TV to the accompaniment of Mozart's Requiem.
10. Hrsg. von Wilhelm A. Bauer, Otto Erich Deutsch, and Joseph Heinz Eibl, *Mozart Briefe und Aufzeichnungen*, 7 vols. (Kassel: Hrsg. von der Internationalen Stiftung Mozarteum Salzburg, 1962–1975). Volumes 1–4 contain the letters, volumes 5–6 the critical commentary, and volume 7 the index. Quotations from the letters in the present book are translations from this German edition.

sometimes has the composer speaking in dignified British rather than his own loose, metaphor-rich prose. Still, her work was pathbreaking, and you should buy a copy of her book if you can afford it (latest online price: $75).[11]

Shorter editions of the letters

Robert Spaethling's translation of 275 of the composer's own letters is highly recommended. He restores Mozart's lively, spiky prose, though he translates only letters *written by* Mozart—with none of his correspondents' replies—thus sharply reducing the book's usefulness. Equally valuable is the Cliff Eisen–Stewart Spencer translation of six hundred letters. An important difference between theirs and Spaethling's is that they include a great many letters from Mozart's father, Leopold. In terms of accuracy and idiomatic nuance, however—a key factor when translating Mozart's colorful German—the two are about equal. Third, but to be avoided: any others, all of which tend to omit the most important letters—the ones telling us how Mozart composed—in favor of gossipy tales and letters containing what sound today like dirty jokes but in their original context weren't regarded as particularly raunchy. Instead, get Spaethling or Eisen-Spencer, both available as inexpensive paperbacks.[12]

Who wrote the letters?

Overwhelmingly, members of the family circle. Most of this correspondence, however, is one-sided—meaning that we have a letter from, say, Wolfgang to Leopold, but not Leopold's answer. This tells us that someone didn't save that letter. It used to be claimed that the composer's wife, Constanze, destroyed them (for whatever reason), but this groundless accusation has mostly disappeared from today's less-biased scholarship. The fact is that we don't know what happened to them; one likely culprit was the composer himself, who apparently rarely kept correspondence. Why? It is impossible to know; but, for whatever cause or causes, we are faced with a great many gaps—places where we know someone wrote him a letter, but we don't have it. Sometimes the contents can be guessed at by what he wrote in his follow-up letter, sometimes not.

Wolfgang Mozart to Leopold Mozart

For two crucially important periods, we have nearly complete two-way

---

11. Emily Anderson, ed. and trans., *The Letters of Mozart and His Family*, 3rd ed. (New York: W. W. Norton, 1985).

12. Robert Spaethling, ed. and trans., *Mozart's Letters, Mozart's Life* (New York: W. W. Norton, 1999); Cliff Eisen, ed., Stewart Spencer, trans., *Wolfgang Amadeus Mozart: A Life in Letters* (London: Penguin, 2006).

correspondence between father and son: 1777–1779 (during Mozart's long, difficult journey to Mannheim and Paris) and 1780–1781 (during his trip to Munich for the premiere of his opera *Idomeneo* and his subsequent, life-changing move to Vienna). These two groups of letters are, from both a musical and a psychological point of view, the juiciest in the whole Mozart correspondence and they deserve slow and extremely careful reading.

The Mannheim-Paris and Munich-to-Vienna letters give us the day-by-day facts of a composer's life—more down-to-earth information than we have for any other composer of any period. They make fascinating reading for this reason alone. But in addition, scholars and armchair psychologists probe them for insights into the complex relationship between father and son. When you read these letters, it's safe to say that you and others will not agree on what they reveal about Leopold and Wolfgang Mozart.

Vienna 1781–1791: very little

We have *none* of the letters Leopold wrote to Wolfgang from any time after January 1781. In March of that year, Mozart arrived in Vienna, the city where he would spend the remainder of his life. His last two letters to Leopold are dated, respectively, June 9, 1784, and, after an unexplained three-year gap, April 4, 1787. Leopold died in May 1787. This means that for the entire last decade of Mozart's life—during which he composed most of the music that we know today—we have almost no two-way correspondence between son and father or, for that matter, between Mozart and anyone, including his wife, Constanze. His affectionate, joking, often musically informative letters to her have mostly survived, but none of her replies to him.

Who is the Mozart we meet in these letters?

All told, these four volumes (of the complete letters, in German) constitute a gold mine—indispensable for anyone seriously interested in Mozart. Yet they leave us with a skewed portrait: chiefly, we see him through the lens of his father. Such a fixed camera angle obscures rather than clarifies the picture, causing people who study this correspondence to come away with sharply contrasting impressions. Unavoidably, you find yourself "reading into" it your own interpretations. You can't help it. First, as twenty-first-century readers—particularly those of us who aren't experts in the language, the idioms, and the letter-writing culture of his time—we simply cannot grasp everything implied as well as stated in these letters. Second, post-Freud, we may go to the other extreme and read too much into them. Third, we inevitably bring to them our own preformed images of the composer and his father. Fourth, we may have our own brothers, boyfriends, and fathers in the back of our mind as models. And so our reading is subject to a host of preconceptions and faulty interpretations. We need to bring to this profoundly emotional correspondence as much care and sensitivity as we can muster, though even then it is nearly impossible not to take sides.

Summary remarks on the letters

How accurate a picture would we have of you, if all we had to base it on were letters (more likely, e-mails) between you and your family from your college years—little or nothing before or after that, and only sparse records of your relationships with any other people? It would be a big help if we could buttress this correspondence with an equal stack of neutral letters—letters to and from people other than Leopold Mozart—but there aren't enough of them. Not much correspondence survives between the composer and anyone other than his father—his sister, his enchanting cousin "the Bäsle,"[13] on rare occasions his mother, a handful of friends, and most especially his wife, to whom he sent his last surviving letter. This whole category of letters, while large for that era, is too small to provide us with much insight into his character, his personality, or his way of composing.

What other sorts of documentation do we have?

First, what we don't have: much detailed information about his day-to-day life, especially his ten years in Vienna (1781–1791), as composer, husband, friend, Freemason, and Viennese citizen. Again, more survives about Mozart than for any other composer of his era—much more—but there are still too many blank spaces.

Composers customarily leave behind piles of evidence of their professional activities— letters to and from publishers, management officials, musical colleagues, and librettists; contracts; and receipts of all sorts. For Mozart, we have relatively few such documents. In addition, many of the people he was doing business with were in the same city he was, so matters could be handled person-to-person. We do, however, have archival records from courts and theaters where his music was performed, and references to concerts in letters or diaries of his contemporaries. Such documents help us learn how much things cost and how much he was paid for certain events. His income and how, when, and why it fluctuated—as incomes do for many musicians today—is surveyed in a growing body of research. Some of this research arrives at radically different conclusions; compare, for example, the

---

13. "The Bäsle" was Mozart's cousin, about his age, with whom he exchanged some spar-klingly bawdy letters in 1777–1778 after he visited her family in Augsburg on his way to Mannheim in the fall of 1777. Predictably, we have none of her letters, only his. *Bäsle* is the diminutive of the German word for "cousin."

"The Bäsle" (Maria Anna Thekla Mozart)

biographies by Volkmar Braunbehrens and Maynard Solomon, both listed in the annotated bibliography at the end of this book.

Two useful sources

Deutsch's *Mozart: A Documentary Biography* is a one-volume collection of items such as reviews, diary entries by contemporaries, newspaper ads (including ads Leopold wrote about Wolfgang and his older sister, Nannerl, during their European tours), edited by Otto Erich Deutsch and subsequently updated in publications of the International Mozart Foundation (Internationale Stiftung Mozarteum).[14] These make engrossing, illuminating reading and are highly recommended.

Mozart's personal library is another treasure. Deutsch gives us a list of what it contained, or at any rate, what was found in it after his death. More recently, Ulrich Konrad and Martin Staehelin have revised the list and accompanied it with a detailed commentary.[15] Mozart's widow, Constanze—

---

14. Otto Erich Deutsch, ed., *Mozart: A Documentary Biography*, trans. Eric Blom, Peter Branscombe, and Jeremy Noble (Stanford, CA: Stanford University Press, 1966); cf. Cliff Eisen, ed., *New Mozart Documents* (London and Stanford, CA: Stanford University Press, 1991).

15. See Deutsch, 583–604; cf. Ulrich Konrad and Martin Staehelin, eds., *"Allzeit ein Buch"— Die Bibliothek Wolfgang Amadeus Mozarts* (Wolfenbüttel: Herzog-August-Bibliothek, 1991).

faced with the sudden loss of her young husband and the need to support herself and their two small children—may have sold some items and given others away. Mozart himself probably lent books and scores to friends; he was generous to a fault with money, time, and possessions. The list, then, does not represent all that had once been in this library. What remains, however, shows us that this was no ordinary musician but a man with wide-ranging musical tastes coupled with a sophisticated intellectual curiosity reaching far beyond the realm of music. In both respects he was his father's son.

In addition to music, Mozart's personal library included:

Works by Ovid
Complete comedies of Molière
Poems by esteemed German poets: Kleist, Wieland, Weisse
Librettos of Metastasio (the leading writer of eighteenth-century
    opera texts)
A history of Germany
Books on mathematics, philosophy, literature, ethics, religion,
    and Freemasonry
The Holy Bible
Journals devoted to music, literature, and current issues
Books on musical pedagogy[16]
Travel guides to Austria, Germany, Russia, and Italy
Biographies of Frederick the Great and Joseph II
Children's books on geography, mathematics, and science; and
    collections of stories[17]

Two sources we wish we had

First, Leopold Mozart's intended biography: imagine the story of Mozart's life as written by his father! True, Leopold did intend to publish a biography of his son; this is why he painstakingly collected and preserved every artifact of Wolfgang's from the time the child was four or five years old. All those letters Leopold wrote back to Salzburg during the childhood European tours (quoted frequently in this book, with further excerpts in an appendix) were meant as grist for his biography. Sometimes he mailed off two copies to ensure that one of them arrived safely. Every sketch, every musical exercise of Wolfgang's was stored away for future publication. But Leopold never

---

16. Mozart had for some years before his death thought about writing a textbook on music. What might that have been like!

17. The composer took a keen interest in his children's education and was particularly curious about new pedagogical approaches. In this respect also, he was very much his father's son.

wrote the book. Why? Perhaps because, in his eyes, his son failed to achieve the international fame his father dreamed of. Indeed, although Mozart did become well known and highly esteemed during his lifetime, he did not reach celebrity status until long after his death. How he ultimately became a veritable icon of Western culture is a strange and convoluted story that will be introduced briefly at the end of this chapter.

Second, we also wish we had a biography by one of Mozart's friends. Composers' first biographies are generally written by contemporaries—if not full-scale studies, at least these are often lengthy descriptions. Sifting through such material gives us a third dimension that we can't get any other way. Based on such information, more complete studies can then be written. Not so with Mozart; we have no biography written by anybody who ever met him, though we do have individual recollections from several of his contemporaries.

Any number of his friends and colleagues were in a position to leave behind extended reminiscences of what it was like to know and work with Mozart, and over the course of this book we'll discover who some of these people were. The sad news is that none of them put pen to paper to give us any sort of substantial biographical sketch. Of course, none of them had any idea that he would suddenly fall ill at thirty-five and die a few weeks later. Nor was he famous enough for a publishing house to search out friends to write about him. Moreover, his business had been, not with an international house such as Breitkopf and Härtel, but with Artaria, which made no move to honor his memory with a biography. Some years later, Breitkopf and Härtel corresponded with his widow about putting together a life of Mozart, but the project never came to fruition.

Thus all we have are some recollections, notably from his older sister, Nannerl, about their childhood and their lengthy tours as child prodigies.[18] Others are from Michael Kelly, who created the roles of Basilio and Don Curzio in *The Marriage of Figaro;* from Luigi Bassi, who sang the title role in *Don Giovanni* and the Count in *The Marriage of Figaro;* and from Lorenzo da Ponte, librettist of *The Marriage of Figaro, Don Giovanni,* and *Così fan tutte.* Da Ponte's memoirs include anecdotes about Mozart, though some are of questionable reliability.

Comparing Mozart's situation once more to Beethoven's: Anton Schindler, Beethoven's secretary and confidant, wrote the first study of that composer's life. Although Schindler portrayed him rather on the heroic side (to put it mildly) and also ran off with his sketchbooks, at least Beethoven

---

18. Deutsch, 451–62. Nannerl's recollections include a long postscript written by someone else, but Deutsch was unable to identify the author. See Nannerl Mozart (Postscript), page 28f., for details about this.

was followed around day after day by someone with his eyes on the future. Haydn had better luck. He was interviewed over a period of years by Georg August Griesinger, hired by Haydn's publisher, Breitkopf and Härtel. Griesinger was an honest man, he took his responsibilities seriously, and he and Haydn became friends.

Nobody stepped forward to do this for Mozart.

The First Four Mozart Biographies, and a Contribution of a Different Sort

1. Schlichtegroll's *Nekrolog auf das Jahr 1791* (1793), published in modern times as *Mozarts Leben* (Mozart's Life), was technically the first biography, though it was actually an extended obituary.[19] Written by a man who was not a musician, had never met Mozart or, apparently, ever been to Vienna or Salzburg, this book is therefore a bit problematic, though fascinating for that very reason!—that is, if you are curious about how the Mozart mythology got started. The author, Friedrich Schlichtegroll, was a small-town high school teacher who supplemented his salary by putting together volumes of obituaries of well-known people. In the Mozart volume, the composer is one of ten. Since Schlichtegroll knew little about the man beyond his name, he wrote to an acquaintance in Salzburg and another in Vienna—neither of them a musician—and published more or less what they furnished him, adding his own gloriously overwritten revisions and interpolations. The rather strange result is *Mozarts Leben*.

2. Niemetschek's *Leben des k.k. Kapellmeisters Wolfgang Gottlieb Mozart* (1798).[20] This second biography is somewhat better. However, its author, Franz Niemetschek, implies—without actually claiming it—that he knew Mozart. Niemetschek, an amateur musician and teacher in Prague, was an ardent fan of Mozart's; in fact, he idolized him. But here's the extent of their acquaintance: Niemetschek's future wife—whom he had not yet met—fashioned hats for Constanze Mozart during the Mozart couple's several visits to Prague. Niemetschek himself never saw the composer; his "firsthand" information came from his wife's recollections several years later. Although his book describes events he supposedly witnessed—concerts where Mozart improvised at the piano as well as the Prague premieres of *The Marriage of Figaro, Don Giovanni,* and *La clemenza di Tito*—Niemetschek didn't move to Prague until 1793, two years after the composer's death. Sad

---

19. Friedrich Schlichtegroll, *Mozarts Leben* (Götha, 1793); facsimile edition of the reprint (Graz, 1794), ed. Joseph Heinz Eibl (Kassel: Bärenreiter, 1974).

20. Franz Niemetschek, *Ich kannte Mozart* [I knew Mozart]: *Leben des k.k. Kapellmeisters Wolfgang Gottlieb Mozart*, ed. Jost Perfahl (Munich: Bibliothek zeitgenossischer Literatur, 1984); cf. Walter Brauneis, "Franz Xaver Niemetschek: His Association with Mozart—Legend?" trans. Bruce Cooper Clarke, accessible at AproposMozart.com.

news, because this book makes fascinating reading despite the fact that it is partly fictitious and much of the rest is copied verbatim from Schlichtegroll. Neither book is in any sense complete. Schlichtegroll emphasizes Mozart's childhood and early life because his Salzburg source sent him a lot more material than his Viennese source did. Niemetschek stresses the composer's adult life; for the childhood, he simply reproduces Schlichtegroll. Word for word. There were no laws against plagiarism, and wholesale copying occurred quite regularly.

We'll close this disillusioning survey with three more entries: first, a contribution of a different sort, and then biographies three and four—though we could go on.

The contribution of a different sort was a collection of *Authentic Anecdotes about Mozart* published in the leading German musical journal of the day by a man claiming to have met Mozart in 1789. Scholars don't agree on whether he did or did not meet the composer (I think he did). This was Friedrich Rochlitz, editor of the *Allgemeine musikalische Zeitung.*[21] His "anecdotes," Rochlitz claimed, were assembled through a combination of personal knowledge and correspondence with the widow Constanze. It's hard to prove this one way or the other. Some scholars regard the anecdotes as rubbish, but I don't—at least not all of them. They give us (for example) not only a composer of enormous personal generosity (verified elsewhere) and a profound admirer of the music of J. S. Bach (verified), but also a composer who jotted down error-free masterpieces in a flash, day after day (mostly nonsense). Later, Rochlitz wrote the most important and influential of the many translations of *Don Giovanni,* in which he refashioned the title figure into a kind of Romantic hero. It was this version of the opera that played all over the German-speaking world and formed the basis for every nineteenth-century commentary on the opera and for many modern ones as well.

After 1800, the availability of genuine documents, printed scores, manuscripts, and letters (especially letters) mushroomed dramatically. Books about the composer grew thicker as writers dug much more deeply into his life and music.

3. Nissen, *Biographie W. A. Mozart's* (two volumes, 1828).[22] Biography number three was begun—though not finished—by Georg Nikolaus von Nissen, a Danish diplomat who became Constanze Mozart's second husband. Through her he had access to trunk-loads of material: what remained of the composer's library; all the correspondence sent to Mozart

---

21. Rochlitz's "Anecdotes" appeared in issues of the *Allgemeine musikalische Zeitung* for 1798 and 1799; i.e., were nearly contemporaneous with Niemetschek's book. Each of them claimed to have published first.
22. Leipzig: Breitkopf and Härtel, 1828.

that had survived; and a great many printed scores, manuscripts, sketches, and fragments. Although Nissen had never known the composer himself, he married an excellent source of firsthand information. Together with an assistant, he began compiling a two-volume biography, reaching out to people who had known Mozart—particularly the composer's sister Nannerl, who had the rest of the correspondence at her home in Salzburg. He put together *what seemed to him the kind of biography the great Mozart deserved.* For by this time, mythmaking had taken over and Mozart was already being turned into an icon. This book helped to get that rolling.

Nissen died before finishing his work, and it was brought to completion in 1828 by Constanze and his assistant. The three of them produced a mess, unfortunately—a jumble of disorganized facts and not-quite-facts, repetitious in the extreme, with large chunks copied verbatim from previous biographies. However, there is a great prize here after all: *for the first time, letters.* None of them had seen the light of day before. But due to Nissen's (and also, no doubt, Constanze's) concern for the great man's image, the chosen letters were cut, slashed, in a word: bowdlerized. Nevertheless, with the magical phrase "Constanze Mozart, widow of the composer" on its cover, the book sold like hotcakes and for decades stood unchallenged as the definitive study of the composer.

The circulation of these first three flawed biographies, plus Rochlitz's anecdotes, was paralleled by an escalating number of fictional works— poems, short stories, plays, and novels. Among them were three masterpieces: Aleksandr Pushkin's play *Mozart and Salieri* (a likely source for Shaffer's *Amadeus*), E. T. A. Hoffmann's short story "Don Juan," and Eduard Mörike's novella *Mozart on the Way to Prague* (i.e., on his way to the premiere of *Don Giovanni* in 1787). Both Hoffmann's tale and Mörike's novella—despite being clearly labeled as fiction—have exerted powerful influences, not just on biographical studies but also on serious *musical* analyses of the opera.[23]

These works were just highly significant examples of what became a floodtide toward the middle of the nineteenth century—fiction, biographies, musical studies—as the fiftieth anniversary of the composer's death approached (1841), and after that, the centennial of his birth (1856). By 1856, Mozart was regarded as a German national hero and monuments had been erected to him in both Salzburg and Vienna. Still no wholly reliable

---

23. The Hoffmann, especially, is a wonderful tale. See Hoffmann, "Don Juan; or a Fabulous Adventure that Befell a Music Enthusiast on His Travels," in David Charlton, ed. and trans., *E. T. A. Hoffmann's Musical Writings, Kreisleriana, The Poet and the Composer, Music Criticism* (New York: Cambridge University Press, 1989), 103–15. The story appeared in 1813; two years later, Hoffmann reviewed a production of Don Giovanni in Berlin. Although the story is "fiction" and the review "fact," they make essentially the same points and it was the story that most influenced critical interpretations of the opera.

study of his life and works had emerged, though there was one very serious contender.

4. Jahn, *W. A. Mozart* (four volumes, 1856–1859).[24] Otto Jahn's monumental biography was both massively documented and thoroughly researched. Yet unavoidably—because at that time so much more storytelling was making the rounds than truth—Jahn, too, fell victim to fiction, even initiating a tale or two of his own. He was, for example, a major bearer of the child-man myth about Mozart and the first to fashion Constanze Mozart as little more than a sexual object, a lousy housekeeper, and an intellectual ninny. Jahn's influence was so widespread—because his book was vastly superior to anything that preceded it—that both myths have survived, despite correction, to this day.

Conclusion

Where does all this leave us now? How much clearer is our understanding of Mozart today than it was then? Happily, the news is good:

- We have a continually updated, modern edition of his music (the New Mozart Edition), available online and free to all.
- The "New Köchel" catalog is on the way.
- More and more performances employ instruments of Mozart's time, with attention also devoted to how his music should be played.
- We're chiseling away at all that fiction surrounding his life and music, much of which gained new vigor because of *Amadeus*.

Yet ironically, *Amadeus* also played a key role in igniting a Mozart revival. Sparking a new curiosity about the composer, it helped to turn the Mozart Bicentennial of 1991 into a yearlong global celebration with nonstop music-making and thousands of new CDs. Much the same thing occurred throughout 2006, the 250th anniversary of his birth. All this public concertizing, publishing, advertising, and open-air celebrating has spurred a new generation of scholars—some of them students whose first acquaintance with the composer may have been that movie—to focus their career on Mozart research and performance. They, along with a great many others around the world, are revolutionizing our understanding of him. Although most of the nonspecialist audience has scant knowledge of the Mozart we now know, you're about to meet him for yourself.

---

24. English translation by Pauline Townsend as *The Life of Mozart*, 3 vols. (London: Novello, 1891).

WHAT DID MOZART LOOK LIKE?

Mozart was short, probably not much over five feet tall, with fine, blond hair (about which he is said to have been vain), large, protruding eyes, a missing earlobe on one side, a face somewhat pockmarked from a childhood bout with smallpox, and a "Salzburg" nose inherited from his mother.

In the pictures above, you see that only one of them does justice to this most dominant feature. In the unfinished portrait (at right) by Mozart's brother-in-law, Joseph Lange, which Constanze Mozart regarded as the best likeness of her husband ever made (pictured in more complete form on the cover of this book), he isn't sad, just looking downward toward the piano that never got painted into the picture.

WAS HE CALLED AMADEUS?

The composer's baptismal name was Joannes Chrysostomus Wolfgangus Theophilus Mozart: Joannes Chrysostomus, because January 27 was the feast day of St. John Chrysostom; Wolfgangus, to honor his maternal grandfather; and Theophilus, for his godfather. He seems not to have used the saint's name; occasionally he used Gottlieb, German for Theophilus ("beloved of God"). He almost never called himself Amadeus (Latin for Gottlieb), though it makes an evocative film title.

Which of these possibilities did Mozart prefer? Not Wolfgang

Amadeus Mozart, which is what you see everywhere today. Most of the time, he signed his name Mozart, W. A. Mozart, or Wolfgang Amadè (or Amadé) Mozart:

MOZART AS CRAFTSMAN

In the eighteenth century, music was viewed as a craft. The Romantic notion of "art" and of the composer as an "artist" awaiting moments of inspiration was just beginning to take hold, but Mozart seemed unaware of it. In fact, he did not regard himself as a genius, but as a master of his craft. A craftsman, whether musician, mason, or carpenter, was expected to command every aspect of that craft. Although few could live up to this ideal, Mozart achieved it through a lifetime of enormous effort to develop his colossal natural gifts. He generally arose around five or six a.m. and wrote for hours every day, composing in every genre: sonatas, symphonies, concertos, operas, church music, small-ensemble music (duets, trios, quartets, etc.), along with shorter vocal works such as canons (some of them with obscene texts), songs, and lots of dance music—his wife, Constanze, said his real gift was as a dancer.

MOZART'S FAMILY

LEOPOLD AND MARIA ANNA MOZART

Leopold Mozart is often depicted as a rigid, domineering man whose attempted railroading of his son's career left the composer with emotional scars from which he never recovered. Such a portrayal is, of course, a caricature, though you see it quite often.

Born in Augsburg, Germany, in 1719, Leopold was a very bright, ambitious young man with multiple talents in acting, languages, music, and philosophy. Leaving Augsburg to enroll in the University of Salzburg, he evidently intended to become a lawyer or priest. At first, he was a superior student. Two years later, however, he was nearly expelled for poor attendance and neglect of his work—this from a man later known for ramrod self-discipline.

Perhaps the reason for Leopold's declining interest in academia was that he really wanted to do music. Whether this was the cause or not, he did quit the university before he was thrown out and very quickly found employment as a violinist with a nobleman in Salzburg. Soon he moved upward, garnering a position at the court of the Prince-Archbishop of Salzburg. It must have already been obvious at the outset, however, that this was no ordinary court musician. His years spent in a university, something quite unheard of for musicians of that day, set him apart. Still, the fact was that musicians were servants. In a nobleman's house they were on a par with the kitchen staff. This low status irked Leopold throughout his life, though he learned to sublimate his anger; it would irk his son to the point of open rebellion.

The elder Mozart was an intellectual not only by education but also by natural bent. He spoke several languages, read widely, owned a microscope and a telescope, kept up with political and scientific ideas—in short, was a man of the Enlightenment. He passed on his voracious appetite for learning to his children, for whom he was the sole teacher.

In 1747 Leopold married Maria Anna Pertl, about whom we know very little—mostly because the women in Great Composers' lives haven't been seen as worthy of study. What has emerged about her so far is that she was born in Salzburg in 1720, where her father, educated as a lawyer at Salzburg's Benedictine University, also sang bass at the Benedictine Abbey of St. Peter's and taught singing at its school. This striking fact tells us that Wolfgang Mozart's musical ancestry may have come more from his maternal than his paternal side—Leopold's father and brothers were bookbinders.[25] Maria Anna's father earned most of his income, however, not from music but from administering several small areas near the city, until he was stricken with a disabling illness in 1715. A person unable to work received no pay, which meant that his debts mounted so high that eventually the family's belongings were confiscated. When he died nine years later, his wife and their only surviving child, Maria Anna, subsisted on charity and whatever they could earn by sewing and embroidering (the portrait of Maria Anna, on the next page, shows her holding a piece of lace). But survive they did, which says something about their fortitude and resilience. Then Maria Anna met Leopold Mozart in 1746, and they were married the following year.

Leopold and Maria Anna—said to be "the handsomest couple in Salzburg"[26]—enjoyed a happy marriage, raising two brilliantly gifted children and sharing an at times salacious sense of humor, which their children picked up as well. (Salzburgers were renowned for their jokes about bodily orifices and functions; you find plenty of these jokes in the family correspondence, from all four Mozarts). Leopold and Maria Anna had seven children, of whom only two lived to adulthood: Maria Anna (nicknamed "Nannerl"), born in 1751, and Wolfgang, born in 1756.

---

25. Jane Glover, *Mozart's Women* (London: Macmillan, 2005), 11.
26. Deutsch, *Mozart, A Documentary Biography*, 462.

Maria Anna Pertl Mozart   *Leopold Mozart with his violin method*

In the same year that Wolfgang was born, his father, by that time a well-known violinist, organist, conductor, and composer, carved a lasting European reputation for himself with the publication of an excellent manual on violin technique.[27] Translated into several European languages, it remained the standard violin-teaching method for decades. In 1763 (when Wolfgang was seven), Leopold became *Vize-Kapellmeister* (assistant director of music) at the Salzburg court. Oddly, though, despite his multiple talents and exceptional education, he never rose any higher than this and, in fact, never applied for promotion. As soon as Wolfgang's extraordinary talents manifested themselves, Leopold redirected his own life's course as much as he dared. After a few years he stopped composing altogether to spend most of his time nurturing and developing his boy's education and planning his future career. So single-mindedly did Leopold pursue this that he occasionally found himself in hot water with the prince-archbishop. When that happened he quickly mended his ways, for getting himself fired would have been a disaster for the family. A man dismissed from one court was virtually unemployable in another.

The whole purpose of parenting in the eighteenth century was to find a niche for your children in the socio-economic system (to use today's term), so that they could support themselves and, later on, support you when you became too old to work. It was a cycle: your family sent you forth prepared

---

27. The title in German is *Versuch einer gründlichen Violinschule.*

to take your place in the world; that was *their* duty. Your payback was to take care of them if and whenever needed. Today's parents expect to receive Social Security in their old age and, if they're lucky, to supplement that with other retirement income, plus medical and long-term care insurance. But in the 1700s *you* were your parents' Social Security and Medicare. It was drummed into every male child at a tender age: your goal was to grow into an adult fully able to support yourself, your wife, your children, *and*, if necessary, your parents.

Like every child in that era, Wolfgang Mozart certainly understood his responsibilities. What set his case apart was his extraordinary talent, which should have guaranteed him international success if he were brought to the attention of the right patrons—which is to say, Europe's largest and richest courts. Preparing his son for a distinguished position in such a court was surely what Leopold had in mind from day one—high on the Mozarts' list of reasons for embarking on a series of European tours in 1762 through 1769: to showcase the children's miraculous talent in public performances (while also filling the family's coffers towards the proverbial rainy day); to draw the attention of Europe's crowned heads to an exceptional *Kapellmeister* they should consider hiring when the boy came of age; and, while they were at it, to keep their eyes open for a better job for Leopold Mozart as well.

Leopold served during these trips as advance man, tour manager, musical coach, and personal advisor. It is hard to imagine how one individual kept this whole traveling circus going for months at a time—despite illnesses (on several occasions nearly fatal), cancellations, two stormy crossings of the English Channel, and most galling, the often egregiously rude behavior of some aristocrats. But adding to his talents was the fact that Leopold was a clever traveling salesman. Before they arrived in a given city, he would mail off advertisements to the papers; and after performances, he penned anonymous reviews. Here is one of his ads. You'll notice that it's Wolfgang's skills that are emphasized:

> The general admiration aroused in the souls of every auditor by the skill, never before either seen or heard to such a degree, of the two children of the music director to the court of Salzburg [which he wasn't] has already entailed a threefold repetition of the concert planned for one single occasion. Indeed, this general admiration and the request of several great connoisseurs and amateurs is the cause of the concert (which, however, will quite definitely be the last) today, Tuesday, 30 August, in Scharf's Hall on the Liebfrauenberg, at 6 o'clock in the evening; whereat the girl, who is in her twelfth year, and the boy, who is in his 7th, will not only play on

the harpsichord or fortepiano, the former performing the most difficult pieces by the greatest masters; but the boy will also play a concerto on the violin, accompany symphonies on the keyboard, completely cover the manual of the keyboard, and play on the cloth as well as though he had the keyboard under his eyes; he will further most accurately name from any distance any notes that may be sounded for him either singly or in chords, on the piano or on every imaginable instrument including bells, glasses, and clocks. Lastly he will improvise out of his head, not only on the pianoforte but also on an organ (as long as one wishes to listen and in all the keys, even the most difficult, that may be named for him), in order to show that he also understands the art of playing the organ, which is entirely different from that of playing the piano. Admission, a thaler. Tickets at the Golden Lion.[28]

Nannerl performed along with her younger brother in childhood, but after that was expected to remain at home to learn the domestic duties expected of a future wife and mother. This did not go down well with Nannerl.

When you think about it, raising the young Mozarts must have been thrilling at times, though perhaps just as often more than a little nerve-racking. What would have been the best approach with such massively talented kids? We have no evidence that Leopold or Maria Anna ever worried about their parental decisions, but surely they did from time to time. What we do know—there is no controversy about this at all—is that the children were happy and they received a quite spectacular and well-rounded education.

Leopold Mozart died at home in 1787. Maria Anna died in Paris in 1778.

MARIA ANNA MOZART ("NANNERL")

Mozart's older sister Nannerl was nearly as gifted as he was. As a pianist, she was among the finest of that generation, which produced a lot of piano virtuosos. Her brother praised her composing as well, once their father began giving her instruction during the winter of 1777–1778. But nothing she wrote has survived because no one took the trouble to save it, so we have only Mozart's word on the subject. To say that she was one of the best pianists of the century and a very good, possibly excellent composer to boot may sound like an extraordinary claim, but then, the Mozart children were no ordinary children.

---

28. Deutsch, *Mozart: A Documentary Biography*, 24–25.

The performing Mozarts

Wolfgang and Nannerl in the hand-me-down outfits given them by Empress Maria Theresa

Born in 1751, Nannerl was five years older than Wolfgang. Like him, she learned piano from the age of three. During their childhood tours, he played violin and piano (or harpsichord); she played keyboard instruments and sang. Their exceptional talents—not only as instrumentalists but as complete, well-rounded musicians—amazed their audiences, who as a result of Leopold's careful planning consisted mostly of royalty and nobility. Empress Maria Theresa presented them with royal hand-me-downs.

It was in December 1769 that the paths of brother and sister diverged. When Wolfgang and his father—just the two of them—climbed into the carriage for the first of three journeys to Italy, Nannerl came apart. Weeping hysterically, with a violent headache and sick to her stomach, she slammed the door to her room and refused to come out until the next morning. Her bubble had burst. She was now eighteen, and Leopold (and/or Maria Anna) determined that she should no longer appear before the public but stay home and be taught domestic skills. After that, except for postscripts at the ends of letters (more material for Leopold's biography of Wolfgang), we hear little about her. She had been removed from the concert stage, from her role as costar in the family drama.

Eight years later, in September 1777, Wolfgang and his mother left Salzburg to begin a long journey in search of a permanent position for the twenty-one-year-old composer. Frau Mozart went with him because Leopold had to remain in Salzburg. Once again Nannerl was told she couldn't go; again she collapsed in tears, became ill, and was for several days inconsolable. As she probably understood all too well, with her mother gone, she was now in a sense Leopold's surrogate wife, responsible for household management including meals, laundry, and cleaning as well as the hosting of social events. As months went by, her father missed Maria Anna terribly, and in his loneliness he and his daughter began to spend evenings playing violin sonatas and, at long last, he began to teach her the rudiments of composition. Predictably, she raced forward, making progress that astonished him. "She can improvise," Leopold wrote to her brother, "like you wouldn't believe."[29] But, as mentioned earlier, he saved none of her compositions.

In July 1778 Maria Anna Mozart was suddenly taken ill in Paris and died a few days later. This tragic event had enormous ramifications for the family. Leopold was at once devastated and angry, implicitly blaming Wolfgang for her death, and the once-intimate relationship between father and son never recovered. But Maria Anna's death also needs to be seen from Nannerl's point of view. For her, it was a third body blow: left behind both in 1769 and in 1777, the death of her mother now sealed her fate. She was to remain in Salzburg for the indefinite future, unmarried, with no possibility of a musical career, and expected to take care of her father's household. In the eighteenth century, there was no alternative for women who found themselves in such straits. Her primary connection with music from then on was as a piano teacher. She became an excellent teacher.

Meanwhile, despite her highly circumscribed existence, a series of suitors found their way to the house, but her father sent them all away on one pretext or another. In 1781, however, she and Captain Franz d'Ippold, who had been in love with each other for several years, announced their plans to marry. Wolfgang sent his congratulations and suggested excitedly that they settle in Vienna, where he felt certain Nannerl could quickly establish herself as a pianist and teacher, and the two of them could play concerts together. (Imagine the ads: "Two Mozarts in Concert Tonight." Like old times.) Wolfgang invited his father to come along as well; they could all find an apartment together. But Leopold would have none of it. The captain didn't have enough money to support a wife; Leopold needed her at home; Nannerl was not to marry this man.

Question: What, in fact, would have been the chances of Nannerl launching a successful concert career? Actually, quite good. In no sense would she have been an anomaly. There were touring women pianists in that generation, two of them well known to her brother: the extraordinary blind virtuoso, Maria Theresa von Paradis, for whom he wrote his Piano Concerto

---

29. My translation is informal. The German reads: *"daß du es dir nicht vorstellen kannst,"* literally, "such as you can't imagine." Letter dated February 25/26, 1778.

in B-flat, K. 456; and his gifted pupil, Josepha von Auernhammer, with whom he played his Concerto for Two Pianos and Orchestra, K. 365/316a, at a concert in the summer of 1783. Those who heard Nannerl Mozart in person would have us believe that she was at least their equal—when she was twelve, Leopold declared that she was already one of the finest pianists in Europe. If he had allowed it, there is little doubt that she could have been a superstar. What makes this topic so depressing is that Nannerl herself was no doubt well aware of the fact.

In 1783, Wolfgang and his wife, Constanze (they were married in 1782), came to Salzburg and stayed for about six weeks. Toward the end of their visit, portions of Mozart's incomplete Mass in C Minor, K. 427/417a, were performed in St. Peter's Church, with Constanze as soprano soloist. This was the last time Nannerl and Mozart saw each other.

In 1784, Leopold expressed his hearty approval when Johann Berchtold zu Sonnenburg proposed to Nannerl. Sonnenburg was a widower, much older than Nannerl, and the father of five ill-tempered, undisciplined children. However, since he was financially well heeled and enjoyed a certain social standing in the area (he lived down the road in St. Gilgen), he was the kind of husband Leopold thought suitable for his daughter. And so Nannerl became Frau Berchtold zu Sonnenburg—chiefly, one speculates, so that someone could take charge of Sonnenburg's unruly kids and bring some order into his household. A few years later she bore him the first of three children, "little Leopold" (!), whom her father took care of during his first year (!) because a new baby was more than she could cope with at that point. Nannerl and Sonnenburg later had two more children, both girls.

When Leopold Mozart died in 1787, Nannerl was with him. He died in her arms. Her brother was in Vienna and heard the news only when she wrote to him about it. After her own husband died, in 1801, Nannerl moved back to Salzburg, teaching piano there and fielding tourists' questions about her now-celebrated brother, dead since 1791. She lost her eyesight in 1825, grew weak and frail, and died in 1829. Neither Salzburg newspaper carried a report of her death.

Nannerl Mozart (Postscript): ### Who Started the Myth of Mozart as a Child-Man?

As you remember, Mozart's first biographer, Friedrich Schlichtegroll—more aptly termed an inaccurate obituary writer—collected information for his *Nekrolog* by getting in touch with people in both Salzburg and Vienna. His contact in Salzburg was Albert von Mölk, a clergyman and friend of the Mozart family.

Schlichtegroll sent Mölk a list of questions about Mozart. Mölk, in turn, consulted Nannerl, who agreed to respond as best she could. As a check against her own memory of the distant past, she enlisted the aid of Johann Andreas Schachtner, a longtime Salzburg court trumpeter who had known both children well. In addition, Schachtner supplied his own recollections. Nannerl scrupulously restricted herself to what she had personally observed—the years of Wolfgang's childhood and young adulthood.

Now for the interesting part. At the end of Nannerl's response, someone has inserted a lengthy postscript—ostensibly authored by Nannerl herself, but the handwriting isn't hers—that gives a highly unflattering picture of her brother. Bruce Cooper Clarke has shown that this postscript is in *Mölk's* handwriting.[30] Included in [Mölk's] fake postscript are two statements that became grist for future biographers' mills, repeated so often that they gained a place on our list of common misconceptions of the composer cited near the beginning of this book:

- Mozart married a most unsuitable girl [Constanze Mozart].
  against the will of his father, and this is why his household was
  such a shambles. (myth 5)
- In everything except music, he remained almost always
  a child. (myth 3)

The first of these remarks has been crossed out (by whom, we don't know). Schlichtegroll didn't use that one, though Otto Jahn did, and after him, a great many others. Schlichtegroll pounced on the second remark, which must have seemed too juicy to pass up: an adult in music but a child in everything else. Fashioning this into a full-blown dichotomy, Schlichtegroll garnished it with a phrase of his own, which he highlighted with italics:

> Just as this rare human being became a man in his art very early, so he remained, on the other hand—*this must in all impartiality be said of him*—in nearly every other respect forever a child. He never learned self-discipline and had no feeling for domestic order, for the proper use of money, for moderation and the sensible choice of pleasures. He always needed a supervisor, a guardian to look after the domestic details of his life.

30. Clarke analyzed both the handwriting and the entire Schlichtegroll-Mölk-Nannerl correspondence in "Albert von Mölk: Mozart Myth-maker? Study of an 18th-century Correspondence," *Mozart-Jahrbuch 1995*:155–91. My comments here summarize one section of his article.

Salzburg, with the Salzach River in the foreground. In the eighteenth century, Salzburg was not a city in Austria but an independent state ruled by a prince-archbishop. It was part of the Holy Roman Empire, which during Mozart's lifetime was ruled by the Habsburgs: first, by Francis I and Maria Theresa (until her death in 1780), then by Joseph II (coregent with his mother from 1765 to 1780 before becoming Habsburg monarch from 1780 to 1790), followed by Joseph's brother, Leopold II.

This seems to be how we got the myth of a childish, irresponsible, yet divinely inspired composer, the Mozart we encounter in too many biographies—even quite recent ones—and see again in *Amadeus*. Somebody made all this up, and it appears that that somebody was a Salzburg cleric named Albert von Mölk.

CONSTANZE WEBER MOZART
Before going out for his 5:00 a.m. horseback ride, Mozart often left a note for his wife, Constanze, that ran something like this:

> Good morning, my darling wife, I hope that you have slept well, and that nothing has disturbed you; I desire you not to get up too early, not to get cold, not to stoop, not to stretch, not to scold the servants, not to fall over the doorstep. Do not be vexed at anything until I return. May nothing happen to you! I shall be back at [. . .] o'clock.[31]

---

31. Jahn, *W. A. Mozart*, transl. by Townsend as *The Life of Mozart*, II: 268.

Mozart adored his wife and their marriage remained loving and affectionate throughout their nine years together, until his premature death in 1791. Yet mythology has portrayed Constanze as lazy, petulant, and so lacking in musical or artistic sensitivity that she was incapable of appreciating her husband, much less understanding him. Although the "Stanzi" we see in *Amadeus* is a pretty insulting portrayal, it is tame in comparison to what you can find in some nineteenth- and twentieth-century biographies.

The Constanze-myth, as you recall, appears to have originated when Albert von Mölk fed to Friedrich Schlichtegroll the tidbit he claimed had come from Nannerl Mozart—that "Mozart married a most unsuitable girl . . . and this is why his household was such a shambles." By the mid-nineteenth century Mozart, now elevated from esteemed composer to monument of Western civilization, was thought to have been a tragic, persecuted, even saintly figure. It was therefore assumed that for him no normal wife would do, and Constanze was vilified to fit the preconceived stereotype.

Who was this woman, really?

Constanze Weber was one of four musically talented daughters of Fridolin Weber, a bass singer, music copyist, and theater prompter in the court of Elector Carl Theodor in Mannheim. Because of that court's outstanding musical establishment, the twenty-one-year-old Wolfgang Mozart was sent there in 1777 in search of a suitably prestigious job. He didn't get one, but he did fall in love with one of the Weber girls—not Constanze but Aloysia, an exceptionally talented soprano who later enjoyed a major career as an operatic soprano in Vienna.

Constanze came into Mozart's life in 1781, after he moved to Vienna. By then, Fridolin Weber had died and his widow and three unmarried daughters had followed Aloysia to the Habsburg capital. The widow ran a boarding house in which Mozart rented a room. Six months later, he described Constanze to his father:

> But the middle [daughter], I mean my good, dear Constanze, is the martyr of them all, and for that reason perhaps the most kindhearted, the cleverest, in a word, the best of them all.—She takes care of everything in the house—but can't do anything right in their eyes. . . . But before I set you free from my chatter, I must make you better acquainted with the character of my dearest Constanze;—she is not ugly, but also not really beautiful;—her whole beauty consists of two little black eyes and a pretty figure. She isn't witty but has enough common sense to fulfill her duties as

a wife and mother. . . . [S]he understands housekeeping and has the best heart in the world—I love her and she loves me with all her heart—now tell me if I could wish for a better wife?

(Letter dated December 15, 1781)

Nevertheless, Leopold Mozart remained suspicious. Not only did the Weber family presumably fail to meet his standard of high-ranking, educated musicians as exemplified by himself;[32] he was also perhaps even more skeptical of his son. Had Wolfgang allowed himself to be morally compromised, and was he therefore *obliged* to marry this girl? Despite Leopold's misgivings, the marriage took place on August 4, 1782, in a chapel of Vienna's St. Stephen's Cathedral.

Constanze and Mozart's courtship was marred by at least one significant spat—serious enough to cause them to break off their engagement for a while. At a party one evening at the house of their friend Baroness von Waldstätten, guests played a game called Forfeit, whose rules required that when ladies lost a round, they had to pull up their skirts to let a man measure their calves. When Constanze returned home, she laughingly told everybody this had happened to her. Mozart—despite being a partygoer and perpetual joker himself—was not amused and gave her a stern lecture on the spot. She retaliated by refusing to see him or even speak to him. All this we deduce from his pleading yet preachy letter to her of April 29, 1782 (in fact, it sounds like one of his father's letters to him). They must have made up fairly quickly, because three months later they were married. If they were the normal human beings we assume they were, this surely wasn't their last argument; but it is the only one for which documentation has come down to us.

The Mozarts had six children, four boys and two girls, of whom two survived to adulthood: Carl Thomas (1784–1858) and Franz Xaver Wolfgang (1791–1844). As an adult, Carl Thomas moved to Italy in an unsuccessful bid to launch a piano business, later working in Naples as a court employee. Franz Xaver Wolfgang, born just five months before his father's death, had moderate success as a composer but fared somewhat better as a touring pianist. At his mother's urging, he advertised himself as Wolfgang Amadeus Mozart; she also gave him his father's piano. His teachers included Antonio Salieri, the man demonized in *Amadeus* who, in actuality, was a fine composer and the teacher of Beethoven and Schubert, among many others. The Mozart boys returned to Salzburg for the 1841 unveiling of the

---

32. Fridolin Weber was perhaps more of an intellectual than Leopold realized: when Mozart bade farewell to Mannheim in March 1778, Weber presented him with a copy of the comedies of Molière as a going-away present.

Franz Xaver Wolfgang and Carl Thomas Mozart

city's first monument to their father, the statue that still stands in the Makartplatz today. They probably never saw each other again, and since neither of them had children, the Mozart line ended there.

Mozart and Constanze lived in a succession of apartments during their nine years together. Their constant moving from one place to another presented serious challenges to Mozart but perhaps more so to Constanze. In that era, a wife was expected to take charge of all aspects of a family's everyday living—their children's health, upbringing, and clothes; the needs of live-in pupils studying with her husband (there were often one or two); and the management of the overall household budget (food, bill-paying, social engagements, clothes for herself and her husband). The Mozarts' home was a busy place. They had parties that sometimes lasted till morning; rehearsals went on nearly every day; friends, students, and music copyists stopped by; and hairdressers came every day—those high-flying eighteenth-century wigs had to be professionally arranged before you allowed yourself to be seen by anyone except your family.

How well did she fare at all this? The only report we have, other than the sweet letter Mozart penned to his father before their marriage—the one quoted earlier in this chapter—comes from no less stern a judge than Leopold Mozart. During a ten-week visit to the Mozarts in 1785, he found himself in a whirlwind of concertizing, rehearsing, music copying, and entertaining ("we never go to sleep before 1 a.m.") and reported to Nannerl that household expenditures (Constanze's responsibility) were "extremely economical" (letter dated March 19, 1785).

Musically, Constanze was both a pianist and a singer. Mozart wrote piano music for her and, during their second year of marriage, composed vocalises (technical exercises for the voice) as preparation for the difficult soprano solos he intended her to sing in his Mass in C Minor, K. 427/417a. She performed these solos during the couple's one and only visit to Salzburg, in the late summer of 1783. Constanze also had a special fondness for fugues (complicated musical counterpoint; see "fugue" in the glossary)—as did Emperor Joseph II—and so her husband wrote a few for her. He liked to have her in the room as he was composing, so that they could chat and joke with each other and sing through arias to hear how they sounded. In one of his last letters to her, he bemoans her absence:

> [W]hat sad, boring hours I am spending here—even my work doesn't give me joy anymore, because I am so used to taking a break now and then and having a few words with you, but this pleasure is unfortunately not possible right now—if I go to the piano and sing something from the opera [*The Magic Flute*], I immediately have to stop—it makes me too emotional—*Basta!* [enough!] . . . Adieu, dearest little wife of mine.
>
> (Letter dated July 7, 1791)

Perhaps this is the place to remind ourselves that, for unknown reasons, we have no surviving letters from her.

Some years ago, a doctoral candidate at an Ivy League university gave a talk at a scholarly conference in which he sneeringly referred to "Constanze running off to the spa again," as if she went there for fun. But the fact is that on numerous occasions from 1789 through 1791 she contracted serious illnesses. Her doctors sometimes sent her to a spa in Baden, near Vienna, for weeks at a time. In the summer of 1791, when Mozart wrote her the letter just quoted, she was there because of a nearly gangrenous leg infection. As the wife of a busy composer leading a hectic life, Constanze had to learn how to handle constant pressures throughout their years together, not the least of which was his ever-changing income, out of which she had to struggle to keep their household on an even keel. Plus the strain of her six pregnancies in nine years, with four babies that lived for a few hours or a few months.

After her husband's unexpected death at thirty-five, Constanze and her two sons (one just five months old) were left in severe financial straits. Though she should have been entitled to a widow's pension (from the Musicians' Society), her husband had never submitted the necessary birth certificate to complete the application for the society, so she was ineligible. Applying to the emperor herself, she was granted a lifetime stipend of one-third of his salary. Then she initiated several moves to improve her situation, giving benefit concerts and making arrangements for others to do so as well;

Constanze Weber Mozart

organizing Wolfgang's music for posthumous publication; and selling his manuscripts to publishers, taking great care with matters of musical accuracy. All in all, the much-maligned Constanze Mozart proved to be a canny and resourceful businesswoman.

Some years later, she met a Danish diplomat stationed in Vienna, Georg Nikolaus von Nissen, whom she married in 1809. Nissen, you may remember, wrote a biography of the composer to which Constanze made invaluable contributions—chiefly a vast collection of manuscripts and her priceless personal memories—and, in fact, it was she who saw the book into print when Nissen died before completing it. She made certain that it got finished, though the final result, as you remember, was unfortunately flawed. The Nissens had resided in Salzburg for years before that, probably in order to avail themselves of Nannerl's help with the biography and to make use of her collection of letters and manuscripts. It was there that Nissen died in 1826 and Nannerl in 1829. The twice-widowed Constanze Mozart Nissen lived on until 1842.

TIMETABLE OF EIGHTEENTH-CENTURY EVENTS

*People and events of musical significance are printed in **boldface**.*

1715	Death of King Louis XIV of France, the Sun King, builder of Versailles
1715–1774	Reign of King Louis XV (whose mistress was Madame de Pompadour)
1732	**Joseph Haydn born**
1733	Voltaire, *Letters Concerning the English Nation* Emperor Joseph II born
1750	**J. S. Bach dies**
1751	**Nannerl Mozart born**
1751–1772	*Encyclopédie*
1756	**Wolfgang Amadè Mozart born**
1760–1820	Reign of King George III (British monarch during the American Revolution)
1762	Rousseau, *Social Contract* and *Émile*
1765–1780	Coregency of Empress Maria Theresa and Emperor Joseph II
1770	**Beethoven born**
1776	American Declaration of Independence
1777–1779	**Mozart's journey to Mannheim and Paris**
1780	Joseph II becomes sole Habsburg emperor after the death of Maria Theresa
1781	**Mozart takes up residence in Vienna**
1783	American colonies win independence, become the United States
1789	Storming of Bastille prison in Paris; beginning of the French Revolution
1790	Joseph II dies; his brother Leopold II becomes Habsburg monarch
1791	**Mozart dies**
1792	**Beethoven moves to Vienna**
1793–1794	Reign of Terror in France; virtual anarchy
1806, 1809	Napoleon's troops occupy Vienna
1809	**Haydn dies**
1827	**Beethoven dies**
1829	**Nannerl Mozart Sonnenberg dies**
1842	**Constanze Weber Mozart dies**

THE AGE OF ENLIGHTENMENT

Mozart lived during the Enlightenment, which traced its roots as far back as the Renaissance but came to full flower in the eighteenth century. Both Leopold and Wolfgang Mozart were steeped in its ideals, ideals that profoundly shaped the thinking of writers, artists, musicians, philosophers—and crowned monarchs—throughout that tempestuous century. Enlightenment goals ignited the French and American revolutions

Europe circa 1780, locating cities most important to Mozart. The map of Europe changed frequently and dramatically during the eighteenth century. This is what it looked like around the time that Mozart moved to Vienna in 1781.

and reshaped dynasties in Prussia, Russia, and the Habsburg Empire. To understand Wolfgang Amadè Mozart, we need to review some key principles of the Enlightenment.

To *enlighten* means "to shed light on"—to illuminate, to make clear, to sweep away the "darkness" of obscurity, superstition, and error. This was the goal of all Enlightenment thinkers, but there was an enormous range of views about how to do that. Opinions were so varied that they sometimes contradicted one another. *There was no one, single "Enlightenment" agreed to by everyone,* though everybody stood proudly under that same umbrella as they argued back and forth.

The Enlightenment in the seventeenth century had produced Descartes, Leibniz, Bacon, Locke, Hobbes, and Spinoza. Its eighteenth-century adherents included, in France, *philosophes* (popular philosophers) such as Voltaire, Montesquieu, Rousseau, and Diderot; in England, David Hume and Adam Smith; in Germany, Kant, Lessing, Goethe, and Schiller; and in the American colonies, such key figures as George Washington, Thomas Jefferson, Thomas Paine, John Adams, Samuel Adams, and Benjamin Franklin.

Intellectually, the period's most stunning achievement was the multivolume *Encyclopédie,* the work of D'Alembert, Diderot, Rousseau, and others, which arrayed the proud discoveries of the Enlightenment in alphabetical order. Politically, the era's masterpieces were the Rights of Man in France and, in America, the Declaration of Independence, Constitution, and Bill of Rights.

Another name for the Enlightenment, the Age of Reason, suggests its central tenet: we should think and act rationally in every facet of existence. If we did, the results would be:

- Judicious and equitable laws
- Equality of all citizens: no slavery, no inherited titles
- Fair criminal codes
- An educated (and therefore rational) populace
- Perfect architecture, town planning, roads, sewage systems, etc.
- Tolerance towards the world's varied cultures and religions
- A clear-thinking, happy, productive society

Empiricism and the scientific method were natural outgrowths of rational thought. We should place our trust in proven facts, not give in to hunches or handed-down wisdom from the past; only empirically tested data can yield unassailable results.

The Catholic Church was regarded not only as having no corner on truth, but as guilty of fostering superstition and intolerance. People should seek knowledge through science, not through blind adherence to religious dogmas or creeds. However, not all Enlightenment thinkers excoriated the church. Many intellectuals (including the Mozarts) felt free to criticize individual churchmen while remaining devout believers themselves.

Certain laws were thought to be inherent in human nature, revealed as such by reason. These were termed *natural laws*. Natural law, it was believed, is innate in all of us; by contrast, *legislated law* is changeable because it can be altered or even thrown out whenever a legislative body (or a monarch) decides to do so. The "unalienable rights" (often misquoted as "inalienable") appealed to in the Declaration of Independence are based on *natural law*.

Optimism was the prevailing spirit of the age, fueled by the unshakable conviction that with reason as our guide, we could build Utopia on earth. This

Francisco de Goya (1746–1828) The Sleep of Reason Produces Monsters

was the fervent belief of those rebellious colonists who crafted the documents leading to the United States of America—a belief shared by those who stormed the Bastille in Paris in 1789.

Criticism and satire flourished as counterweights to this starry optimism. Newspapers were invented in the eighteenth century, and with them came cartoons lampooning the grandiose ideas floating through Europe. Jonathan Swift's *Gulliver's Travels* ridiculed the Enlightenment's naive self-confidence, and his darkly satirical essay "A Modest Proposal" cut deeper still, proposing that the solution to hunger lay readily to hand: "A young healthy child well nursed, is, at a year old, a most delicious, nourishing, and wholesome food, whether stewed, roasted, baked, or boiled." Yet the most scathing attack had already come towards the end of the previous century from Hobbes's *Leviathan,* which defined human nature as intrinsically bestial and our lives as "nasty, brutal, and short."

The Sleep of Reason Produces Monsters, by the Spanish artist Francisco de Goya, portrayed the Age of Reason as both dream and nightmare. Goya's famous etching can be interpreted in contrasting ways: as a depiction of what reason might produce (those terrifying bats)—but also of what can result if reason falls asleep.

ENLIGHTENED DESPOTISM

It may come as a shock to discover that this Age of Reason, despite its vaunted democratic and egalitarian ideals, fostered absolute monarchy. This was regarded, not as contrary to Enlightenment principles, but as their perfect, even divinely ordained embodiment. The surest way to build Utopia was to entrust the task to one all-powerful, Enlightened ruler.

The Enlightened monarchs of the eighteenth century were Frederick the Great of Prussia, Catherine the Great of Russia, and Joseph II. Joseph ruled the Habsburg monarchy from 1780 to 1790 and Mozart resided in its capital, Vienna, from 1781 until his death in 1791. None of these despots was interested in creating a democracy. All of them studied the French *philosophes* assiduously. Frederick paid Voltaire to reside at Berlin for three years. Later, Voltaire corresponded with Catherine for years but felt too old to journey to her court. Catherine subsequently hosted Diderot for six months. Joseph II, in France to see his sister, Marie Antoinette, afterward sneaked off to meet Rousseau in person. These were all brilliant, progressive, highly educated rulers, who struggled with single-minded devotion to bring their empires in line with the newest, most rational ideas.

However, they brooked little or no argument about what needed to be done or how and when to do it. This is why they are called despots. Still, they accomplished amazing things. Essential to all of these monarchs was absolute power and their subjects' total subservience to it; otherwise their reforms could not be carried out.

The ruler closest to the Mozarts was Joseph II, who pursued the reform efforts begun by his mother, Empress Maria Theresa, though with much greater intensity. By the end of his brief decade as emperor he could cite the following achievements:

- Many aspects of serfdom had been abolished.
- Legal and judicial codes had been streamlined.
- Peasants were allowed to marry, learn skills, and provide for the education of their children.
- Censorship was greatly reduced. (You could even criticize Joseph himself, either in public or in the newspaper, and not be punished for it.)
- Nobility were subject to the same laws and punishments as everyone else.
- Protestants and Greek Orthodox believers were no longer persecuted, but could live freely and worship publicly.
- Jews, no longer driven out of the empire, were permitted to live in cities, to apply for a wider array of jobs than previously, and to practice their faith (though only in private).
- The Order of Freemasons, abolished by the pope in 1738, was allowed to establish itself in the empire and to flourish (until 1785, when Joseph placed restraints on it, without, however, shutting it down).[33]

Enlightenment Rulers and the Arts

As part and parcel of these despots' efforts to shape their countries into ideal societies, the arts were cultivated at the highest level and without regard to cost. Rulers vied with one another in the size, scope, distinction, and—to be sure—the manifest expense of their artistic establishments. Later in this book, Mozart will undertake a sixteen-month journey in search of a permanent appointment. He won't find one, but along the way he will experience at firsthand the extraordinary orchestras, choruses, ballets, opera houses, and marionette theaters maintained not only at Versailles but even in a smaller (though politically quite significant) court such as Mannheim. To be sure, Joseph II's court in Vienna was no small potatoes, either.

---

33. The ideals of Freemasonry and the Enlightenment were virtually synonymous, with one exception: Freemasonry was democratic.

Emperor Joseph II and his brother, later to become Leopold II

COMPOSERS AND ENLIGHTENED RULERS

What was the role of composers in these magnificent courts? Were they prized celebrities, as were famous thinkers such as Voltaire? Hardly. *They were effectively servants; they wore the livery (uniform) of their court; they ate, were housed, and performed their expected duties alongside other servants.* Mozart's problem was unique: his childhood tours had introduced him to queens, kings, empresses, all sorts of royalty. Year after year he had chatted, dined, and played music with them. How could he now, as an adult, consent to be treated as inferior to such people? The reality was that he had no other choice.

A MOZART CHRONOLOGY

1751 Maria Anna Mozart ("Nannerl," or "little Anna") is born. She, too, is a musical prodigy.

1756 On January 27, Wolfgang is born. It was a difficult birth; his mother nearly died.

1758 "Woferl" (or "Wolfgangerl," family nicknames) enjoys the sound of thirds his little fingers pick out on the family harpsichord. His father begins to teach Nannerl the following year, using a music book he has written for her.

1760 Wolfgang learns to play eight little minuets from Nannerl's book and "composes" a keyboard concerto, mostly ink splotches because he can't control a quill pen yet. When Leopold declares the music too difficult to perform, Woferl replies that concertos are supposed to be hard.

1763 In January, the children perform at the Habsburg Court in Vienna for Empress Maria Theresa, after which she presents them with outfits from two of her sixteen (!) children. Later the whole family embarks on a three-and-a-half year concert tour of European capitals including Munich, Paris (twice), London, The Hague, Amsterdam, and Brussels.

1764 At Versailles, the children play for King Louis XV and Madame de Pompadour and celebrate New Year's festivities with the royal family. Leopold arranges for the publication in Paris of Wolfgang's first keyboard sonatas, K. 6, 7, 8, and 9.[34] They are considerably touched up by the father's hand before seeing print. In London, Woferl meets Johann Christian Bach (youngest son of J. S.), whose progressive musical style, featuring fast-moving, "singing" themes, exerts a lasting influence on the young Mozart.

1765 In London, Wolfgang's musicianship is examined and tested by members of the Royal Society: can he play unknown music at sight, improvise bass harmonies to unfamiliar melodies, name pitches sounded from across the room, and play with the keys covered? Of course, he can—as could an unusually gifted, well-taught child musician today: Mozart's talent was prodigious but not unique. What was most astounding about him was his compositional mastery of every musical genre, an achievement that showed itself only in adulthood. The Mozarts leave London for Holland in late July. Nannerl contracts typhoid fever and nearly dies; later Wolfgang also succumbs and lies seriously ill for several weeks.

1766 The family return from their three-year journey at the end of November. Leopold shows off

---

34. When Mozart's compositions for a given year are cited in this chronology, they are intended as examples, representing only a fraction of his output.

their princely gifts and souvenirs to friends and neighbors, inviting them to the Mozarts' apartment, where he has arranged the items in a special exhibit.

1767 The Mozarts travel to Vienna in late fall, but Leopold decides to leave because of a threatened smallpox epidemic. Nannerl and Wolfgang catch the disease anyway, but recover and the family goes back to Vienna.

1768 The children are received by Empress Maria Theresa and her son, who will rule as Emperor Joseph II during most of Mozart's decade there (1781–1791). Joseph suggests that twelve-year-old Wolfgang write an opera. He does (*La finta semplice*), but when it doesn't get staged, Leopold writes a long letter to the empress to complain. This wasn't a good idea; she views it as impertinence and remains bitingly critical of the family from then on. Wolfgang composes *Bastien und Bastienne*, K. 50, a one-act opera, which is performed at the home of Dr. Mesmer, a Mozart family friend who experimented with an early form of hypnotism (mesmerism), which Mozart later caricatures in *Così fan tutte* (1790). Wolfgang also writes "Mass for an Orphanage" (*Waisenhausmesse*), K. 47a, which is praised in a Vienna newspaper following its performance, during which Wolfgang sang some of the (soprano) solos.

1769 Archbishop Schrattenbach appoints the thirteen-year-old as (unpaid) third concertmaster in the Salzburg orchestra. In December, father and son set out on the first of three journeys to Italy.

1770 Wolfgang's voice changes and he begins to grow facial hair. He concertizes in Verona, Florence, Rome, and Naples. In Milan, his first significant opera, *Mitridate, rè di Ponto*, is performed twenty-two times to great applause. In Bologna, he meets the music theorist and historian Padre Giovanni Battista Martini, who is so impressed with the fourteen-year-old boy that he arranges for him to be appointed to the Philharmonic Society of Bologna, a great honor. Wolfgang later sends compositions to Padre Martini for criticism. In Rome, the pope awards Wolfgang the Order of the Golden Spur. While in St. Peter's during Holy Week, he writes out Allegri's *Miserere* from memory after hearing it sung by the Sistine Chapel choir; the music was considered the private possession of the Vatican and no outsider was supposed to have a copy. But the *Miserere* is stylistically simple and full of repeats, rendering his achievement perhaps somewhat less remarkable than was traditionally claimed.

1771 Father and son return home, then travel to Italy a second time, where Wolfgang's *Ascanio in Alba* is staged in Milan; then they journey back to Salzburg.

1772 Archbishop Schrattenbach dies

in 1771, succeeded by Archbishop Colloredo, whose Enlightenment reforms include a radical shortening and simplifying of sacred music and a reluctance to grant lengthy leaves-of-absence. Such restrictions, added to his dour manner and insensitivity to the arts, infuriate the Mozarts. Yet Leopold and Wolfgang are permitted a third trip to Italy, once again to Milan, for Wolfgang's opera *Lucio Silla.*

1773   Father and son are off to Vienna again in mid-summer, in hopes of a job in the court of Empress Maria Theresa. No luck: she already has a full complement of musicians. Wolfgang plays concerts in various churches and homes, including the residence of Dr. Mesmer, where *Bastien und Bastienne* had been staged in 1768. Compositions this year include the Symphony in G Minor, K. 183/173dB, and his first fully original piano concerto (K. 175).

1774   Munich commissions *La finta giardiniera* (The Pretend Gardeneress) and Leopold and Wolfgang travel there for rehearsals in December. Among other works, he writes a concerto for bassoon (K. 191).

1775   Nannerl joins her father and brother in Munich for the premiere of *La finta giardiniera* in January. Mozart, now second concertmaster of the Salzburg orchestra, writes the last four of his violin concertos (the first had been composed in 1773) and,

to honor a visit from Empress Maria Theresa's youngest son, *Il rè pastore* (The Shepherd King). Across the Atlantic Ocean, there are skirmishes at Lexington and Concord that lead to the American Revolution.

1776   The whole family spends the year at home for the first time since 1761, depriving us of family letters, which means we have little information about Mozart (now twenty) except that he writes two piano concertos, a good deal of church music, and a number of divertimentos and serenades including the "Haffner" Serenade, K. 250, for a friend's wedding. In September, Mozart—rather, his father, who still takes over at such moments—pens a warm letter to Padre Martini in Bologna asking his opinion of Mozart's new church motet (K. 222). The priest's reply praises its "natural" changes of key and its smooth voice-leading.

1777   At twenty-one, Mozart needs a regular appointment, not in Salzburg, which he and Leopold despise, but in some major court. Leopold's petition to go job-hunting with his son is denied. Mozart then applies on his own behalf—not to travel, but to leave the court's employ altogether. In response, the archbishop terminates them both and wishes them good luck! Leopold manages to get reinstated but decides he'd better not leave town.

1777–1779   Mozart and Maria Anna, who is acting as chaperone, launch what turns into a sixteen-month journey, most of it spent in Mannheim and Paris. At Augsburg, their first stop, Mozart plays concerts and enjoys the company of his cousin, "the Bäsle." In Mannheim, he is smitten by the gifted seventeen-year-old Aloysia Weber, who will later take the role of Donna Anna in his *Don Giovanni;* but he receives no offer from that fabulous court, probably because he is seen as no longer a cute child prodigy nor yet a mature composer. In Paris he writes the Symphony in D Major, K. 297/300a ("Paris") and the Piano Sonata in A Minor, K. 310. On July 3, 1778, after a brief illness, Maria Anna dies. On his way home, he is jilted by Aloysia Weber, who later marries Joseph Lange. Despite personal tragedies, this long trip proves hugely important both musically and intellectually. Mannheim was the home of Europe's finest orchestra, a great theater, and outstanding musicians. Paris was the capital of the European Enlightenment, with *philosophes* including Baron Grimm, the Mozarts' Parisian guide in 1763 through 1764, with whom Mozart resides for three months in 1778, after the death of his mother.

1779–1780 Mozart is back in Salzburg, again in the dreaded Colloredo's service (now as court organist, responsible for both church music and any other music he is ordered to write). Despite his frustration, he creates probing, suddenly mature works such as the "Coronation" Mass, K. 317;

the *Vesperae solennes de confessore,* K. 339; the Sinfonia Concertante for Violin and Viola, K. 364/320d; and the opera *Idomeneo,* K. 366.

1781 *Idomeneo* premieres in Munich in January with both Leopold and Nannerl in the audience. The three of them vacation for three weeks afterwards, Mozart ignoring Colloredo's summons to come to Vienna at once. At last, he does go. After volcanic arguments with Colloredo and his chamberlain, he quits/is fired and, at twenty-five, excitedly begins a freelance career in Vienna. Many of his best-known works date from his decade here—a period which, tragically, turns out to be the last years of his life. But his new career has a shaky start; he earns very little until the summer of 1782, when his new *Singspiel, The Abduction from the Seraglio* (Die Entführung aus dem Serail), has a smashing success. (A *Singspiel* is a type of opera.)

1782 *The Abduction from the Seraglio* debuts in July. Shortly afterward, he marries Constanze Weber (one of Aloysia's three sisters) against his father's wishes. He begins his association with Baron Gottfried van Swieten, who introduces him to the sacred music of Handel and J. S. Bach, music that will profoundly influence Mozart's own music, both secular and sacred. A stunning early example is the Mass in C Minor, K. 427/417a (unfinished). This is also the year of his "Haffner" Symphony, K. 385, cobbled together from his earlier "Haffner" Serenade, K. 250; three piano concertos, K. 413, 414, and 415; and the first of what were to become his six "Haydn" String Quartets.

1783 Wolfgang and Constanze's first baby, Raimund Leopold, is born in June, but, left with a wet nurse in Vienna (a customary practice then), he dies during his parents' six-week visit to Salzburg from August to October. Mozart writes the "Linz" Symphony, K. 425, on their way home. Also composed this year: one of his four horn concertos; two more of the "Haydn" String Quartets; and the sacred work mentioned above, the Mass in C Minor, K. 427/417a (unfinished), performed in Salzburg during the young couple's stay there. In September, England and the American colonies sign the Treaty of Paris, ending the American Revolution.

1784 Mozart performs widely and with great success both as improvising pianist and as soloist in his six new piano concertos: K. 449, 450, 451, 453, 456, and 459. His income soars. Carl Thomas is born, one of two Mozart children to live to adulthood; the other, Franz Xaver Wolfgang, arrives in July 1791. Mozart is inducted into the Freemasons in December.

1785 During Leopold's ten-week (!) visit to the Mozart family—dramatized with breathtaking inac-

curacy in *Amadeus*—the proud father is astounded at the impressive amount of money his son is making; at his exhausting schedule, which takes him all over the city to perform and rehearse; at his popularity; and at his well-ordered household (a tribute to Constanze, so maligned in the movie). Leopold is a guest performer for several of his son's brand-new "Haydn" String Quartets. Mozart and Lorenzo da Ponte start work on *The Marriage of Figaro*. Other works this year: piano concertos K. 466, 467, and 482, and the last two of the six "Haydn" Quartets, including the "Dissonance." In December, Emperor Joseph II promulgates a sweeping, frightening reform of Freemasonry.

1786 Johann Thomas Leopold is born in October but dies a few weeks later. Mozart composes and performs three more piano concertos, among them the Piano Concerto in C Minor, K. 491. *The Marriage of Figaro* debuts in May. The Mozarts are invited to visit Prague in early 1787; in anticipation, the composer writes his "Prague" Symphony, K. 504. Also dating from this year are the piano concertos K. 488 and 503; another of the four horn concertos, K. 495; the "Kegelstatt" Trio for Clarinet, Viola, and Piano, K. 498;[35] and the moving farewell aria he wrote for Nancy Storace, the first Su-

---

35. The nickname comes from a legend that Mozart wrote this piece while playing a game of ninepins (*Kegeln*). The first performer of its difficult viola part was the composer himself.

sanna in *The Marriage of Figaro,* "Ch'io mi scordi di te," K. 505.

1787 *The Marriage of Figaro* and the "Prague" Symphony, K. 504, enjoy great success in Prague in January, prompting the management to ask Mozart to compose another opera for the following fall; this will be *Don Giovanni.* In April, he writes Leopold, who is seriously ill, an important letter affirming the Freemasons' view of death as "the true and ultimate purpose of our life." Leopold dies in May. *Don Giovanni* premieres in Prague in November to great acclaim, and in Vienna in May 1788. A seventeen-year-old musician from Bonn, Ludwig van Beethoven, travels to Vienna to audition for Mozart, in hopes of becoming his student. At first, Beethoven doesn't make much of an impression, but then (or so legend has it) he plays something more striking and Mozart predicts "great things for this young man." But by the time Beethoven can get back to Vienna again, in 1792, Mozart is dead. The Mozarts' daughter Theresa, born in December, dies six months later. In January, Mozart is appointed chamber-music composer to Emperor Joseph II. War with the Ottoman Empire is declared soon thereafter, causing Joseph, leading his troops, to be away from the city for months. War costs coupled with widespread crop failures trigger inflation, reducing support for the arts; theaters (including opera houses) shut their doors. Like a great many

others, Mozart has trouble making ends meet and begins to borrow money from his friend and fellow Mason, Johann Michael Puchberg. Compositions this year include the "Coronation" Piano Concerto, K. 537, a good deal of small-ensemble music, and his last three symphonies, including the "Jupiter," K. 551.

1789 Mozart spends two months traveling to Prague, Dresden, Leipzig, Potsdam (summer residence of the Prussian king, Friedrich Wilhelm II), and Berlin. In Leipzig he visits St. Thomas's Church, where J. S. Bach had been music director. Though he gives numerous performances on this trip, he garners no new commissions. Both he and Constanze suffer bouts of illness this year. Their daughter Anna Maria (reversing the names of his mother) is born in November and dies the same day. There are more letters to Puchberg, requesting loans. Compositions include an "updating" of Handel's *Messiah* (i.e., from Baroque to Classic-era vocal and instrumental style); the Clarinet Quintet, K. 581, for his fellow Mason, Anton Stadler; and the "Prussian" string quartets. He begins to write the opera *Così fan tutte* to a libretto by Lorenzo da Ponte. *The Marriage of Figaro* is revived with great success. In Paris, the prison known as the Bastille is stormed, marking the onset of the French Revolution.

1790 *Così fan tutte* (That's How Women Act) packs the house at its

January premiere; a triumph for Mozart. Emperor Joseph II dies in February; Vienna observes a period of mourning, during which no public concerts or theatrical performances are held. Joseph's brother is crowned Emperor Leopold II. Mozart, hoping to catch the eye of royalty or nobility during regional coronations of the new emperor, travels to Frankfurt, Mainz, Mannheim (where he sees a performance of *The Marriage of Figaro* in German), and Munich; but to no avail. Works this year include, in addition to *Così fan tutte,* two string quartets and a string quintet.

1791 In July, Constanze gives birth to Franz Xaver Wolfgang, one of two Mozart children to survive infancy (the other was Carl Thomas, born in 1784). But complications before and after preg-

nancy send her to Baden (not far from Vienna) to recuperate from a serious leg infection. Mozart visits often and composes a motet, *Ave verum corpus,* K. 618, for the choir there. Guaranteed stipends are offered, in exchange for new compositions, by merchants in Amsterdam and another group in Hungary.[36] On September 6, *La clemenza di Tito* debuts in Prague and on the 30th, *The Magic Flute* in Vienna, the former opera earning a mixed reception but the latter a triumph. Mozart is happy and extremely busy. Working simultaneously on several compositions including the Requiem, he is suddenly taken ill in mid-November and dies on December 5.

---

36. See Braunbehrens, *Mozart in Vienna 1781–1791,* transl. Timothy Bell (New York: Grove Weidenfeld, 1990), 141; and Julian Rushton, *Mozart* (Oxford, UK: Oxford University Press, 2006), 210.

2

CHILDHOOD AND YOUTH, 1756–1773

Mozart's boyhood reads like a fairy tale—except that it was true. At three, he was delighted by the sound of thirds he picked out on the harpsichord; at four, he learned to play a minuet in half an hour; at five, he started composing; at six, he performed before royalty for the first time. Not even the children of nobility traveled as widely as he did—to England, France, the Netherlands, Austria, Germany, and Italy—all the while performing, conducting, even publishing his own music. During this well-traveled childhood he met leading composers, European monarchs, and the pope; learned a bit of French, Italian, and English to add to his native German; lost his boy-soprano voice; and, by the time he returned home from the last of these tours, was a young man of seventeen. How did this amazing childhood come about; what was it like for him; and where did it ultimately lead?

The answer to how it came about is, of course, Leopold Mozart. This cultivated man of the Enlightenment seemed to sense just how to nurture his two children to artistic maturity, particularly his son, the "miracle that God allowed to be born in Salzburg."[1] The composer's boyhood affection for his father was beyond question. Every night Woferl sang the same Italian nursery song, to which Leopold sang the harmony; then the boy kissed him good night. Years later, as their relationship was threatening to unravel, Mozart recalled those days when he used to say, "Right after God comes Papa."[2]

LIFE IN SALZBURG

Until Wolfgang was seventeen, the Mozarts lived in a third-floor walkup apartment in a house owned by Lorenz Hagenauer, a prosperous businessman and friend of the family. Hagenauer served as Leopold's

1. Letter from Leopold Mozart to Lorenz Hagenauer dated July 30, 1768.
2. Letter from Mozart to his father dated March 7, 1778.

banker during the childhood tours, arranging letters of credit in strategically located cities where he had business connections. The family's apartment, advertised today as "Mozart's Birthplace," is reached by a stairway from the street. There was, of course, no running water or refrigeration; water had to be carried upstairs in buckets for cooking and for bathing. Garbage was disposed of and the family's "chamber [toilet] pots" were emptied in the same way. Groceries were shopped for a day or so in advance to keep them from spoiling. The Mozarts, like other families of better than average income, employed a housemaid to help with cooking, cleaning, and shopping. Nannerl and Wolfgang were probably assigned a few chores as well.

If you travel to Salzburg today you may get the seriously mistaken impression that the Mozarts were the town's most celebrated family. That certainly wasn't true then. Leopold Mozart was viewed as a standoffish and conceited man who looked down on most of his fellow musicians as musically and intellectually inferior (which in many cases was probably true). Years later, Wolfgang—who seems to have imbibed his father's contempt for the city—cursed it in the German equivalent of four-letter words.

In fact, however—although no member of the Mozart family is recorded as ever having said so—Salzburg is postcard-beautiful, nestled in a stunning alpine landscape.[3] Its location placed it within the musical and cultural orbits of Munich, Vienna, and northern Italy. The river Salzach, which runs through the city, was the prime attraction for its earliest settlers: *Salz* (salt) was transported from nearby mines down the river. Salzburg's boundaries extended so far in several directions that it was more of a county than a city. A distinct political entity, it did not become part of Austria until 1815, after the fall of Napoleon. There has always been a large number of churches, monasteries, and convents in the area: in the city itself, St. Peter's Abbey was founded by Benedictine monks in the seventh century; the cathedral, seat of the ruling prince-archbishop, dates from the eighth century. Salzburg University, also Benedictine, was established much later, in 1622. All three became important venues for Mozart's music.

Although Salzburg was the most important German-speaking archbishopric on the Continent, musicians viewed it as small-minded and oppressive. There was not much public music-making except for services in the cathedral, on a much smaller scale in the abbey and in the many churches

---

3. The 1965 movie *The Sound of Music* starring Julie Andrews was made nearby, and a bus will take you on "*The Sound of Music* Tour."

in the surrounding area, and on festive occasions at the university. Salzburg had no opera house. All in all, the musical horizon was pretty narrow.

EDUCATING NANNERL AND WOFERL

Leopold took charge of their education himself. Instead of sending Nannerl and Woferl to school, he homeschooled them. Probably no other teacher in Salzburg was more splendidly qualified. University trained and a voracious reader in several languages, he taught them not only music but foreign languages, mathematics, geography, science, plus that absolute necessity for properly brought up children in those days: dancing. Both children were swift learners. Wolfgang, who loved to dance, was also a whiz at math, decorating walls, floors, and any nearby furniture with endless rows of numbers. All his life he delighted in it—as an adult he doodled in the margins of some of his autograph manuscripts with what today is called number theory.[4]

Musical instruction started with Nannerl, who worked her way through "Nannerl's Music Book," a collection of short pieces Leopold compiled for her, some of which he had composed himself. Unlike her brother, she was taught only keyboard performance, not how to compose. Woferl began playing from her book when he was about four, and within a year was adding pieces of his own.

In teaching the boy musical composition, Leopold was evidently something of an innovator.[5] The standard method was to have students learn the rules of harmony and form by copying out examples that demonstrated them. The next step was to imitate the models, showing that they had grasped the rules. Eventually, they were allowed to write their own pieces. Leopold, however, seems to have let Wolfgang invent musical ideas freely, without prior imitation of textbook models. Instead, the child would scribble something down, or perhaps sing or play it, and his father would correct it. The result, of course, was a boy who loved to compose and who, in a sense, was teaching himself, his imagination darting off wherever it wanted to go. He was writing his own music—replete with Leopold's corrections, but his own compositions nevertheless (Leopold continued to edit his son's music until at least 1766 and perhaps well beyond that).[6] There is no record of Woferl having been assigned

---

4. According to Daniel N. Leeson's presentation, "Mozart and Math," at a conference of the International Society for Eighteenth-Century Studies in Dublin, July 25–31, 1999.
5. Braunbehrens, "Aus der Ferne," 17–18.
6. Cliff Eisen and Stanley Sadie report that "until the early 1770s scarcely a single autograph of Wolfgang's is without additions or alterations in his father's hand. Even later, the attributions and dates on Mozart's autographs are frequently by Leopold." *The New Grove Mozart* (New York: Macmillan, 2002), 3; also accessible at www.grovemusic.com.

standard musical textbooks; for the most part, Leopold apparently created his own curriculum.[7]

Besides the boy's budding talents as a composer and his rapidly growing skill at the keyboard, he displayed an astonishingly precise sense of pitch and a painful sensitivity to loud music: a blast from a trumpet would reduce him to tears. Neither child had to be reminded to practice—especially Woferl, who at night sometimes had to be ordered to get up from the keyboard and go to bed.

THE CHILDREN'S SPARE TIME

We have to imagine that with two very active kids added to nearly constant music-making—plus a dog—the Mozarts' house wasn't a very quiet place. But how did Nannerl and Wolfgang spend their unscheduled time? Since they didn't go to school, how much contact did they have with other children? We simply don't have much of an answer to such questions. The family as a whole enjoyed a rich social life, spending many of their evenings with other musicians either at home or at their friends' houses. The family's favorite game, referred to many times in their letters, was *Bölzlschiessen,* target-shooting with air guns at hand-drawn targets caricaturing themselves and the friends they'd invited for the occasion; favorite targets included pictures of people's rear ends.

Woferl's sense of fun extended in many directions and lasted all his life. An avid punster and prankster, he liked to create silly poems about people (often in a polyglot of languages) and wasn't above subjecting friends to sometimes hurtful practical jokes. His imagination took characteristically theatrical forms, forecasting his future as a composer of operas. As a little boy he invented the Kingdom of Back, assigning to this imaginary realm quite specific geographical features, including particular names for its cities and streets. He ruled as its king, with Nannerl its queen. His favorite time of the year was Carnival season (the weeks between Christmas and Lent), with its upside-down rules and normally forbidden privileges. As an adult, he once wrote both words and music for a Carnival skit in which he cast himself as Harlequin, writing home to ask that certain costumes be mailed to him. At various points in his career he set musical canons (a type of counterpoint) to comic, sometimes obscene Latin texts. In January 1787 while on his way to Prague, a city with a largely Slavic population, he made up Slavic-sounding nicknames for everybody in the coach, including his dog:

---

7. Stanley Sadie notes that Leopold Mozart's library included that era's standard text on counterpoint, Johann Fux's *Gradus ad Parnassum* (Ascent to Mount Parnassus, 1725), which the young Mozart would presumably have mastered. See Sadie, *Mozart: The Early Years, 1756–1781,* edited posthumously by Neal Zaslaw (New York: W. W. Norton, 2006), 114. For a definition of *counterpoint,* see "Glossary of Musical Terms."

I [am] Pùnkititi.—*My wife,* Schabla Pumfa. *Hofer,* Rozka-Pumpa. *Stadler,* Nàtschibinitschibi. *Joseph, my servant,* Sagadaratà. *Gauckerl, my dog,* Schamanuzky.—*Mad.me Quallenberg,* Runzifunzi.—*Mad.selle Crux,* Ps.—*Ramlo,* Schurimuri. *Freystädler,* Gaulimauli.[8]

Throughout Mozart's hectic life, however, leisure hours may have been scarce, extremely so in childhood, when he and Nannerl lived in a grown-up world most of the time, surrounded by adults and measured by adult standards. They were away much more often than they were at home, particularly Woferl. From the time he was six until shortly after his seventeenth birthday he spent a total of three and a half years in Salzburg. You might say he had no Salzburg childhood.

Yet we hear of no complaints from either of them; on the contrary, they seem to have had a rollicking good time traipsing from court to court and performing before unknown audiences twice or even three times a day. Amazingly, or at least as far as we know, they behaved like model citizens. Their father's copiously detailed travel reports make no mention of troublesome conduct on the part of either Woferl or Nannerl—not even occasional episodes of grouchiness or whining. Nor, apparently, was there ever a need to punish either one of them. This is the most startling fact of all, and stands in such contrast to the typical pattern of child-rearing in that era that it bears discussion.

RAISING A CHILD IN THE EIGHTEENTH CENTURY: TWO THEORIES

In the eighteenth century, harsh physical punishment of children was the norm.[9] In 1739 a Lutheran pastor explained that this is why God gave us "so many bushes . . . so that we would not lack for instruments of punishment." The goal was to transform children—by force, if necessary—into morally upright, civilized, economically productive adults. Beginning at a very early age, they were to be kept under tight control and assigned specific tasks, lest they acquire habits of idleness.

The most widely respected German educator of that period was August Hermann Francke. Pastor and professor of Hebrew at the University of Halle, Francke created a school for poor children that was so highly praised by the aristocracy that many of them not only supported

---

8. Letter to his friend Gottfried von Jacquin dated January 15, 1787. The Mozarts' dog Gauckerl came along for the journey. There are references here and there in the family correspondence to pets the family owned, including dogs, cats, and birds.

9. Barbara Beuys, *Familienleben in Deutschland: Neue Bilder aus der deutschen Vergangenheit* [Family Life in Germany: New Images from the German Past] (Reinbek bei Hamburg: Rowalt, 1980), especially 324–31.

it financially but sent their own children there. The future Frederick the Great was raised in strict accordance with Francke's principles. To begin with, the professor believed, you must break a child's will; until that is accomplished, the necessary perfect obedience cannot begin. Francke's views on corporal punishment, however, were considered moderate. His teachers were ordered

> not to pull hair [or] strike [a child's] head with objects, and not to hit [children] at all on Sundays or holidays.

At the opposite educational pole from Francke was the Swiss-born French *philosophe* Jean-Jacques Rousseau, who argued that the purpose of a child's education was to foster the emergence of a "natural man." We are all born good, loving, and free-spirited, he argued, and it is these innate qualities that education must nourish. Up to the age of twelve, children should learn spontaneously, from life and nature, not books, and must be shielded as long as possible from society and civilization, whose evil and corrupt ways might destroy their native-born innocence. Rousseau's absolute belief in the innocence of children was soon taken up by Romantic poets (for example, by William Blake in his *Songs of Innocence* and *Songs of Experience*), exerted a decisive influence on nineteenth-century Romantic philosophy, and continues to form the bedrock of modern educational theories.

Rousseau first proclaimed his radical ideas in *Émile, or Education,* which appeared in 1762, when Wolfgang was six. Presumably Leopold Mozart at least heard about these ideas, because they provoked violent reactions both pro and con and the book was burned in Paris and Geneva. Significantly, Rousseau restricted his novel ideas to boys; girls were to be trained as future wives and mothers, as had always been the case. He sent his own five children, all illegitimate, to an orphanage.

Thankfully, Leopold Mozart appears to have subscribed wholeheartedly to neither of these extremes. If anything—despite the myth of him as a relentless taskmaster—he seems to have leaned a bit more toward Rousseau than toward Francke. Not only did he employ no physical punishment, as far as we know, but he seems never to have forced either child to learn; instead, he encouraged them. Still, his single-minded mission was clearly to turn them into productive adults—à la Francke—with no reliance on Mother Nature to be their teacher—à la Rousseau. Nor did he share Rousseau's fear of exposing them to the evil influences of the world: he took Nannerl and Woferl straight to the center of that world, where they explored for themselves its colorful whirl of languages and customs. And what was the kids' reaction to all this? Not only were they not at all frightened, as Rousseau would have predicted; they adapted easily to each new environment and performed like pros in all of them. How much of their astonishing adaptability we should attribute to the way their parents raised them, and how much to their own natural dispositions, is impossible to say.

As the years wore on, however, tragic repercussions scarred both children's lives. Nannerl suffered badly from her traumatic removal from the family concert stage. Leopold and/or Maria Anna's actions were fully in line with that era's conventional thinking; even the otherwise progressive Rousseau would have agreed with them. But it broke their daughter's heart and brought a cruel end to her potentially brilliant professional career. She never again performed outside Salzburg.

Wolfgang returned home from his three Italian journeys (1769–1773) a highly promising seventeen-year-old. But the other side of the coin wasn't so attractive: the endless praise reaped over the course of eleven years impressed upon him how exceptional he was, a fact (and it was a fact) that in later years he took pleasure in pointing out to other musicians— then wondered why they looked annoyed. Added to this was that, after dining with monarchs in city after city, how was he to cope with putting on a servant's livery and bowing to the whims of a prince-archbishop, an emperor, or indeed anyone? His enchanted boyhood had provided him with an incalculably rich musical and cultural education, but at a high price, leaving him with a sense of superiority capable of inflaming his enemies and sometimes even exasperating his friends.

WHY MAKE THESE TOURS?

Why, we might wonder, would parents subject their children to this? What did they expect to gain that could possibly make the risks of long-distance travel with a six-year-old boy and an eleven-year-old girl worthwhile? Leopold and Maria Anna Mozart probably had several quite specific goals in mind. First and foremost, they planned to exploit that century's fascination for child prodigies; in fact, our modern curiosity about exceptionally gifted children dates from that time. But because prodigies were so much in vogue, there were lots of them. Woferl met two in Italy: the English violinist Thomas Linley and the Italian keyboard player Giuseppe Pallavicini.

A second purpose—never mentioned straight out, but you get a clear sense of it here and there in Leopold's letters—was to put *Leopold* on the job market. Certainly (he must have thought), some discerning court would make an offer to the father of two prodigiously gifted children who was a respected composer himself as well as the author of a well-regarded treatise on violin playing. Occasionally his letters hint at a potential opening, but none of them panned out and he remained in Salzburg until his death.

But the tours' primary goal was to lay the groundwork for Woferl's future career. The problem with this was that people were starting to realize that *Wunderkinder* rarely make it into adulthood with their miraculous talents intact. Gradually, their gifts tend to peter out, leaving them to lead normal lives as adults. How could anyone know that this little boy was going to break that mold?

After a three-week journey to Munich in January 1762—perhaps intended as a trial run—the family's decade of travel really got underway when they spent four months in Vienna from October 1762 to January 1763. During these tours (though not the later ones to Italy), Leopold sent frequent letters to his landlord, friend, and creditor Lorenz Hagenauer containing detailed reports of expenditures, difficulties encountered, celebrities the family met (musical, clerical, and royal), and, of course, audiences' astonished reactions to the children's performances. Leopold meant for Hagenauer to pass around these letters, particularly at the Salzburg court, where important people, he hoped, would be impressed. Leopold also intended to use them in the biography of his son which he planned to write, but never did.

CHALLENGES AND HAZARDS ON TOUR

How did the family prepare for these lengthy journeys, which took them over roads that, depending on the season, were muddy, rutted, dusty, or icy; to cities that none of them had seen before, where they encountered people who spoke languages, wore clothes, used types of currency, and ate kinds of food all quite unknown to them? What were they most worried about as they set out? To begin with, where, exactly, did they intend to go?

That is our first shock: the Mozarts apparently had no carefully prepared itinerary in mind. In those days the mecca for musicians was Italy, as it had been for 150 years; Italian singers and instrumentalists still commanded top salaries in courts all over Europe, regularly receiving more perks and more distinguished appointments than native Germans. Despite this, the Mozarts didn't head south until several years later—in 1769, when Leopold took his son to Italy for the first of three tours.

Although the family had no precise plan, they did heed good advice when they got it. In Vienna, the French ambassador urged them to go to Paris; so they went to Paris.[10] In Paris, everyone said London was a must;

---

10. Important stops en route to Paris included Augsburg (Leopold's home town), Ludwigsburg, Munich, Schwetzingen, Mainz, Frankfurt, Coblenz, Aachen, and Brussels.

so they went to London. In London, The Hague was highly touted—and so on. Actually, it was in London that the necessity of going to Italy was urged upon them, which may be why Leopold and the boy turned up there later on.[11]

Leopold proved quite savvy at finding his way to the person or persons in each city who could be of most help. Undoubtedly the most significant of these was the Baron Friedrich Melchior Grimm in Paris, who would later become at once indispensable and a thorn in the side of the twenty-two-year-old Wolfgang when he visited the city in 1778 looking for a job.[12] On this 1763–1764 trip, Grimm, a well-known *philosophe* as well as a highly supportive fan of little Woferl, simply took charge of everything, getting the Mozarts into Versailles, arranging concerts, and taking care of all those details without which no concert can take place (tickets, lighting, etc.); in short, befriending and aiding them in every conceivable way. It is safe to say that a Grimm-less Paris would have either failed or been incomparably more difficult.[13]

Financially, this three-year journey was partly underwritten by Archbishop Schrattenbach, who was eager for his musicians to bring glory to his court while expanding their own horizons. Leopold's request for an extended leave of absence was granted and, as the trip grew ever longer, Schrattenbach appears to have either okayed all subsequent requests or to have stopped paying attention. Hagenauer's letters of credit in city after city had, of course, to be repaid. Leopold's salary could by no stretch of the imagination support European travel for four people even with Schrattenbach's contribution, so how was all this paid for? By the children's music-making. Everything was up to them—a spectacular risk. It then fell to Leopold to organize their appearances, sometimes one right after the other (he appears to have never taken part himself). He wrote from Vienna on October 19, 1762:

> Today we were at the French ambassador's. Tomorrow we're invited to Count Harrach's from 4 to 6, but I don't know what for. . . . Everywhere we go, we are picked up in a carriage by a servant and then brought back home. From 6 to 6:30 we are to perform for six ducats at a big concert given by a certain rich nobleman, where Vienna's finest virtuosos will

---

11. As they headed back to Salzburg in 1766, Leopold was tempted to veer off toward Italy, but decided not to delay his return any longer—they had been gone since 1763!

12. See the entry for Grimm in "Important People in Mozart's Life."

13. Yet it was almost by happenstance that Leopold met Grimm. As he reported to Lorenz Hagenauer in a letter dated April 1, 1765, a merchant's wife in Frankfurt provided him with a letter of recommendation to Grimm.

perform. . . . Once we drove at 2:30 to a place where we stayed until 3:45; there, Count Hardegg had us picked up in his carriage and drove at a full gallop to a lady's house where we stayed till 5:30. From there, Count Kaunitz had us picked up and we were at his house until almost 9. . . .

Did the children's performances manage to keep the family solvent? The answer to this is hard to nail down from surviving records, but the best guess is that things were often nip and tuck. They made out well in Paris and London, even though their expenses were considerably higher in those cities than elsewhere. Whenever either Woferl or his father took ill, appearances stopped; there were no instances of Nannerl going it alone, or of the kids' appearing in the absence of their father. Can you imagine your family's income being entirely dependent on one little boy's ability to open people's pocketbooks? Any time Wolfgang was unable to perform, his family earned nothing, though their expenses continued unabated.

Nor did their earnings always arrive in cashable form. Frequently the children were rewarded with elegant trinkets—delicate items of jewelry, a miniature sword, say, or watches (these were Wolfgang's favorite, he once sarcastically remarked, because he accumulated such a stash of them). Such gifts could not be pawned, which meant that they were of no help in paying innkeepers or buying meals. Still, some of these presents were pretty impressive. Leopold reports from Vienna:

> On the 15th the empress [Maria Theresa] had her paymaster deliver via two sets of clothes, one for the boy and one for the girl.
>
> (Letter dated October 16, 1762)

From Paris:

> My Master Wolfgang . . . has received from Madame la Contesse de Tessé a gold snuffbox and a gold watch, valuable on account of its smallness, the size of which I trace here. . . . Nannerl has been given an uncommonly beautiful, heavy, solid-gold toothpick case. From another lady, Wolfgang received a traveling writing-case in silver and Nannerl an unusually fine tortoiseshell snuffbox, inlaid with gold. . . . We have also received . . . a host of trifles which I do not value very highly, such as sword-bands, ribbons, and armlets, flowers for caps for Nannerl . . . and so forth.
>
> (Letter dated February 1, 1764)

Among Leopold's canny decisions, albeit an expensive one, was to dress the family not only well but in the style of each new city—both for dignity's sake and, as we would say, to "dress for success." A third reason was to ward off muggers and con artists, for whom tourists were easy prey (as they still are today). In those days you could instantly identify a Viennese or a Parisian by their wardrobe. As a matter of fact, Leopold was miffed by the way ladies in Paris got themselves up:

> Whether the women in Paris are pretty, I really can't tell you because they are painted so unnaturally, like Berchtesgarten dolls,[14] that even a naturally beautiful woman wearing this detestable makeup is unbearable to the eyes of an honest German. . . . That you see remarkably beautiful and precious things here, you can imagine; but you also see astonishing follies. In winter, the women wear not only clothes trimmed in fur, but also collars or ties of fur, and instead of flowers, all sorts of fur in their hair and fur armlets and so forth. . . .
>
> (Letter to Frau Hagenauer dated February 1, 1764)

But he was smitten by the radiantly beautiful Madame de Pompadour, Louis XV's mistress. From the same letter:

> Now I am going to jump from the ugly to the charming and moreover to someone who has charmed a king. You surely want to know what Madame Pompadour[15] looks like, don't you? She must have been beautiful once, because she is still pretty. She is a tall and imposing person, fat or rather well-covered, but very well proportioned, blond, and . . . in her eyes [you see] a resemblance to Her Majesty the empress [Maria Theresa]. She exudes dignity and an exceptional intelligence. Her apartments at Versailles are like a paradise, looking out on the gardens. In Paris, she has a most splendid house in the Faubourg St. Honoré, all newly rebuilt. In the room where the harpsichord is (which is all gilt and most artistically lacquered and painted) is her life-size portrait, and beside it, a portrait of the king. . . .

At the outset of their trip, less than a day's coach ride from home, the Mozarts faced an all-too-predictable hazard of eighteenth-century travel: a wheel on their rented carriage broke. It took nearly forty-eight hours to make a new one, during which they had to pay for two days' food and lodging for themselves, their driver, and his horses.

---

14. Berchtesgarten is a town near Salzburg famous for its painted figurines.
15. The Marquise de Pompadour was also said to have vast political influence. Note that Leopold (1719–1787) describes her (1721–1764) as past her prime.

Carriages also caused personal injury. Leopold was badly hurt one day in Italy:

> [T]he postilion [who rode alongside the coach] whipped the horse that was between the shafts and thus keeping the coach on track. The horse reared, caught in the sand and dirt—which was more than half a foot deep—and fell heavily on one side, pulling the front side of the coach down with him, because there were only two wheels. I held Wolfgang back with one hand so that he wouldn't be thrown out, but the plunge forward pulled my right foot toward the middle bar of the falling dashboard so violently that I gashed half the shinbone of my right leg about a finger wide. . . . On the second day my injury looked rather dangerous, because my foot was very swollen, and I stayed in bed most of yesterday and today. But today, as I write this, it is much better and the wound, which is very long, looks good; there is less pus and I now have no pain. . . . You must not worry, for with God's help, it will heal. . . .
>
> (Letter to Frau Mozart dated June 30, 1770)

In Italy, however, in contrast to the years when the kids were still young, the show could go on without Leopold. Wolfgang, now fourteen, kept busy by composing nonstop until his father was able to get around again.

The worst and most frightening danger, which was also the most disastrous financially, was life-threatening illness. Most feared at that time was smallpox, for which doctors were experimenting with different types of vaccination. (Catherine the Great had herself and all her court vaccinated as a way of persuading her subjects to follow suit. It worked, and neither she nor anyone in her court contracted the disease.) A 1767 epidemic in Vienna caused the death of a young archduchess, after which Leopold quickly left the city. Both of his children succumbed nevertheless, though with relatively mild cases from which they soon recovered. Wolfgang and presumably also Nannerl retained facial scars for life, as did many thousands of others.

In 1765 in The Hague, however, Nannerl and Woferl both nearly died from what we now believe was typhoid fever. At first, they only seemed to have caught colds; but as they grew much sicker, a physician was summoned. When he seemed to be on the wrong diagnostic track—Nannerl, the first to fall ill, continued to get worse—the royals' own physician came, altered the treatment, and she very slowly recovered. Leopold and Maria Anna, who fully expected both children to die, never left their rooms, watching and praying at their bedside in shifts of five to six hours. A priest came to each child in turn to pronounce the last rites. Leopold's letters recount the harrowing details, including his request that Masses be said at certain churches and shrines in Salzburg—something he frequently asked for on behalf of the children, the whole family, or some unusually significant upcoming event. Priests were paid to do this service, further adding to the family's expenses. The Mozarts were forced to remain in The Hague for five months—September to January—with no income to compensate for the costs of physicians, medicine, food, and lodging.

JOYS AND TRIUMPHS

The Mozarts' successes were nearly endless. The following are a few examples:

The family's and especially the children's easy camaraderie with royalty seems mind-boggling when you consider how far up the ladder His or Her Highness was from a midlevel court employee like Leopold Mozart. In the United States we have nothing to compare this to; we need to imagine how very rigid class distinctions were in eighteenth-century Europe. Note this from Mozart, age six, in Vienna:

> Wolferl [*sic*] jumped up onto the empress's lap, put his arms around her neck, and kissed her warmly.
>
> > (Letter to Lorenz Hagenauer dated October 16, 1762)

At Versailles, where they celebrated New Year's:

> You can easily imagine how impressed and amazed these French people . . . must have been when the king's daughters . . . stopped when they saw my children, came up to them, and not only allowed them to kiss their hands but kissed *their* hands innumerable times. . . . But what appeared most extraordinary to these people was that . . . on the evening of New Year's Day, not only was it necessary to make way for us to go up to the royal table, but my Herr Wolfgangus had the honor to stand next to the Queen, to talk constantly to her, entertain her, and kiss her hands repeatedly, as she fed him from the table.
>
> > (Letter to Lorenz Hagenauer dated February 1, 1764)

And in London:

> [T]he graciousness with which both His Majesty the king [King George III of American Revolution fame] and Her Majesty the queen [Charlotte] received us was indescribable. In short, their easy and friendly manner made it impossible to think of them as the king and queen of England.

At all courts up to the present we have been received with extraordinary courtesy, but what we have experienced here exceeds all the others: 8 days later went walking in St. James's Park. The king came driving through with the queen, and although we had on different clothes [from those we had worn at court], they recognized us right away and not only greeted us, but the king opened the window, leaned his head out, and smilingly greeted us with waves, especially our Master Wolfgang.

(Letter to Lorenz Hagenauer dated May 28, 1764)

In Rome, the pope presented Wolfgang with the Order of the Golden Spur:

It is the same order Gluck has[16] and reads: [*translation of the Latin:* We create you a Knight of the Golden Spur]. He must wear a beautiful gold cross, which he has received, and you can imagine how I laugh when I hear everybody calling him "Signor Cavaliere" now.... Tomorrow we have an audience with the pope.

(Letter to Frau Mozart dated July 7, 1770

Over and over again—in Salzburg, Vienna, Paris, London, and several cities in Italy—Wolfgang was subjected to tests of his abilities. The keyboard was covered with a cloth to see if he could play without looking at the keys. He was asked to play a piece of music at sight (i.e., without practicing it first). When handed the soprano part to a song, could he add a harmonically correct bass accompaniment? These and similar tests he passed with flying colors, as, in fact, would a well-trained, exceptionally talented young pianist today. Although Mozart was beyond question a truly extraordinary prodigy, the most remarkable fact about his musicianship was how it continued to develop, deepen, and widen throughout his life until he achieved encyclopedic mastery of every genre and style. This is what eventually set him apart, more so than his acing of these childhood tests.

Yet two such tests deserve special mention: one in London, the other in Bologna, Italy. His London examiner was the lawyer Daines Barrington, a fascinating man whose interests ranged from planned expeditions to the North Pole to studies of birdsongs. In the august presence of other members of the Royal Society, Baines ran the boy through the usual proofs including the composing *and singing* of an Italian operatic aria, which Woferl delivered with proper pomposity in his nine-year-old voice, his face

---

16. Christoph Willibald Gluck was among Europe's most esteemed composers. Although he adopted the title *cavaliere,* Mozart used it only a very few times.

reddening with emotion. Then he jumped down and scampered over to play with a cat he'd just seen on the other side of the room.

The examination of fourteen-year-old Wolfgang Mozart in Bologna was conducted by the most famous music theorist in Europe, Padre Giovanni Battista Martini. After being impressed with the teenager's performance the night before, Padre Martini invited him over for conversation the next day, then arranged for him to take the entrance examination for the distinguished Philharmonic Academy of Bologna (Accademia filarmonica di Bologna). Despite its membership's restriction to musicians twenty years old or older, Mozart passed the test—it is thought with some help from Martini—and was admitted.

As they traveled, young Wolfgang had the chance to hear the best music being written at that time—symphonies, concertos, sonatas, opera, church music—and to meet some of Europe's top composers. Although many of their names are unfamiliar today to anyone who hasn't taken a music history course, these composers taught this gifted child invaluable lessons just through performances of their music that he was able to hear: Hasse, Jommelli, Schobert, Abel, Johann Christian Bach, and many others. As one example: Christian Bach, the youngest son of Johann Sebastian Bach, composed in a "singing," Italianate style that captured the young boy's imagination when he heard it in London during his fifteen months there (April 1764–August 1765). The two of them met, and right away Wolfgang's music began to sound very much like his mentor's; indeed, the influence continued throughout his life. In his letters, when he refers to "Bach," it is usually Christian Bach that he means.

Wolfgang composed throughout the touring years, beginning with the keyboard sonatas K. 6–9, "which can be played with violin accompaniment" (to make them more saleable), advertised on their cover as written by a seven-year-old boy and published in Paris (after a good deal of editing by Leopold). In London his first symphonies appeared (K. 16, 19, perhaps also 20) and were also performed in concert there. In Vienna in 1768 he wrote a Mass for an orphanage (K. 47a), conducted it, and sang the soprano solos.

During the Italian tours, when he was a teen and more musically experienced, opera houses offered him *scritture* (contracts or commissions) and the operas he wrote won consistent applause, even roaringly so. His *Mitridate, rè di Ponto* (1770) for Milan was given twenty-two performances. Also well received was his *Ascanio in Alba* the following year. The situation in Italy was, in fact, altogether different from what he and his father had experienced elsewhere. Opera was king, and Wolfgang seemed to know already that he was born to compose it. For the rest, however—

instrumental music, performances at the keyboard—musical activity was largely controlled by individual aristocrats, who financed events privately; there were no public concerts for which tickets were sold, which meant that the Mozarts had to rely on the personal generosity of these aristocrats. But thankfully, they were generous, Wolfgang was a hit wherever he went, and he came home victorious.

HOME AGAIN

Leopold and his son returned to a different Salzburg from the one they had left. The simpatico, genial, fiscally undisciplined Archbishop Schrattenbach had died and his successor, Count Hieronymus Colloredo, seemed his exact opposite: "Enlightened," a reformer, unpleasant, and unyieldingly strict with his employees. Worse, he showed little interest in the arts. Nevertheless, he approved of the position to which Schrattenbach had appointed Wolfgang—assistant leader of the orchestra—and even awarded it a salary. But the Mozarts disliked and distrusted him.

They moved into a much larger, sunnier apartment on the other side of the River Salzach. The family needed more space now that the children were older and required separate bedrooms (Nannerl was twenty-two, Wolfgang seventeen). Leopold also needed a room for teaching, ensemble practice, and the storing of the keyboard instruments he was now selling. Sometimes the family took over that room for *Bölzlschiessen*. Leopold's position at court had not improved, however. Colloredo had appointed a new, Italian *Kapellmeister*—once again giving the choice job to an Italian. Though he could not have realized it, Leopold would never be promoted beyond *Vize-Kapellmeister* (assistant director of music).

But for his son, prospects looked very bright. Wolfgang assumed that more opera *scritture* would be coming his way from Italy; in fact, he still had one or two to fulfill in the immediate future, which took father and son back down south the following year. Strangely, after that Wolfgang was never contacted by anyone in Italy; that fertile source simply dried up. But in 1773 he surely looked forward to more of the same.

Wolfgang came home from his long years of touring with the widest and richest musical and cultural education anyone could imagine; no composer at any time has been able to match it. Thanks to his extraordinary talents and his father's remarkable ingenuity, he had learned about everything it was possible to learn, which included a great deal more than music. He had also been showered with adulation year after year. It would be a challenge for any boy to keep a level head after that.

Yet for a composer this had all been a jump-start to what looked like an outstanding future career. Before the year was out he finished two brilliant, forward-looking works: his first wholly original piano concerto (K. 175) and the startling Symphony in G Minor, K. 183/173dB.

Mozart wearing the Order of the Golden Spur. Inscription at the top: member, Accademia filarmonica di Bologna, another honor conferred in 1770.

3

MOZART IN HIS MUSIC: MAJOR FORMS AND HOW TO LISTEN TO THEM

INSTRUMENTS OF MOZART'S DAY

Instruments in Mozart's time played about one-quarter tone lower than they do today. This makes them sound less brilliant to ears accustomed to today's higher pitches. Eighteenth-century acoustical spaces were far smaller, requiring much less volume to fill them than do modern concert venues. There were also no subways, no airplanes, no car horns, and no backhoes.

In vocal music, lowering the pitch can make a note either easier or harder to sing. When a soprano's high notes are lowered one-quarter tone, she can get to them with less effort. But a bass reaching down to the bottom of his range will have to go lower still.

Changing the pitch also changes the *timbre,* a word denoting the quality of a sound, what it "sounds like." When a friend phones you, you recognize whose voice it is mainly through *timbre.* That's also the way you tell a flute from a trumpet or a bird from a cow.

Woodwind instruments (flutes, oboes, clarinets, bassoons) had far fewer keys then, and thus could play fewer notes. Flutes were made entirely of wood, giving them a recorder-like sound. The clarinet was a mid-eighteenth-century invention, which Mozart was among the first to exploit. Modern manufacturing techniques have made reeds (used for all woodwinds except the flute) easier to deal with today—though any player will tell you what a problem they remain nevertheless.

Stringed instruments (violins, violas, cellos, basses) were strung with uncovered gut and the strings were far less taut than on modern instruments, lending them a soft, "stringy" sound. The violin's bridge (the small, upright piece hinged between the strings and the body of the instrument) was lower; the fingerboard was smaller; and the "neck" was shorter, wider, and angled less sharply downward from the body of the instrument. All this resulted in a violin with a smaller range than violins of later times.

Bows were lighter than they are today, with hairs that were bunched more loosely. When you pick up a Mozart-era bow it feels like a feather, making those delicate, quick little ornaments and runs so characteristic of eighteenth-century music easier to negotiate than they are with today's much heavier bow, which wants to dig in.

Brass instruments (trumpets, trombones, horns—although horns were also considered members of the woodwind family) had no valves until the mid-nineteenth century. Instead, "crooks" were inserted between

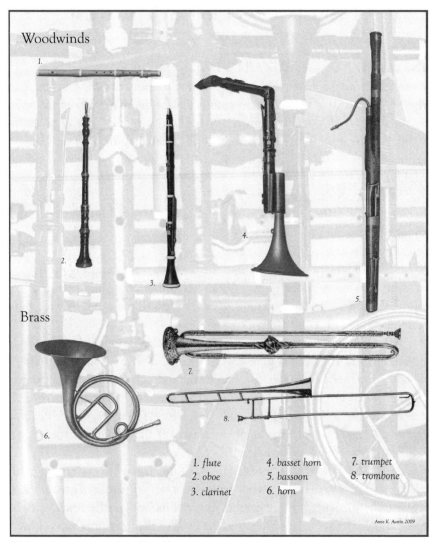

1. flute   4. basset horn   7. trumpet
2. oboe   5. bassoon   8. trombone
3. clarinet   6. horn

Anne K. Austin 2009

Eighteenth-century woodwinds and brass

the mouthpiece and the body of the instrument to increase its length of tubing and therefore its range. Players found crooks annoying because they sometimes had to be inserted and then removed again very quickly. The invention of valves in the nineteenth century solved this problem. Trombones, softer-sounding than their counterparts today (because of narrower "bells" and smaller mouthpieces), were used chiefly in church music until ca. 1800. Tubas didn't exist before ca. 1830.

Timpani (kettledrums, usually two of them, tuned to different pitches), covered with animal skins (usually calfskin), were played with bare wooden drumsticks; drumstick heads were not covered, as they are today, with lamb's wool or felt. The "kettles" were much smaller then.

MOZART AND THE PIANO

Both Mozart children were fabulous pianists, though we shall never know how extraordinary Nannerl might have become if Leopold had bestowed upon her the attention he devoted to her brother, and if he had allowed her to perform outside Salzburg after she turned eighteen. That would have enabled her to test her mettle against the touring pianists of that era—a group that, as you already know, included a few women.

But now we have to lay aside Nannerl's sad story and move to the case of her brother, whose facility as pianist, harpsichordist, and organist is well documented. He seems to have kept his skills burnished to a high gloss even in adulthood, though he rarely had time to practice; he once semijoked to his father that he was so busy performing that practicing was unnecessary and in any event impossible.

The eighteenth-century *fortepiano*,[1] so-called today to distinguish it from the modern piano, sounds quite different from a harpsichord, because its thin wire strings are struck by hammers rather than plucked by quills. The instrument acquired its name for its ability to play gradations of *forte* (loud) and *piano* (soft), allowing for nuances of dynamics possible on the eighteenth century's more delicate keyboard instrument, the *clavichord*, but not on a harpsichord. The fortepiano's range in the 1780s (when Mozart bought the one pictured on the following page) was around five octaves, in comparison to today's seven and a half. Its "touch"—the amount of force required to depress a key—was much lighter than on its modern counterpart. Today's piano strings are strung so tight that the instrument must be reinforced by an iron frame to keep it from breaking apart; a fortepiano, made almost entirely of wood and requiring no such reinforcement, weighs a great deal less. Finally, whereas modern pianos have pedals to raise the dampers off

---

1. All references to the piano in this book are to the eighteenth-century *fortepiano*.

Mozart's fortepiano

the strings and sustain the sound, fortepianos had hand stops and/or knee levers. Mozart's had two knee levers, one to raise only the bass dampers and one to raise them all. He also had a pedal piano made that fit beneath this one and gave him two more octaves of bass notes that he played with his feet, like an organist. He used this when improvising or playing concertos with an orchestra.[2]

A 1789 newspaper describes a Mozart concert on both harpsichord and the new fortepiano:

> On 14 April the famous composer Herr W. A. Mozart of Vienna was heard at the fortepiano by His Elect. Highness—furthermore he also played here at Dresden in many noble and private houses with boundless success; his agility on the clavier [harpsichord] and on the fortepiano is quite inexpressible—and to this is added an extraordinary ability to read at sight, which truly borders on the incredible:—for he himself is hardly able to play a thing better after practice than he does the very first time.[3]

What dazzled Mozart's audiences more than anything was his genius for improvisation. Eighteenth-century music had much more spontaneity in it than we may realize, and amateurs as well as professionals were expected to be able to improvise on the spot. You gave them a tune and after playing

2. I am indebted to Kathryn Libin for correcting and greatly adding to my understanding of the fortepiano and particularly for her specialist's knowledge of Mozart's own instrument.
3. Deutsch, *Mozart: A Documentary Biography*, 347.

it "straight" they took it through a series of melodic, harmonic, and rhythmic changes. This Mozart did on a great many occasions both formal and informal—either as a scheduled portion of a concert or on the spur of the moment at someone's house. To be in that room must have been thrilling:

> Mozart then performed on the fortepiano at a great concert in the opera house [in Prague]. Never had the theater been so full of people as it was on this occasion; never had there been greater or more unanimous delight than his divine playing aroused. . . . [A]t the end of the concert, when Mozart extemporized alone for more than half an hour at the fortepiano, raising our delight to the highest degree, our enchantment dissolved into loud, overwhelming applause. And indeed, this extemporization exceeded anything normally understood by fortepiano playing, as the highest excellence in the art of composition was combined with the most perfect accomplishment in execution.[4]

Despite Mozart's acknowledged superiority at the keyboard—or perhaps because of it—challengers appeared from time to time, among whom the most impressive was the well-known Italian pianist and composer Muzio Clementi. On Christmas Eve 1781 the two of them were summoned to a pianistic playoff by Emperor Joseph II, who was a good musician himself (you can forget the caricature of him in *Amadeus*). Joseph bet on Mozart and won. Mozart reported his version of the evening to his father in less than modest tones:

> Now about *Clementi*.—He is a solid keyboard player.—but that's all you can say.—he has very great facility in his right hand.—his best passages are thirds.—beyond that that he doesn't have a *kreuzer* [penny] of taste or feeling—a mere *mechanicus*. The emperor declared, after we had paid each other enough compliments, that *he* [Clementi] should play first. . . . He played a prelude and then a sonata;—after that the emperor said to me: "*Allons*,[5] Take off!"—I played a prelude too and then some variations. Then the grand duchess gave us sonatas by [Paisiello] that Paisiello had miserably written out; from these I was to play the Allegro and he the Andante and Rondo. Then we each chose a theme from the sonatas and developed it on 2 pianos.—What's strange is that Countess Thun had lent me her pianoforte,[6] but I could use it

---

4. The performance took place in Prague on January 19, 1787; quoted in Neal Zaslaw with Neal Cowdery, eds., *The Compleat Mozart* (New York: W. W. Norton, 1990), 305.
5. French for "Let's go!"
6. Pianos could be carried by a few stout men; hence the references in Mozart's letters to taking his piano—here, someone else's—to a certain house or concert venue for a particular event. Countess Thun was one of his good friends and supporters.

only when I played alone, because the emperor wanted it that way.—and N.B.,[7] the other piano was out of tune and 3 of its keys stuck.—*It doesn't matter*, the emperor said.—Well, I am giving this the best light; the emperor already knows my art and my knowledge of music, and only wanted to size up what the foreigner could do.

(Letter dated January 16, 1782)

In those days the piano was a centerpiece of family entertainment. People spent whole evenings playing solo or four-hand music, singing songs to piano accompaniment, or reading through whole operas or symphonies transcribed for four-hand piano. All this triggered a vast market for composers—not only for amateur-level music, but also for works demanding the skills of an advanced player, even a professional such as Mozart.

Mozart's compositions for piano embraced every genre:

- Music for solo piano: sonatas, variations, fantasies, rondos, etc.
- Chamber [small-ensemble] music for piano and/or other instruments: duets for two pianos or one piano four-hands, sonatas for violin and piano, piano trios (piano, violin, and cello; piano, clarinet, and viola), piano quartets (piano plus violin, viola, and cello), and a piano quintet (piano, oboe, clarinet, bassoon, and horn).
- Concertos for piano and orchestra: twenty-three,[8] including one for two pianos (K. 365/316a) and one for three pianos (K. 242).

In this book we will introduce a piano sonata, two piano concertos, and, in what follows, an example of his piano variations as an illustration of musical variation form.

VARIATION FORM
■ Twelve Variations for Piano on "Ah, vous dirai-je, maman," K. 265/300e
(Vienna, 1781 or 1782)
Variation form, or theme and variations, is a form we hear all the time in

---

7. *Nota bene:* "note well; pay special attention to this."
8. The oft-cited total of twenty-seven includes isolated single movements and works from childhood derived from works by composers whom Wolfgang was imitating. The figure of twenty-three includes only whole concertos beginning with K. 175, his first truly original work in this genre. When citing them by number ("Mozart's twenty-fourth concerto") people are thinking of the total as twenty-seven. In this book, to avoid confusion, concertos are referred to by K. number and key only.

jazz. It starts with a "theme" (a tune)—either a golden oldie or something newly invented—which is followed by a series of musical "variations" on that theme, all having the same format and length (the same number of bars) as the theme. If the format doesn't remain the same, jazz players won't know when to come in with their individual variations—successive new versions of the theme. How many of these might there be? As many as the jazz combo, or in classical music the composer, wants to give us—anywhere from three or four to several dozen. The fun for us is to listen for the outlines of the theme in each of the variations. Predictably, they take us progressively farther and farther away from where we started. The overall design is simplicity itself:

> Theme
> Variation I
> Variation II
> Variation III (etc.)

In music of the Classic era (the generation of Haydn, Mozart, and Beethoven), the theme—and consequently the variations as well—generally takes one of these forms:

> aabb (called *binary* form: two sections, each repeated)
> Or: aababa (called *rounded binary* form: two sections, the *a* returning to "round off" each *b*)

The letters are lowercase to denote the fact that they are subdivisions of the theme.

Repeat Signs

||: and :||

The customary way for composers to instruct musicians to repeat a segment of music is to use these signs rather than having to write out the repetitions note by note. At the beginning of the segment, the composer writes: ||: and at the end, the same thing backwards: :||. You'll see these signs in many places in this book. If employed above, they would change aabb to ||:a:|| ||:b:|| and aababa to ||:a:|| ||:ba:||.

The basic tune (the theme) of Mozart's K. 265/300e is a French song called "Silvandre's Loves," which we know as "Twinkle, Twinkle, Little Star." You are probably wondering: can this be the great Mozart, stooping so low he's using a *nursery song*? Absolutely; just as in jazz, the idea is to start with something so simple it allows for plenty of new possibilities.

Remember the song?

a melody:	Twinkle, twinkle, little star,
	How I wonder what you are. (*repeated*)
b melody:	Up above the world so high,
	Like a diamond in the sky.
a melody:	Twinkle, twinkle, little star,
	How I wonder what you are![9] (*b–a repeated*)

Mozart's piece begins with the theme in the right hand and its harmony in the left. There are then twelve variations, the form in every case remaining the same: ||:a:|| ||:ba:||.

Over the course of these variations, Mozart challenges the pianist to execute fast, accurate runs in each hand; to play passages smoothly (*legato*) as well as detached (*staccato*); in minor keys and major keys; with and without embellishments; and so on. The comprehensive, quite methodical digital workout provided by K. 265/300e suggests that it was meant for one of his pupils as a practice piece. For a listener, it is pure delight.

Time

0'00"	Theme			:a:				:ba:			
0'54"	Variation I			:a:				:ba:			quick notes in right hand
1'47"	Variation II			:a:				:ba:			quick notes in left hand
2'38"	Variation III			:a:				:ba:			triplets[10] in right hand
3'33"	Variation IV			:a:				:ba:			triplets in left hand
4'22"	Variation V			:a:				:ba:			offbeat rhythms in both hands
5'15"	Variation VI			:a:				:ba:			chords in right hand, quick notes in left
6'02"	Variation VII			:a:				:ba:			majestic; triumphant
6'52"	Variation VIII			:a:				:ba:			minor key; melody imitates itself in the two hands
7'46"	Variation IX			:a:				:ba:			again, melodic imitation; childlike

---

9. Dr. Stanley Hamilton has kindly translated the opening stanza of the French song:
Let me tell you, dear Mommy,
What is making me so irritable!
Papa wants me to think
Like a real grownup.
As for me, I think that candy [acting my age]
is more important than reason [acting like a grownup].
10. Triplets are groups of three notes occupying the rhythmic space of a single note: three for one, with each of the three given the same duration.

8'31"	Variation X			:a:				:ba:			grand style; loud
9'18"	Variation XI			:a:			:ba:			adagio (extremely slow), meditative, languid
12'33"	Variation XII			:a:				:ba:			triple meter; quick in left hand, then both hands

Note: The K. number 265/300e was assigned to this work when it was thought to date from 1778. It has more recently been assigned to 1781 or 1782.

Timings based on András Schiff, piano. ©1990 London 421369-2

DIVERTIMENTOS, SERENADES, ETC.

Divertimentos and serenades, in Mozart's era, were lighthearted instrumental compositions written for a wide variety of circumstances. Divertimentos were meant to *divert* listeners in some amusing, charming way; serenades were often composed to honor or pay tribute to a person or an event. But the lines between the two were blurry, and scholars today offer differing interpretations of them. What follows is a general description.

Divertimentos, composed for a mixed group of winds and strings, winds alone, or occasionally strings alone, generally employed one player to a part. Some were performed indoors, as background music; others were played outside, for a party or celebration. The number of movements varied from three or four up to nine, each with its own form, tempo, dynamics, instrumentation, and style. Reams of such easy-listening music were composed in the late eighteenth century, though little of it saw print because when the occasion for which it had been composed was over, that was it. Curiously, in view of their less than serious purposes, a large number of Mozart's divertimentos have survived—though we have only one of the more than thirty such works composed by his father.

A serenade had for centuries been a song crooned outside your lover's window.[11] In the late eighteenth century it could either be that (a piece to be sung) or, more often, an instrumental work to celebrate whatever needed celebrating—a couple's engagement, a friend's promotion, a new job, or students about to graduate. *Finalmusik* marked the end of the academic year. *Nachtmusik* (nocturne) was performed at night. The word *cassation* may be a Frenchified version of *gassatim gehen*—to stroll down a street while tootling music. But all these terms referred to essentially similar kinds of music. Like divertimentos, serenades were multimovement compositions, some of them nearly an hour long.

Although it's certain that Mozart wrote the Divertimento in D Major,

11. As, for example, Don Giovanni's "Deh vieni alla finestra" in Act II of *Don Giovanni*.

K. 131, during the summer of 1772, we don't know what the occasion was. Maynard Solomon believes it "may well have been composed as wedding music" because the Adagio (the third movement) sounds like a love song. But *A Mozart Compendium* suggests that it might be *Finalmusik* for the end of Salzburg University's summer term, and Stanley Sadie calls it a serenade.[12]

If K. 131 was *Finalmusik*—but to repeat, we have no knowledge that it was—we can read a bare-bones description of how such a piece might have been performed in Nannerl Mozart's diary entry for August 9, 1775 (written three years *after* our divertimento):

> On the 9th the *Finalmusik* was presented. At 8:30 it started out from our house for the Mirabell [the castle], where it lasted until 9:45, and from there it went to the university, where it lasted until 11:00.[13]

While terse, this description nevertheless conveys useful information: first of all, how very informal the whole affair was. The musicians gathered, started playing as they walked toward the designated spot, and were still playing when they got there. Many of these pieces (regardless of title) began and ended with movements labeled "March"—music performed while playfully "marching" to and from the party. Finally, unstated but implied is the fact that the instruments should be portable—unless a keyboard instrument was involved (Mozart wrote only one such work, K. 254, for piano, violin, and cello).[14]

Nearly all of Mozart's serenades were written while he still lived in Salzburg (i.e., before he moved to Vienna in 1781). Two of his best-known works in this genre are the "Posthorn" Serenade, K. 320, and the "Haffner" Serenade, K. 250. He later converted the "Haffner" into a symphony, also known as the "Haffner" (K. 385). Years later, in Vienna, he composed *A Musical Joke* (*Ein musikalischer Spass*, K. 522), a hilarious parody of inept composition, with lots of sour notes, brainless repetitions, and illogical modulations. We used to think Mozart wrote this comic piece shortly after his father died, in a crass display of insensitivity; but paper studies have shown that he composed most of it before he knew his father was ill, and the rest some months after that. The title of Mozart's well-known *Eine kleine Nachtmusik*, K. 525, tells you what sort of piece it is: the German means "A Little Nocturne." Although we often hear the work played by a full string

12. Maynard Solomon, *Mozart: A Life* (New York: HarperCollins, 1995), 128; H. C. Robbins Landon, ed., *A Mozart Compendium* (New York: Schirmer Books, 1990), 273; Sadie, *Mozart: The Early Years*, 276.

13. Quoted by Solomon, *Mozart: A Life*, 126. The translation of Nannerl's diary entry is Solomon's.

14. Sadie, *Mozart: The Early Years*, 405.

orchestra, it was perhaps intended for the one-on-a-part ensemble typical of works of this type. Written in August 1787, it was his last work in this genre.

In a magical scene near the beginning of *Amadeus,* Antonio Salieri is mesmerized by the sounds of musicians performing (indoors) the ethereal slow movement of the Serenade for Thirteen Instruments, K. 361/370a. The serenade's seven movements, of which this is the third, span slightly more than three-quarters of an hour.

Its thirteen instruments are:

- two oboes
- two clarinets
- two basset horns
- four horns
- two bassoons
- one double bass—a strange choice![15]

Just when and for what circumstances Mozart wrote this work has been the subject of controversy. Formerly thought to have been intended for a 1784 concert by his friend and fellow Freemason,[16] the brilliant clarinetist and basset hornist Anton Stadler, the serenade has now been dated to 1781 by Dexter Edge. Edge bases his argument on studies of the paper Mozart used and on concerts during that year for which this work might plausibly have been written.[17]

The serenade's Adagio (very slow) third movement featured in the film lasts just under six minutes and is divided into three sections: **A–B–A.** If you listen closely, you'll recognize the **B** section (which starts a bit after two minutes) when the music slips into minor keys and darker moods.[18] **B** lasts slightly more than a minute, after which **A** returns. (If you listen to the second **A** section carefully, you will hear it as **A¹**—i.e., not note-for-note what you heard the first time; but calling it **A** is quite good enough.)

Throughout this Adagio, eleven instruments (two of the horns are silent) divide into three groups, each playing different music, in contrasting rhythmic patterns:

- Two low-pitched instruments (one bassoon and the double

---

15. Why this one stringed instrument, one that is just barely portable? A much-debated issue.
16. For Mozart's membership in this order and its significance to him, see "Mozart and Freemasonry."
17. Edge presented his evidence at a panel discussion about the serenade at Boston's New England Conservatory of Music on February 28, 2006.
18. For "major" vs. "minor" keys, see "Notes for Musical Beginners."

bass) mark out a slow, steady walking rhythm. The two horns sometimes accompany them.

- Moving twice as fast as the bass instruments is a pulsating *oom-pah, oom-pah-pah* played by four instruments: oboe, clarinet, basset horn, and bassoon.
- Above all this steady, scarcely varying rhythm, an oboe, a clarinet, and a basset horn croon tender, long-breathed, delicately poignant melodies that sometimes alternate with one another, sometimes overlap, and sometimes harmonize with each other.

Because of its slow tempo and stately rhythmic foundation, this whole movement exudes a quality of peace, a kind of classical serenity. Although Mozart's divertimentos and serenades—including the Serenade for Thirteen Instruments—are full of frolicsome movements, you also encounter unexpected moments like this one. In fact, whenever he writes *adagio*—a very slow tempo, which he uses rarely—he invites us into another world. Then, immediately afterward, he jolts us back into a party mood.

Despite their great variety, most works of this type—whether labeled divertimento, serenade, *Nachtmusik, Finalmusik,* or cassation—shared important features. With exceptions, they

- were commissioned (i.e., formally requested and paid for) to mark a specific occasion
- were sometimes preceded and followed by a march
- contained as many as eight or nine movements
- included at least one minuet

Mozart gave no title to what is known today as his Divertimento in D Major, K. 131. Someone wrote "Divertimento" at the top of the first page a long time ago, and we have called it that ever since. So much for the significance of those terms. Whatever its original purpose, the work includes four horns, as does the Serenade in B-flat Major—and in the eighteenth century, these would have been "natural horns," without valves and therefore more difficult to play than modern horns. (Throughout this book, *horn* refers to the French horn.)

The Divertimento K. 131 is typical of Mozart's compositions in this genre—if any single work could be—and our study of it will focus on its dance forms: movements three and five, both minuets.

DANCE FORM
■ Two Minuets from Divertimento in D Major, K. 131
(Salzburg, 1772)
For flute, oboe, bassoon, 4 horns, 2 violins, viola, double bass

This divertimento has six movements: Allegro, Adagio, Minuet, Allegretto, Minuet, and Adagio-allegro molto.[19] The two minuets (each has its own music; they are not the same) illustrate *dance form*, whose design remains the same regardless of the particular dance it is used for—whether a minuet or some other favorite such as the contredanse ("country dance," less formal than the minuet) or a waltz. All of them employ this same form:

Dance	Trio	Dance
aabb	ccdd	ab
		(i.e., this time without repeats)

The Trio, the middle section of a dance movement, is so-named because in olden times it was played by only three instruments. Mozart-era Trio sections pay homage to this antique custom by lightening and thinning the texture and sometimes—though not here—even changing the meter from triple (*one*–two–three) to duple (*one*–two).

In this Divertimento, the *fifth movement* has two trios. The *third movement*, whose timings are indicated below, has three trios, the second played by all four horns with no other instruments—a pretty distinctive sound! The coda brings all the players together.

Minuet	Trio 1	Minuet	Trio 2	Minuet	Trio 3	Minuet	Coda
aabb	ccdd	ab	eeff	ab	gghh	ab	
53"	54"	1'43"	2'09"	2'50"	3'16"	3'59"	4'25"

Timings based on Camerata Salzburg, Sándor Vegh, conductor. © 1994 Capriccio 10 333.

VIOLIN CONCERTOS
A concerto is a work for (usually) one solo instrument and orchestra, typically in three movements: the first is fast, the middle one is slow, and the finale fast. Although most of Mozart's concertos featured the piano, he also wrote two for flute, four for horn, one for bassoon, one for oboe, one for clarinet, one for a combination of flute and harp, and five for violin.

You might think of eighteenth-century violin concertos as serenades with a violin soloist, and that wouldn't be far off, since a number of Mozart's

---

19. Translations of Italian terms can be found in "Glossary of Musical Terms" at the end of this book. They are not titles, but indications of tempo telling musicians how fast or slow the music should go. There are no markings for the minuets because everybody knew how to play them! A coda is a final, flourishing conclusion to a composition.

serenades have middle movements that sound like mini-concertos. Besides their serenade- or divertimento-like functions, however, Mozart-era violin concertos were also performed indoors, at intermission between the acts of a play, or in church during moments for reflection during Mass or Vespers. All this takes his concertos far away in both concept and style from the much larger, louder, and more symphonic works by Romantic composers such as Brahms or Tchaikovsky.

Mozart wrote five violin concertos, the first probably in 1773 (a recent redating), the other four in 1775. It's uncertain who the intended soloist was for these concertos, although the Salzburg concertmaster, Antonio Brunetti, performed them in later years. Mozart himself played the Concerto for Violin and Orchestra in G Major, K. 216, in Augsburg one night after dinner in 1777, writing to his father that "it went like oil. Everyone praised my beautiful, clear tone." Notice that he makes no mention of his technical mastery of the instrument, just the quality of his tone. Like his father, Mozart prized beauty of sound and nuance of expression above all else, viewing with contempt what he regarded as mere digital showmanship. Leopold's *Violin Method* stresses tone and expression, and it was Leopold who taught him violin.

Wolfgang began his career as a violinist at the age of six, after receiving a child-size instrument from the emperor and empress during the Mozarts' trip to Vienna in 1762. Shortly after returning home, he walked into a room where his father and others were sight-reading some string trios, with Leopold taking the viola part and Andre Schachtner playing second violin. Schachtner later recalled that Wolfgang

> asked to be allowed to play the 2nd violin [part], but Papa refused him this foolish request, because he had not yet had the least instruction in the violin. . . . Wolfgang said: You don't need to have studied in order to play 2nd violin, and when Papa insisted that he should go away and not bother us any more, Wolfgang began to weep bitterly and stamped off with his little violin. I asked them to let him play with me; Papa eventually said: Play with Herr Schachtner, but so softly that we can't hear you, or you will have to go; and so it was. Wolfgang played with me; I soon noticed with astonishment that I was quite superfluous . . . and so he played all 6 trios. . . . Wolfgang was emboldened by our applause to maintain that he could play the 1st violin, too. For a joke we made the experiment, and we almost died for laughter when he played this too, though with nothing but wrong and irregular [finger positions], [yet nevertheless] in such a way that he never actually broke down.[20]

20. Deutsch, *Mozart: A Documentary Biography*, 453.

Although Mozart evidently became as skilled on the violin as he was on keyboard instruments, he put down his fiddle—at least as a public performer—during his pivotal journey to Mannheim and Paris in 1777–1779, a decision that may well have rankled his father. Was this in some sense a rejection of fatherly influence?

The orchestra in Mozart's early years (i.e., in Salzburg) was essentially a string ensemble, to which woodwinds, horns, trumpets, and/or drums (timpani) might sometimes be added if they were available and the occasion called for a grander or fuller sound. This particular concerto employs, besides strings, a pair of oboes in the opening and closing movements. In the second (slow) movement, oboes are replaced by flutes. During that generation, oboists could also play flute, so composers could alter the tone color from movement to movement without having to switch players or hire two more.

Our focus will be on the final movement, in *rondo form*. Rondos were favorite choices for finales because they are (usually) brisk, upbeat, witty, and in duple meter.[21] This rondo is brisk, upbeat, witty—but in *triple* meter. As you will hear, however, it also has some strange un-rondolike content—some of it very slow and in *duple* meter. Exploding conventional form with unexpected "asides" is a regular feature of Mozart's music.

RONDO FORM
■ Concerto for Violin and Orchestra in G Major, K. 216, "Strasbourg"
(Salzburg, 1775)
For solo violin, 2 oboes [these switch to flute in the slow movement], bassoon [plays the same music as cellos and double basses], 2 horns, strings
   3. Allegro (rondo form, triple meter)

R	E¹	R	E²	Cadenza	R
tutti	solo	both	solo	solo alone	solo
	31″	1′34″	1′46″	2′46″	2′52″

transition	Silence	E³,⁴	Cadenza	R
tutti		tutti	solo alone	both
3′04″		3′19″ 4′25″	5′29″	5′36″
		[duple] "gypsy": slow, then fast: "the Strassbürger"		

---

21. For explanations of duple and triple meter, see "Notes for Musical Beginners."

R = the main, "rondo" theme

E = an episode (i.e., not the rondo theme)

In this period, rondo movements generally have four statements of **R,** as here. That makes for three episodes, as here. But there are several unusual features in this movement:

- The soloist has two cadenzas.
- There is an instant of dead silence near the center of the movement.
- Episode 3 is actually two different episodes (3 + 4)—one of them a dance-hall theme called the "*Strassbürger*," well known in the town of Strasbourg.

Timings based on CD by Stephanie Chase, violin, and Roy Goodman conducting The Hanover Band, CAIA CD 1014, ©1992

SYMPHONIES

How many symphonies did Mozart write? The traditional numbering yields forty-one, but four of them were composed by someone else (Numbers 2, 3, 11, and 37) and others that Mozart *did* write hadn't yet come to light when the list was compiled. Scholars now give the total as fifty-two. This book will play it safe by avoiding numbers altogether, identifying symphonies only by key and Köchel number.

Mozart, who grew up as the symphony was being born, wrote his first when he was eight years old (in London, in 1764) and his last when he was thirty-two (in Vienna, in 1788). The symphony emerged gradually during the middle third of the eighteenth century, assuming its now familiar shape in the late 1770s. By the time Mozart reached young adulthood, it was universally understood to be an orchestral composition in (usually) four movements, each with its own music—its own distinct themes, form, meter, and style:

First movement: on the fast side (in sonata form, with or without a slow introduction; see below for explanation of this form)
Second movement: slow (often in ABA form, variation form, or sonata form)
Third movement: a dance form (most often a minuet)
Fourth movement: fast (usually in rondo or variation form, or sonata form)

Of the formal designs most frequently used in classical music, we have so far encountered *variation form, dance form,* and *rondo form.* We now meet that era's most important and most complex instrumental design, one that evolved alongside the symphony itself: *sonata form.*[22] As the overwhelming choice of composers (not just Mozart) for the first movements not only of symphonies but of concertos, sonatas, and small-ensemble music of every sort, sonata form crops up everywhere—in second and fourth movements, too, as you see above. Once you understand this form's general outlines and gain some experience with it, it becomes easy to follow, and then you will have opened up for yourself an enormous musical repertory—literally tens of thousands of compositions from the time of Haydn, Mozart, and Beethoven right down to the present. Sonata form is alive and well in the twenty-first century; it worked back then and it works today.

Here is an abbreviated diagram of the form (sometimes an Introduction precedes the Exposition; if so, it will be slow):

[Introduction]	Exposition	Development	Recapitulation	Coda
optional; slow; not repeated	A–Bridge–B–C (Exposition repeated)		Returns to main key & complete statement of A; all themes in main key	

SONATA FORM

The Exposition introduces one, two, or sometimes three musical ideas (themes **A, B,** and/or **C,** a Closing Theme), each of them played twice,[23] with a transitional section (the *bridge*) separating theme **A** from the rest. The purpose of the bridge is to modulate—to change key—and whether you're a trained musician or not, you will clearly hear this happening; a helpful clue is that the bridge usually rises to a *higher key,* that is, listening to the bass instruments, you hear them climb upward. Themes **B** and/or the Closing Theme (**C**) are all in this second, higher key. Often the last few notes of the Exposition are slightly different the first time through, so that the Exposition's repeat can begin in the main key. Note that the whole Exposition is played through *twice,* note for note—a nice idea, since it helps us to identify the main themes clearly.

22. Although it is frequently called sonata-allegro form, such movements are by no means always fast (allegro), so this book calls it sonata form.
23. To conserve space, these repeats are not indicated in the diagram. If they were, the Exposition would read: AA–Bridge–BB–CC. These themes are generally also played twice in the Recapitulation.

The Development, unlike the Exposition, has no formal order or rules. Rather, its agenda is to explore harmonic, melodic, and rhythmic possibilities of *parts* of one or more of the Exposition's themes. You can usually count on the following features in a Development section:

- No theme will be heard in its entirety; fragments or portions only.
- No theme will be heard in its original key; foreign keys only.
- Composers may "develop" all of the themes, some of them, or only one.

With the Recapitulation, order is restored:

- The main theme (occasionally, another theme instead) is heard, complete and in its original key: when this happens, the Recapitulation has begun.
- This is followed by the other themes from the Exposition, though not necessarily in their original order and not necessarily all of them.
- The bridge is replaced by a transition which, though it modulates, *returns to the main key* instead of leading to a different key.
- All themes in the Recapitulation are in the main key, giving us the sense that they are all related. That thematic contrast we heard in the Exposition is now smoothed over.

The Coda ("tail"), usually brief in music of this period, closes off the movement with a final flourish, frequently by echoing portions of the main (**A**) theme.

Note that sonata form is a design, not for a whole composition, but for a *single movement*.

The four movements of the Symphony in G Minor, K. 183/173dB are marked as follows:[24]

- Allegro con brio ("fast and lively"; sonata form)
- Andante ("somewhat slow"; sonata form)
- Minuet (minuet form)

---

24. These Italian (or sometimes German) words aren't titles, but indications of approximate speed (tempo). See "tempo" in "Notes for Musical Beginners" and in "Glossary of Musical Terms."

- Allegro ("fast"; rondo form)

We'll focus on the opening movement, which has one rather unusual structural feature: the Exposition *and* the Development and Recapitulation are repeated:

Exposition	Development, Recapitulation	Coda
(played twice)	(this whole section is played twice)	

What one hears in most sonata-form movements, however, is this:

Exposition	Development, Recapitulation, Coda
(played twice)	(played once)

The first movement of the "Little G-minor" Symphony, K. 183/173dB—heard to chilling effect near the beginning of *Amadeus*—opens with harsh minor-key leaps and unsettling rhythms (Theme **A**). After this is repeated (with slight variation), suddenly a mysterious solo oboe sings into the void. Then the bridge moves us into a higher key where the second, rather chirpy theme emerges, in a major key (Theme **B,** played twice; the repeat is a varied version of the theme). Following a brief, transitional **Closing** section, the entire Exposition is repeated, note for note.

The Development is rather brief, though tense and dramatic, before the return of the complete first theme (**A**) announces the beginning of the Recapitulation. At its completion (as in *some* sonata-form movements of this period), the entire Development and Recapitulation are repeated. Then the Coda closes off the movement.

The ominous quality of this symphony's **A** theme may have derived either from the style of operatic storm scenes (it certainly sounds like a storm), or from the influence on the young Mozart of the pre-Romantic movement called Sturm und Drang (Storm and Stress), which burst onto the musical scene in the 1760s and '70s with dense harmonies and tortured rhythms. Still a third possible model may have been Haydn's powerful Symphony No. 39—although dark, throbbing music is not at all rare in Mozart's own music; the image of him as candy-sweet is, as you know, pure myth.

The next page presents a detailed diagram of the first movement of the "Little G-minor." (The "big" G-minor, though it's never called that, is his much later symphony in the same key, K. 550.) After several hearings, you should feel pretty comfortable with this movement's form—though not, perhaps, with such astonishing music from a seventeen-year-old composer.

■ SYMPHONY IN G MINOR, K. 183/173DB
(Salzburg, 1773)
For 2 oboes, 2 bassoons, 4 horns, and strings
1. Allegro con brio (sonata form, duple meter)

‖: Exposition :‖		‖: Development	Recapitulation :‖	Coda
0'00"	4'13"	4'14"	7'17"	10'17"

Note: The Development and Recapitulation are repeated, as a unit.

Breakdown of this movement:

Exposition	A	A'	solo oboe	Bridge	B	B'	Closing
		18"	25"	44"	1'28"	1'40"	1'53"
repeat:	2'06"	2'23"	2'30"	2'49"	3'34"	3'46"	3'58"
Development	4'14"						
repeat:	7'17"						
Recapitulation	A	solo oboe	transition	B	Closing		
	5'04"	5'30"	5'49"	6'37 "	7'01"		
repeat:	8'08"			9'40"			
Coda	10'17"–10'36"						

Timings based on Ton Koopman conducting the Amsterdam Baroque Orchestra.
Erato 2292-45431-2©1990.

Hieronymus Colloredo, Count and Prince-Archbishop of Salzburg, 1772–1800. When he succeeded Prince-Archbishop Schrattenbach in 1772, Colloredo found a court mismanaged and deeply in debt. An admirer of Joseph II, he moved quickly to reinstate fiscal solvency and institute sweeping reforms. Among his reforms were a streamlined bureaucracy, radically simplified church music, and rules forbidding employees from taking off to play concerts elsewhere. For the Mozarts and their colleagues, the free-spending, cavalier management style of Archbishop Schrattenbach was now just a fond memory. Worst of all, Colloredo showed little affinity for music or indeed for any arts.

4

IN SEARCH OF EMPLOYMENT, 1777–1779

Toward the end of September 1777, Mozart, now twenty-one, set out to look for a permanent, well-paying position. The journey would be of critical importance to the family's future. Could he take it on by himself? His parents thought not. Its responsibilities would far exceed those of the childhood tours, during which the family had employed a division of labor. The children performed; their parents did everything else:

- Deciding where to go next, and when
- Packing
- Paying the bills
- Arranging for transportation, lodging, and food
- Searching out contacts in each new city
- Dealing with foreign languages and unfamiliar customs
- Arranging concerts
- Keeping track of expenses
- Turning a profit; each city had to pay for travel to the next city
- Sending regular, detailed reports home (in those days, to Hagenauer)
- Keeping both themselves and their children healthy and rested

Mozart had zero experience with any of this, but now he would have to add his own list:

- Performing as often and for as many influential people as possible
- Lining up commissions for new works
- Composing those works plus any others that might impress the right people

- Writing home to keep his father abreast of everything on these two lists

Obviously, someone had to go with him, but this time it would not be Leopold, because the Salzburg administrative landscape now made that impossible. Archbishop Colloredo, who had replaced Archbishop Schrattenbach, kept a tight rein on his servants: no longer could they take off for months or years at a time while expecting to receive full pay. But Wolfgang had to get out of there—had to find a job somewhere else—both to escape Salzburg's provinciality and to contribute to the family's support (as he already had done as a child). Colloredo, surprisingly, had made him a paid *Konzertmeister* of the court orchestra upon the family's return in 1773, but the salary wasn't sufficient for an adult to live on, and the position was no match for his extraordinary abilities.

The original plan was for Leopold to take up his usual role as mentor and guide. His petition for a leave of absence, which has not survived, was evidently turned down, because he reapplied. This time Wolfgang also applied, on his own behalf—not to search for a job, but to be released from Colloredo's service altogether.

The prose in Wolfgang's document, which was written by Leopold, is embarrassing, trumpeting forth like a preacher (to an archbishop!) that "[t]he Gospel tells us to use our talents . . . to improve [our] parents' and [our] own circumstances." Colloredo's sarcastic response set *both* men free—to "seek [their] fortune elsewhere, according to the Gospel." Leopold, terrified, begged to be reinstated, and was; but under the circumstances he dared not leave town. The job of traveling companion now fell to Maria Anna. Nannerl, once again told she must stay home, broke down in tears, as Leopold later wrote to his wife and son, and remained in her room for several days.

ITINERARY: MUNICH, AUGSBURG, MANNHEIM, PARIS

The trip had three major targets in mind: first, Munich, the seat of the elector of Bavaria (followed by a brief visit to Leopold's hometown, Augsburg); second, Elector Carl Theodor's magnificent court in Mannheim; and third, Versailles, which carried by far the most prestige, though unfortunately, neither Leopold nor Wolfgang cared much for France or French music.

As mother and son drove off, how did Wolfgang feel about the radically changed circumstances for this all-important undertaking, with his father humiliated and his sister emotionally devastated? He said nothing about it in his first letter home. All we hear is jubilation and ebullient self-confidence:

> *Viviamo come i Principi* [We're living like princes]. The only thing missing
> is Papa, but then, that's God's will. Everything will go well. I hope Papa is
> well and as pleased as I am. . . . I'm the other [i.e., second] Papa. I take care
> of everything. I just asked to pay the postilions [outriders] as I know how
> to talk to these guys better than Mama. . . . I'm sitting here like a prince.
> Half an hour ago—Mama had just gone to the bathroom—the innkeeper
> knocked and asked about all kinds of things, and I answered him with all
> seriousness, the way I look in my portrait [see page 67]. I have to stop,
> Mama has gotten undressed. Both of us ask Papa to look after his health,
> not to go outside too early, not to get worked up, to have a good laugh
> and be jolly, and all the time remember joyfully, as we do, that Mufti H.C.
> [Hieronymus Colloredo] is a prick, but God is merciful, compassionate,
> and loving. I kiss Papa's hands 1,000 times and embrace my scoundrel of
> a sister as often as I've—taken snuff today.
>
> P.S. This pen is coarse and I am rude.
> Wasserburg, 23 Sept. 1777, *undecima hora nocte tempore* [11 p.m.]
> I think I left my diplomas at home—please send them . . . ?

"I'm a second Papa" sounds pretty cocky—yet in the same breath he
"asked to pay the postilions," as if he were still a little boy, not a man taking
charge of his life. Then comes the patronizing admonition to his father to
"have a good laugh." At the end Mozart jokes that he realizes his prose
was over the top ("This pen is coarse and I am rude"); then, after playfully
rendering the time of day in Latin, he suddenly remembers what this trip
was all about: I'll need those diplomas, he says (the documents attesting to
his papal Order of the Golden Spur and his membership in the Accademia
filharmonica di Bologna).

Leopold, remarkably, wasn't upset, but delighted to receive "dear
Wolfgang's" letter. In a few months he would react to such borderline
impertinence with barely contained rage, but for now he was content
to reassert his role as family manager, providing his son with a sheaf of
instructions. Here are a few of them:

> In Augsb. you should stay at the Lamb in Holy Cross Street, where
> you'll pay only 30 kreuzer for lunch and the rooms are nice and the most
> respectable people [stay there]. . . .
> You must also visit Herr Christoph von Zabuenig . . . , [who] *can arrange*

for something nice and impressive to be published in the papers. . . .

My brother or his daughter [the Bäsle] will probably take you to His Grace, . . . the magistrate Herr von Langenmantel [a childhood friend of Leopold's]. . . .

You needn't wear your cross [the papal order] except in Augsburg, where you must wear it every day because it will earn you esteem and respect [there]. . . .

Wherever you stay, always make sure the innkeeper puts boot-trees in your boots [at night]. . . .

Your music bag can always stay at the front of the trunk, but you should buy a big oilcloth and use this one and the old one to wrap up the music to make sure it's well protected. . . .

The pants to your pike-gray suit remained behind. . . .

Don't forget to get letters [of recommendation] in Munich. . . .

(Letter dated September 25, 1777)

His follow-up letter three days later makes a special request:

Now I ask you, my dear Wolfgang, not to do anything in excess; you've been accustomed since youth to good order, so you should avoid hot drinks, since you know that you will get hot and that you prefer cold to warmth—clear proof *that your blood has a tendency to heat up and boil immediately.* Strong wines and drinking a lot of wine are harmful to you. Just imagine the unhappiness and distress you would cause your dear mother in a far-off country.

MUNICH, AUGSBURG, AND THE BÄSLE

Although Mozart and his mother spent over two weeks in Munich, they had little to show for it. He interviewed with both the former and the current opera intendants (managers). Nothing. Several members of the aristocracy asked hopefully if he planned to remain in Munich—but without a job, he couldn't. Finally he met with the elector himself, who praised him, then said, "Yes, my dear boy, but I have no vacancy."

The Mozarts left on October 11 and pressed on to Augsburg, where the Bäsle—Mozart's fun-loving cousin—lived. These two peas in a pod had a jolly time together, hurling puns and bawdy jokes back and forth. Some scholars think they indulged in a few bedtime amusements. Leopold suspected as much but said nothing until months later, writing on February 12, 1778, that "you had your little scene, amusing yourself with my brother's daughter." Wolfgang retorted on February 19 that the

National Theater at the court of Elector Carl Theodor in Mannheim. The entire court moved to Munich in 1778, when Carl Theodor became elector of Bavaria.

accusation was false and "insults me greatly." Here is a sample of the cousins' correspondence, from Wolfgang's letter to her dated November 5, 1777, as translated by Robert Spaethling (no letters from her have survived):[1]

> Dearest Coz Fuzz!
> I have received reprieved your dear letter telling selling me that my uncle carbuncle [Leopold's brother], my aunt can't and you too are very well hell. ...Today the letter setter from my Papa Ha! Ha! dropped safely into my claws paws. I hope that you too have got shot the note dote which I wrote to you.... If so, so much the better, better the much so.... You write further, you pour out, disclose, divulge, notify, declare, signify, inform, acquaint me with the fact, make it quite clear, request, demand, desire, wish, would like, order me to send lend you my portrait.... I shall certainly dispatch scratch it to you.... Why, a fox is no hare, well ... Now, where was I? ...
>   Now I must close, though it makes me morose.... I kiss you 1,000 times and remain, as always, your little old piggy wiggy
> Wolfgang Amadé Rosy Posy

In Augsburg Mozart played several concerts, one of them featuring two piano concertos (K. 242 and 238); for another, private performance he played his Violin Concerto, K. 216. He also shared ideas with the important Augsburg piano maker Johann Andreas Stein, trying out instruments and writing excited descriptions of their innovations to his father.

---

1. Spaethling, *Mozart's Letters, Mozart's Life,* 86ff.

MANNHEIM

On October 30, 1777, the travelers arrived in Mannheim, where Elector Carl Theodor ruled over a fabulous court—an imitation Versailles with (in addition to his palace) an opera house, a theater for spoken drama, a ballet theater, a marionette theater, and a concert hall. On the elector's payroll were dancers, set designers, musicians, singers, actors, and lighting specialists ("lighting" of course meant candles). Carl Theodor lived life to the hilt, displaying excellent taste in the arts and encouraging the new and experimental; he also kept mistresses and fathered a number of illegitimate children (referred to in the Mozart correspondence as his "natural" children, in line with the era's customary circumlocution).

Mannheim's Orchestra

In Mannheim Mozart encountered a level of music-making so superior to Salzburg's that it fundamentally altered the way he composed. Mannheim's orchestra could play anything he could imagine writing. The string playing was unbelievably in tune and rhythmically precise, the brass exceptional, and the woodwinds—above all, it was the woodwinds that astonished him. After hearing what these instruments were capable of in the hands of such musicians, he began writing solo parts for flute, oboe, bassoon, and horn that were freer, more expressive, and more demanding than those of any other composer of his time including Haydn or, later, Beethoven. You can actually identify his music as pre- or post-Mannheim by the richness and variety of its writing for winds.

Mozart quickly forged friendships among musicians there, lunching and dining with them time and again. His letters mention in particular the principal flutist, Johann Baptist Wendling (whose wife was a leading soprano in the Mannheim opera), and the principal oboist, Friedrich Ramm. He also formed a close colleagueship with the conductor and chief composer, Christian Cannabich. Mannheim's music-making made Salzburg's look pathetic. Salzburg also had no opera house, and opera was what he wanted to compose more than anything else.

Opera in Mannheim

The *Kapellmeister* (director of music) at Mannheim was Ignaz Holzbauer, a central figure in Carl Theodor's support of new music. Holzbauer's *Günther von Schwarzburg* was the first opera seria (serious opera) written in German, and Mozart wrote home with great enthusiasm about seeing it rehearsed and performed. German writers such as Goethe and Schiller were urging that poets, artists, and musicians strive to create German-language works to match those of France and England; up to that time, German had been thought incapable of such heights. Holzbauer's new opera was a deliberate step toward this goal, and Mozart was deeply impressed by it. He also impressed Holzbauer, who graciously volunteered to speak on his behalf to the court's music manager. Holzbauer did so, but to no avail.

Another Mannheim experiment involved a genre called *melodrama,* which wasn't eighteenth-century soap opera but spoken drama with musical accompaniment. Rousseau wrote a melodrama called *Pygmalion;* 150 years later, George Bernard Shaw recycled the same Greek myth as a play, which, still later, spawned the musical *My Fair Lady.* Goethe also contributed to the genre. Melodrama piqued Mozart's interest, and he set about writing one with a Mannheim diplomat who furnished the text, but they never finished it.

A SINGLE COMMISSION?

A major purpose of Mozart's job-seeking trip was to show off his gifts as performer and, more importantly, as composer. Curiously, he wrote no music for the fabulous Mannheim orchestra. In fact, he composed precious little during his stay there. His only money-making opportunity came from a man he at first called "the Indian." The man wasn't Indian at all, but Dutch, and his only connection with "India" was as a physician with the [Dutch] East India Company (which was heavily invested in the American colonies). His name was Ferdinand Dejean or DeJean, and he was a fine amateur flutist.

Dr. Dejean admired the young man's music and commissioned him to write some flute concertos (there is some confusion about the number requested) and (probably) six flute quartets (a flute quartet comprises flute, violin, viola, and cello, the flute taking the place of the first violin). Mozart, however, fulfilled only part of the commission—he said he disliked the flute—and cheated on that, writing only one quartet, parts of a second, and one concerto. A second concerto was actually an oboe concerto he'd written earlier; Ramm, Mannheim's principal oboist, liked it so much he played it around town *after* Mozart presented it to Dejean as a flute concerto. Wolfgang complained to Leopold that Dejean had paid him only 96 of the promised 200 gulden, never confessing why; but Leopold wasn't fooled.

MOZART'S FRIENDS IN MANNHEIM

Mozart's circle of friends switched quite dramatically and suddenly while he was there. At the outset, his closest friends were the composer-conductor Christian Cannabich, his wife, and his talented thirteen-year-old daughter

Rosa. The Cannabichs entertained him many times. Mozart sat in on orchestral rehearsals and Cannabich presented his case to the elector's music manager, though without success. Mozart, who spoke glowingly of Rosa's pianistic talents, composed a sonata expressly for her (K. 309/284a), describing its slow second movement as her musical portrait. This is the only time he is known to have claimed that he portrayed someone in music.

During his first weeks in Mannheim, Mozart also developed ties with Ramm and Wendling. The three of them, along with the court's ballet master, Lauchéry, hatched a plan to travel to Paris together. Mozart's mother was to be settled into a Mannheim apartment for the winter, then take a coach to Salzburg alone. Ramm and Wendling, already well known in Paris, knew their way around the city's musical venues and could guide Mozart toward jobs and commissions. During that period the cross-traffic and reciprocity of influence between Mannheim and Paris were well established; musicians traveled back and forth all the time. Mozart wrote his father about this idea with great excitement and added that his mother liked the group and fully supported their plan.

Then, practically overnight, he describes his traveling partners as morally deficient (Wendling's daughter is a "mistress"; Wendling "is without any religion"; Ramm is "a libertine"). The Paris trip was off. Wolfgang and Maria Anna had been in Mannheim since October 30. In December the elector's music manager had told him he could expect no appointment. It was now February. Leopold's patience was nearly at an end; why was Wolfgang hanging around a court where there was no job?

There were two reasons why Mozart wanted to stay. One, quite practical, was the severe risk of long-distance travel in wintertime. Although he himself could face this unperturbed, it would have been imprudent to subject his mother to such potential discomfort, even danger. He suggested to his father that she come home by herself (which would have left him free to go to Paris whenever he liked), but Leopold refused to entertain such a thought. You will stay with your mother, ordered his father, and she will join you wherever and whenever you go.

ALOYSIA WEBER

Mozart's main reason for not leaving was a seventeen-year-old girl named Aloysia Weber, a very promising young soprano, a good pianist, and beautiful. Mozart met her *after* he planned to go to Paris with Ramm, Wendling, and Lauchéry and *before* he decided not to go.

His letters to Leopold immediately begin to focus on Aloysia, escalating rapidly to grandiose travel and career plans. He would escort her to Italy (he, who was unemployed), where he would establish her as a prima donna in an opera house (she is 17 and with virtually no stage experience); after that, he casually remarks, "I think we shall go to Switzerland and maybe also Holland." On the way they would stop at the Mozarts' for two weeks— Wolfgang, Aloysia, her father, mother, and three sisters. Mozart, head over heels in love, wasn't thinking straight.

Fanciful as his pipe dream was, his instincts about Aloysia's career prospects were right on target. All four Weber daughters were musical, but she was easily the most gifted, establishing herself a few years later as a celebrated soprano in Vienna. It was not Mozart's musical judgment that was faulty, but his lack of common sense. To his father:

> I would bet my life that [Aloysia] will do me great honor. She has already profited a great deal in a short time [from my instruction]. . . . Please do everything possible for us to go to Italy. You know my greatest desire—to write operas. For Verona I will gladly write an opera [for very little money] if only she can make herself famous. . . . By that time I will have made so much money on the other journeys we want to make together that it won't hurt me [financially]. . . . A propos, you must not be too surprised that of my 77 gulden only 42 gulden are left. . . . [But] the thought of helping a poor family . . . pleases my whole soul. . . .
>
> (Letter dated February 4, 1778)

Mozart's next letter includes a rare and forthright self-assessment. Explaining why he wasn't interested in teaching untalented pupils, he continued:

> I am a composer and was born to be a *Kapellmeister.* I dare not and cannot bury the talent for composition that God in his goodness has so richly given me (I may say so without conceit, for I feel it now more than ever) . . .
>
> (Letter dated February 7, 1778)

On February 12, Leopold responded to this barrage "with amazement and shock." He had never heard such "groundless, poorly considered plans." He reminded his son why he undertook this journey: "either to find a substantial post, or if that fails, to go to some large city where great profits can be made." But now, with no money yourself, you want to write an opera for Verona, "although you know the Veronese have no money and never commission new operas." And even if Aloysia "sings like [the greatest of divas]. . . what impresario wouldn't laugh if you tried to recommend a girl of 16 or 17 who has never appeared on stage? . . . Your letter was written like a novel." Leopold complains that he himself is lonely and his debts now totaled 700 gulden. His clothes are so threadbare that "I look like Lazarus." Nevertheless, he has pulled himself together to send instructions for what Wolfgang is to do in Paris—whom he is to see, how much everything would cost, and how he should proceed. How much money do you have now, he inquires. Why didn't you write all the music Dejean paid you to write? At his wit's end, Leopold fairly shouts: "Get yourself to Paris! And soon!"

Aloysia Weber Lange, Mozart's first love, in costume for an operatic role

Now Mozart backpedals. Of course (he writes on February 19), he wouldn't have gone through with such plans in his present financial circumstances. Of course, Aloysia is young and still has much to learn. However (he wrote on February 28), he has composed an aria for her. More than this his father never learned, because Mozart never referred to her again. But Aloysia was the love of Wolfgang's young life and he could not give her up so easily. On his way back to Salzburg months later, he made a beeline for her door—a fact he never mentioned to Leopold.

DEPARTURE FROM MANNHEIM

When Mozart left Mannheim, the court he wanted so badly to be a part of, he took with him a cluster of memorable experiences both good and bad. He had heard a matchless orchestra; witnessed a new kind of opera, composed in his native language; enjoyed the warm companionship of first-class musicians; fallen passionately in love—and he had experienced all of this for himself, without the constant tutorial presence of his father. But he had spent a great deal of his father's money and failed to land a job. Why was no job offered to him? There were several likely causes: first, he was only twenty-two. Second, he was perceived to be inexperienced as a composer. In fact, most of his music that we know today dates from years later, during his decade in Vienna. Third, he was unusually short (a source of continual embarrassment), so that when people saw him, they still thought of him as a charming little boy. He complained about this in letters, but there was no way he could stop it. Fourth, there was simply no job available.

The Mannheim court was also in the process of moving. The elector of Bavaria had died of smallpox in December 1777, and Carl Theodor became his successor. The Mannheim court, with its musical establishment nearly intact, relocated to Munich during the course of 1778. Carl Theodor himself moved there in late summer.

Mozart and Maria Anna left Mannheim on March 14, after a farewell concert-and-party that brought Mozart to tears with its tender-hearted good wishes. As a farewell gift, Fridolin Weber presented him with the comedies of Molière (very useful for an opera composer). Aloysia gave him a set of lace cuffs she had embroidered. Oddly, his "best friends," the Cannabichs, didn't show up. After a nine-day journey in miserable weather, Mozart and his mother reached Paris on March 23, 1778, thoroughly worn out and drenched to the bones.

PARIS

Mozart hit the ground running in the French capital, presenting himself the day after his arrival to the two most important people on the list of more than fifty that Leopold had sent him: Baron Grimm, the Mozart family's Parisian tour guide from years before, and Count Sickingen, Mannheim's ambassador to Paris. Grimm not only welcomed him warmly but also undertook to visit Frau Mozart from time to time, a courteous gesture that was much appreciated; Sickingen invited him to dinner that very night. Mozart quickly sent a detailed report to Leopold, telling him not to worry, that this was a city where you could make a lot of money and everything was going to be fine.

In response, Leopold's letters cease their constant moralizing for a while and become amiable, leisurely, even chatty. He regales his wife and son with lengthy anecdotes about what's going on in Salzburg. He also proudly reports that Nannerl is "playing like a *Kapellmeister*"; at long last he was teaching her composition, and (as he could have predicted) she took to it at once. The two of them have the usual coterie of friends over for weekly *Bölzlschiessen* target practice (Mozart sometimes sent suggestions for hand-drawn targets), and the family's dog, Pimperl, is enjoying herself as always:

> [W]henever she stands on the table she very gently scratches the rolls with a paw so that somebody will give her one, then [scratches] the knife so someone will slice it for her. And if there are 4 or 5 snuffboxes lying on the table, she scratches the one with Spanish tobacco in it until someone takes a pinch and lets her lick their fingers.
>
> (Letter dated April 20, 1778)

Picking up on his son's positive tone, Leopold—ever the mentor—urges him to figure out what pleases French audiences and set about composing exactly that. He praises Wolfgang's "innate industriousness," which will "bring him fame throughout the world," because anyone who succeeds in Paris will be esteemed everywhere:

> You'll become a real Frenchman now and I hope you'll concentrate on acquiring a correct accent. Nannerl and I are well, praise God, and I'm no longer worried but actually pleased to know that our good friend Baron Grimm has taken you on and that you are now in the place which, with your innate industriousness, can bring you fame throughout the world. . . . These are now your years, which you must use for yourself and for all of us.
>
> (same letter as above)

Maria Anna, however, was not so thrilled. Although she wrote her husband that she was happy to see her son so well remembered that he was practically the toast of Paris (which, to put it mildly, was not the case), she spent all day in their cold, dark room—it's like being in prison, she said; I scarcely see the sun; it is so dark I can hardly see to knit, and I cannot keep warm. . . . Wolfgang has to go out searching for pupils, drumming up commissions, and composing—he can't work in their room because it has no keyboard and the stairs are too narrow to carry one up. Unfortunately, since Maria Anna knew very little French, she was of no help to her son as he made the rounds of Parisian salons. She also found French food inedible and prices twice as high as fifteen years before.

Rescue from their grim accommodations came from a woman whom the Mozarts remembered with much pleasure from the 1760s. Generally described, insultingly, as Grimm's mistress, Madame Louise d'Épinay was the baron's friend, literary colleague, and intellectual partner. Decades before, following her divorce from an alcoholic husband with a habitually roving eye, she had retired to her château north of Paris. Here she supported the impecunious Rousseau for over a year, putting him up in a cottage on her estate that she dubbed the Hermitage, famous today as the place he idealized in his novel *La nouvelle Héloïse*. But when she penned articles critical of Rousseau's educational theories, he struck out against her quite vehemently in his own writings; he also neglected to thank her for supporting him during a trying time. The formidably intelligent Madame d'Épinay was well known among French *philosophes*. She and Grimm shared a house in Paris, d'Épinay occupying the first floor and he the second. It was she who took the trouble, in mid-April, to locate a warmer and more spacious apartment for Frau Mozart and her son.

The Concert Spirituel

Things did seem to go swimmingly for Mozart at the beginning. His first significant musical contact, with Joseph Legros, the new director of the Concert Spirituel, resulted in several commissions. The Concert Spirituel, formed in 1725 by singers and musicians from the Paris Opéra who wanted a way to perform on days when the Opéra was closed, was so named because its repertory included sacred choral music as well as orchestral works. It boasted an excellent chorus and orchestra. Legros arranged for Mozart to write several choruses for insertion into a Miserere by Ignaz Holzbauer, composer of the Mannheim opera Mozart had so admired, *Günther von Schwarzburg*. For the internationally known choreographer and ballet master Jean-Georges Noverre, whom he had met in Italy, he contributed some of the music for the ballet *Les petits riens*, K. 299b. He was also to write a four-soloist sinfonia concertante for Mannheim woodwind virtuosos Ramm, Wendler, and Ritter, to be joined by Europe's star horn player, Giovanni Punto. (A sinfonia concertante is a kind of hybrid between a concerto and a symphony). The largest commission from Legros was for the "Paris" Symphony, K. 297/300a.

How did all this pan out? The symphony, performed by the Concert Spirituel on June 18, was a rousing success. At the performance of the Miserere, however, no one seemed to identify any of the music as Mozart's, and he wasn't paid for it. Reviews of the ballet didn't mention his name and he received no payment for that, either. The woodwind sinfonia concertante was never performed, and the story about that is not pretty.

The composer Giuseppe Cambini, also commissioned to write a

sinfonia concertante for the same quartet of soloists, not only saw his work performed as scheduled but heard it played a second time a week later. When Mozart angrily confronted Legros to find out what happened to his work, the director said he had lost the music. There was no performance, no payment, and today all we have are portions—widely regarded as spurious— of a composition lovingly tailored for four of the finest woodwind players he ever heard.[2]

Yet Mozart knew exactly what had made this work "disappear," and it was his own fault—a classic display of Mozartian arrogance toward a fellow composer, but this time the victim struck back. As Wolfgang blandly reported to Leopold:

> [T]he cause of it all was *Cambini*. . . . because when I met him for the first time at Legros's, I unintentionally put him down. He has written some [string] quartets, one of which I heard in Mannheim; they are rather pretty, and I praised them to him and played the beginning of [one of them] to him [i.e., from memory], but Ritter, Ramm, and Punto were there and gave me no peace until I kept going, making up whatever I couldn't remember, so that's what I did, and Cambini was really beside himself; he couldn't stop saying [sarcastically, presumably], *questa è una gran testa*! [What a great mind!] Well, he definitely didn't like it.
>
> (Letter dated May 1, 1778)

Amadeus offers a fictionalized version of this humiliating scene with a more impressive cast of characters. Emperor Joseph II is haltingly performing a simple dance that Salieri has composed for him as Mozart, summoned to an audience with the emperor, walks into the room. Mozart sits down and plays through the entire piece from memory, pausing at one of Salieri's unimaginatively chosen chords to observe, "This doesn't work, does it?" Recognizable to knowledgeable viewers is Mozart's segue into the mocking aria Figaro sings to close Act I of *The Marriage of Figaro* (an opera actually written years later).

PRIVATE PUPILS AND PATRONS

Music in Paris also included first-rate amateur music-making in aristocrats' private homes. Baron Grimm introduced Mozart to Count de Guines, a

---

2. In 1866 Otto Jahn found a sinfonia concertante for oboe, clarinet, bassoon, and horn (the original was for flute, oboe, bassoon, and horn), though not in Mozart's hand. Some scholars believe this was the composer's own revised version; others think only its solo parts are Mozart's; still others regard the whole work as spurious. See Sadie, 471, and for a contrary view, Robert D. Levin, *Who Wrote the Mozart Four-Wind Concertante?* (Stuyvesant, NY: Pendragon Press, 1988). Levin has also reconstructed the work with its original scoring.

superb flutist whose daughter was a harpist. Mozart described her playing as "*magnifique*" and marveled at the fact that she never needed the music in front of her ("she has an incomparable memory"). For the two of them he composed the Concerto for Flute and Harp, K. 299, an exquisitely beautiful combination of solo instruments despite Mozart's earlier complaint, back in Mannheim composing for Dejean, that he didn't like the flute. Mlle. de Guines was also one of his three piano pupils. In this capacity, though, she proved frustratingly inept at elementary composition—which Mozart, like the best teachers today, included as an element of piano instruction:

> She simply has no [musical] ideas at all; nothing comes. I have tried everything conceivable with her. Among other things, I wrote out a really simple minuet to see if she could write a variation on it.—Well, that was hopeless.—Oh, I thought, she doesn't know how to start—so I began a variation on the first measure, and told her to continue in this manner and stick with that idea—that went finally more or less okay.... Then I wrote out 4 bars of a minuet and said to her—you see what a numbskull I am; I begin a minuet but can't even get to the end of the first part—please be kind enough to finish it; she thought it would be impossible; but at last, with much effort, she put something together, and I was glad that finally something came....
>
> (Letter dated May 14, 1778)

Getting around Paris, whether to teach his aristocratic students or to ingratiate himself with potential patrons, was difficult. This wasn't Salzburg or Mannheim; distances were vast, streets were often muddy ("the dirt in Paris is beyond description"), transportation expensive, and the financial rewards insufficient to make it all worthwhile. To meet up with a hoped-for patron, you had to present yourself at their home, not they at yours; and once there, you awaited their pleasure, which might take hours—remember, musicians weren't "artists" but hired entertainers, and Wolfgang Mozart was a foreigner with a German accent. The following description records his frustration at one such encounter. Recommended by Grimm to the Duchess of Chabot, he arrived at her house, where

> I had to wait half an hour in a large, ice-cold, unheated room without even a fireplace.... I said, I want very much to play something, but right now it is impossible because my fingers are so cold I can't feel them; ... [might the Duchess] have somebody lead me to a room with a fireplace with a fire in it? "Oui, Monsieur, you are right."... All the windows and

doors were open. . . . I started to get a headache . . . [though] I did play on that wretched, miserable piano. But what most annoyed me was that Madame and her [guests] never left off their drawing for a moment; they just kept on going, and so I had to play to the chairs, the tables, and the walls. . . . [Finally I stopped, and] they showered me with praise. . . . [At last] her husband came. He . . . sat beside me and listened to me with total concentration, and I—I forgot about the cold and my headache and played without noticing how wretched the piano was—the way I play when I am in a good mood. If you give me the best piano in Europe, but with listeners who don't understand or don't want to understand, and who don't feel what I'm playing, then I lose all joy. I told this whole story to Monsieur Grimm afterward.

(Letter dated May 1, 1778)

Even in childhood Mozart would stop playing if people began to talk or be disruptive. His own focus was intense and he expected the same intensity from those listening to him. But if you gave him undivided attention, he would play for you all night long.

Mozart's mood began to sour on everything Parisian. Solo vocalists don't sing, he griped to his father; they "screech," all the more so in Italian music, of which they haven't the slightest grasp; and French vocal music is simply beyond the pale. People there had no taste; "I am among cattle and beasts where music is concerned." Being outmaneuvered by Cambini and Legros and receiving only partial payment from Count de Guines didn't help. There may have been an offer to become court organist at Versailles, a well-paid position requiring only a half-year's work, but when Leopold asked for details, probably skeptical that there really was such an offer, none were forthcoming and the post was never mentioned again.

Mozart's letters grew increasingly angry and resentful. In response, his father's ceased being supportive and newsy and turned toward sermonizing lined with self-pity. One wonders if Leopold still planned to publish a biography of Wolfgang based on their correspondence. Would he have wanted such letters to appear in print?

I don't know the cause of your bad mood. Having to take care of one's own everyday expenses is indeed quite different from being able to live without having to worry about such things because someone else is taking care of them for you. . . . Now you can understand all the work, the burdens, and the daily worries that I've had in the *30 years* since I got married in order to support a family, *worries* that will not leave me until the hour of my death. . . . You are young!—But I must plague myself with *5 pupils* in my *59th year for very little money!*

(Letter dated June 11, 1778; emphases are Leopold's)

MOZART'S MOTHER DIES

Around the time that Leopold was writing this letter, Maria Anna took to her bed with what developed into a fatal illness. It may have been typhus or perhaps typhoid fever, the disease that had nearly killed both of her children in The Hague. Water may have been the culprit; Parisians never drank it, but the Mozarts had always done so, unsuspectingly, wherever they were. As her condition worsened, Frau Weber bled herself (without help of a doctor), and a few days after that, Mozart summoned a physician. She insisted on a German doctor but got no better under his care. When at last Mozart confided her illness to Grimm and Madame d'Épinay, they sent their personal physician, but it was too late. She died on July 3. Leopold knew only that she was ill, and Mozart didn't tell him of her death right away. First, he sent a letter to a close Salzburg friend and advisor, the Abbé Bullinger, describing his mother's last days and asking Bullinger to break the news to Leopold personally—a thoughtful gesture intended to soften the blow temporarily. Then Mozart himself wrote.

I hope you are prepared to hear one of the most sorrowful and painful messages with steadfastness— . . . on the 3rd at 21 minutes after 10 o'clock at night my mother went blessedly to sleep in God.—When I wrote to you [on the day she died] she was already enjoying the joys of heaven— everything was already over—I wrote to you late that night—and I hope that you and my dear sister will excuse my small but necessary deception— when I thought about my own pain and sorrow in comparison to yours, I simply could not bring myself to shock you with this news. . . . You can easily imagine what I went through—what courage and fortitude were necessary to endure it all . . . —and indeed, the merciful God bestowed on me this grace—I felt such pain, and cried a lot—but what help is that?—I had to console myself; may you do the same, my dear father and sister! Cry, cry yourselves out! But then console yourselves.

. . . She died peacefully. . . . Now, the divine, all-holy will is fulfilled—let us pray a devout Paternoster ["Our Father," the Lord's Prayer] for her soul— and then turn our thoughts to other things, for everything has its time. . . .

(Letter dated July 9, 1778)

In the months that followed, his father's letters referred several times to his wife's death. The marriage had been a strong and affectionate one. Leopold and Maria Anna had survived much together, and his inability to be at her bedside during her final illness gnawed at him. For some time thereafter, he insinuated that if he had been with her she would not have died.

MOZART, MADAME D'ÉPINAY, AND GRIMM

During Mozart's remaining three months in Paris—he didn't leave until late September—he resided on the first floor of the Grimm–d'Épinay house, her part of the house, "where I have a pretty little room with a very pleasant view." Thoughtfully, they had invited him over immediately following his mother's death so that he didn't have to remain in the room where she had died.

How did Mozart spend these months, and why, his father wanted to know, didn't he come directly home after his mother died? Mozart explained that he had to stay to collect fees due him from the Concert Spirituel (which wasn't possible, since they owned the "Paris" Symphony and claimed they'd lost the woodwind sinfonia concertante), and from Count de Guines, who seems never to have come up with more than a partial fee. Mozart's second stated reason was that he wanted to arrange publication of a number of compositions—Paris was a world center of music publishing—but he also failed in that regard.

Meanwhile, on July 27 Grimm sent a kind of report card to Leopold, describing Wolfgang as

> not very active, easily distracted, too little concerned with the means that lead to fortune. Here . . . you have to be cunning, entrepreneurial, audacious. . . . I would wish him half the talent that he has and twice the entrepreneurial spirit . . . [T]his business will not suit him because it will keep him from composing, and *that* he loves beyond anything else. . . . [I]n this country most of the public is not very knowledgeable as far as music is concerned. You are acclaimed for your name, and the artistic value of your work can often only be judged by a very small number of people. The public, at this moment, is so ridiculously torn between Piccinni and Gluck, and all the explanations you hear about music are pitiful. For your son, it will be very difficult to succeed between these two parties.[3]

A CONTROVERSY ABOUT OPERA

The Piccinni-Gluck debate was indeed embroiling Parisian salons (can you imagine people today arguing furiously about the best kind of opera?).

---

3. Translation (from the French) abridged and slightly altered from H. C. Robbins Landon, *The Mozart Essays* (New York: Thames and Hudson, 1995), 66.

Twenty years earlier, when the controversy had centered on French vs. Italian opera, Grimm had published an anonymous pamphlet—though everybody soon identified him as its author—in which he satirized French vocal music. Now the opponents were different: one was Gluck, who was not French, but German, internationally admired though castigated by some for his radical reforms of opera. After he transferred his sphere of operations to Paris, a battle royal ensued between his works and those of the Italian composer Niccolò Piccinni. Essentially, the quarrel pitted beautiful singing and tuneful melody (Piccinnists) against credible dramatic action and minimal vocal display (Gluckists).

Mozart lived in Paris at the height of this debate, and it seems beyond question that at the Grimm–d'Épinay house opera was talked and argued about for hours at a time; the friends who came and went in that household included *philosophes* who were actively engaged in the debate. Mozart complained to his father that Grimm avidly supported the Italians; he himself sided unequivocally with Gluck. Although he apparently didn't attend any of the celebrated composer's operas, he must have seen some of the music, because his own breakthrough opera of a few years later, *Idomeneo* (1781), demonstrated how much he had grasped and appreciated Gluck's reforms.

As the weeks wore on, Mozart's arguments with Grimm moved toward more mundane concerns. He declared to Leopold that it wasn't Grimm who had invited him to live there in the first place, but Madame d'Épinay. It was she who was kind to him and understood perfectly why he couldn't succeed in Paris: "they treat me like a seven-year-old boy"—the same problem he had in Mannheim. Grimm, by contrast, was no help at all; he "might be able to help children but not grown-ups." In short, the two men got on each other's nerves so badly that Mozart finally left—or was thrown out—on September 26, Grimm writing Leopold that his son still owed him money.

Wolfgang, in fact, owed Leopold many times more than he owed Grimm, and the debts kept mounting. In letter after letter his father urged him to cut his losses, stop this catastrophic job search, and head for home. Leopold was now in such financial straits that the only way out, he pleaded, was a concentrated effort by *both* of them for about two years; Wolfgang must return to Salzburg at once to get this going. Leopold would try to have him reinstated in the archbishop's service, probably as cathedral organist, a position carrying with it compositional duties as well. The previous organist had died and Archbishop Colloredo was looking for a replacement. At the same time, Colloredo was searching all over Europe for a new *Kapellmeister*, coolly bypassing the man right in front of him: his own

Vize-Kapellmeister, Leopold Mozart. Leopold did not give voice, at least not to his son as far as we know, to what must have been unspeakable rage at this public humiliation. Meanwhile there was also a Salzburg opening for a *prima donna* (lead soprano). Wolfgang excitedly proposed that his father nominate Aloysia Weber! Which Leopold did not do. Leopold had nevertheless heard complimentary things about Aloysia's singing, which he passed along to Wolfgang without any hint of recrimination. He also conveyed the news that she had been appointed to the Munich [formerly Mannheim] opera. Wolfgang, pining for her throughout his months in Paris, also missed Mannheim's glorious orchestra and its superb conductor, Christian Cannabich.

Return to Aloysia Weber

Leaving Paris in late September 1778, Mozart at last started his long and, to Leopold, frustratingly circuitous journey back to Salzburg. After stopovers in Nancy and Strasbourg, he headed straight for Mannheim—curiously, not in the first instance to Munich, where Aloysia now was. After a fond reunion with the Cannabichs, and despite insistent orders from his father to come straight home, he traveled to Munich to see her again at last. Maybe he intended to propose to her; maybe he did so.

Who knows why, but she reacted quite coldly to him and he was devastated, weeping, we are told, for hours. Perhaps it was because she was now a professional singer in a significant court—no longer an ingenue—and couldn't picture herself marrying an unemployed musician who, despite his colossal talent and unequalled professional connections, couldn't seem to land a job. At all events, about a year later she moved up the ladder to Vienna. There she sang leading roles and married the actor and portrait painter Joseph Lange. In 1788 she portrayed Donna Anna in the Vienna production of Mozart's *Don Giovanni*. When she and Lange separated some years after that, he lamented to friends that she still carried a torch for Wolfgang Mozart, who had died in 1791.

Mozart stayed on in Munich, savoring the company of his Mannheim friends in their new surroundings and possibly also deepening his acquaintance with persons of influence such as the tenor Anton Raaff, whose opinions appear to have carried great weight in that court.

Back to Salzburg

As Mozart continued to invent excuses for not getting to Salzburg faster, Leopold's letters climbed from impatience to fury. He claimed that he was now in debt to the sum of 863 gulden (nearly twice his annual salary): you'll destroy me if you keep this up! But Mozart did not leave Munich until January 13, 1779. Before that, he wrote to his Augsburg cousin the Bäsle, asking her to join him on his homeward trek, perhaps as a shield against his father's wrath. She did come, and their coach arrived in Salzburg on January 15. He had been gone since September 1777.

Two days later, on January 17, Archbishop Colloredo signed Mozart's contract as organist-*Konzertmeister*, responsible for the supervision of church music and for composing any other music required by his employer. His salary was 450 gulden, sufficient in a town such as Salzburg, where he could live and eat at home for free. Aloysia's salary in Munich was 600, a fact of which he was doubtless aware.

Mozart was to remain in Salzburg until November 1780—nearly two years—until he went to Munich again, this time to complete *Idomeneo*, K. 366, which had been commissioned the previous summer. The composer's wide acquaintance at that court—perhaps most especially with Raaff—had garnered him this distinguished prize. *Idomeneo*'s success, in turn, became the opening wedge of his escape from the city he so despised. From there he went to Vienna, where he lived for the rest of his life. He visited Salzburg only once, for about six weeks in the late summer of 1783.

A TURNING POINT

This whole Mannheim-Paris journey, so agonizing in many respects, can nevertheless be viewed as a turning point, perhaps *the* turning point, of Mozart's life—personally, intellectually, and musically.[4] Documented in letters peppered with Leopold's annoyance at his son's inability to deal with the realities of job-hunting—one of only two such father-son exchanges that we have[5]—this long trip confronted him with major disappointments. He failed to secure a job, Aloysia Weber rejected him, and his relationship with his father was strained nearly to the breaking point. Worst of all was the profound family tragedy of Maria Anna's death. For all these reasons, writers tend to describe the journey as a failure.

Yet these sixteen months also provided him with experiences that exerted an immediate and profound impact on his own music. For five months he had listened to the incomparable Mannheim orchestra demonstrate what he could write if superior musicians were at hand; once he moved to Vienna

---

4. I am indebted for the title and general idea of this section, though not its content, to chapter 8, "A Turning Point," in Georg Knepler, *Wolfgang Amadé Mozart*, trans. J. Bradford Robinson (London and New York: Cambridge University Press, 1994).

5. The other is their correspondence while Mozart was in Munich completing work on *Idomeneo*. That correspondence, quite unlike the Mannheim-Paris letters, vividly portrays two musicians sharing ideas as equals. The difference: Leopold now appears to acknowledge his son's status as a fellow professional.

in 1781, they were. In Paris, he had his first chance to compose music for virtuoso woodwind players, although the resulting sinfonia concertante has unfortunately not come down to us. Finally, he spent three months in the company of two Enlightenment *philosophes,* Baron Grimm and Madame d'Épinay, during which a new concept of opera seems to have taken shape in his mind.

Back in Salzburg, despite the frustration of being trapped there again, Mozart created four quite extraordinary works: *Idomeneo;* the Mass in C Major, K. 317 ("Coronation"); the *Vesperae solennes de confessore,* K. 339; and the Sinfonia concertante for violin and viola, K. 364/320d.[6] In each of them, Mozart shows full mastery of his craft. He may have been young at the start of this trip, but he is a fully mature composer now.

THE "PARIS" SYMPHONY

The "Paris" Symphony is noteworthy for several striking features:

First, it requires the largest orchestra of any he had written for up to that time, including not only martial-sounding trumpets and timpani but also clarinets, which make their first appearance in his music. Salzburg had no clarinets, but Mannheim, Paris, and other major cities did; from now on, they figure regularly in Mozart's orchestral music—whenever he was not composing for Salzburg.

Second, it has only three movements. This is because the French preferred three. In this they were influenced by the Mannheimers, who in an odd historical twist had pioneered the four-movement symphony in the 1740s, then changed back to three in the 1770s.

Third, the first movement's Exposition is not repeated—again, a bow to French taste; it was not the custom there to repeat expositions.

Fourth, the stunning figure at the opening of the first movement is played many times during the course of the movement. Known as a *coup d'archet,* this sort of gesture was a favorite in Mannheim and therefore also in Paris. It still makes a sensational effect today, as the strings in unison (i.e., all playing the same notes) race up the scale in a quick, dramatic crescendo; the point was to demonstrate an orchestra's musical discipline.

Fifth, the slow movement exists in two versions, the second composed after Monsieur Legros complained that the first one was too long and harmonically too complicated. The problem is that today, Mozart specialists aren't sure which version came first. Their task isn't made easier by the fact that the two versions are about the same length.

---

6. Volkmar Braunbehrens, in a private communication, has speculated that the Sinfonia concertante may have been a peace offering meant for performance by Leopold (violin) and Wolfgang (viola).

On July 3, Mozart wrote his father that the *coup d'archet* achieved its effect (Leopold frowned upon such "mannerisms") and the concert—after a lousy rehearsal that sent him to bed "with an anxious heart and a dissatisfied and angry mind"—was a triumph.

■ Symphony in D Major, K. 297/300a, "Paris"
(Paris, 1778)
For 2 flutes, 2 oboes, 2 clarinets, 2 bassoons, 2 horns, 2 trumpets, timpani, and strings
    1. Allegro assai (sonata form, major key, duple meter)

Exposition (not repeated)	A	A1	Bridge	B	B1	Closing (codetta)
			43"	1'24"		2'00"
Development	3'25					
Recapitulation	4'30"					
Coda	8'16"					

Timings based on Sir Charles Grove conducting the English Sinfonia.
IMP Classics PCD 892, n.d.

THE MYSTERIOUS PARIS PIANO SONATA
A keyboard prodigy as a child, Mozart announced to his father in a letter from Paris in 1778 that he was now more interested in composing than performing. However, since audiences in the eighteenth century were just as dazzled by keyboard pyrotechnics as people are today, displaying his pianistic gifts from time to time—especially in piano concertos—remained a prime source of income, particularly during his first years in Vienna (1781–1786).

Most of Mozart's eighteen piano sonatas were not intended either for public performance or for the subjective expression of feelings; here he differed from Beethoven, for whom they were an intensely personal and subjective medium. For the most part, Mozart's were written less often for himself than for his students, as practice pieces, or for patrons and would-be patrons. Thus these works did not assume the degree of importance for him that, say, his concertos and operas did. This is at least partly explained by the fact that in his generation the piano (i.e., the fortepiano) was chiefly—though certainly not exclusively—associated with amateur music-making.

But the Sonata in A Minor, K. 310/300d is not only highly unusual in style; the circumstances surrounding the composition of this starkly probing work remain a mystery today. We know that Mozart wrote it in Paris during the spring or summer of 1778. It is one of his very few minor-key works, only two of which are piano sonatas. Because his mother died in that city on July 3, 1778, it has been suggested that this demonic sonata must have emerged out of his profound grief at her passing. But perhaps it stemmed from his anger at being forced to leave Aloysia Weber, or from any number of other causes—or none of them; perhaps he simply wanted to write it. At all events, there is no evidence that this sonata was performed in Paris by Mozart or anyone else. There is no record of a commission, and it is not mentioned in the family letters.

Mozart's sonatas for piano typically have three movements (i.e., no dance movement). In this sonata, these are marked

- Allegro maestoso
- Andante cantabile con espressione
- Presto

As you listen, concentrate on the anguished first movement; but there is also the slow movement with its dark, unsettling middle section and the restless, turbulent finale. However this sonata came into being, it is surely among Mozart's most remarkable achievements.

■ PIANO SONATA IN A MINOR, K. 310/300D
(Paris, between March 23 and September 26, 1778)

1. Allegro maestoso (sonata form, minor key, duple meter)

Exposition				Development	Recapitulation	Coda
‖: A	Bridge	B	Closing :‖			
	31″	43″	1′26″	3′11″	4′10″	5′20″
repeat:						
1′35″	2′07″	2′19″	2′43″			

2. Andante cantabile con espressione (sonata form, major key, triple meter)

3. Presto (rondo form, minor key, duple meter

Timings based on Malcolm Bilson, fortepiano. Hungaroton HCD 31011-12, ©1990

5

RETURN TO SALZBURG, 1779–1780

NEW GENRE: THE SINFONIA CONCERTANTE

Suddenly, in the 1770s and especially in Paris, a new genre sprang up called the *symphonie concertante* or *sinfonia concertante*. Instantly popular, it quickly migrated first to Mannheim and from there to London, Vienna, various courts in Italy, and other major cities across Europe. Before it mysteriously died out in the 1830s, the genre attracted composers of the first rank: Joseph Haydn; Mozart's beloved London mentor J. C. Bach (again, not to be confused with his father, J. S. Bach); and his good friend from Mannheim, Christian Cannabich. Mozart himself wrote, or began to write, three such pieces: the Sinfonia Concertante K. 297B, featuring outstanding woodwind players, the one the Concert Spirituel "lost"; the Sinfonia Concertante for Violin, Viola, and Cello, K. 320e, which he never finished; and the (complete) Sinfonia Concertante in E-flat Major for Violin and Viola, K. 364/320d. All three date from 1778 to 1779, making them direct outgrowths of his pivotal journey to Mannheim and Paris.

What was this new kind of music? Part symphony, part concerto, part divertimento or serenade, it was an orchestral composition in three (sometimes only two) movements, with concertante (i.e., soloistic) writing for several instruments. The solo instruments could be a mix of strings and winds, strings only, or winds only.

We know next to nothing about the specific origins of the Sinfonia Concertante in E-flat Major for Violin and Viola, K. 364/320d. No autograph manuscript survives; we have no record that the work was ever performed; we don't know what soloists Mozart had in mind. Possibly it was intended as a musical peace offering to his father, as Volkmar Braunbehrens has suggested. You can imagine the glow in Leopold's eyes if they did perform it together.

The work is scored for pairs of oboes and horns—no clarinets, since

Salzburg had none. Unusually and to remarkable effect, the violas are divided into two parts, yielding (along with the absence of flutes) a warm-hued sound unlike any he had called upon before. Oboes and horns are given opportunities to shine, rather than merely filling out the harmony as they had in Mozart's pre-Mannheim compositions. The solo viola is notated in the "wrong" key, D major, the player instructed to tune the instrument up a half-step so that it sounds in the proper key, E-flat major. Called *scordatura*, this was no Mozartian innovation, but a well-known device more than a century old: here, its function is to brighten the viola's characteristically dusky sound and keep it from being outshone by the violin.

There are three movements. The opening Allegro, in concerto-first movement form, will be our focus (see diagram on the following page). This is followed by an elegiac, minor-key pastoral mvovement in triple meter, marked *andante*. The finale—in a characteristic Mozartian about-face—is a Presto in rondo form, so lighthearted that you think the slow movement must have been a figment of your imagination. In this as in most of Mozart's concertos, there is a striking lack of soloistic display; instead, you hear an ongoing friendly dialogue between *soli* and *tutti*. As he once remarked, "I am no lover of difficulties." He had no appetite for showoff stunts.

Mozart's previous compositions for orchestra are far outdistanced by this sinfonia concertante. Its depth of sonority, richness and variety of musical ideas, formal complexity, and compositional scale have no precedent in anything he had written before. Nor can we discern a step-by-step progression leading him to this point; it is as if yesterday he was an extremely promising young composer and now, at twenty-three, his style is fully mature. Eight months after this he would write a similarly unprecedented work, *Idomeneo*. His long, painful trip to Mannheim and Paris had indeed marked a milestone in his career.

COMPARING SONATA FORM TO CONCERTO FIRST-MOVEMENT FORM

- Instead of a single exposition played twice, there are two *different* expositions: one for the orchestra and one dominated by the soloist.
- The bridge is delayed until the Solo Exposition, awarding this major responsibility to the soloist. This means that *there is no change of key in the Orchestral Exposition.*
- The Development is short, and is dominated by the soloist rather than by the orchestra.

- At the end of the Recapitulation, the soloist plays alone, extemporizing for a minute or so on one or more themes in the movement; this solo moment is called the *cadenza.*
- The Coda immediately follows the cadenza.

SONATA FORM
(in sonatas, symphonies, string quartets, etc.)

[Introduction]	||: Exposition :||	Development	Recapitulation	Coda
optional; slow; not repeated	A–bridge–B–C (Exposition repeated)		returns to main key and complete statement of A; all themes in main key	

CONCERTO FIRST-MOVEMENT FORM

Orchestral Exposition	A–B &/or C (not repeated) ends with tutti*
Solo Exposition	A (or new theme)–bridge–B &/or C (or can be all new themes) (not repeated) ends with tutti*
Development	short; dominated by soloist
Recapitulation	starts with tutti* return to main key; all themes now in this key; ends with tutti*
cadenza	played by soloist alone
Coda	tutti*

*Tutti ("everybody") here means the orchestra, as opposed to the solo or soloists.

■ SINFONIA CONCERTANTE IN E-FLAT MAJOR FOR VIOLIN AND VIOLA, K. 364/320D
(Salzburg, 1779)
For solo violin and viola, 2 oboes, 2 horns, and strings
   1. Allegro maestoso (concerto first-movement form, major key, duple meter)

Orchestral Exposition:
0'00" **A**

0'50" **x**	a transition (not the bridge: the bridge occurs in the Solo Exposition)
1'11" **B**	horns with a hunting-horn theme, answered by oboes
1'28" **C**	a very dramatic gesture, heard first in the violins

Solo Exposition:

2'11"	emerges out of misty clouds: octave E-flat played by solo violin and viola
2'25"	tutti restates **A(a)**—i.e., only the theme's first half
2'29"	soloists introduce a *new theme* (**D**)—rather brief; tutti barges in; then
2'54"	three soft, mysterious chords
2'59"	soloists play a *second new theme* (**E**), which becomes the **bridge**
4'03"	soloists play a *third new theme* (**F**), disjunct and rhythmic
5'08"	the orchestra closes off the exposition, ending with *its* third theme (**C**)

Development:

5'38"	dominated by soloists; listen for **C** (6'05")

Recapitulation:

7'35"	opens with **A** (both parts of it)
7'54"	the entire *solo* exposition is recapped, inside this tutti recapitulation
9'58"	orchestra's **B** theme reappears
11'09"	recapitulation ends with a loud tutti

Cadenza:
11'34" (written out by Mozart rather than improvised by the two soloists)

Coda:
based on **C**

Timings based on Stephanie Chase, violin, Roger Chase, viola, the Hanover Band, Roy Goodman, cond. CAIA CACD 1014. ©1992

6

VIENNA, 1781–1791

MOZART'S LIFE IN VIENNA
Breakout, March–June 1781

In March 1781, Archbishop Colloredo required the presence of his entourage in Vienna for the ceremonies attending Joseph II's accession as Habsburg monarch. Mozart, who didn't show up, had to be summoned. In January, Leopold and Nannerl had joined him in Munich for the premiere of *Idomeneo*, after which they all enjoyed several weeks' travel. Colloredo had granted Mozart a six-week leave of absence to finish writing the opera, rehearse it, and conduct the first performances—but that was four months ago. Mozart finally arrived in Vienna on March 16.

At once he ran into the kinds of situations that so galled him. Required to don the livery identifying him as Colloredo's employee, he was also to eat his meals sitting "next to the cooks." In Colloredo's mind this prickly twenty-year-old was not a future world-class composer but a nice ornament to his court, at least as long as he behaved; but Mozart saw himself quite a bit more favorably, bragging that "I tickle his pride." Maybe so; but he still had to perform for the archbishop and his guests that afternoon at four and again that evening. No allowance was made for the fact that he had traveled all night to get there.

Yet in his first days in Vienna Mozart also forged his way into the upper reaches of Viennese society, ingratiating himself with musically inclined nobility who obviously enjoyed both his company and his music. In a letter dated March 24 (the same letter quoted above), he wrote Leopold:

> I'm going tonight . . . to Court Councilor Braun's, who everyone says is
> the greatest lover of the piano; I have already had lunch twice at Countess
> Thun's and go there almost every day—she is the dearest, most charming
> lady I have ever seen; and she likes me very much—her husband is a

bit unusual— . . . I've also lunched at Count Cobenzl's [Joseph's vice chancellor], invited there through Countess Rumbeke, his cousin. . . .

Countess Thun, Count Cobenzl, and Countess Rumbeke were all notably helpful to him during his first years in the Habsburg capital. Delighted to be in a city he already knew, where he didn't have to speak a foreign language, and where people seemed to value him highly, Mozart didn't want to leave. He exclaimed to Leopold that Vienna is "magnificent— and for my *métier* [type of work] the best place in the world—everybody will tell you that" (letter dated April 4, 1781).

Unfortunately, as soon as he arrived in Vienna, the two-way father-son correspondence stopped. From here on, we have Wolfgang's letters but none of his father's replies. Yet since he generally began his own letters with a summary of his father's main points, we can reconstruct the essential parts of their dialogue.

Their topic from March until June—virtually their only topic—sparked a harsh father-son debate: should Wolfgang quit Colloredo's service and move to Vienna, leaving Salzburg, his father, and his sister behind? He had to have Leopold's approval for such a move because the archbishop would not release him without it.

In letter after letter, Mozart builds his case. Frequently welcomed into aristocratic homes, he is unable to turn this to his advantage because Colloredo has him boxed in. If he could perform before Joseph II, the doors of the city would open to him and that, in turn, could lead to a court appointment. But Colloredo makes the whole scheme impossible:

> What makes me almost desperate is that on the same evening as our shitty concert here [a few days before], I was also invited to Countess Thun's—but wasn't permitted to go, and who was there?—*the emperor*— Adamberger [star tenor at the opera] and Madame Weigl [star soprano] were there, and each of them got 50 ducats [about 225 gulden; i.e., roughly half of Mozart's annual salary]! What an opportunity [that would have been for me]!

As he saw it, there was good money out there but Colloredo was preventing his getting it. His father, of course, couldn't believe what he was reading. Are you really willing to forfeit a *guaranteed* income of 450 gulden without anything to replace it? To be sure, Leopold's own well-being was riding on this as well; a son was expected to provide support for his father's old age.

Events now begin to take their own course. On April 8, the archbishop notifies employees that they must now return to Salzburg. If they choose to remain longer in Vienna, it will have to be at their own expense. Mozart stayed; when he was finally ordered out, he moved to a rooming house run by Aloysia Weber's mother. Frau Weber lived there with her other three daughters (Aloysia, now married, lived elsewhere, and Herr Weber had died). Nothing could be worse, in his father's eyes, than for his son to move into the Weber nest again.

Mozart now initiates a series of violent meetings, the first of them with Colloredo, during which the archbishop

> called me a rogue, a slovenly, immoral lout! ...[F]inally, as my blood started to boil, I said—so is Your Highness not satisfied with me?—[Colloredo's reply:] What, are you threatening me? ...There is the door, right over there, look at it; I want nothing more to do with such a miserable rogue.— At last I said, and I don't want to have anything to do with you either! ... I hate the archbishop to the point of fury.
>
> (Letter dated May 9, 1781)

Mozart then presents a formal letter of resignation to the archbishop's steward, Count Arco. Arco, who has no doubt been instructed by Colloredo not to accept it, declares that he needs to have Leopold's permission first—which, of course, Leopold will never give him. Now Mozart's exchanges with his father get out of hand, turning so venomous on both sides that he writes on May 19, "I must admit I can't recognize my father in anything in your letter!"

Things come to a head in early June. Count Arco, actually a family friend who truly wants the best for Mozart, warns him that the Viennese are fickle: "[Here] a man's fame lasts only a short time—at first you get nothing but compliments and earn a lot, true—but for how long?—after a few months the Viennese want something new" (Mozart's letter to Leopold dated June 2). Predictably, Arco's words fall on deaf ears. Mozart keeps trying to get his resignation accepted, and Arco keeps saying no. More angry words follow until Arco—as Mozart tells his father on June 9—threw him "out the door with a kick in the ass." In fact, Mozart's resignation was never formally acted upon. His salary, however, was stopped, effectively terminating his employment.

To make up for or, ideally, to exceed that lost salary, Mozart needed generous patrons, pupils willing to pay high fees, and a stream of lucrative commissions. He was now a freelancer—a word not yet in existence because he was the first major composer to surf the ups and downs of the emerging market economy.[1] It is unlikely that he would have described himself in such dramatic terms; but at all events, Leopold urged the necessity of a salary. For someone with his son's gifts, that meant, ideally, a post as *Kapellmeister* in a major court. Wolfgang was unable to attain that and, truth be told, it was probably fortunate that he didn't.

It is hard to imagine Mozart in charge of a court's musical establishment, reporting every morning to be given that day's assignments, supervising a staff of musicians, checking to make sure that instruments were kept in good repair, and performing a host of mind-numbing duties. As a composer, his works would belong to his employer and he could write for others only with permission. Did he truly want such a job? For the income and prestige, yes, absolutely; but with all those responsibilities plus sharply reduced time for composing? It seems ludicrous to picture him in such a life.[2]

WHAT WAS VIENNA LIKE IN MOZART'S DAY?

If you have visited Vienna, you are familiar with its overall layout: in the center stands the old city with its narrow, winding streets; encircling that is the Ringstraße (Circle Street) with its imposing state buildings, among them the Vienna State Opera. Beyond the Ringstraße lies the rest of Vienna, a large, modern metropolis. The Danube flows by on the north and east; to the south and west, graceful hills offer magnificent views of the old city, topped by the spires of St. Stephen's Cathedral.

In Mozart's day, the space now occupied by the Ringstraße was a vast tree-lined park scattered here and there with benches. Called the glacis, it was used both for military drills and for recreational enjoyment. On one side of it a high, fortresslike wall separated the inner city from the suburbs. When the Turks laid siege to Vienna in 1683, the glacis and wall protected the city, but by Mozart's time there was no fear of invasion. In the nineteenth century, the wall was demolished and the Ringstraße covered over what had once been the glacis.

The inner city, in Mozart's day, was peopled by royalty, wealthy

---

1. The term *free lance* (two words) appeared for the first time in Sir Walter Scott's *Ivanhoe* (1819) to describe a lancer (soldier) offering his services to anyone who would pay him—in other words, a mercenary. As a single word used in its modern sense, *freelance* originated in the twentieth century. Traditionally a noun, it is now more generally an adjective.
2. Joseph Haydn's contract with Count Esterházy, standard for the time, included additional responsibilities and restrictions as well; see James Webster, art. "Haydn, Joseph," *The New Grove Dictionary of Music and Musicians* (New York: Grove's Dictionaries, 2001). Cf. Braunbehrens' more detailed discussion of this possibility in Mozart's case in his essay, *"Hier ist doch gewiß das Clavierland"*—Mozart in Vienna," trans. Bruce Cooper Clarke, at www.AproposMozart.com.

The Augarten, a park in Vienna where Emperor Joseph II chose to live, in a (relatively) small house

merchants, tradesmen, skilled artisans, and the poor. Aristocrats resided in grand mansions inside the wall, retreating in summertime to their country estates, often a twenty- or thirty-minute carriage ride away. The ground floors of most buildings served as storefronts, as did both sides of major streets such as the Graben, which leads from St. Stephen's Cathedral toward the Hofburg, or royal palace, several blocks away. Joseph II, however, was rarely seen in the Hofburg. Strongly opposed to pomp and ceremony of any sort, he lived most of the time in a modest residence in one of Vienna's parks, the Augarten. Usually dressed in normal attire rather than an emperor's regalia, Joseph could be seen riding his horse, walking the streets, or strolling the Augarten's paths, saying hello to one and all. Both the Augarten and Vienna's other large park, the Prater, had formerly served as royal hunting preserves, but Joseph opened them to the public.

In addition to its native Viennese, the city's 1780 population of around 200,000 included Turks, Hungarians, Romanians, Italians, and a variety of others—a cultural and linguistic mix probably unmatched anywhere else in Europe. Its total population, however, was a far cry from London's 900,000 or Paris's 700,000. Salzburg had about 15,000 inhabitants.

Although oriented toward Paris during Empress Maria Theresa's reign—not only intellectually and philosophically but in everything down to matters of fashion and dress—Vienna turned Anglophilic under Joseph II. Aristocrats traveled to England and Ireland to tour the new English gardens laid out on country estates of the landed gentry. Inspired by the nature philosophy of Rousseau, such gardens—meandering, informal, often open to the public—were constructed in deliberate political and philosophical opposition to the rigidly organized French gardens exemplified by Versailles. Because of the association of English gardens with democracy, Maria Theresa prohibited them. Joseph, however, an admirer of Rousseau, actively fostered them; soon, nearly a score of the new-style gardens dotted the city and its suburbs.

Count Cobenzl's English garden outside Vienna

Count Johann Philipp Cobenzl, one of the first aristocrats to welcome Mozart to Vienna, drove the composer out to his country estate several times during the summer of 1781. There Mozart met other top officials in Joseph's court and strolled through the empire's most distinguished English garden. Situated on a hill known as the Reisenberg and commanding a splendid view of the city, it was probably the first such garden Mozart saw and seems to have had a powerful effect on his creative imagination.

In Vienna as in England, these gardens were also the site of Masonic meetings, and Cobenzl, like nearly all of his guests, including Mozart himself later on, was an active Freemason. All of Mozart's Viennese operas—*The Abduction from the Seraglio, The Marriage of Figaro, Don Giovanni, Così fan tutte,* and *The Magic Flute*—make thematic use of gardens, and without exception they evoke values associated with the democracy-inspired English garden—in no case those of a straight-lined, hierarchical French garden.

Reading through the "Sketches of Vienna" of Johann Pezzl, a contemporary of Mozart, we find out why the nobility spent summertime away from the city.[3] Vienna was notorious for lung-clogging dust:

> Servants, runners, hairdressers, coachmen, soldiers, etc., who have to be out on the streets a great deal, often die of pneumonia, phthisis [tuberculosis of the lungs], consumption, chest infections, etc. . . .
>
> The wheels of sixteen thousand carriages and their horses' hooves, plus an army of more than two hundred thousand pedestrians, [cover] Vienna in fog. The worst situation occurs when, after several warm days, a strong wind springs up. . . .
>
> (Pezzl as quoted in Landon, p. 55)

Pezzl also described, tongue-in-cheek, the latest fashions of the mid-1780s:

> Gentlemen nowadays wear everything short and close-fitting. Their hair-dress [i.e., their wig] is flat. . . . [N]ow the fashionable headgear is the small, round, English sort. . . . Laced shoes and striped stockings are becoming popular, stockings matching the color of your clothes being the latest fashion. For everyday wear, red and dark-green frock coats are preferred. Rings are now set with cameo portraits of famous men. Swords [note: swords are still carried by gentlemen, as a matter of fashion] are inlaid with brilliants [cone-shaped diamonds or other gemstones].
>
> And as for the ladies! . . . The country hat with its thousand kinds of ribbons, flowers, garlands, lace, feathers, decorative pins, etc.—how much more charmingly does it flatter the wearer compared to the former stiff head-dress! . . . How like nymphs are those vivacious girls with their white summer dresses and a ribbon around their waist as they float across the Promenade. . . . And the furs in winter. . . what Grecian simplicity. . . . How they complement the charms of a rounded bosom!
>
> [Footnote by Pezzl:] By 1787 all hooped skirts had disappeared [Pezzl had condemned them as "frightful, clumsy, and accursed"].
>
> (Pezzl as quoted in Landon, pp. 69–70)

---

3. Johann Pezzl, "Sketch of Vienna," translated and abridged by H. C. Robbins Landon in *Mozart and Vienna* (New York: Schirmer Books, 1991), 54–191.

The Turks' siege of the city in 1683 brought Turkish coffee to town, spawning the creation of Europe's first coffeehouses. By Mozart's time there were around seventy of them, in which

> one studies, plays cards, chats, sleeps, does business, talks politics, reads the newspapers, and so on. . . . People are beginning to smoke tobacco [another Turkish import].
>
> (Pezzl as quoted in Landon, p. 155)

Although Mozart-era coffeehouses sound much like ours today, eighteenth-century musical venues were anything but. There were no public concert halls because there was no tradition of public concerts; the shifting economic situation—above all, the gradual decline of aristocratic patronage—was changing all that, but it hadn't done so yet. Even orchestral works like symphonies or concertos might be performed in the private homes of the aristocracy or in the ballroom of a restaurant. Of course, orchestras were not the hundred-member giants of today, but were generally composed of around twenty to twenty-five players, up to perhaps forty. In addition to performances in aristocratic houses or rented halls, there were open-air concerts. Mozart played in the Augarten several times, joining his pupil Josephine von Auernhammer for a performance of his Concerto for Two Pianos, K. 365/316a in 1782.

Vienna had two opera houses: the Burgtheater and the Kärntnertortheater, both owned by the court and managed by its appointees.[4] No opera could be staged during Lent. The big season was Carnival (post–Twelfth Night [January 6] to Ash Wednesday), with a second season starting up after Easter. The same schedule was followed in England and everywhere on the Continent. In addition, operas were produced in the homes of aristocrats, some of whom were singers and musicians of professional or near-professional caliber, but their code of etiquette forbade them to be seen on a public stage. Mozart's *Idomeneo* was given privately in 1786, its only performance in the Habsburg capital.

When an opera was staged in a public theater, the composer received a flat fee, typically one hundred ducats (its equivalent in gulden varied from time to time), to which might be added the net proceeds from one or more "benefit" performances given on his behalf. Subsequent stagings, whether at that theater or elsewhere anywhere in the world, were unpaid, as were translations. Mozart's Italian operas were all translated into German soon after their premieres—this is what spread his name—but he had no control

---

4. The Burgtheater and the Kärntnertortheater were also used for orchestral concerts.

over them and reaped no profit from them. *Don Giovanni* was translated some twenty times during the decade following its premiere, altering the opera so drastically that it would have been unrecognizable by its composer and librettist. No one needed to ask their permission to do this, and there were no copyright laws.

Viennese church music was extravagant, featuring top singers and orchestras—until Joseph II's hostility toward ceremonial display resulted in stringent new rules that drastically simplified all church-related rituals. For a composer looking for well-paying employment, by far the best church position was at St. Stephen's Cathedral, whose *Kapellmeister* earned an annual salary of two thousand gulden. In 1791, the final year of his life, Mozart became (unpaid) assistant *Kapellmeister* with a guarantee of inheriting the job upon his predecessor's death. Unfortunately, though the man was in poor health and expected to die soon, he outlived Mozart by two years.

As for concert managers and agents in the modern sense, such people did not exist—hence the desirability of steady employment. If, as in Mozart's case, you had no employer, you hoped to garner fees or commissions from wealthy patrons, theaters, or the emperor; or you could attempt to self-manage.[5] Mozart pursued all of these angles during his decade in Vienna, with varying but often quite remarkable success.

1781–1786: *The Abduction from the Seraglio*, Marriage, "The Land of the Piano," Leopold's Visit

In the months just after his breakup with Colloredo, however, Mozart had poor luck trolling the city's "fickle" waters. With most of the nobility away for the summer at their country homes, there was no one in town to offer commissions or invitations to perform. Countess Rumbeke was his only piano pupil.

His living situation at the rooming house run by Frau Weber, however, seemed ideal. She served him meals whenever he was ready, regardless of how late that might be; no one minded if he came to the table sloppily dressed; and her unmarried daughters—Josepha, Constanze, and Sophie— waited on him hand and foot. Within weeks he was gossiped about for living in that all-female house. The rumors made their way to Salzburg, causing Leopold to fire off blistering letters telling him to get out of there. Mozart did, though not before staunchly defending himself, claiming that he had no plans to marry anybody:

---

5. Mozart was, however, appointed *Kammermusikus* (chamber musician) to Joseph II in 1787, although that was not a full-time appointment.

[T]here is no question of my being in love. . . . God hasn't given me my talent for me to hang it onto a woman and live my young life in idleness. . . . I don't have anything against marriage, but for me it would be a bad thing. . . . I am not in love with [Constanze Weber]. . . . If I had to marry everybody I've been having fun with, I'd easily have 200 wives.

(Letter dated July 25, 1781)

But the gossip not only failed to abate even after he moved out; it swelled to a climax. This, plus his dwindling resources, made him consider going to Paris again (letter to Leopold dated September 5, 1781), but he didn't go.

There was, fortunately, one very happy prospect. Joseph II's German-language theater, featuring *Singspiel,* commissioned a work from Mozart in June. *Singspiel* was a type of comic opera mixed with fairy tales and the exotic, in which spoken dialogue alternated with musical numbers; much later, Mozart would write another one, *The Magic Flute.* In July 1781 the theater's manager, Gottlieb Stephanie, gave him a libretto—the words—for Act I (Stephanie had plagiarized the libretto from a *Singspiel* recently performed in Berlin, though he appears not to have told the composer that). Mozart was so excited that he finished Act I's music in three weeks, racing because the opera was to form part of the festivities for the upcoming visit of Russia's Grand Duke Paul, son of Catherine the Great. But then the project stalled. First, Stephanie got too busy with other duties; then the court decided to go with an esteemed composer, Gluck, instead of a newcomer. Eventually—in fact, a year later, in July 1782—*The Abduction from the Seraglio (Die Entführung aus dem Serail)* came to the stage, filling the house night after night despite midsummer heat and making Mozart well known very fast. Gluck requested a special, additional performance so that he could see it, afterward praising the opera and becoming the young composer's friend from then on.

We have wonderfully rich letters from Mozart to Leopold during this period, describing in vivid detail how he goes about composing an opera. The story of *The Abduction* is of an Englishman, Belmonte, who sails off to rescue his beloved Constanze from a presumably evil Turkish pasha, who keeps her locked up in his seraglio (harem). (Although it was the original Berlin librettist, not Mozart or Stephanie, who gave her the name Constanze, everyone noticed the coincidence, and Mozart most assuredly did.)

Like all comedies, this one has a happy ending, the best and most touching part of which is a feature that became typical of Mozart's operas: the pasha, not the European, is the hero; he turns out to be decidedly more moral than the Westerners. Mozart and his librettists consistently assign qualities of generosity and kindness to those from whom we would least expect such virtues, and grant power to those who normally have no power. The "evil" character in *The Abduction* is not the pasha but the pasha's overseer, Osmin; but he's comically bad, not to be taken seriously. Here is a portion of what Mozart said about the music he wrote for Osmin—and notice also that he affirms his fundamental belief that "music must never offend the ear":

> Osmin's anger will be made comic through Turkish music [with piccolos, quick, circular melodic figures, and other conventions identifiable as "Turkish" by his audience]. . . . [A]nd as his anger keeps growing,—just when you think the aria is over—the *allegro assai* ["very fast"] will produce a really great effect. . . . Someone who finds himself in such violent anger oversteps all [sense of] order, moderation, and boundaries; he doesn't know himself anymore—so the music must no longer know itself either— although . . . passions, whether violent or not, must never be expressed to the point of disgust, and music even in the most terrifying situations must never offend the ear, but must nevertheless please, in other words, must always remain music. . . .
>
> (Letter dated September 26, 1781)

His letter continues with pages of fascinating explanations of how he brings a libretto's characters into three-dimensional life through a vast array of pinpointed gestures: here a certain instrument, there a particular rhythm, chord, or sudden shift in harmony. Sometimes he spotlights a crucial word buried inside many lines of text. These letters illustrate what was clearly his operatic creed: that each character's music—phrase by phrase and note by note—must sound like that character and no one else. At the same time, you have to make sure that your audience doesn't go home at intermission:

> [T]hat's really everything you need for the end of an act—the more noise the better;—the shorter the better—so the audience's applause won't cool off.

Regrettably, Leopold and Nannerl did not come to Vienna to see this triumph. Mozart sent his father the score (i.e., the complete text and music), but Leopold seems to have never looked at it—a far cry from his eager, blow-by-blow sharing in the composition of *Idomeneo*. Neither of them ever mentioned *The Abduction* again.

Mozart's next operatic commission came three years later, for *The Marriage of Figaro* (*Le nozze di Figaro*, 1786), the first of three collaborations with his finest librettist, Lorenzo da Ponte. For that opera, discussed in detail in a later section of this book, we have no written comments by the composer and no surviving letters to Leopold—though we know that they did correspond about it, because Leopold mentioned the fact in his letters to Nannerl, without indicating what was said. In one instance he simply wrote that he was sending her Wolfgang's letter. This was probably Mozart's description of the premiere, but it has not survived.

Shortly after *The Abduction* premiered, Mozart and Constanze Weber were married. He had told his father months before, in a letter dated December 15, 1781, that he had several good reasons to marry: "[N]ature speaks as loudly in me as it does in everybody else, louder maybe than in some big, strong ox." Besides, think of how much money you can save with a wife to cook and do the laundry! And so they were wed—one day before Leopold's half-hearted assent arrived. The Baroness von Waldstätten, a frequent and supportive friend, hosted a joyous feast following the ceremony, sending them forth on a marriage that remained sweetly loving until Mozart's death nine years later.

Apart from this one operatic success in 1782, the years from 1781 through 1786 were mostly keyboard years for the composer. Although he had come to the city intent on seeing *Idomeneo* staged there—he played sections of it for Countess Thun, individual scenes were performed for her guests, and he talked it up everywhere—it just wasn't going to be produced, because when he first arrived he was too young and too unknown. As a pianist and improviser, however, he was sought after from the start. Beginning in 1782 and climaxing during 1784 through 1786, concerts and private performances were frequent and the money flowed in.

Mozart had exclaimed to his father early on that Vienna was "quite definitely the land of the [fortepiano]" (June 2, 1781). As the new instrument's popularity rose, it gradually replaced the harpsichord. Sometime around 1784 or 1785, Mozart was able to buy his own fortepiano, made by the Viennese master craftsman Anton Walter (the instrument is pictured on page 72).[6]

There were as many as six thousand fortepianos and/or harpsichords in Vienna at that time, along with scores of highly skilled performers and

---

6. Kathryn Libin, cited in reference to the fortepiano in chapter 3, bases her estimate of the purchase date on stylistic features of certain piano concertos that seem to indicate that they were written for this particular piano (private communication).

teachers. Ladies were expected to learn to play. Evenings at home featured the latest songs, sonatas, duets, trios, and so forth, accompanied by family members or friends who sang or played along.

Mozart, however, was at the highest imaginable level, recognized in his first year there as Vienna's finest pianist.[7] He put on what might be described as musical variety shows: orchestral works such as a newly written concerto and perhaps also a symphony, an aria or two sung by leading lights of Viennese opera, and, as centerpiece, a half hour or so of his own improvisations. The fortepiano was new and his versatility, pianistic skill, and spontaneity were unrivalled.

From 1781 to 1786 he wrote fifteen piano concertos, a handful of piano sonatas (most of them for his students), and small-ensemble compositions such as the piano and woodwind quintet (K. 452) and the two piano quartets, K. 478 and K. 493 (i.e., for piano, violin, viola, and cello).

Leopold Mozart came for a ten-week visit in February 1785 and was both impressed and exhausted by his son's schedule. Here is part of that schedule while he was there:[8]

February 11	Leopold arrives. Evening: Mozart plays his Piano Concerto in D Minor, K. 466, at the first of six concerts he had organized unrelated to Leopold's visit.
February 12	Joseph Haydn comes over to hear three of Mozart's "Haydn" Quartets. Leopold and Wolfgang play first and second violin, while two of Mozart's friends play viola and cello.
February 13	Concert by Madame Laschi before Joseph II; Mozart plays a concerto.
February 15	Concert at which he again performs the D-minor concerto.
February 16	Concert by a piano student of his, at which he probably also plays.
February 18	The second of his six concerts.
February 21	Mozart performs at Count Zichy's.
February 24	Fräulein Auernhammer's concert, at which Mozart probably also plays.
February 25	The third of his six concerts.

7. *The New Grove Mozart*, ed. Cliff Eisen and Stanley Sadie (Palgrave: New York, 2002), 20.
8. Adapted from Deutsch, *Mozart: A Documentary Biography*, 236–41.

February 28	Another concert at which he may have performed.
March 4	The fourth of his six concerts.
March 10	Another concert, including the premiere of his Piano Concerto in C Major, K. 467.
March 11	The fifth of his six concerts.
March 13	Benefit concert for the Society of Musicians, at which Mozart conducts the premiere of *Davidde penitente,* a recasting of his Mass in C Minor, K. 427/417a.
March 15	Repeat of the March 13 concert.
March 18	The last of his six concerts.

Actually, Leopold should have expected such nonstop music-making. His son's letter of March 3, 1784, had listed twenty-two appearances between February 26 and April 3, and this was more of the same. Still, he was overwhelmed, writing to Nannerl (who had married the previous year and therefore couldn't come) that "since I got here, your brother's piano has been carried out of the house to the theater or some other house at least 12 times" (letter of March 12, 1785). He praised Constanze's management of the household as "extremely economical" and observed that, if his son continued at his current pace and "has no debts to pay," he could be putting "2,000 gulden in the bank" (March 19, 1785).

After this happy visit Leopold and his son never saw each other again. Mozart had already seen his sister for the last time, when he and Constanze traveled to Salzburg in the late summer–early fall of 1783.

1787–1791: OPERAS, *KAMMERMUSIKUS*, DEBTS, CHURCH MUSIC, JOURNEY TO BERLIN, A DAY AT THE MOZARTS'

In trying to gain a picture of the last four years of Mozart's life, we are seriously hampered by the absence of correspondence with his father. Leopold died in May 1787 and the last surviving letter from his son was written that April. It is the only piece of correspondence we have from either of them during that year (for the letter, see page 209). After that—actually, from January 1787 on—almost all of Mozart's surviving correspondence is addressed to his wife, to his Viennese friend Gottfried von Jacquin, or to his Freemason brother and creditor Johann Michael Puchberg. We have none of their replies. In what follows, some questions will therefore have to remain unanswered.

Ironically, although events from 1787 until his death are not entirely clear to us, the manner in which his life ended is now pretty well established (though still not widely known), including the illness that struck him in mid-November 1791, the probable causes of his death three weeks later, and the nature of his burial. These topics are addressed later in this book.

Mozart's musical output changed dramatically in 1787, and we can only speculate why. His orchestral compositions for piano fall off sharply: after fifteen new concertos in the previous five years, he wrote only K. 537 in 1788 and K. 595 in 1791. His new focus seems to be opera: *Don Giovanni* in 1787, a revival of *The Marriage of Figaro* in 1789, *Così fan tutte* in 1790, and both *La clemenza di Tito* (The Clemency of Titus) and *The Magic Flute* in 1791. With the notable exceptions of *The Abduction from the Seraglio* and *Idomeneo*, all of his operas that are most widely known today were staged and all but one of them (*The Marriage of Figaro*) composed during this five-year period.

Several explanations have been proposed for this remarkable shift from instrumental to vocal music, all of them negative:

- The novelty of the new piano and of his improvising ability wore off.
- Hostilities between the Habsburg and Ottoman empires threatened in late 1787. From his declaration of war on February 1, 1788, until the end of 1789, Joseph II was scarcely in Vienna at all, and when he was, his mind was on military affairs.
- Joseph imposed a huge "war tax" to pay for the army of 300,000 he led into battle early in 1788.
- Crop failures throughout the empire, on top of the war tax, caused inflation, depleting the nobility's available cash.

Although any one of these reasons could have been decisive, we have no direct evidence of their impact on Mozart. Nor do they account for his turn toward opera—his first love, though many times more expensive to produce than concerts. Whatever the cause or causes, his ability to draw crowds for public or private performances appears to have dried up—or, to be more accurate, we have no documents attesting to them, which by no means indicates that they never took place.

Overall, what sort of income did he earn during these ten years in Vienna? This topic has been much researched, yielding five facts that now seem clear:

- In most years he did extremely well.
- Although he borrowed money fairly regularly, he appears to have paid most of it back more or less promptly.

- He liked to live well, entertain frequently, and "dress for success."
- He was generous to a fault, well known for his spontaneous acts of charity.
- He was most definitely not poor. Short on cash flow sometimes, but not poor.

This brings us back to the financial realities faced by freelance musicians. Neither in Mozart's time nor in ours can such a life provide a stable income; the money comes in fits and starts. A Pulitzer Prize–winning composer with several Grammy recordings once explained to me the impossibility of getting a mortgage because of the ups and downs of her bank account. No lender will take the risk. So she rents.

Of course, if Mozart had squirreled away some of the really good money he earned from 1784 through 1786 instead of spending it about as fast as he got it, any problems he encountered would have been solved. But he was not Leopold, and he appears not to have saved a kreuzer.

A deeply touching and depressing topic arises with the pleading letters Mozart sent to Michael Puchberg beginning in 1788. They make embarrassing reading. From July 12, 1789:

> God! I'm in a situation I wouldn't wish on my worst enemy, and if you, my best friend and [Masonic] brother, leave me, unfortunate and innocent man as I am, then along with my poor sick wife and my child I will be lost. . . . O God! instead of gratitude here I am with more requests. . . . My situation is so bad, *though only in Vienna,* that I can't earn anything no matter how hard I try. 14 days ago I sent around a [subscription] list, and on it is just one name. . . . My only friend, will you or can you lend me another 500 gulden?

When he failed to get the money by return post, Mozart wrote again five days later:

> You must be angry with me, because you don't answer me. . . . If it is absolutely impossible for you to help me with the sum I mentioned, . . . I beg you to support me *right now* with whatever you can spare. . . .

The amounts the composer received were rarely more than a fraction of what he requested. How much of it Puchberg ever saw again, we do not know; but he placed no lien on the composer's estate in 1791, either out of kindness or because Mozart had, in fact, paid him back. It is also unclear whether these letters—more than twenty in all—represent an underlying financial need or merely temporary, occasional difficulties.

In December 1787 Emperor Joseph II had appointed Mozart *Kammermusikus* (chamber musician), a part-time appointment earning him eight hundred gulden a year. What this entailed was the performing of music for the emperor's enjoyment. Joseph, who sang and played piano and cello, took pleasure in reading through music in the evening hours after dinner. For this he engaged a group of top woodwind players (called his *Harmoniemusik*) as well as a small number of singers and string players, with Mozart as composer (perhaps also as pianist?). Scholars believe Joseph gave him the post both to keep him in Vienna and to stabilize his income during the upcoming war. Unfortunately, Leopold Mozart didn't live to celebrate his son's appointment to an imperial position at the relatively young age of thirty-one. Mozart's duties included writing dance music—he and Constanze adored dancing—for the annual balls in the imperial ballroom, the *Redoutensaal*. He wrote reams of such music (and a lot more of it in his operas, symphonies, and concertos). As far as his position was concerned, however, he is said to have complained that the salary was "too much for what I do, too little for what I could do." Still, eight hundred gulden was at the least a very nice cushion—though Mozart continued to have trouble making ends meet.

He and Constanze moved around a lot—ten times during their nine years together. Some of their apartments were large, some small; some were in the center of the city, some in the suburbs (outside the glacis). Most writers have taken this impressive degree of mobility as evidence of a financial roller coaster. Braunbehrens disagrees, offering convincing justifications for at least some of the moves.[9] Perhaps the largest of the Mozarts' apartments was the one they lived in from September 1784 until April 1787, during the height of the composer's popularity. Transformed years ago into a museum called Figarohaus, it was greatly expanded during the "Mozart Year" of 2006 and is now known as Mozarthaus Vienna. You can visit it the next time you're there. It's where Leopold stayed in 1785 and where Mozart kept his billiard table, which probably cost him around three hundred gulden. The tenor Michael Kelly recalled being able to beat him only rarely.

From April to June of 1789, for reasons we're not quite sure of, Mozart traveled to Prague, Dresden, Leipzig, Potsdam, and Berlin with Count Carl Alois Lichnowsky. Lichnowsky, better known in today's musical world for

9. Braunbehrens, *Mozart in Vienna 1781–1791*, 110–19.

his enthusiastic support of Beethoven later on, was also a patron of Mozart's, and they were members of the same Masonic lodge. The trip was the count's idea, and he evidently covered Mozart's expenses until they parted company halfway through, leaving Mozart to pay his own way home. The composer mentioned in a letter to Constanze that he had lent the count one hundred gulden—was Lichnowsky temporarily short of cash, or did he just have none with him at the moment?

Whenever the Mozarts were apart from each other, they exchanged letters every couple of days. His usually began with a quick summary of what was going on, followed by an onslaught of emotion saying how much he missed her. His first letter from this trip was written on departure day (April 8, 1789), as the carriage's horses were being changed:

> While [the count] is negotiating for fresh horses, I'll happily grab the chance to write you a few words, dearest little wife of my heart.—How are you?—Do you think about me as often as I think of you?—I gaze at your portrait [inside a locket?] every minute—and cry—half from joy, half from sorrow!—Please take care of your health, so important to me, and be well, my dear!—Don't worry about me, because I'm experiencing no hardship on this trip—no difficulty—nothing but your *absence*—which, since it can't be otherwise, can't be helped.—I am writing this with tearful eyes;—adieu—I'll write more from Prague—and more legibly, because I won't have to hurry so—adieu—I kiss you a million times most tenderly and am forever your
>
> > Stu—stu—Mozart,
> > faithful unto death.[10]

At their first stop, Prague, Mozart was delighted to rendezvous with the wonderful Mannheim (later Munich) oboist Friedrich Ramm. He also looked up the manager of Prague's theater, who had commissioned *Don Giovanni* two years before. The manager offered him a commission to write a new opera for 250 gulden, but the deal collapsed when the manager moved to another city. Then on to Dresden, where Mozart collaborated with a longtime friend, the excellent soprano Josepha Duschek, for a concert including arias from *The Marriage of Figaro* and *Don Giovanni*. The next day he performed the piano concerto (K. 537) that he had written in 1788 for the elector of Saxony, who rewarded him with a snuffbox full of money—100 ducats.

---

10. "Stu—stu" seems to have been some private code between them. Nobody today knows what it meant.

Mozart's visit to Leipzig, their next stop, offered what was surely the journey's emotional climax for him: an afternoon in St. Thomas's Church, whose music director had once been J. S. Bach. The composer roamed through the church's library, savoring, page by page, church works by his great predecessor. The choir sang one of them for him and presented him with a copy of the score (the musical notation) as a memento. Having performed major works by Handel and Bach at the weekly musical gatherings sponsored by Baron van Swieten since 1782—as well as recasting some of these works in his own, more modern style—Mozart had already come under the influence of this music, a fact dramatically evident first in his Mass in C Minor, K. 427/417a, and later in works including his "Jupiter" Symphony, K. 551, *The Magic Flute,* and the unfinished Requiem.[11]

In Berlin, Mozart felt sure he would be offered a commission by King Friedrich Wilhelm II—Ramm had told him it was being arranged—but when he got there, his reception followed standard protocol and he didn't even see the king. He and Lichnowsky returned to Leipzig, where Mozart played a concert at the Gewandhaus (later to become famous before the fall of the Iron Curtain in 1989 as the site of anti-Soviet protests). The program featured symphonies and, once again, arias by Madame Duschek, though there weren't very many people there due to poor advance publicity. At this point, Count Lichnowsky left Mozart's company. The composer, after staying on for a while, went back to Berlin. This time he did get to play for the king and queen, who commissioned six string quartets, for which they paid him eight hundred gulden. He ultimately wrote three of these "Prussian" quartets, K. 575, 589, and 590, but never finished the others. He returned to Vienna on June 4, 1789.

During the "Mozart Year" 1991, the Austrian Mozart scholar Walter Brauneis discovered that Lichnowsky—this good friend, patron, and Masonic brother—had sued Mozart for an unpaid debt of 1,435 florins, 32 kreuzer, and that on November 9, 1791, the court had supported his claim.[12] Nine days after that, Mozart was struck by the illness that killed him three weeks later. What happened to the lawsuit, and why had no scholar over the previous 250 years uncovered it? So far, no one can answer either question. Perhaps another of Mozart's admirers, or a group of them, paid off the debt. Perhaps he did so himself. Or perhaps Lichnowsky dropped the suit

---

11. Mozart's association with van Swieten is discussed more fully on page 200.
12. Walter Brauneis, "'... owing to indebtedness of 1,435 Gulden 32 Kreuzer': A new document on Mozart's financial plight in November 1791" ("'... wegen schuldigen 1435 f 32 xr': Neuer Archivfund zur Finanzmisere Mozarts im November 1791"), trans. Bruce Cooper Clarke, accessible at AproposMozart.com.

after learning that his friend was dying. We have no clue what this was all about or how it was resolved, if it was. We do know that Constanze settled all of her husband's financial affairs within a few years after his death; but this is just one more instance of the serious gaps in our knowledge. People think his life and times, and of course everything about his music, were all wrapped up a long time ago. How wrong they are.

For example, we know precious little about his everyday life in Vienna, but here is some idea of a typical day, gleaned from letters and other documents. He generally arose around five or six a.m. and rode his horse around town—out to the Prater perhaps?—before dressing for the day, receiving his hairdresser, and sitting down to breakfast. He might devote the rest of the morning to composing. Lunch, usually not before one, would be eaten either at home or out, with friends. After this he taught pupils, including one or two live-ins (this was a customary mode of teaching, there being no music schools; Leopold had done this also). Franz Xaver Süssmayr, famous for completing Mozart's Requiem after the composer's death, wasn't a pupil but an assistant and composer's helper. He would have presumably lived either in the house or nearby.

Like his parents' homes in Salzburg, Constanze and Mozart's apartments were probably noisy, with all-day performing and rehearsing, people coming in and out, and Carl Thomas running around with the current family pet. During late afternoons and early evenings Mozart and Constanze sometimes took a carriage ride through one of Vienna's parks. More often, he was attending rehearsals either at home or elsewhere, maybe grabbing time afterward to enjoy his pipe and a mug of coffee at a nearby coffeehouse before going with his wife and others to the theater (spoken drama), opera, or a concert (these began earlier than they customarily do today). Dinner at a restaurant followed. If he stayed home, he likely spent the time composing. He rarely went to bed before one a.m., sometimes much later. He once wrote his father that he and Constanze had rolled up the rugs and invited friends over to dance the night away—each guest contributing two gulden toward the wine and food—with Mozart at the piano playing dance music from six that night until seven the next morning (letter dated January 22, 1783).

For three years, one of the family's pets was a much-beloved starling. Mozart had fun teaching it the main theme from the finale of his Piano Concerto in G Major, K. 453, and when the bird died in 1787 the family held a burial ceremony in the back yard. The bittersweet poem Mozart composed for the occasion may be tempting to read as a prophecy of the composer's own short life:

Here rests a bird called Starling,
A foolish little darling.
He was still in his prime
When he ran out of time,
And my sweet little friend
Came to a bitter end,
Creating a terrible smart
Deep in my heart.
Gentle reader, shed a tear!
For he was dear.
Sometimes a bit too jolly,
And at times quite folly,
But nevermore
A bore.
I bet he is now up on high
Praising my friendship to the sky,
Which I render
Without tender;
For when he took his sudden leave,
Which brought me such grief,
He was not thinking of the man
Who writes and rhymes as no one can.[13]

But Mozart had no premonitions of an early death; that is myth. Nor was he unhappy: his income in most years was substantial, he had a loving family, and he was held in high esteem as a composer. To be sure, he had to deal with endless twists and turns in his freelance life—inevitably so—but this was a man who, in 1791, looked forward to the possibility of stipends from a group in Hungary and another group in Amsterdam, as well as a preferred trip to England. He was also still madly in love with his wife. Reading through his letters to her, you get a sense of the fun they had together. From June 6, 1791:

> I got your dear letter this very moment and see with pleasure that you are well and happy—Madame Leitgeb [a neighbor] helped me fasten my tie today; but how!—dear God!—I kept saying over and over, *No, she does it this way!*—but it didn't help . . . Adieu—my love—my only!—catch them in the air—2,999½ kisses are flying from me, waiting to be snapped up. —

13. The poem is dated June 4, 1787. Translation by Spaethling, *Mozart's Letters, Mozart's Life*, 191–92.

Now I'm saying something in your ear– – – – –now you in mine– – –and more– – . . . you can think of anything you want—that's just what makes it so easy to do—adieu—

1000 tender kisses and eternally your

Mozart

Who is this man? You see this picture often— sometimes only the face—but you realize at once that it isn't Mozart. This man is too tall, too chubby, and his expression is far too smug: Mozart as a wax monument. His left hand rests on delicate rococo flowers; his right hand holds a music sketchbook. A nineteenth- century writer, in an ostensibly factual article that was widely accepted as true, originated the myth that the composer carried such a book with him at all times (pencil at the ready) to record his divine inspirations. Salzburg, the city Mozart loathed, is here his celestial backdrop.

OPERA AND *SINGSPIEL*

Opera, which was invented— yes, invented—during the late Renaissance, still reigned supreme in the eighteenth century. Every court and major city had at least one opera house and they all vied for the most celebrated singers, set designers, and choreographers. Opera was big business—as it is today—and the competition was, and still is, fierce.

There were three main types of opera in Mozart's day: serious (*opera seria*), comic (*opera buffa*), and *Singspiel*. Opera seria portrayed characters and situations from ancient history or myth (Julius Caesar, Cleopatra, Orpheus, Hercules), and its audiences were composed mostly of royalty and the aristocracy. Opera buffa drew its plots from current issues and attracted a wider audience; it was also less expensive than opera seria because it used modern dress and required no elaborate machinery to transport divinities down from the heavens. *Singspiel* (German for "sung play") was opera written in the language of the audience. It employed spoken rather than sung dialogue, making its words more easily understood, and its stories tended toward fantasy, magic, and the exotic. All three genres featured Hollywood endings. No matter how complicated or even tragic the situation became, by the close of the last act everything was resolved. If this meant rewriting history or myth, so be it.

In the descriptions that follow, all statements apply equally well to opera buffa, seria, and *Singspiel* except where otherwise noted.

GENERAL DESCRIPTION OF OPERA (AND *SINGSPIEL*)

Opera brings together many elements—singing, acting, an orchestra, scenery, costumes, sets, and lighting. If the work is a good one and if by some miracle everything works and no unexpected disaster befalls, the production is a success. But in such a complex, multimedia affair, anything and everything can go wrong. In the days of Mozart, when there were no computers, no photocopiers, no cell phones or even telephones, communication among the various parties had to be person-to-person or by letter. Both music and libretto (the script) had to be copied out by hand, with quill pens. Lighting consisted of a row of shaded candles across the front of the stage; candles were also affixed to the backs of stage flats. A chandelier (of candles) hung above the audience.[14] Scenery meant generic (often quite beautiful) paintings, hauled out from the wings on rollers, to represent a palace's facade, a country village, or someone's drawing-room.

Definitions

What exactly is an "opera"? Not a play set to music (i.e., with musical accompaniment in the background), nor a collection of songs linked by some nonsense of a plot. Opera at its best is a blend of music with drama in which every note of music drives the action forward. The characters are three-dimensional human beings caught in urgent situations, and we come to care about them because of the way the music portrays them. Opera, then, is *drama propelled by music.*

The Libretto

An opera's text was (and still is) written first, in the form of a *libretto,* or script. Music is set *to* the libretto, not the libretto to the music. Mozart waited to see the words to the first act, say, or the first scene, before he got down to serious composing, although he sometimes suggested ideas to his librettist or already had certain patterns of melody or rhythm in mind for a particular character. All through this gestation process, composer and librettist negotiated back and forth. Eventually, perhaps following an outburst or two, enough of the libretto was finished (more or less) for musical composition to begin.

---

14. Around 1780, gaslights appeared in some theaters, though not yet in Vienna.

The role of librettists was crucial and in modern times has too often been downplayed or misunderstood. To begin with, in the eighteenth century they were generally not novelists or poets, but specifically librettists, trained to do just what they were doing. Second, a good libretto (whether then or now) should furnish each star singer with at least one aria (song) per act, so that no individual star seems to rank higher than the others; secondary roles receive proportionally fewer arias. Accommodating all this while maintaining plausibility in both individual characterization and overall plot is no mean feat: when a character comes onstage to sing, we hope it's for a dramatic reason and not simply to fulfill that act's quota of arias. Third, a libretto isn't meant to stand on its own as literature; the words should spring to life only when inspired by and bonded to the music, not in some general sense but note by note. These are words to be *sung*, which demands a very special sort of writing. Fourth, eighteenth-century librettos were usually in poetic form, with rhymes and stanzas and so forth. Fifth, librettos are much, much shorter than plays. As you know from pop, rock, and most especially jazz, when you sing words you really expand them. It takes much longer—pleasantly so!—to sing "I love you" than to say it.

Musical Forms
Musically, opera consists of arias, recitatives, ensembles, sometimes choruses, sometimes dancing, all of it with the underpinning of an orchestra. *Singspiel* has all of these elements except recitatives: in *Singspiel*, dialogue is spoken.

Arias are emotional outpourings sung by *individual* characters—an aria is always a solo event. In Mozart's era, arias took one of four forms:

Aria da capo: This is a three-part form: **A** (main emotion) – **B** (subordinate or contrasting emotion) – **A** (reprise of the main emotion, now sung with added vocal embellishments). An archaic form by the 1780s, there are none of these in *The Marriage of Figaro, Don Giovanni, Così fan tutte,* or *The Magic Flute.*

Binary aria: **AABB** or (more often) **ABAB.** This is the form heard most frequently in Mozart's Viennese operas.

Rondò aria: This is in two parts, an opening three-part slow section, **ABA,** followed by a fast section sung twice, **CC.** Rondò arias are rare but quite special, reserved for leading characters in pivotal situations who are also great singers. Note the accented *ò;* this vocal design is not to be confused with the instrumental rondo form.

Cavatina: An abbreviated aria, usually **AB.** Mozart uses this short form often.

How to locate where an A section ends and a B section begins: Look (in the words) for a shift in subject matter and a terminal mark of punctuation (period, exclamation point, or question mark). You can also count the total number of lines in the aria and expect to hear the break halfway through. If there appear to be more than two sections in the aria—a C section, even a D—the same principles still apply: look for changes of topic, terminal marks of punctuation, and a symmetrical division of lines (such as two, four, or six lines in each section).

Recitatives are *musical speech,* used for narration, dialogue, and monologues. Characters converse in recitatives (in arias, they reflect, usually alone). They are not melodic, and words are not repeated—unlike arias, in which important words are often given emphasis through repetition. Recitatives are free-form, musically; they don't break down into A and B sections because they wander here and there. There are two kinds of recitatives:

Semplice ("simple"; sometimes called *secco*), accompanied in Mozart's generation by a keyboard instrument, fortepiano or harpsichord, plus cello and violone (perhaps also a bassoon) to strengthen the bass line.[15] Simple recitatives are the most nonmelodic of recitatives and convey fairly pedestrian content; there are yards of them in most operas. They are operas' connective tissue, the closest thing to ordinary speech.

Accompagnato ("accompanied," i.e., by orchestra) or ***stromentato*** ("instrumented") recitatives are reserved for special moments; you won't hear more than four or five of them in any opera. They serve to introduce major arias sung by leading characters at dramatic climaxes or turning points. More melodic and character-revealing than "simple" recitatives, they express a character's conflicted or as yet unformed feelings, with sometimes explosive punctuation by the orchestra. Once the feelings coalesce, the aria can begin.

---

15. The violone was the ancestor of the modern double bass.

Ensembles are sung by a group of *individual* characters—duets, trios, quartets, and so on. Ensembles are not the same as *choruses,* which are sung by a homogeneous group of characters (the army, your servants, etc.).

The Orchestra

In operas and *Singspiels* (the correct German plural is *Singspiele*) by great composers, the orchestra is almost another character. A dedicated operagoer once remarked to me, "But isn't opera all about the singing?" No, it's all about the drama. For a composer like Mozart, with vast experience in symphonies, small-ensemble music, concertos, and sonatas, "speaking" through an orchestra was as natural as talking in words is to you or me. His operatic writing is many-colored, exact, and so pinpointed you will hear it turn on a dime from pathos to snappy repartee. If you ignore what the orchestra is doing at the microlevel—second by second and word by word—you miss at least half the drama.

Opera *overtures* in this period (with a few notable exceptions, among them Mozart's *Don Giovanni*) do not anticipate the music we are about to hear in the opera, nor do they introduce the action except in a very general

The Burgtheater, Vienna, where The Marriage of Figaro *(1786),* Don Giovanni *(1788), and* Così fan tutte *(1790) had their Viennese premieres, and where Mozart played many concerts*

sense. Mozart's overtures are often in sonata form, with or without a slow introduction, and they frequently lead directly into Act I, Scene 1, without a pause. Dramatic credibility, fluidity, and continuity were important to him.

No Authoritative Versions!

Operas in the eighteenth century were works-in-progress; rarely were they definitively finished. Whenever singers in certain roles were replaced by others, certain arias might need to be revised, deleted, or replaced (both words and music). For example, if Madame So-and-So could no longer sing comfortably above a certain note, her replacement, unhindered by that problem, might get a new aria allowing her to soar to great heights. By the same token, when Mozart (or any composer) took an opera premiered in one city for performances in another city, he faced a whole new cast and orchestra, a situation that often called for some rewriting. An aria should fit a singer "like a well-made suit of clothes," he said, which is another way of saying that there is nothing generic about his music—each aria was tailor-made for one particular singer's voice, expressive power, and acting skill (or lack thereof).

TWO OPERAS WITH LORENZO DA PONTE
THE MARRIAGE OF FIGARO, K. 492 (LE NOZZE DI FIGARO)
(Premiere: Vienna, May 1, 1786)

"Here they talk of nothing but *Figaro*," Mozart famously exclaimed in a letter to a friend from Prague in January 1787. "Nothing is played, blown, sung, or whistled but *Figaro* . . . it's all a great honor for me." Eight months earlier, in Vienna, *The Marriage of Figaro* had enjoyed a moderately successful run. In Prague it was such a hit that Mozart was asked to write a new opera for the following season, which would turn out to be *Don Giovanni*. The difference between Prague's and Vienna's reactions to *Figaro* could not have been more dramatic. In Vienna, so many obstacles were thrown in its path that it almost didn't get staged at all. This story is full of frustrating twists and turns from the time the opera was conceived until it finally received its long-delayed premiere in Vienna's Burgtheater in 1786.

First, the Burgtheater. From 1778 to 1783 this was the home of Emperor Joseph II's noble though ultimately futile effort to establish a German-language musical theater in his empire's capital city, an idea he felt certain would please his German-speaking subjects; but in fact, they stayed away because they wanted their opera in Italian. Mozart's *The Abduction from the Seraglio*, which played to full houses in 1782, was one of the few

Singspiels that proved successful. Only a few months after its run, Joseph II bowed to box-office reality and converted the Burgtheater back to an all-Italian house. Upon hearing this, Mozart, aching to compose another opera, wrote his father that he "would love to show what I can do in an Italian opera"—if only he could find a decent libretto; he had read through "at least 100." Recently he had met "a certain Abbate da Ponte," who promised to write him a new one, but "you know well that these Italians are very polite to your face!" What did finally emerge two years later was a colleagueship that resulted in *The Marriage of Figaro* (1786), *Don Giovanni* (1787), and *Così fan tutte* (1790).

What was Mozart looking for in a libretto? One of the little-known facts about him is that he was an avid and quite discerning theatergoer. Europe's top writers—Diderot, Goldoni, Lessing, Goethe, and Schiller—had called for greater naturalness and realism in the theater. Opera buffa—the reigning genre of comic opera—was formulaic: stock characters, stereotypical plots, boilerplate dialogue. This is why Mozart had trouble finding a good libretto; what he wanted existed only in the finest spoken dramas. These he knew firsthand, since he went to the theater quite often, seeing plays by Europe's leading dramatists. On top of this, a Shakespeare revival swept through Germany in the 1770s and '80s—Shakespeare was previously unknown there—and Mozart knew personally many of its stars: Friedrich Ludwig Schröder, a dynamic actor-director who, more than anyone, was the star of the revival; Emanuel Schikaneder, later the librettist of *The Magic Flute*, who played Hamlet in the first Shakespeare play Mozart ever saw; and Joseph Lange, the composer's brother-in-law (Aloysia Weber's husband), who was an accomplished actor as well as an artist. Mozart, who knew theater inside out, insisted that opera be true to life. The audience must believe that what they see onstage "is really *so*."

What brought Mozart and da Ponte together was an explosive political satire from Paris: *La folle journée, ou Le mariage de Figaro* (The Crazy Day, or The Marriage of Figaro) by Pierre Augustin Caron de Beaumarchais. This was a sequel to the playwright's hugely successful *Le barbier de Séville*, which was turned into an extraordinarily popular Italian opera by Giovanni Paisiello—an opera that still remained popular as late as 1816, when Gioachino Rossini composed his *Il barbiere di Siviglia*. Beaumarchais's play centers around the clever stratagems of the barber-poet Figaro, which enable Count Almaviva to make the beautiful Rosina his countess. It features fast-paced dialogue and characterizations that are more realistic than the comedic norm. Beaumarchais wanted to leave us not just amused, but touched. Paisiello's opera likewise moves well beyond conventional buffa.

Beaumarchais's *Le mariage de Figaro* was the longest play staged in France in the eighteenth century, lasting around five hours; it was also the most successful, its stinging attacks on the French nobility making it seem like forbidden fruit and thus all the more enticing. The play was quickly translated into other languages, so that by 1785 both Mozart and da Ponte most certainly knew it. Schikaneder proposed staging it in Vienna, but the emperor said no. Joseph II's sister, Marie Antoinette, had written him about what was brewing in France, and only four years later, the Bastille would be stormed. Nevertheless, he allowed the play to be published, though only after it had been cleansed of its most incendiary lines.

Turning this political firebomb into an opera was Mozart's idea; librettist da Ponte then set to work and did a masterful job: condensing the plot, deleting extraneous characters, and dialing down the politics. Both composer and librettist were evidently more interested in the play's human drama than in its scathing political attacks, which after all had been aimed at French rather than Viennese targets. Da Ponte's most important changes involved, first, shortening Figaro's comprehensive diatribe against French society in Act V (now Act IV) into a generalized attack on women; and second, reshaping the role of the Countess. Whereas in Beaumarchais she is a quick-witted, sometimes rather brittle Parisian, da Ponte makes her a lonely, elegant figure. Mozart's music goes further still, allowing her deep inner resolve to strengthen until, at the end of the opera, it is she who, in one extraordinary gesture, resolves, at least temporarily, the fractious tensions in the house.

The Marriage of Figaro has two parallel plots, one dealing with the marriage between the Count and Countess Almaviva (which is coming apart because of his philandering), the other with the impending marriage of Figaro, the Count's valet, and Susanna, the Countess's maid. Newcomers to this opera may find it helpful to focus on these two couples and the lovesick young pageboy, Cherubino, who keeps turning up in the wrong place at the wrong time. The role of Cherubino is written to be portrayed, not by an adolescent boy, but by a woman dressed as a boy.

Central to the opera (though scarcely a factor in the play) is the opposition between the values of the world inside the Almavivas' villa, riddled by domestic chaos, and the pastoral values symbolized by the garden just outside. The opera begins indoors, at the frantic urban pace adumbrated in its sparkling overture. As the action proceeds, we hear increasing references to the garden. At first, these are comic, as in Cherubino's aria "Non so più, cosa son, cosa faccio" discussed later on; but during Acts II and III the allusions grow more serious, pointing to the garden as a spiritual haven, where reconciliation between the Count and Countess might conceivably be possible. A pivotal moment occurs with the Countess's aria in Act III followed by her pastoral "Letter Duet" with Susanna ("Sull'aria"). All of Act IV takes place outside the turbulent house, in the garden, as night is falling.

Mozart's music for *Figaro* is boldly innovative. The opera is driven, not by individual star turns, but by "action ensembles" (a modern term used to describe this opera's most characteristic feature) composed, very often, of characters from different social classes. While ensembles were a feature of opera buffa, da Ponte and Mozart brought their action-component to glowing heights. The opera begins with such an ensemble for Figaro and Susanna, to be discussed later on. Mozart instructed singers to "speak" rather than sing their recitatives, and in a normal speaking tempo. Arias, unlike those in traditional opera, are short and, except for those of the Countess, employ short-breathed phrases as well. In place of grand operatic rhetoric, we have three-dimensional people, reacting to one another spontaneously— as people do in real life. Mozart's orchestra is very nearly a member of the cast, so involved at every instant of the action that "accompaniment" seems a strikingly inappropriate term. Reviewers criticized him for overwriting, particularly in the way he used woodwinds, whose expressive potential had fascinated him ever since he first heard the virtuosic Mannheim orchestra in 1777. In *Figaro*, flutes, oboes, clarinets, bassoons, and horns all play leading roles.

Da Ponte claimed that Mozart wrote the opera in about six weeks, which isn't so. It was probably begun during the late spring or early summer of 1785, worked on from time to time that fall, and finished shortly before the premiere in May 1786.[16] Joseph II, eager to use it as a moral scold for his philandering nobles, had his theater impresario, Count Rosenberg, push Mozart to get it done. Yet the premiere was postponed again and again. First, the Burgtheater's schedule was crammed; then there were so many cabals that the composer grew "as touchy as gunpowder," threatening to burn the score. Joseph II dropped in on the dress rehearsal, da Ponte writes in his memoirs, where there may have been one more infuriating episode. According to this possibly apocryphal story, Count Rosenberg reminded the emperor that he had forbidden the inclusion of ballet sequences in operas— yet Act III of *Figaro* has such a scene, and it is dramatically quite important. Da Ponte says that when Joseph saw the scene danced silently in rehearsal, it looked so stupid that he ordered the music restored on the spot.[17]

---

16. According to Dexter Edge's paper "The Genesis of *Le nozze di Figaro*," delivered at the American Musicological Society's conference in Columbus, Ohio, on November 2, 2002.
17. Elisabeth Abbott, trans., Arthur Livingston, ed., *Memoirs of Lorenzo da Ponte* (Philadelphia and London: J. B. Lippincott, 1929), 159–61. The scene is dramatized in *Amadeus*.

The first few performances went off reasonably well, considering the music's extraordinary complexity and difficulty. Several arias and ensembles brought down the house and had to be repeated, making the opera so long that the emperor decreed that thereafter, only arias could be encored. Tenor Michael Kelly reported in his memoirs that "no opera ever had a stronger cast." The Italian company at the Burgtheater was indeed superb. Francesco Benucci, the outstanding buffo of his generation, amazed Mozart with his "stentorian" rendition of *Figaro*'s showpiece, "Non più andrai," at the close of Act I, an aria to be discussed later on. The role of the Countess was taken by the gifted Luisa Laschi, and Susanna was sung by Nancy Storace, a close friend of the composer. Typical of the time, all these actor-singers were in their twenties except Benucci, who was forty. Despite their sterling performances, however, *Figaro* lasted only a few months. Not until it reached Prague many months later did *Figaro* find an audience of people who fell in love with it, coming out of the theater already singing its tunes by heart.

Scenes from The Marriage of Figaro

These brief scenes will illustrate how Mozart's music breathes three-dimensional life into the words of an already fine libretto. As you read through this section and listen to the music being described, imagine yourself as the opera's stage director, plotting—line by line—not only what the various characters should be thinking but also what they should be physically *doing* in response to what composer and librettist have written for them. The best way to imagine this is to become the character or characters yourself: sing along (yes: actually sing) while also making each gesture or movement implied by the music, the libretto, or both. This is not as easy as it sounds, as professional singer-actors can tell you. Doing it fairly accurately will take some practice, but the excerpts are short and so can be repeated. Try to avoid stereotypical "operatic" gestures in your acting; in the best performances, you never see them. As you undertake to sing and act each role yourself, you will experience the fact that Mozart's music *is* the stage director: it tells you, note by note and rhythm by rhythm, what your character should be thinking, doing, and feeling. Final instruction: be sure to listen to the orchestra at every moment. Those instruments don't just accompany the singer; they are a significant part of the role.

Figaro and Susanna (*duettino* [short duet]): "Cinque . . . dieci . . . venti . . . "

Cherubino (aria): "Non so più, cosa son, cosa faccio"

Figaro (aria): "Non più andrai"

■ FIGARO AND SUSANNA *(DUETTINO)*: "CINQUE . . . DIECI . . . VENTI . . . "
Bass-baritone, soprano, 2 flutes, 2 oboes, 2 bassoons, 2 horns, strings

We are in Figaro and Susanna's quarters. Figaro, yardstick in hand, is measuring the dimensions of either their room (as it's often staged) or their marital bed (as it sometimes is); the stage directions don't specify. What is clear is that they hope the Count will perform their wedding ceremony sometime that day, and they're planning for that. Susanna, seated before a mirror, is trying on the new hat she plans to wear for the occasion. They are each trying to get the other's attention.

FIGARO
Cinque . . . dieci . . . venti . . . trenta . . .
trentasei . . . quarantatré . . .

FIGARO
Five . . . ten . . . twenty . . . thirty . . .
thirty-six . . . forty-three . . .

SUSANNA
(guardandosi nello specchio)
Ora si ch'io son contenta,
sembra fatto inver per me.
Guarda un po', mio caro Figaro,
guarda adesso il mio cappello.
(seguitando a guardarsi)

SUSANNA
(looking at herself in the mirror)
Finally, I'm pleased with it,
it really seems made just for me.
Please take a look, dear Figaro,
take a look at my hat.
(continuing to look at herself)

FIGARO
Sì, mio core, or è più bello:
sembra fatto inver per te.

FIGARO
Yes, my love, it's very pretty;
It really looks made for you.

SUSANNA, FIGARO
Ah, il mattino alle nozze vicino
quanto è dolce al mio/tuo tenere sposo,
questo bel cappellino vezzoso
che Susanna ella stessa si fé.

SUSANNA, FIGARO
On the morning of our wedding
how sweet to my/your dear fiancé
is this charming little hat
that Susanna has made for herself.

In this first scene of the opera, which follows immediately on the incredibly fast, bustling overture, we meet Figaro, jack-of-all-trades and valet to the Count, and Susanna, the Countess's maid. This excerpt, a miniature action ensemble, leads into simple recitative between the two characters (i.e., nonmelodic musical conversation) and then to a second *duettino*. Lorenzo da Ponte's words here are not great poetry, nor were they meant to be. This is ordinary conversation between two people who at this particular moment are not listening to each other, though they are politely pretending to. By the time they come together in the final stanza, however, they achieve musical harmony, symbolizing their premarital harmony as well. They seem a model of what we come to wish for in their aristocratic master and mistress.

After a brief orchestral introduction, Mozart dramatizes their initial ignoring of each other by giving them different *types* of music. Figaro's absentminded counting with his yardstick sounds like the supporting harmony for an upper melody that isn't there. The music for Susanna's preoccupied gazing in the mirror, on the other hand, is temptingly seductive and most definitely a melody. Which of these two will take the lead here, who will seem to be in charge? Quickly, we hear Figaro's counting-motif slide between the phrases of Susanna's melody, dovetailing with them perfectly; then, as the duet continues, he copy-cats her melody note for note, singing, "Sì, mi core, or è più bello: sembra fatto inver per te" (Yes, my love, it's very pretty; it really looks made for you). After that, they merge into a sugar-sweet duet for their closing stanza, Susanna providing the melody and Figaro its (lovingly supportive) accompaniment.

What has happened here dramatically? Quite subtly and by means of a few deft musical strokes, we have been given to understand that in this adoring couple Susanna is not only the gentler but also somewhat the stronger of the two. Figaro is as yet unaware of this (quite the contrary, he regards himself as a master fixer), but will eventually find out for himself.

■ CHERUBINO (ARIA): "NON SO PIÙ, COSA SON, COSA FACCIO"
Soprano, 2 clarinets, 2 bassoons, 2 horns, strings

The teenaged pageboy Cherubino, suffering the pangs of adolescence, has dropped by midway in Act I to cry on Susanna's shoulder. Confusingly, he finds himself in love with every woman in the house, in fact, with every woman he sees, though most of all with the Countess, whom he worships. He has just confided to Susanna that he's written a poem to the Countess, which in Act II he will be commanded to sing to her, with Susanna accompanying on the guitar. That performance will both thrill and terrify him, but right now he is just trying to calm himself down.

Non so più, cosa son, cosa faccio.	I don't know who I am or what I'm doing.
Or di foco, ora sono di ghiaccio.	First I'm on fire, then I'm all ice.
Ogni donna cangiar di colore,	Every woman makes me blush,
ogni donna mi fa palpitar.	every woman makes me tremble.
Solo ai nomi d'amor, di diletto	If anybody speaks of "love" or "delight"
mi si turba, mi s'altera il petto	I get jumpy, my heart pounds,
e a parlare mi sforza d'amore	and I seem forced to talk about love
un desio ch'io non posso spiegar!	by a desire I cannot explain!
Parlo d'amor vegliando	I talk about love when I'm awake,
parlo d'amor sognando,	I talk about love when I'm dreaming—

all'acqua, all'ombra, ai monti,	to the water, to the shadows, to the mountains,
all fiori, all'erbe, ai fonti	to the flowers, to the grass, to the fountains,
all'eco, all'aria, ai venti,	to the echo, to the air, to the breezes
che il suon dei vani accenti	which carry away with them the sounds
portano via con sè.	of my fruitless words.
E se non ho chi m'oda	And if there's nobody listening to me,
parlo d'amor con me.	I talk of love to myself.

The role of Cherubino, performed by a woman dressed as a boy, is a "trousers role." This is a centuries-old tradition based on two facts: the voices of male adolescents are vocally unpredictable, and they are also not usually powerful enough to carry in a large opera house unless they shout, which is not what you want to hear unless there's a specific dramatic justification for it. One of the connotations of trousers roles is a hint of androgyny. In European art, cherubs are tiny, winged angels, at once girl-like and boylike. The name Cherubino ("little cherub") suggests a still more delicate creature. Figaro, when he sings the boy off to war, calls him an "amorous butterfly" and taunts him for his "girlish, rosy cheeks" and smooth, beardless face. In art, the figure of Cupid is characteristically rendered as a cherub, and indeed our opera's pageboy is utterly consumed with love, aiming his arrows at every woman in the house.

The first half of Lorenzo da Ponte's poem—the opening two stanzas—graphically conveys a teenager's jumbled feelings; more than feelings, they are physical sensations: "First I'm on fire," Cherubino laments, "then I'm all ice." It's not just one woman who gives him the jitters; all women do. If he even hears anybody utter the word *love*, he freaks out.

Mozart's music casts these two stanzas into an ABA format: stanza one, then stanza two, then a reprise of stanza one. The orchestral accompaniment, with violins playing *con sordino* (muted, to keep the sound from resonating), is soft and silvery, a brushed landscape for Cherubino's feverishly short, breathless phrases. Mozart scores the aria for the warmer, lower-register woodwinds—no flutes or oboes; instead, clarinets, bassoons, and horns. Underneath these opening stanzas, on-the-beat thumping in the basses makes the page seem to blurt out these phrases one on top of the other. The tempo marking is *allegro vivace*, "fast and lively," and indeed Mozart races Cherubino through these two stanzas, allowing him to repeat just one word: *desio* ("desire"). He sings this key word—the one that so frightens and excites him—no less than four times, the music elongating it almost to the point of onomatopoeia.[18]

Then there is an unexpected shift. In the poem's second half—the longer,

---

18. In onomatopoeia, a word's sound conveys its meaning, as in *hiss, fizz, honk, quack.*

final stanza beginning with "Parlo d'amor vegliando" ("I talk about love when I'm awake")—Cherubino shows us his poetic side through allusions to flowers, grass, water, fountains, and breezes in a subtle evocation of classical style, a style with which da Ponte was intimately familiar.[19] The shift is so sudden and unexpected—from the page's mixed-up interior feelings to an idyllic outdoor world—that da Ponte clearly intends to lift him, for one quick moment, above the domestic disorder of the Count's house toward a calmer, pastoral realm. In eighteenth-century gardens, as da Ponte and Mozart both knew from many examples in Josephine Vienna, sculptures of cherubs—and Cupids—were characteristic features. The words of this aria seem to point toward Cherubino as such a figure, one who, like Cupid, flits back and forth from boudoir to garden. In Act IV, at the close of this frantic day, it is in the garden that a tentative reconciliation occurs between the Count and Countess.

Musically, this final stanza yields longer phrases and note values. We slow down a bit, though not much, and Cherubino's melodic lines convey a poignant yearning rather than the frantic confusion of previous stanzas. The music for all but the last two lines is sung twice; then we encounter another shift, this one created by Mozart more than his librettist.

For the first line of the poem's final couplet ("E se non ho chi m'oda" ["And if there's nobody listening to me"]), the tempo abruptly drops down to very slow, repeating that idea, almost contemplating it, as if Cherubino isn't quite sure what he will say next. Then it's back to the breathless blurting we started with: "Parlo d'amor con me" ("I talk of love to myself"). Did you ever know a teenager who, after complaining loud and long about the tragedy of his life, suddenly reversed himself to say, "Oh, not to worry; I'll be okay"?

■ FIGARO (ARIA): "NON PIÙ ANDRAI"
Bass–baritone, 2 flutes, 2 oboes, 2 bassoons, 2 horns,
2 trumpets, timpani, strings
Cherubino, whom the Count has just discovered hiding in Susanna's room, has been banished from the house and ordered to report immediately to the Count's military regiment. After the Count leaves the room enraged at having caught the page in yet another embarrassing moment (though, in fact, it was entirely innocent), Figaro sings this parting farewell to Cherubino:

---

19. Lorenzo da Ponte had been trained in classical literature in Italy, and decades after his colleagueship with Mozart he moved to New York City, where he became a professor of classics at Columbia University. In each of his three librettos for Mozart, da Ponte employed classical imagery whenever the situation seemed to call for it.

Non più andrai, farfallone amoroso,	You amorous butterfly, you'll no longer
notte e giorno d'intorno girando,	flutter around night and day,
delle belle turbando il riposo,	disturbing the peace of beautiful ladies—
Narcisetto, Adoncino d'amor.	you little Narcissus, little Adonis of love.
Non più avrai questi bei pennachini,	You'll no longer sport those little feathers,
quel cappello leggero e galante,	that light and stylish little cap,
quella chioma, quell'aria brillante,	those curls, that sparkling air,
quel vermiglio, donneco color.	those rosy, girlish cheeks.
Tra guerrieri, poffarbacco!	You'll be with soldiers, by Bacchus!
Gran mustacchi, stretto sacco	Long mustaches, backpack stuffed,
schioppo in spalla, sciabla al fianco,	rifle on your shoulder, saber at your side,
collo dritto, muso franco,	neck straight, face forward,
un gran casco, o un gran turbante,	tall helmet or grand turban,
molto onor, poco contante,	lots of honor but not much pay—
ed invece del fandango,	and instead of dancing the
marcia per il fango.	fandango[20] you'll be marching through mud.
Per montagne, per valloni,	Over mountains and through valleys,
con le nevi e i solleoni,	in snow and summer heat,
al concerto di tromboni	with concerts by blunderbusses,
di bombarde, di cannoni	bombs, and cannons—
che le palle in tutti e tuoni	shells of every kind
all'orecchio fan fischiar.	to set your ears ringing.
Cherubino, alla vittoria,	Cherubino, on to victory
alla gloria militar!	and military glory!

In this rousing aria that brings down the curtain on Act I, Figaro bids good-bye and good luck to young Cherubino, who is ostensibly on his way to serve in the Count's regiment. Already suspicious of the boy for his presumed flirtations with the Countess, the Count is so angry that he banishes him forthwith. Actually, Cherubino never leaves the house, although everyone assumes he does. We find out only later that he never went.

Imagine a teenager listening to Lorenzo da Ponte's words, their opening two stanzas a confusing mix of flattery (you're such a loverboy) and condescension (you're not even old enough to shave). In the two longer stanzas that follow, the tone darkens toward irony, though again complimentary at first (you'll look great standing at attention, weapon at your side) before piling on the facts (you'll be exhausted, broke, covered with mud, and dodging bullets), culminating in a sarcastic salute: "Cherubino, on to victory!"

---

20. A fandango is a slowish courtship dance in triple meter that originated in Spain. Figaro and Susanna, then others as well, dance a fandango in Act III. For "meter" see the glossary and "Notes for Musical Beginners."

Mozart's music rearranges da Ponte's asymmetrical poem—two short stanzas, two long ones, followed by a brief finale—into rondo form, deploying the opening stanza as the recurring (rondo) theme. He paints that stanza with a devil-may-care rhythm, a lighthearted march (dum–da–*dum*, dum–da–*dum*, dum–da–*da*–dum), alternating it with differing treatments of the other stanzas (the rondo's episodes) and the final couplet. The overall design is:

Stanza 1: **Rondo**
   Stanza 2: **Episode 1**
Stanza 1: **Rondo**
   Stanzas 3 and 4: **Episode 2**
Stanza 1: **Rondo**
Couplet: **Coda**

But as you see, Mozart's plan is as asymmetrical as the poem's. The poem's first two stanzas each have four lines, so that **Episode 1** (stanza 2) is the same length as the **Rondo** (stanza 1); but the third and fourth stanzas, especially the third, are much longer, making for a radically outsized **Episode 2**. So much for symmetry! Mozart seems more interested in spotlighting these vignettes of army life than in formal exactitude, and da Ponte has furnished him with rhyming, half-line snippets. If you read stanza three aloud to yourself in the original Italian, you hear how irresistible they are—just the sound alone, never mind the images:

Tra guerrieri, poffarbacco!
Gran mustacchi, stretto sacco,
schioppo in spalla, sciabla al fianco,
collo dritto, muso franco,
un gran casco, o un gran turbante,
molto onor, poco contante,
ed invece del fandango,
un marcia per il fango.

This stanza, midway in the poem, becomes the aria's musical climax. The orchestra, up to this point mainly strings, with woodwinds joining in at certain points, now adds the two trumpets and timpani for the first time. The resulting louder, brassier, more percussive sound punctuates each half-line of the poem, spotlighting each individual image with a burst of orchestral color—thus taking our minds away from Susanna's room and out onto the battlefield. Figaro checks out the new recruit like a drill sergeant—are knapsack, rifle, saber, and helmet all in place?—before anticlimactically warning him about low pay (the music dwells for a while on that reality) and marching, not gloriously on some parade ground, but through mud (here the orchestra blasts with triumphant sarcasm).

The still harsher vignettes of stanza four (mountains and valleys, snow and heat, shells whizzing around the new recruit's ears) are made to seem ridiculous because of Mozart's choice of flutes and oboes to join the strings—not brass and timpani, which would ennoble them. If Cherubino had any momentary thoughts of teenage battlefield heroics, they have been laughed away here.

The aria's coda serves as Figaro's chest-thumping, mock-heroic farewell: "Cherubino, on to victory, on to military glory!" set to a marching rhythm played by full orchestra—including, for the first time since stanza three, trumpets and timpani. In this marvelous conclusion to the opera's hectic first act, Figaro has treated poor Cherubino to a full-dress tease. How would you have the boy react, stanza by stanza, if you were the stage director for the show—proud, excited, petrified, or just confused?

DON GIOVANNI, K. 527
(Premiere: Prague, October 29, 1787; Vienna, May 7, 1788)

We don't know whose idea it was to write this opera—Lorenzo da Ponte's or Mozart's—but by 1787 the story was a well-worn cliché. It had already played in Vienna earlier that year as both a one-act opera, also called *Don Giovanni*, and as a marionette show you could take the kids to in the park. The earliest treatment of the theme had probably been Tirso de Molina's *El burlador de Seville* (1630), followed by Molière's *Don Juan* (1665) and a host of other versions in various languages, including several operas in the months preceding this one. Additionally, Gluck had written a ballet based on Molière's play in 1761, which Mozart doubtless knew. Da Ponte's libretto, borrowing freely from these predecessors, is episodic—that is, it consists of fast-moving, loosely connected scenes. Mozart's music turns them into an opera that races to its fiery conclusion like a whiplash.[21]

As you remember, this opera was commissioned by Prague to capitalize on the huge success of *The Marriage of Figaro* in January 1787. *Don Giovanni* was scheduled for the following fall. By the time Mozart and da Ponte arrived in October of that year to tidy up loose ends and oversee rehearsals, most of their work was done, but not all of it. As always, Mozart custom-tailored each role to the vocal strengths of the singers, which meant leaving some scenes unwritten until he could work directly with the people

---

21. Notable later versions of the story include Byron's unfinished poem "Don Juan" and George Bernard Shaw's play *Man and Superman* (1905), in which Act III carries the title "Don Juan in Hell."

who were going to perform them. Also characteristic of him was that he had not yet composed the overture, which he is said to have written between midnight and seven a.m. on the day of the premiere. Following the first performance, he sent a note to a friend back in Vienna saying that everything had gone off pretty well, considering, though lots of notes had fallen on the floor, particularly during the overture.

That overture is an astonishing piece of work, opening with *fortissimo* blasts of D-minor chords followed by a series of mysterious-sounding, fragmentary melodies; so far, we seem to be headed toward a tragic opera. Then, out of nowhere, a bright, perky theme in D major appears and we spend the rest of the overture in the jolly realm of opera buffa.

The opera's title page calls *Don Giovanni* a *dramma giocoso* (jocose, or comic drama), a term which might suggest an in-between status, a mixture of comic and serious. But Mozart's own thematic catalog labels it [pure] opera buffa. Problem unsolved! The fact is that *Don Giovanni* defies classification. For the most part, it is an opera buffa in two acts (both opera buffa and opera seria often had three[22]), with a lot of comedy and with characters who are modern and earthbound rather than mythological or celestial—except for a terrifying statue at the end.

Also characteristic of opera buffa is the reliance on ensembles, rather than arias, for dramatic climaxes. As in *Figaro,* these are action ensembles— people don't just stand there and sing; they simultaneously act, move, "live." Yet—as is also typical of *Figaro*—certain principal figures are cast in opera seria mode: Donna Anna, the Commendatore, to some extent Donna Elvira, and, during his confrontations with the Commendatore, Giovanni himself. The opera opens with a possible rape and a murder and closes with eternal damnation for the hero, certainly no standard-issue buffa plot.

Above all, however, it is Mozart's music that takes this opera beyond categories. Even in the gayest party scenes there is an undertone of foreboding. The music shifts back and forth from major to minor keys and from cries of anguish to pastoral idyll to raw sexual innuendo. The total effect is at once thrilling and unsettling.

More has been written about this opera than about almost any other work of art in Western civilization. There are now two hundred years of such commentary, and its influence continues to be so powerful that it is

---

22. The fact that *The Marriage of Figaro* has four acts is perhaps explained both by its unusual length and by the fact that Beaumarchais's original play had five. Throughout the nineteenth century and well into the twentieth, *Don Giovanni* was divided into four acts. Act II began with the peasant wedding-party of Zerlina and Masetto; Act III, with Don Giovanni, Leporello, and the statue of the Commendatore in the cemetery.

nearly impossible for us to view the opera with fresh eyes and ears. Some of this inherited criticism—literally hundreds of works, both fiction and nonfiction—dates back more than two centuries, to the earliest writers on *Don Giovanni*. But curiously, many of those writers never saw the "real" opera, because after the final Viennese performance in 1788 it was often staged as a *Singspiel*—that is, in German, with spoken dialogue instead of recitatives.

Actually, converting (Italian) opera buffa into (German) *Singspiel* was done all the time back then, because audiences wanted to understand the words. Mozart was aware of this custom and, as far as we know, wasn't bothered by it. But the switch to spoken dialogue (i.e., with no musical accompaniment) made possible wholesale cuts, rewrites, and improvised ad libs, all of which, over time, refashioned both the plot and the main characters, transforming Don Giovanni from a sleazy (though dashing and charismatic) sexual predator into a Hamlet-esque tragic hero. Between 1788 and 1800—a mere twelve years—the opera was translated some twenty times, acquiring so many alterations in the process that what Mozart and da Ponte wrote was scarcely recognizable anymore.

The Marriage of Figaro and *Così fan tutte* were also turned into *Singspiels*. But in the case of *Don Giovanni* more so than in the case of the other two, there was no clear original to begin with. Following its premiere in Prague, the composer made changes for its debut in Vienna the following June, not only writing new arias and scenes for a different cast of singers, but reshaping the end of the opera, after Don Giovanni is sent to Hell for his sins.[23] While we are pretty sure how the first Prague performance ended— with a final scene for all the surviving characters (option 3 below)—we don't know how it ended in Vienna.[24] Here were the possibilities, based upon what survives in the original manuscripts:

1. To end with the Don's descent into hell
2. To end with that, followed by a choral scream by the other characters
3. To end the same way the Prague premiere ended, with each of the surviving characters announcing what he or she plans to do now that Don Giovanni is dead

---

23. Besides the revised ending, the most significant changes were a new aria for Don Ottavio, "Dalla sua pace" to replace "Il mio tesoro," and an added accompanied recitative and aria for Donna Elvira, "In quali eccessi . . . Mi tradì quell' alma ingrata." In modern performances, both the replacement arias and the originals are generally sung.
24. Julian Rushton (*Mozart*, 160) believes the Vienna production ended with the death of Don Giovanni.

Although option three is standard practice nowadays, as recently as the 1960s people were debating whether that was anticlimactic. How to choose? Mozart left us no clear roadmap. During the nineteenth century and well into the twentieth, option 1 was regarded as not only the most appropriate, but the one Mozart himself had authorized. People thought the opera should end with Don Giovanni's demise, and they felt certain that a genius like Mozart would have written it that way.

This opera is laced with special effects:

- A swordfight ends in death.
- Two women are nearly raped; one of them, Donna Anna, perhaps is raped, according to some interpreters of the opera.
- Three onstage bands play dance music in three different meters at the same time.
- The principal characters sing "Long live liberty!" ("Viva la libertà") during Don Giovanni's party in Act I, giving no explanation for it. Was this intended to incite political rebellion in the Habsburg Empire, two years before the storming of the Bastille in Paris, or was it (merely) encouraging sexual license?
- An onstage band performs hit tunes from current operas, including *The Marriage of Figaro*, before an audience that can sing them by heart.
- A statue walks, talks, comes for supper, and condemns the hero to Hell.
- A trapdoor in center stage opens, fire shoots upward, the earth quivers, and the Don drops out of sight forever.

Making opera seem real—not "staged"—was important to Mozart. Young, exciting cast members helped to achieve this. Prague's Don Giovanni was incredibly handsome and sexy. Vienna's was twenty-two years old and very good looking. In Vienna, the role of Donna Anna was taken by Aloysia Weber Lange, who had been the composer's first love back in Mannheim and was now his friend, sister-in-law, and colleague. In Prague, during a rehearsal of the end of the first act, when Zerlina is supposed to scream in fright as Don Giovanni corners her in a back room at his party, Mozart hid behind the curtain and poked a hairpin into her backside. When she let out a startled shriek, he told her that that was just what he wanted.

At the center of this funny, violent, exciting drama stands the enigmatic figure of Don Giovanni himself. Traditionally, dramatists tell us who characters truly are through soliloquies (monologues); in opera, these are arias. But the Don's aria that comes closest to a soliloquy, his "Champagne Aria" ("Fin ch'han dal vino"), tells us nothing about who he is or what he feels but is simply a toast to wine, women, and himself. In fact, and most oddly, there are no monologues in *Don Giovanni* at all—no arias sung by a character alone onstage, except Leporello's "Notte e giorno faticar" in Act I, Scene 1, which he doesn't get to finish because of the sudden appearance of Donna Anna and Don Giovanni.

Yet, in fact, we do know who Don Giovanni is, because we have all encountered him in our own lives. How would you describe him? Dashing, Hollywood handsome, suave, worldly, rich, the essence of cool—but at the same time, cruel and heartless. Sexually and in every other way, he is a gorger. In the opera he lies, cheats, manipulates, seduces, beats up his servant, blasphemes, and kills an old man—all without showing the slightest remorse.

Following along by the Don's side is his servant Leporello, who, while viewing his ethically challenged master with contempt, nevertheless aspires to be like him someday. Leporello's opening aria showcases these two sides: he hates his job ("Notte e giorno faticar" ["Working night and day"]) and would rather be a Don himself ("voglio far il gentiluomo" ["I want to be a gentleman"]).

The cast features three women:

- Zerlina, an innocent peasant lass, is about to marry Masetto, who seethes with anger when the Don cavalierly makes a pass at his betrothed yet is powerless to stop it, because a peasant has to give way to a nobleman.
- Donna Elvira, to whom the Don promised marriage before our drama begins, was abandoned by him and has come back to reclaim her rightful status.
- Donna Anna is engaged to Don Ottavio.

In Act I, Scene 1, Donna Anna chases a masked man (guess who) out of her boudoir, screaming that she will pursue him "like a Fury"—which, by the end of the opera, she does. Hearing her cries, her father, the Commendatore (Commander) of Seville, challenges Don Giovanni to a duel. When the Don insults him by refusing to fight an old man, the father insists and is killed. Thus this "comic" opera starts off with what may have been rape and what amounts to a murder. A few minutes later, Donna Elvira is humiliated, first by the Don and then—still more excruciatingly—by Leporello, who sings in his "Catalog Aria" ("Madamina, il catalogo è questo") that she shouldn't feel too badly; she's just one of hundreds of the Don's conquests, which include "1,003 in Spain."

The opera's blazing Act II finale begins with a self-celebratory party for the Don to which he has jokingly invited the statue of the late Commendatore. While Don Giovanni stuffs himself with food and wine, his private band amuses him with snatches of popular tunes, including Figaro's "Non più andrai" from Mozart's own *The Marriage of Figaro*. In the midst of his festivities, the statue of the Commendatore suddenly arrives to demand that the sinner repent. The sinner refuses, the trapdoor opens, and Don Giovanni is gone.

This awesome scene—propelled by what may have been the most dissonant music composed during the eighteenth century—is followed by an utter stylistic about-face (which is why the nineteenth century felt certain that Mozart never wrote it). The stage fills with the surviving characters, who tell us, one by one, what they intend to do now that the archfiend is no more. Leporello plans to search for a new master. Zerlina and Masetto can finally get married. Donna Anna and Don Ottavio will also wed—though not right now, she pleads; give me a year to think about it. Donna Elvira is off to spend the rest of her days in a convent. Then they all join together to sing the opera's moral, in a breathlessly quick fugal conclusion that leaves the drama suspended in midair, not quite resolved—which, as you will discover, is the case with many of Mozart's mature operas:

Questo è il fin	This is the end
di chi fa mal,	Of one who does evil,
e de'perfidi la morte	And the death of evildoers
all vita è sempre ugual.	Is always equal to the life they led.

Scenes from Don Giovanni

Leporello, Donna Anna, Don Giovanni, and the Commendatore (ensemble): Opening scene of Act I

Don Giovanni and Zerlina (recitative and duet): "Alfin siam liberati . . . Là ci darem la mano"

Don Giovanni, Leporello, and the Statue of the Commendatore (recitative): "Don Giovanni, a cenar teco m'invitasti"

■ LEPORELLO, DONNA ANNA, DON GIOVANNI, AND THE COMMENDATORE (ENSEMBLE): OPENING SCENE OF ACT I

Soprano, baritone, bass-baritone, bass, 2 flutes, 2 oboes, 2 bassoons, 2 horns, strings

Leporello, Don Giovanni's valet, has been ordered to stand guard outside while his master cavorts in yet another lady's boudoir. So far in this opera, we have been subjected, first, to dark, ominous foreboding (the introduction to the Overture), then, without transition, to cheery opera buffa (the remainder of the Overture). If we take overtures as predictors of plots (which they sometimes are), we may wonder, as the curtain rises on Act I, Scene 1: Is this opera going to be comic or tragic? The answer comes in the form of the complex action ensemble with which the opera begins. In just under five minutes, we meet four highly contrasted characters, each of them sharply etched (Leporello, Donna Anna, Don Giovanni, the Commendatore); we witness a servant's clowning, a possible rape, and a murder; and we hear, in quick succession, four utterly different musical styles. The answer to our question therefore seems to be: *Don Giovanni* is neither tragedy nor comedy, but an ever-changing mixture of both.

To introduce this multifaceted scene, perhaps the clearest way is to break it down into segments. This destroys its dramatic integrity, of course, as the scene is continuous; there are no breaks. But to focus on its features one by one, this may be the best solution.

Here is the first segment, in which Don Giovanni's servant, Leporello, is onstage alone:

LEPORELLO (*solo, che vi passeggia*)
Notte e giorno faticar
per chi nulla sa gradir;
piova e vento sopportar,
mangiar male e mal dormir. . .

Voglio far il gentiluomo,
e non voglio più servir.
Oh, che caro galantuomo!
vuoi star dentro colla bella,
ed io far la sentinella!

Voglio far il gentiluomo,
e non voglio più servir.
Ma mi par . . . che venga gente;
non mi voglio far sentir.
(*S'asconde.*)

LEPORELLO (*alone, as lookout*)
Slaving night and day
for somebody who's never satisfied;
putting up with rain and wind,
eating badly, sleeping badly. . .

I want to be a gentleman,
and not be a servant any more.
Oh, what a generous guy!
He's over there with the beauty
while I'm standing guard outside!

I want to be a gentleman,
and not be a servant any more.
But look out . . . people are coming.
I don't want them to spot me.
(*He hides.*)

Leporello paces slowly back and forth across the stage, the orchestra banging out a march as he lugs his aching body around. The melody he sings as he gripes about his master continually repeats the same simpleminded up/down/up/down motif, suggesting that Leporello is not overly bright.

He tells us that, with Don Giovanni, you have to work all night and all day, in the wind, the rain, whatever. The music rises in pitch line by line, as people's voices do when they are frustrated. Ending his list, temporarily, by mentioning lousy food and lack of sleep, he suddenly has a vision: what if he himself were a gentleman! This bright thought inspires new music—no longer the march but a real tune, higher than his bored pacing motif and decorated with a flourish from the orchestra. In this way, da Ponte's words combine with Mozart's three musical gestures: the march, the up/down motif, and the flourish, to tell us in the first forty seconds of the opera that Leporello dislikes and disapproves of his master, but oh, how he would love to live his life![25]

Suddenly, Leporello's brief aria is interrupted by the sounds of a panicked exodus from the very house he is guarding, the residence of Seville's military Commendatore and his daughter, Donna Anna. Donna Anna is engaged to Don Ottavio (a tenor, whom we don't meet in these excerpts). Hearing the commotion and probably suspecting what it's about, Leporello breaks off his complaints and visions and leaps away to hide. This is one of numerous places in Mozart's operas where moving the drama forward wins out over formal symmetry; in a "normal" opera, Leporello would finish his aria and the music would stop before the next scene would begin.

This is where the action ensemble begins. Leporello, Donna Anna, Don Giovanni, and the Commendatore enact and express their own thoughts, sometimes individually, sometimes in duets, trios, or quartets. The result, from a dramatic point of view, is astonishingly close to real life; from a musical perspective, it is counterpoint.[26] What's challenging here, for the composer, is that all three men sing in lower registers. It would help if at least one of them were a tenor, but *Don Giovanni* was written for Prague, whose opera house had but one tenor, which meant that he had to sing Don Ottavio.

Here is the beginning of the action ensemble, the scene's second segment:

Donna Anna esce tenendo forte pel braccio Don Giovanni, ed egli cercando sempre di celarsi.	*Donna Anna rushes out hanging on to Don Giovanni's arm, while he tries to keep his face hidden.*
DONNA ANNA	**DONNA ANNA**
Non sperar, se non m'uccidi, Ch'io ti lasci fuggir mai, *ecc.*	Don't think you'll get away except over my dead body!

25. A 1980s production of *Don Giovanni* conducted by Craig Smith and staged by Peter Sellars, available on DVD, cast twin brothers as Leporello and Don Giovanni. Smith and Sellars didn't plan it that way; it was just a happy coincidence.
26. For a definition of *counterpoint*, see the glossary.

DON GIOVANNI
Donna folle! indarno gridi!
Chi son io tu non saprai.

DON GIOVANNI
Crazy woman! Your shouts are useless!
You'll never find out my name.

LEPORELLO
Che tumulto! o ciel, che gridi!
Il padron in nuovi guai!

LEPORELLO
What a mess! O God, what yelling!
The boss is in trouble again!

DONNA ANNA
Gente! servi! al traditore!
Scellerato!

DONNA ANNA
Everyone! Servants! Grab this
evil man! Criminal!

DON GIOVANNI
Taci, e trema al mio furore!
Sconsigliata!

DON GIOVANNI
Shut up and don't make me angry!
Crazy woman!

LEPORELLO
Sta a veder che il malandrino
mi farà precipitar.

LEPORELLO
I can see this jerk
is going to get me into big trouble.

DONNA ANNA
Come furia disperata,
ti saprò perseguitar.

DONNA ANNA
I will chase you down
like an avenging Fury.

DON GIOVANNI
Questa furia disperata
mi vuol far precipitar.

DON GIOVANNI
She's going to chase me down
like an avenging Fury.

First, Donna Anna races out, screaming (in the decorous vocal style appropriate to both her class and the seriousness of this moment—a total contrast to Leporello's monotonous up/down/up/down)—that she is chasing an intruder she found in her bedroom and she demands to know who he is. Don Giovanni (the mystery man) retorts—imitating her musical style—that he has no intention of identifying himself and, in fact, if she doesn't shut her mouth he may have to hurt her. Then, with eerie clairvoyance, he prophesies that this "Fury" will bring about his downfall, which, eventually, she does.

In the voices of Donna Anna and Don Giovanni, we move into the style of opera seria, a difference you hear immediately; underneath them, however, Leporello patters along in comic, opera buffa style, mostly going up and down the notes of a chord over and over again. The result is a serious verbal confrontation following what may have been a sexual assault, undercut by Leporello's frantic repetitions.

Characteristic of our hero, however, is that he mimics the vocal idiom of whoever he is addressing, which means opera seria when he is talking to

Donna Anna. He will switch to another idiom when confronting her father, the Commendatore, and to still another when he tries to seduce the peasant lass Zerlina, later in Act I. Musically, the man is faceless—or, put another way, he has an infinite number of faces. This is part of his con: as we know, when someone seems to "speak our language," we relax and let down our guard.

Here is the third segment:

Appare il Commendatore colla spada sguainata. Donna Anna fugge in casa.	*The Commendatore appears, his sword drawn. Donna Anna runs into the house.*
COMMENDATORE Lasciala, indegno! Battiti meco.	COMMENDATORE Let go of her, you brute! Fight with me.
DON GIOVANNI Va, non mi degno di pugnar teco.	DON GIOVANNI Get out of here. I won't stoop to fight with you.
COMMENDATORE Così pretendi da me fuggir?	COMMENDATORE Is this how you expect to get away from me?
LEPORELLO Potessi almeno di qua partir!	LEPORELLO If only I could get out of here!
COMMENDATORE Battiti!	COMMENDATORE Fight!
DON GIOVANNI Misero! attendi, se vuoi morir!	DON GIOVANNI Miserable creature, stick around if you want to die!
Combattono. Il Commendatore cade, mortalmente ferito.	*They duel. The Commendatore falls, mortally wounded.*

Donna Anna's father storms out to defend her and, as honor required, challenges Don Giovanni to a duel. Unfortunately, this dramatic scene is sometimes trivialized or even played for laughs. There are two reasons for this. First, we forget that swords can kill and that, in the eighteenth-century, gentlemen routinely carried them. Second, we may not be listening clearly enough to the music. Don Giovanni and the Commendatore address each other in the solemn tones of church music, this scene's third distinct musical style. By elevating their verbal confrontation to an idiom heard in Handel's great oratorios—which Mozart knew—as well as in his own sacred music, the composer erases any notion that this is supposed to be funny.

Now for the fourth and final segment:

COMMENDATORE	COMMENDATORE
Ah, soccorso! son tradito!	Ah, help me! I'm done for!
L'assassino m'ha ferito,	The assassin has wounded me,
e dal seno palpitante sento	and my throbbing breast tells me
l'anima partir.	I'm dying.

DON GIOVANNI	DON GIOVANNI
Ah! già cade il sciagurato	Ah! The miserable wretch is down
. . . affannosa e agonizzante	. . . terrified and agonizing,
già dal seno palpitante	and in his throbbing breast
veggo l'anima partir.	I see his life ebbing away.

LEPORELLO	LEPORELLO
Qual misfatto! qual eccesso!	What a crime! How horrible!
Entro il sen, dallo spavento,	I'm so scared I can feel
Palpitar il cor mi sento.	my own heart pounding!
Io non so che far, che dir.	I don't know what to do or say.
(*Il Commendatore muore.*)	(*The Commendatore dies.*)

This multisection action ensemble concludes with music we would never have expected: not loud, violent music to dramatize the murder, but a soft, almost melancholy trio. It is an emotionally confused yet meditative ending. The Commendatore groans as he lies dying, Don Giovanni seems startled that his evening's fun has been interrupted (though he is clearly not upset), and Leporello is so terrified that all he can do is stammer out the bass notes of the harmony. Amazingly, considering everything that's happened since, Mozart ends this scene by returning us to the minor key with which the opera's Overture began.

■ DON GIOVANNI AND ZERLINA (RECITATIVE AND DUET): "ALFIN SIAM LIBERATI . . . LÀ CI DAREM LA MANO"
Bass-baritone, soprano, 2 flutes, 2 oboes, 2 bassoons, 2 horns, strings
Midway through Act I, Giovanni and Leporello meet up with a group of peasants on their way to a wedding. (Some writers interpret this scene as following rather than preceding the wedding. While Zerlina's description of Masetto as her *marito* can mean either husband or fiancé, the thrust of the plot seems to move us forward, toward rather than away from their wedding.) What follows is the opera's most vivid portrait of the Don Giovanni in action. Zerlina is about to marry Masetto, but Don Giovanni doesn't see why that should stand in the way of enjoying this innocent young country girl for a few minutes himself. He commands the wedding procession to stop, and Leporello is instructed to escort Masetto and the others to his villa to wine and dine them. Masetto angrily refuses to leave, and only the

threat of Don Giovanni's sword persuades him otherwise. Zerlina and Don Giovanni are now onstage by themselves. Their conversation begins in the form known as simple recitative, then slides smoothly into a duet.

Recitativo semplice

DON GIOVANNI
Alfin siam liberati,
Zerlinetta gentil, da quell scioccone,
Che ne dite, mio ben, so far pulito.

ZERLINA
Signo, è mio marito!

DON GIOVANNI
Chi? colui? Vi par che un onest'uom,
un nobil cavalier, qual io me vanto,
possa soffrir che quell visetto d'oro,
quel viso inzuccherato,
da un bifolcaccio vil sia strapazzato?

ZERLINA
Ma signore, io gli diedi parola di
sposarlo.

DON GIOVANNI
Tal parola non vale un zero,
Voi non siete fatta per essere paesana,
un'altra sorte vi procuran
quegli occhi bricconcelli,
quei labbretti sì belli,
quelle dituccia candide e odorose;
parmi toccar giuncata e fiutar
rose!

ZERLINA
Ah, non vorrei ...

DON GIOVANNI
Che non vorreste?

ZERLINA
Alfine ingannata restar. Io so
che raro colle donne voi altri cavalieri
siente onesti e sinceri.

DON GIOVANNI
È un impostura della gente plebea!

Simple recitative

DON GIOVANNI
At last we're free,
my dear little Zerlina, of that dolt!
What do you think—wasn't that well
done, the way I got rid of him?

ZERLINA
But sir, I'm engaged to him!

DON GIOVANNI
Who, him? You can't think that an
honest guy, a high-class gentleman
like me, could allow this pretty little
face, this face as sweet as sugar, to
be touched by such an oaf?

ZERLINA
But sir, I've given my word to marry
him.

DON GIOVANNI
Such words are worthless.
You weren't born to be a peasant;
you're meant for a different life,
with those mischievous little eyes,
those dear little cherry lips,
those slender fingers, so white, so
fragrant, as soft as cream and as sweet
as roses!

ZERLINA
Ah, I wouldn't like ...

DON GIOVANNI
What wouldn't you like?

ZERLINA
To find out I'd been tricked. I know
that you fine gentlemen are rarely
honest and sincere with women.

DON GIOVANNI
That's a lie put out by the common

La nobilita ha dipinta negli occhi
l'onestà. Orsù, non perdiam tempo:
in quest'istante io ti voglio sposar.

ZERLINA
Voi?

DON GIOVANNI
Certo, io!
Quel casinetto è mio; soli saremo,
e là, gioiello mio, ci sposeremo.

Duet
DON GIOVANNI
Là ci darem la mano
là mi dirai di sì.
Vedi, non è lontano;
partiam, ben mio, da qui.

ZERLINA
Vorrei e non vorrei,
mi trema un poco il cor.
Felici, è ver, sarei,
ma può burlami ancor.

DON GIOVANNI
Vieni, mio bel diletto!
io cangerò tua sorte.

ZERLINA
Mi fa pietà Masetto! . . .
Presto, non son più forte!

DON GIOVANNI, ZERLINA
Andiam, andiam, mio bene,
a ristorar le pene
d'un innocente amor!

folk! We aristocrats have honesty
written in our eyes. Come on, don't
waste time. I want to marry you at once.

ZERLINA
You?

DON GIOVANNI
Of course, me!
That little cottage is mine; we'll be
alone, and there, my little jewel, we'll
get married.

Duet
DON GIOVANNI
There we'll join hands,
There you'll tell me yes.
Look, it's not far;
Let's go there, my love.

ZERLINA
I would, and then I wouldn't;
my heart isn't sure about this.
I guess I should be happy,
but he might be fooling me.

DON GIOVANNI
Come on, my dear delight!
I'll change your life.

ZERLINA
What about poor Masetto! . . .
Quick, I'm losing strength!

DON GIOVANNI, ZERLINA
Let's go, let's go, my dear one,
to soothe away the pain
of our innocent love!

Alone with Zerlina at last, Don Giovanni chats her up before nonchalantly enticing her into a duet. Before she knows what has happened, she has given in, and they dance away (literally: their duet's closing stanza and its orchestral postlude are set to the rhythms of a dance). Suddenly, Donna Elvira arrives. Appalled and once again humiliated by this man's raw-edged conniving right in front of her, she furiously shoos him away.

In Mozart's time and for many years thereafter, audiences regarded this as a garden scene: an idyllic moment amid the opera's otherwise more city-oriented situations. During the 150 years when this opera was played in four acts, Act II began here.[27] This made for a sharp contrast with the opera's opening scenes, all of which deal with aristocratic characters and situations and take place at night. Now we are both outdoors and in sunlight for the first time; and if we missed those signals, the music introducing this scene, sung and danced to by Zerlina, Masetto, and their friends, is a country jig. We have heard no such music in any previous scene. The implication is clear: Don Giovanni is an interloper, invading a bucolic paradise.

Whereas Masetto is suspicious and has to be ordered out of the way, Zerlina is all innocence: she has never met an operator like Don Giovanni and hasn't the savvy to recognize him for what he is. After a moment's questioning, she believes him when he proposes marriage (he had done the same to Donna Elvira, then left town), and is ready to follow him home, where she would have lost her innocence, like so many others before her.

Granted, Don Giovanni's come-on is brilliant—after all, it was written by a librettist who was himself a notorious womanizer, well experienced in this line of work. Once again, as in all three of his collaborations with Mozart, da Ponte has created poetic verbiage tailor made for the situation. The compliments Don Giovanni bestows on this country girl are luscious. Read some of the lines aloud and savor their erotic suggestiveness for yourself, not only the words, but the very sounds—a hallmark of da Ponte's style:

Voi non siete fatta per essere paesana,
un'altra sorte vi procuran
quegli occhi bricconcelli,
quei labbretti sì belli,
quelle dituccia candide e odorose;
parmi toccar giuncata e fiutar rose!

It is, of course, Giovanni who begins their duet, selecting from his repertory of musical cons the one filed under "peasant girls." Constructed of four balanced phrases, it is a bewitchingly simple tune, as if it carried the label, "You can rely on me." Contrast this schmoozing melody with the kind of music he sang to Donna Anna!

---

27. The first division into four acts occurred in 1798, in a production conducted by Mozart's assistant, Franz Xaver Süssmayr. Well into the 1950s, people still debated whether two acts or four should be the norm. Since then, almost all productions have reverted to the original two-act format.

The shy, bashful Zerlina is, musically, overcome at once. Although her *words* say she isn't sure what to do, her first *musical* reply ends with its fourth phrase going on for too long: she doesn't balance his four phrases with four of equal length, but gilds the lily on the last one, which is Mozart's way of telling us that she has already capitulated. Next, she completes each of Don Giovanni's phrases: he sings a line, she provides the musical answer. After that, she begins to come in before he even finishes his lines. Could anything be clearer? At last, they join together for the final stanza, the one referred to earlier that is set to a dance rhythm. Off they go! But Donna Elvira arrives unexpectedly, sees what's going on, and ends it.

■ Don Giovanni, Leporello, and the Statue of the Commenda-
tore (recitative): "Don Giovanni, a cenar teco m'invitasti"
Bass-baritone, baritone, bass, 2 flutes, 2 oboes, 2 clarinets, 2 bassoons, 2 horns, 2 trumpets, 3 trombones, timpani
Earlier in this next-to-the-last scene of the opera, Don Giovanni enjoyed a private feast for himself, served up by Leporello, with music by his private [onstage] band. Donna Elvira then appeared, uninvited, to urge him to change his ways; Don Giovanni humiliated her and sent her away. Hearing loud knocking at the door, Leporello reports that something horrible is happening. He hides, and Don Giovanni, annoyed, goes to the door himself. To the sounds of ear-splitting chords from the orchestra, a statue of the dead Commendatore enters.

LA STATUA
Don Giovanni, a cenar teco
m'invitasti, e son venuto.

THE STATUE
Don Giovanni, you invited me to
dinner, and I have come.

DON GIOVANNI
Non l'avrei giammai creduto,
ma farò quell che potrò.
Leporello, un'altra cena
fa' che subito si porti!

DON GIOVANNI
I never thought you'd come,
but I'll do what I can.
Leporello, set another place
at the table at once!

LEPORELLO
Ah, padron, siam tutti morti!

LEPORELLO
Ah, boss, we're dead men!

DON GIOVANNI
Vanni, dico . . .

DON GIOVANNI
Go on, do as I say . . .

LA STATUA
Ferma un po'.
Non si pasce di cibo mortale
chi si pasce di cibo celeste.

THE STATUE
Wait a minute.
Those who have eaten celestial food
do not eat mortal food any longer.

Altre cure più gravi di queste,
altra brama quaggiù mi guidò.

Other, graver issues have guided
me here tonight.

LEPORELLO
La terzana d'avere mi sembra,
e le membra fermar più non so.

LEPORELLO
I'm shaking as if I had fever,
and I can't stop.

DON GIOVANNI
Parla dunque: che chiedi, che vuoi?

DON GIOVANNI
Tell me, then, what do you want?

LA STATUA
Parlo, ascolta, più tempo non ho.

THE STATUE
I will tell you; listen, I don't have much
time.

DON GIOVANNI
Parla, parla, ascoltando ti sto.

DON GIOVANNI
Speak, speak, I'm listening.

LA STATUA
Tu m'invitasti a cena,
il tuo dover or sai.
Rispondimi: verrai tu a
cenar meco?

THE STATUE
You invited me to dinner;
you know your obligation.
Answer me: will you have dinner
with me?

DON GIOVANNI
A torto di viltade tacciato mai sarò!

DON GIOVANNI
No one can ever say I'm a coward!

LA STATUA
Risolvi!

THE STATUE
Decide!

DON GIOVANNI
Ho già risolto.

DON GIOVANNI
I've decided.

LA STATUA
Verrai?

THE STATUE
Will you come?

LEPORELLO
Dite di no, dite di no!

LEPORELLO
Say no, say no!

DON GIOVANNI
Ho fermo il core in petto:
non ho timo, verrò!

DON GIOVANNI
My pulse is steady;
I am not afraid; I accept!

LA STATUA
Dammi la mano in pegno!

THE STATUE
Give me your hand as pledge!

DON GIOVANNI
Eccola! . . . Ohimè!

DON GIOVANNI
Here it is . . . Oh, my God!

LA STATUA
Cos'hai?

THE STATUE
What's the matter?

DON GIOVANNI
Che gelo è questo mai!

LA STATUA
Pentiti, cangia vita!
E' l'ultimo momento!

DON GIOVANNI
(cercando di liberarsi)
No, no, ch'io non mi pento!
Vanne lontan da me!

LA STATUA
Pentiti, scellerato!

DON GIOVANNI
No, vecchio infatuato!

LA STATUA
Pentiti, pentiti!

DON GIOVANNI
No, no!

LA STATUA
Sì, sì!

DON GIOVANNI
No, no!

LA STATUA
Ah, tempo più non v'e!
(Parte. Fuoco da diversi parte,
tremuoto.)

DON GIOVANNI
Da qual tremore insolito sento
assalir gli spiriti!
Donde escono quei vortici di
fuoco pien d'orror?

DEMONI (sotto terra)
Tutto a tue colpe è poco!
Vieni! e'è un mal peggior!

DON GIOVANNI
Chi l'anima mi lacera!
Chi m'agita le viscere!
Che strazio, ohimè!
Che smania, che inferno, che terror!

DON GIOVANNI
I've never felt anything so cold!

THE STATUE
Repent, change your life!
This is your last chance!

DON GIOVANNI
(trying to free his hand)
No, no, I will not repent!
Get away from me!

THE STATUE
Repent, you wretch!

DON GIOVANNI
No, you miserable old man!

THE STATUE
Repent, repent!

DON GIOVANNI
No, no!

THE STATUE
Yes, yes!

DON GIOVANNI
No, no!

THE STATUE
Ah, there is no more time!
(He leaves. Fire appears from all sides of
the room; the ground trembles.)

DON GIOVANNI
What kind of terror is this,
one I've never felt before!
Where did this horrible whirlwind of
fire come from?

DEMONS (from underground)
They can never match your crimes!
Come! Even worse than this awaits you!

DON GIOVANNI
What spirits are tearing at me!
How they are eating my insides!
What torture, Oh, my God!
What misery, what hell, what terror!

LEPORELLO
Che ceffo disperato!
Che gesti da dannato!
Che gridi! Che lamenti!
Come mi fa terror!

DON GIOVANNI
(*sprofnodondosi*)
Ah! (*Resta inghiottito della terra.*)

LEPORELLO
Ah!

LEPORELLO
What desperation in his face!
What gestures of someone damned!
What screams! What groans!
It terrifies me!

DON GIOVANNI
(*sinking through the ground*)
Ah! (*The earth swallows him up.*)

LEPORELLO
Ah!

The set changes and the surviving characters come out to begin the last scene, during which each person says what he or she plans to do, now that Don Giovanni is dead. The opera closes with a victorious, symphonic-style coda sung by these characters, in which they pronounce final moral judgment on the sinner.

This concluding segment of the opera's next-to-the-last scene is among the most thrilling in all opera. Remarkably, throughout the scene as a whole, including this segment, there are no arias, no ensembles, and no choruses—no set pieces of any kind—nothing but continuous accompanied recitative. Much later, the composer Richard Wagner would write whole acts in which he studiously avoided any arias at all; but in Mozart's day and for decades afterward, a scene such as this was unique. Its climax, of course, was the terrifying entrance of the statue.

The Romantic poet, conductor, and critic E. T. A. Hoffmann reminded us that the figure that suddenly appears at Don Giovanni's door is not a ghost, but a statue. Hoffmann argued that it should not be some towering, oversized figure, but a regular man in height and build—thoroughly lifelike and thus all the more frightening. He also urged that the statue remain motionless except when offering his hand to Don Giovanni, making that the statue's one, startling move. During the more than two centuries since the opera's premiere, this scene has been staged in every way you can imagine. In the movie *Amadeus,* a huge twenty-foot statue makes its entrance by crashing through what looks like about a twelve-foot brick wall, while acrobats costumed to look like bats fly at Don Giovanni from every corner of the stage.

What probably concerned Mozart most of all was how to convince the audience that the statue was real. If the audience thinks this is a joke, the scene falls apart. He solves the problem by so many means that it is a challenge to hear them all. First, the statue's violent entrance music shatters the rules of eighteenth-century harmony; after that, it remains unnervingly fragmentary and harmonically unstable for nearly five minutes, a very long time in music. Second, the orchestra is larger than at any other point in the opera, making this scene shockingly loud. Third, the action is nonstop, offering no release of tension. Fourth—this he had also done for the Act I duel between these two—Mozart elevates the level of discourse from buffa to church music, convincing us that the statue, far from being a figure of comedy, is pronouncing divine judgment. Fifth, Mozart adds three trombones to the orchestra. Chiefly associated then with church music—they were not used in symphonies before Beethoven—we hear them every time the statue speaks, but nowhere else; they do not accompany any of Don Giovanni's replies.

When nineteenth- and early twentieth-century productions ended with this scene, omitting its comic follow-up because they regarded it as un-Mozartian and therefore unworthy of being performed, the result, of course, was that audiences (and critics) came to view the opera as a tragedy and Don Giovanni as a hero unafraid of even cosmic powers. This interpretation of the opera and its title character was handed down for generations.

After writing the opera's last pages, Mozart had about twenty-four hours to come up with an overture. Perhaps as a way of forecasting the Don's demise—although overtures in those days did not customarily do that—he decided to lift the overture's introduction nearly note for note from this towering scene. Thus it came to pass that the statue's terrifying music—undoubtedly still ringing in Mozart's ears—became the opera's powerful opening as well.

PIANO CONCERTOS

Mozart's favorite genres were opera and the piano concerto. Opera naturally fascinated him because it brings music to full, three-dimensional life in the voices and actions of real people—people who, in many instances, were personally known to him. But a piano concerto is also a kind of theater, in which the pianist is the star. Concertos are a highly personal medium as well—particularly so in Mozart's case, since he himself was the intended soloist for most of them. Yet unlike the pugilistic concertos of the nineteenth century, here there is no conflict between soloist and orchestra, no vying for the limelight; the atmosphere is collaborative rather than combative.

The themes in Mozart's concertos often remind you of those you've heard in his operas. This is because so much of his music is grounded in musical gesture—melodies, rhythms, harmonies, or sudden shifts from loud to soft that suggest, evoke, or even choreograph specific human actions,emotions, or patterns of speech.[28] Gestures range from walking or running to sighing, moaning, laughing, drawing a sword, marching, screaming, saluting, bowing—the possibilities are endless. This does *not* imply that the music tells a story, only that it is peopled with gestures translated into music. A characteristic tune or rhythm can make you think that Figaro just walked into the room, or Susanna or Leporello. Once you start listening to Mozart's music with an ear for this language—which he uses constantly—you are in for a rich experience. Before you realize it, a concerto's exchanges between piano and orchestra start to bear an uncanny resemblance to actual dialogue. Although this may sound far-fetched, it is a fact. The more of his music you know, the richer it becomes. And while gestures permeate all of his music, the kinship between concerto and opera—because they are both theatrical—is especially close.

Before Mozart, the piano concerto was not a major genre; he brought it to center stage. The piano came of age in his hands, and so did the piano concerto. He wrote twenty-three concertos in all, not counting some precocious childhood works that were actually arrangements of other composers' music. As mentioned earlier, the traditional numbering yields twenty-seven, but this includes those arrangements. In this book, to avoid confusion, numbers will not be used—only K numbers and keys.

The concerto's ancestors (think of Bach's Brandenburg Concertos or the concertos of Vivaldi) were written before sonata form had evolved. The idea then was thematic alternation between the *orchestra* (designated *tutti*, meaning "everybody") and the *soloist* (or soloists, in the case of the Brandenburgs). There were generally five tuttis, which left four sections for the soloist:

Tutti–Solo–Tutti–Solo–Tutti–Solo–Tutti–Solo–Tutti

In contrast, the formal design for first movements in Mozart's day—sonata form—was based, not on an *alternation* of themes, but on thematic *change* (the Development section), leading to *resolution* (the Recapitulation). How could these two opposite principles be reconciled?

The solution was arrived at by Mozart more than by anyone else. It was a compositional merger, *grafting sonata form onto the tutti-solo idea*. We've already heard the resulting format in the first movement of the Sinfonia concertante in E-flat Major for violin and viola, K. 364/320d.

---

28. See also "gesture" in the glossary. Music of this period was a language of gestures, instantly recognizable to everyone in that era, composers and audiences alike. The path-breaking study of Mozart's use of gesture is Wye Jamison Allanbrook, *Rhythmic Gesture in Mozart: Le nozze di Figaro and Don Giovanni* (Chicago and London: University of Chicago Press, 1983).

How did it work? There are still five tuttis and four appearances of the soloist, as in the old scheme. Fused onto that is a slightly altered version of sonata form, with two Expositions, an Orchestral Exposition and a *different* Solo Exposition, followed by a Development, Recapitulation, and Coda. Interrupting the Recapitulation is a gala appearance by the soloist called a *cadenza*, which explores in improvisatory fashion any or all of the preceding themes, including some virtuosic fireworks, the whole thing lasting only a minute or so. During the cadenza the orchestra remains silent. In Mozart's day (and with increasing frequency today), cadenzas were improvised on the spot. The result, called *concerto first-movement form*, is diagrammed below. You saw the same diagram in our discussion of the Sinfonia concertante, K. 364/320d.

Second (slow) movements in Mozart's concertos explore a variety of designs—rondo, ABA, or variation form.

Third movements are usually rondos, though the finale of K. 491 is in variation form. The third movement also may include a cadenza; if so, it occurs just before the coda, as it does in first movements.

Concerto First-Movement Form

Orchestral Exposition	A – transition – B &/or C (not repeated) ends with tutti
Solo Exposition	A (or new theme) – bridge – B &/or C (or can be all new themes) (not repeated) ends with tutti
Development	short; dominated by soloist
Recapitulation	starts with tutti return to main key; all themes now in this key; ends with tutti.
cadenza	played by soloist alone (no orchestra)
Coda	tutti

In establishing this form as the gold standard, Mozart made solo piano concertos a leading genre for the first time and from 1782 through 1786 earned a good deal of his income from them. This was exciting, it was new, and he was a brilliant pianist. On at least one occasion, he performed a piano part that was as yet unwritten: he just made it up as he went along.

Beginning in 1785 and continuing into 1786, Mozart was engrossed in a new and innovative opera, *The Marriage of Figaro*. During spring 1786, he also wrote three piano concertos for a series of concerts: the Concerto in E-flat Major, K. 482, the Concerto in A Major, K. 488, and the Concerto in C Minor, K. 491.

CONCERTO FOR PIANO AND ORCHESTRA IN C MINOR, K. 491

The C-minor concerto dates from March 1786, two months before the premiere of *The Marriage of Figaro*. This was one of only two concertos he wrote in minor keys; the other, from 1785, is in D minor (K. 466). These two were Beethoven's favorites, and he not only performed them many times (supplying his own cadenzas for both of them) but actually modeled his own Piano Concerto No. 3, Op. 37, which was also in C minor, on Mozart's K. 491.

Mozart gave tempo indications to only one of this concerto's three movements, the second, which he marked *larghetto* (somewhat slow). Since first and last movements are, with rare exceptions, both fast—in this instance, the first perhaps a bit quicker than the third—tempo markings aren't really needed; but editors have added the words *allegro* and *allegretto*, respectively, as a guide to performers. The Allegro is in *concerto first-movement form*, as expected; the Larghetto is a *rondo* (you can write slow rondos as well as fast ones; recall the rondo finale to Violin Concerto, K. 216); and the Allegretto finale is in *variation form (theme and variations)*.

The *first movement* is not only in a minor key but also in triple meter, a meter Mozart used for the first movement of only one other concerto (K. 449). After a tense orchestral exposition with *three* different themes, the piano—ignoring or defying everything the orchestra has played— introduces its own three themes, making a total of six for us to keep track of. One of the hallmarks of Mozart's concertos is their melodic profusion—so much thematic material you can't keep it all in your head. He also delighted in exploiting solo woodwinds ever since his experience in Mannheim. Both the second and third themes of the solo exposition (**E** and **F**) are accompanied by elegant melodic figures in the winds. Happily, despite the number and coloristic variety of themes, once you get your bearings in this movement the form becomes crystal-clear, the overall design revealing itself as not only straightforward but somehow inevitable.

Development sections in Mozart's concertos are generally short. This one begins, not with one of the orchestra's themes, but with **D**, the first of the new ideas introduced by the soloist. Actually this is logical, since concerto development sections are dominated by the soloist. As in all of Mozart's concertos written after 1782 (i.e., after he began spending Sunday mornings at the Baron van Swieten's), this one features a notably contrapuntal development section. With the arrival of the recapitulation, the orchestra again takes charge, at least at the outset, by restating the **A** theme.

Mozart wrote out no cadenza for this movement—not even shorthand notes, as he sometimes did. The soloist must supply his or her own cadenza, either making one up or (as is often the case) checking one out of the library, where you can find volumes devoted to cadenzas for concertos by Mozart and other composers, written by famous pianists of the past and by some composers as well, notably Beethoven. In addition to lacking a cadenza, this movement presents the soloist with another oddity: Mozart ignored his own custom of allowing the orchestra to perform its final tutti alone and undisturbed. Instead, the piano plays softly all through it, right to the end of the movement. The delicate close to what began as an angry, tense movement is one of this concerto's ineffable moments.

■ Piano Concerto in C Minor, K. 491
(Vienna, 1786)

For 1 flute, 2 oboes, 2 clarinets, 2 bassoons, 2 horns, 2 trumpets, timpani, and strings

1. Allegro (concerto first-movement form, minor key, triple meter)

Orchestral Exposition							
	35"	1'06"	1'20"	1'35"	1'58"		
A a,b a = rising notes of chord b = sharp jagged rhythm	transition	B woodwinds; begins with 3 repeated notes	A a,b	C	A b only		
Solo Exposition							
2'08"	2'34"	2'56"	3'11"	4'18"	4'45"	5'41"	
D new theme; piano alone	A (a,b) piano plays only b	bridge	E piano, then woodwinds (major key)	F oboe, other woodwinds, then piano	A (a) solo flute above piano doodles	tutti	
Development							
6'03"	6'39"	7'04"					
D piano's new theme	A tutti	Series of loud tuttis answered by piano runs					
Recapitulation							
7'42"	8'17"	8'43"	9'13"	9'33"	9'59"		
A (a,b) tutti and piano	F led by piano	E led by piano	A b only	B piano	A (a,b) tutti		
Cadenza (piano alone): 10'20"							
Coda (tutti joined by piano: 10'53" – end							

Larghetto (rondo form, major key, duple meter)

A (major key)			52"		1'11"
	a	a	b		a
	piano alone	tutti	piano + woodwinds, especially bassoon		
B (minor key)	1'29"				
A (brief reprise)	3'01"				
C (also minor)	3'23"				
	Listen for the pedal point (a sustained note) played by horn, cello, and double bass from 4'42" to 4'53"				
A	4'54"				

2. Larghetto (rondo form, major key, duple meter)

3. Allegro (theme and variations, minor key, duple meter)

See if you can follow this! There is a surprise appearance of a pastoral section in triple (actually, compound) meter about two-thirds of the way through.

Timings based on Peter Toperzcer, [modern] piano, Latislav Slovák, cond. Point Classics 26721262, n.d.

■ Piano Concerto in E-Flat Major, K. 482

(Vienna, 1785)

For 1 flute, 2 clarinets, 2 bassoons, 2 horns, 2 trumpets, timpani, and strings

Whereas C minor is the main ("tonic") key of K. 491 and is therefore used for both opening and closing movements, its related major key, E-flat major, is used for the slow movement.[29] In K. 482 the tonic key is E-flat, which puts the slow movement in C minor.

2. Andante (theme and variations, triple meter, minor key)

0'00"	**Theme**	Muted strings in soft, hesitant phrases, like sighs; a radical darkening of mood after the cheery first movement.
1'12"	**Variation I**	The piano plays a languidly elaborated version of the Theme. Toward the end, strings quietly join in.

---

29. For major and minor keys, "relative major" and "relative minor," see Appendix E, "Notes for Musical Beginners."

2'22"	**Variation II**	Woodwinds only (flute, clarinet, bassoon, horn—there are no oboes in this concerto).
3'23"	**Variation III**	Piano, with rapid arpeggios[30] in the left hand; occasional light accompaniment from the strings.
4'32"	**Variation IV**	Changes to a major key, with a delightful duet for flute and bassoon.
5'23"	**Variation V**	Back to C minor; stark, majestic challenges from the orchestra, gentle responses from the piano.
7'40"	**Coda**	Quiet piano arpeggios backed by soft woodwinds lead to a blissful close.

This second movement, though clearly written in variation form, also has a large-scale A-B-A design because the switch to major keys with the bright duet for flute and bassoon occurs right in the middle of it; on the other hand, the movement's alternation between piano and (especially) woodwinds gives it the feeling of a rondo as well. However you hear it, this is a poignant yet serenely classical movement. At the premiere, the audience was so moved by this andante that they demanded to hear it again.

3. Allegro (rondo form, triple meter, major key)
The Allegro finale, though also in triple meter,[31] is light-footed, quick, and energetic: a rondo in the idiom of a country dance (as opposed to the more aristocratic minuet). Like the concerto as a whole, this Allegro is bursting with star turns for woodwinds—solo runs and pirouettes, graceful duets, sweet four-part harmonies, everything a wind player could dream of. No other composer for a long time afterward challenged and delighted great woodwind players the way Mozart did.

There are *three* cadenzas: one a little past four minutes into the movement, a second about two and a half minutes after that, and the third perhaps three minutes after that. Since Mozart wrote out none of them, each pianist—as is also true for K. 491 and numerous other concertos—must

---

30. For a definition of *arpeggio*, see the glossary. Briefly, the term refers to chords whose notes are played, not all at once, but one at a time.
31. More accurately, it is in compound meter (6/8), but you can certainly hear this movement in threes as well as in sixes.

either compose or improvise his or her own, or consult those written and handed down by earlier soloists. Not quite halfway through this ten-minute movement, right after the first cadenza, the music shifts into a *different* triple meter (3/4 this time) and slows down to half the previous tempo (the new marking is *andantino cantabile*, "a little slow, and as if singing"). This interruption comes in the form of close harmony from two clarinets, two bassoons, and two horns. Soon the piano enters, and the section closes with soft strings playing *pizzicato* (plucking rather than bowing). The second cadenza follows, leading to a return of the original tempo, meter, and rondo theme. The final, third cadenza precedes a jolly coda.

Timings based on Robert Levin, fortepiano, Christopher Hogwood, cond. L'oiseau-lyre
452 052-2.©1999

SYMPHONIES

For Mozart, symphonies were neither the compositional bread and butter they were for Haydn (who wrote 104 of them), nor the intense personal outpourings they would become for Beethoven (who composed only nine, though he sketched a tenth). Still, it seems odd that, in a city boasting outstanding orchestral musicians, he wrote only six symphonies in these ten years. Why so (relatively) few? The probable reason is lack of that necessary commodity mentioned so often in this book: *commissions.* To survive, a composer has to be paid. In the 1780s, one hoped to be asked for a composition or group of compositions by a publisher, a rich patron, a friend, an organization, or a theater's management—perhaps encouraging their generosity through written or oral hints. Mozart sometimes set up his own concerts during this period, and he had varying luck at it. For the first few years, attendance numbers held strong; by the late 1780s, however, the numbers grew smaller. Such concerts featured one or more symphonies, one or more concertos, and a few arias by leading singers. Some of the music was freshly composed and all the rest both current and familiar—unlike today's "classical" concerts, which often restrict themselves to museum pieces, with little or nothing contemporary. Not back then!

Mozart's symphonies from this period include the "Haffner," K. 385, based on his earlier "Haffner" Serenade, K. 250, written to honor his Salzburg friend Sigmund Haffner; the "Linz," K. 425, composed in that Austrian city en route to Vienna; the "Prague," K. 504, and the "final three": K. 543, K. 550, and the "Jupiter," K. 551. The circumstances and possible performances of the "final three" remain unclear, as we shall see.

Opening pages of Mozart's thematic catalog, in which, beginning in 1784, he kept a record of works he had composed (the entire catalog is accessible at www.bl.uk/onlinegallery).

THE "PRAGUE" SYMPHONY

Mozart's "Prague" Symphony was the next-to-last composition recorded in the composer's thematic catalog for 1786. His final work that year was a concert aria (an aria for voice and orchestra that stands alone, rather than being part of an opera) for Nancy Storace, who had created the role of Susanna in *The Marriage of Figaro*. Madame Storace and her composer brother, Stephen Storace, were about to move back to England and wanted the Mozarts to go with them. She promised the composer great success with London audiences. Michael Kelly (who had sung Basilio and Don Curzio in *The Marriage of Figaro*) and Mozart's pupil Thomas Atwood were part of the journeying group as well, and the composer, declaring himself an "Arch-Englishman," was excited at the prospect, even studying English for several months (his textbook was in his library at his death). But Leopold refused to babysit for the children—How long will they be gone? he must have wondered. What if they never come back? So everyone else took off and the Mozarts stayed home.

Just before that, Mozart was invited by his favorite city, Prague, to bring *The Marriage of Figaro* there and, while he was in town, to play a series of concerts. If he couldn't travel to England, at least he could spend time in the company of good friends, excellent musicians, and warmly responsive audiences in a city whose people adored him. In the end, *Figaro* proved such a sensation in Prague that he was commissioned to write a new opera for the following season; this was to be *Don Giovanni*, his second collaboration with Lorenzo da Ponte.

The new symphony Mozart wrote for the occasion, known ever since as the "Prague," has only three movements, like the "Paris"; in both cities, audiences preferred it that way. Also like the "Paris" is the brassy scoring with trumpets and timpani, but this time, no clarinets—perhaps because Anton and Joseph Stadler, Mozart's friends as well as his favorite clarinetists (and basset hornists), were unavailable for this trip.

The "Prague" Symphony's three movements are all in sonata form. The first opens with a slow introduction—one of the few times Mozart began a work this way. In Haydn's late symphonies, slow introductions were the norm; all twelve of his "London" symphonies (Nos. 93–104) employ them, but for Mozart they were rare. The solemn, mysterious, minor-key prelude of the "Prague" lasts over three minutes before sliding almost imperceptibly into the quiet, repeated-note first theme. (Incidentally, symphonic introductions are usually not repeated when the Exposition comes around the second time.) The finale of the "Prague" surely brought the audience to its feet, because the first theme is a refashioning of the prestissimo Act

II duet of *Figaro*'s Susanna and Cherubino, just before he leaps out the window and crashes into the garden below—a stunning conclusion to a symphony for *Figaro*'s favorite city!

■ SYMPHONY IN D MAJOR, K. 504, "PRAGUE"
(Premiere: Prague, 1787)
For 2 flutes, 2 oboes, 2 bassoons, 2 horns, 2 trumpets, timpani, strings

1. Adagio [Introduction] – Allegro (sonata form, major key, duple meter)

Introduction: slow, solemn, modulates between major and minor; very long!			
Exposition			
A	Bridge	B	Closing
repeated-note theme, syncopated, then oboe; circles back to A, which becomes the Bridge	(based on A)	violins; restated in minor; then feathery	soft; returns to A
3'04"		4'49"	5'35"

Exposition	**Development**	**Recapitulation**	**Coda**
(repeat begins)	weirdly airy, then contrapuntal; near close, a pedal point leads to…		
6'12"	9'20"	11'15"	13'07"

2. Andante (sonata form, major key, compound meter)

Exposition			
A	Bridge	B	Closing
graceful, chromatic ascent at end	poignant violin theme echoed by cellos	minor key; with ornamentation	A theme returns, at first with horn drone
		1'08"	2'10"

Development	**Recapitulation**
begins with sighs; dissonant, contrapuntal	
7'21"	9'48"

3. Presto (sonata form, major key, duple meter)
The main theme is based on the duet of Susanna and Cherubino in Act II of *The Marriage of Figaro*, "Aprite, presto, aprite."

Timings based on Sir Charles Grove, conductor, English Sinfonia. IMP Classics
PCD 892 [n.d.]

■ **SYMPHONY IN C MAJOR, K. 551, "JUPITER"**
(Vienna, 1788)

For reasons that have never come to light, Mozart in midsummer 1788 wrote three symphonies in quick succession, finishing them off in just under two months. We don't know why he did this or where he expected they would be performed, though he surely didn't compose them without a concrete plan in mind—Mozart never wasted valuable time writing into thin air. We just don't know what his plan was. These were the last works he was to write in this genre, though of course such a thought never entered his mind. He was thirty-two years old and had no idea that in three years he would be dead.

These three symphonies are all quite extraordinary:

- Symphony in E-flat Major, K. 543
- Symphony in G Minor, K. 550 (not to be confused with K. 183/173dB, the "Little G-Minor")
- Symphony in C Major, K. 551, later given the nickname "Jupiter"

During the summer of 1788 Mozart found himself—not for the first time in his life—in financial straits. Although the life of a freelance musician is always unpredictable, his available income seems to have spiraled downward around this time. At this point in our study of him we realize that he was not a pauper—the image of a starving Mozart is sheer myth; still, there were times when the cash level dropped. There could have been various explanations for this—increased expenses, unpaid debts, Constanze's medical expenses; we don't have sufficient facts to say more.

Actually, though, 1788 was a tough year for nearly everyone in Vienna. Mozart was hardly the only person—certainly not the only musician—trying to make do. Economic realities being what they were, why then, in the middle of the summer—when potential patrons were away from the city enjoying themselves at their country estates—why did Mozart pick this moment to turn out a trio of symphonies? There are three possible reasons, all of them having some basis in fact:

- He again dreamed of going to England, and perhaps thought of taking along some new symphonies.

- He was planning to schedule concerts of his music in Vienna.[32]
- He could maybe cobble together a series of subscription concerts with these works as come-ons, reestablishing himself in the public eye as a composer not just of operas, but also of large-scale instrumental works.

We do not know the answer; especially because of the absence of correspondence following his father's death the previous year, we are lacking a crucial source of information.

The "Jupiter" Symphony, the last of the trio, is at once the most complex, the most boisterous, and the loudest of the three; yet at the same time, it's deadly serious. Mozart revels in his fluency with counterpoint—the whole symphony is a polyphonic masterpiece—but this flamboyant display exists side by side with an almost religious quietude. All these qualities come together most exuberantly in the last movement, the densest and most complicated symphonic movement he ever wrote.

The finale, in sonata form, is at the same time also a fugue, an elaborate and extended kind of counterpoint, for which Mozart's model was J. S. Bach. See if you can recognize four of this movement's themes (there are seven in all) as you hear them. This is not easy, because they fly by at lightning speed:

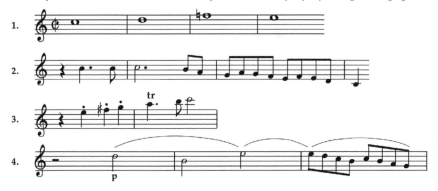

Themes from the "Jupiter" finale

---

32. An undated Mozart letter to Michael Puchberg from sometime in 1788, perhaps even 1787, may refer to such concerts. Scholars offer differing scenarios for the likely date of the letter and for which concerts—in Vienna or elsewhere—Mozart may have intended these symphonies. For a summary of their arguments up to the date of her book, see Elaine R. Sisman, *Mozart: The "Jupiter" Symphony* (Cambridge, UK: Cambridge University Press, 1993), 21–27. A very different scenario is proposed by Konrad Küster, *Mozart: A Musical Biography*, trans. Mary Whittall (Oxford, UK: Clarendon Press, 1996), ch. 33. Dexter Edge, in an unpublished essay, argues that "there is no known independent documentation of [a 1788 concert] series ... and no good reason for associating the undated letter with the last three symphonies" (private communication). For the letter, see Anderson, 914–15, where it is dated "June 1788."

CHAMBER MUSIC

In the eighteenth century, music was divided into three broad categories:

- Church music
- Theater music
- Chamber music

Composers were expected to become fluent in all of them. As you may remember, eighteenth-century musicians didn't think of themselves as "geniuses"—above the rest of us and therefore able to pick and choose what they would or wouldn't write—but as masters of their craft, which required mastering every aspect of it.

Chamber music was instrumental music to be played in a "chamber" of almost any size—someone's living room, the music salon of an aristocrat's mansion or palace, or a public concert venue. Today, the term refers to works for a small group of instruments. But in the eighteenth century it included almost any composition that wasn't classifiable as church music or opera:

- Piano sonatas (these were not considered concert-hall music, but were for home use)
- Piano-ensemble music (piano plus other instruments)
- String ensembles (from duets on up)
- String-plus-wind ensembles
- Symphonies
- Concertos

There are two surprises here. First, purely wind ensembles are excluded because such music was usually performed outside, for acoustical reasons, although Joseph II, for his after-dinner entertainment, fostered a new genre of woodwind music called *Harmoniemusik,* most of which was played indoors. The second surprise is that symphonies and concertos *are* included—because orchestras were still quite small, with anywhere from twelve or fifteen players to something in the mid-twenties, sometimes higher. As they expanded to forty or fifty players, rented halls began to be used more often than living rooms. All these developments took place over a period of years, but as they unfolded, the whole face of music making changed radically.

JOSEPH HAYDN AND THE STRING QUARTET

The leading genre of chamber music was unquestionably the string quartet,[33]

---

33. A string quartet = two violins (which play different music), a viola, and a cello. "String quartet" describes both the musical genre and the musicians (a quartet of string players) who perform it.

which had virtually been invented by Joseph Haydn (1732–1809) during the 1770s. Over the course of his life Haydn wrote eighty-three such works. Mozart, still in his teens as Haydn was bringing this genre to its zenith, knew that in order to master it, he would have to measure up to Haydn's towering achievement.

String quartets are structurally identical to symphonies and sonatas: four (sometimes three) movements employing the formal designs customary in instrumental music:

> *First movement:* on the fast side (in sonata form, with or without a slow introduction)
> *Second movement:* slow (often in ABA form, or sonata form)
> *Third movement:* a dance form (most often a minuet)
> *Fourth movement:* fast (usually in rondo or variation form, or sonata form)

What's different about string quartets—and, in fact, nearly all solo or small-ensemble genres—is that their gestures are usually more compact and faster-changing than those of a symphony. Orchestral music, even when written for a chamber-size group, is conceived in broader strokes. For this reason, you may find symphonies easier to follow than quartets.

Mozart's "Haydn" String Quartets (1782–1785)

The six "Haydn" quartets (so-called because they were dedicated to Haydn) were composed over a span of almost three years. Think about it: this is the same man who wrote whole operas in a couple of months and dashed off three symphonies in a matter of weeks.[34] As he confessed in his flowery, affectionate dedication, these quartets cost him "long and arduous work." For evidence we have autograph manuscripts that plainly show signs of sweat.

These six quartets were first heard in Mozart's Vienna apartment during Leopold's ten-week visit in 1785, with Haydn himself as guest of honor and sole audience member. In Mozart's opinion—which was correct—Haydn was the only composer in Europe who was his equal; in string-quartet writing, his superior. The performers that evening were Leopold Mozart, first violin; his son, second violin; and two friends of the composer, fellow Freemasons, playing viola and cello. The evening went off splendidly. Leopold proudly reported in his letter to Nannerl that Haydn had said to him, "I tell you before God, as an honest man, that your son is the greatest composer I know, either personally or by name."[35]

---

34. Mozart wrote twenty-three string quartets in all, from K. 80 in 1770 to K. 590 in 1790.
35. Letter from Leopold to Nannerl, February 16, 1785.

When the "Haydn" Quartets were published a few weeks after that magical premiere, they were prefaced by this lengthy dedication, written in Italian:

To my dear friend Haydn:

A father who had decided to send his children into the world at large thought it best to entrust them to the protection and guidance of a famous man who fortunately happened to be his best friend as well. Behold here, famous man and dearest friend, my six children. They are, to be sure, the fruit of long and arduous work, yet some friends have encouraged me to assume that I shall see this work rewarded to some extent at least, and this flatters me into believing that these children shall one day offer me some comfort. You yourself, dearest friend, have shown me your approval of them during your last sojourn in this capital. Your praise, above all, encourages me to recommend them to you, and makes me hope that they shall not be entirely unworthy of your good will. May it please you, therefore, to receive them kindly and to be their father, their guide, and their friend. From this moment I surrender to you all my rights in them, but beg you to regard with leniency the faults that may have remained hidden to the partial eye of their father, and notwithstanding their shortcomings to preserve your noble friendship for him who loves you so dearly. Meanwhile, I am, with all my heart,

W. A. Mozart[36]

Of the six quartets in this set, the last is not only the most famous; for a long time it was also notorious. Its nickname, "Dissonance," comes from the adagio introduction that opens its sonata-form first movement. Once you hear this, you'll realize at once what the problem was. For two minutes of slow, weird, polyphonic[37] music, we can't even tell what key the piece begins in; it's minor, but in a succession of possibilities. People have described this Introduction as "mystical," "mysterious," or, less positively, "incoherent." The hue and cry about it erupted as soon as the quartets were published. People demanded to be sent "corrected" copies. But the music was correct to begin with. To listeners today, who've experienced Beethoven, Wagner, Bartók, Schoenberg, and heavy metal, these tortured few minutes may come across as relatively tame; but they can still singe your ears, more than two hundred years later.

After this introduction, the Exposition begins blithely, as if nothing

---

36. Translation by Alan M. Kriegsman in Zaslaw with Cowdery, eds., *The Compleat Mozart*, 264.
37. For a definition of the term *polyphony*, see the glossary.

ever happened, with an innocuous, lyrical theme **A** tossed from instrument to instrument in clear, unambiguous C major. The movement proceeds in normal fashion after that, with perky, buoyant themes.

The second movement is an andante, also in sonata form (though abbreviated, i.e., without a Development section), which is followed by a minuet and a final rondo.

When Haydn came to hear these quartets on February 12, 1785, the ink was barely dry on this one. Mozart had written its final notes the day before.

■ STRING QUARTET IN C MAJOR, K. 465, "DISSONANCE"
(Vienna, 1785)

1. Adagio [Introduction] – Allegro (sonata form, major key, duple meter)

Introduction	0'00"–2'03"				
Exposition					
‖: A	Bridge	B	C	Closing :‖	
2'04"	2'31"	3'00"	3'29"	4'07"	
Repeat					
4'34"	5'04"	5'31"	5'59"	6'37"	
Development (based entirely on the A theme)					
7"05"					
Recapitulation					
A	Transition	B	C	Closing	
8'31"		9'08"	9'37"	10'14"	
Coda	10'41"–end				

Timings based on Salomon String Quartet (playing on reproductions of Mozart-era instruments). Hyperion CDS 44001-3©1993.

■ QUINTET IN A MAJOR FOR CLARINET AND STRINGS, K. 581
(Vienna, 1789)

The Clarinet Quintet was composed for Mozart's Masonic friend Anton Stadler, who was also probably the best clarinetist in the Habsburg Empire. There were two Stadler clarinetists: Anton and his brother Johann. Anton preferred the instrument's lower, darker register—so much so that he manufactured a device to extend its range downward by four half-steps, creating the basset clarinet. It was for this new instrument that Mozart wrote not only this quintet but also the Clarinet Concerto, K. 622, and the accompaniment to a climactic aria in the opera *La clemenza di Tito,*

K. 621. Today these pieces are customarily played on normal clarinets, which requires some rewriting here and there to avoid the basset clarinet's lower notes. Wherever you hear a solo clarinet in Mozart's music from about 1782 on—in a symphony, a concerto, or an opera—imagine that you're listening to Mozart's gifted friend playing it.

The Clarinet Quintet has four movements: an Allegro in sonata form, a ravishing Larghetto in pastoral mode, with strings *con sordino* ("muted"), a Minuet with two trios, and for the finale, an Allegretto con variazioni. The finale's toy-march-like theme leads to four variations. The third is a kind of eighteenth-century tango in minor mode, followed by a fourth as bubbly as champagne; the movement concludes with a long, improvisatory-sounding coda.

Did you ever see the final, two-hour episode of *M*A*S*H*? Charles, the snobbish classical-music lover, teaches the first movement to Koreans, who play it on their folk instruments so movingly it breaks your heart.

CHURCH MUSIC

To hear the Mass in C Major, K. 317 ("Coronation"), from Mozart's Salzburg days alongside his unfinished Mass in C Minor, K. 427/417a, of 1782/3 is to experience the vast range of his church music. First, the "Coronation" Mass.

As a young composer, Mozart wrote a good deal of sacred music including Masses, Vespers, motets, and various sorts of instrumental music for religious ceremonies. Such works were expected from composers employed by a prince of the church, as both Leopold and Wolfgang Mozart were, first by Archbishop Schrattenbach and, after his death, by Archbishop Colloredo.

The Mozarts' laundry list of complaints against Colloredo included some that were valid. Empathy wasn't the archbishop's strong suit, and his manner could be dictatorial. But chief among his faults, from the Mozarts' point of view, was his reformist (i.e., Enlightened) concept of church music—which, in fact, conformed perfectly to the rules promulgated by Joseph II, whom they both admired. These rules specified that a Mass should last no longer than forty-five minutes and contain no solo arias and no fugues (elaborate counterpoint); above all, it should nurture a devotional atmosphere rather than drawing attention to itself.

At the same time, we need to understand that a solemn Mass on a major feast day—Easter, for example—might last well over an hour even without music. A queen's coronation or the installation of a prince-archbishop might take longer than that. So the Enlightenment came down hard on all aspects of the Catholic Church's pomp and ceremony—which also entailed radically scaling down the music. This, of course, frustrated composers. As Mozart wrote to his Italian mentor and friend, Padre Martini,

> Our church music is very different from that of Italy, all the more so because a complete Mass ... even the most solemn ones, during which the prince-archbishop himself presides, may not last more than three quarters of an hour. One needs particular training for this kind of composition; and furthermore it must be a Mass with all instruments—trumpets, timpani, etc.
>
> (Letter dated September 4, 1776)

Mass in C Major, K. 317 ("Coronation") (1779)[38]

Mozart's first assignment in 1779—right after his return from that complicated sixteen-month journey to Mannheim and Paris—was to write a full-length Mass for soloists, chorus, and orchestra, one that would fill Salzburg's massive cathedral with opulent music in a style befitting the splendor and joy of Easter Sunday, but lasting less than forty-five minutes. He managed to bring it in under thirty.

How did he do this?

- By treating the four soloists as a quartet—as a sort of mini-choir—rather than assigning arias to each of them (except for the Agnus Dei: see page 195).
- By replacing the traditional fugues that normally closed the Gloria and Credo with quick, sharp chords.
- By setting most of the words *homophonically* rather than *polyphonically*.

Homophony and polyphony are contrasting kinds of musical texture. When a choir sings words together—i.e., in the same rhythm and at the same time—the resulting texture is *homophonic* (from *homo*, "same"). Rhythmically, it sounds something like this:

sopranos:	Glory to God in the highest.
altos:	Glory to God in the highest.
tenors:	Glory to God in the highest.
basses:	Glory to God in the highest.

In polyphony (from *poly*, "many"), individual sections of the choir sing

---

38. This Mass acquired its nickname after its use for the coronation of Emperor Leopold II in 1791.

the words at *different* times. This means that you hear portions of the text first in one part of the choir, then in another, then still another—hypothetically, something like this:

sopranos:	Glory to God	in the highest.
altos:		Glory to God in the highest.
tenors:	Glory to God	in the highest.
basses:		Glory to God in the highest.

For the listener, homophony makes the words both distinct and understandable; it's a kind of choral recitation. From Mozart's point of view, setting words homophonically meant getting through a long text quickly. The fact that this Mass had to be over in forty-five minutes was a good reason to compose most of it homophonically. But that in no sense meant that the music is boring; quite the contrary.

When a composer sets the text of the Catholic Mass to music, the words are those of the Ordinary of the Mass. "Ordinary" means those texts recited (in this case, sung) in all Masses throughout the year except funerals, for which the Mass takes a somewhat different form (see the discussion of Mozart's Requiem later in this book). The Ordinary consists of the following sections, each of which becomes, musically, a movement:

Kyrie
Gloria
Credo
Sanctus
Benedictus
Agnus Dei

From its opening bars, the "Coronation" Mass sparkles with vivid orchestral colors and pulsating energy. The majestic rhythms of the Kyrie sound even more triumphant with the addition of brass and timpani. The Gloria explodes in a fast, dancelike triple meter, opposing choral tuttis to passages for vocal quartet and climaxing with dramatic solo-tutti exchanges at the final Amen. The Credo also opens with choral declamations, this time amid rushing violin figures and joyful blasts from brass and timpani.

Then, suddenly, there is a kind of quiet musical genuflection at the words "And he was incarnate by the Holy Spirit of the Virgin Mary, and was made man." Here, where worshippers were expected to kneel, the harmony shifts magically into a major key, as the solo quartet intones the words softly and slowly to the accompaniment of an angelic solo violin. The triple-meter Sanctus is marked *maestoso* ("majestically"), its strong rhythms underscored by brass and timpani. The Osanna ("Hosanna in the highest"), brisk and joyful, contrasts with the vocal quartet's gentler, duple-meter Benedictus ("Blessed is he who comes in the name of the Lord").

For the Agnus Dei ("Lamb of God, who takes away the sins of the world"), Mozart breaks into this Mass's format with a transcendent aria for soprano solo—in defiance of Colloredo's rules against solo display. Written in pastoral style,[39] this is Mozart's moving response to the image of Christ as the Lamb of God (Agnus Dei). Its languid tempo and triple meter, with pizzicato (plucked) cellos and basses supporting songful countermelodies for oboes and violins, seem to evoke a peaceable kingdom, where all is calm and the sins of the world are forgiven ("qui tollis peccata mundi"). Later, the composer employed very nearly identical music, changing its meter from triple to duple, for the Countess's moving aria in Act III of *The Marriage of Figaro,* "Dove sono."

■ MASS IN C MAJOR, K. 317, "CORONATION"
(Salzburg, 1779)
For soprano, alto, tenor, and bass soloists; chorus; 2 oboes, 2 horns, 2 trumpets, 3 trombones, timpani, organ, and strings

Kyrie

Kyrie eleison.	Lord, have mercy on us.
Christe eleison.	Christ, have mercy on us.
Kyrie eleison.	Lord, have mercy on us.

Gloria

Gloria in excelsis Deo.	Glory to God in the highest.
Et in terra pax hominibus bonae voluntatis.	And on earth, peace to people of good will.
Laudamus te. Benedicimus te.	We praise you. We bless you.
Adoramus te. Glorificamus te.	We adore you. We glorify you.
Gratias agimus tibi propter magnam gloriam tuam.	We give thanks to you for your great glory.
Domine Deus, Rex coelestis,	Lord God, heavenly King,
Deus Pater omnipotens,	God, the Father almighty,
Domine Fili unigenite, Jesu Christe,	Lord, the only-begotten Son, Jesus Christ,
Domine Deus, Agnus Dei, Filius. Patris	Lord God, Lamb of God, Son of the Father.
Qui tollis peccata mundi, miserere nobis.	You who take away the sins of the world, have mercy on us.
Qui tollis peccata mundi,	You who take away the sins of the world,

39. Mozart's pastoral music, a key feature of his mature style, seems inspired here by the image of lambs strolling in a green pasture. See "pastoral" in the glossary.

suscipe deprecationem nostram.
Qui sedes ad dexteram Patris,
miserere nobis.
Quoniam tu solus sanctus,
tu solus Dominus,
tu solus altissimus,
Jesu Christe,
cum Sancto Spiritu in gloria
Dei Patris. Amen.

receive our prayer.
You who sit at the right hand of the Father,
have mercy on us.
For you alone are holy,
You alone are the Lord,
You alone are most high,
Jesus Christ,
with the Holy Spirit in the glory of
God the Father. Amen.

Credo

Credo in unum Deum,
Patrem omnipotentem,
factorem coeli et terrae,
visibilium omnium et
invisibilium.
Et in unum Dominum Jesum
Christum,
Filium Dei unigenitum.
Et ex Patre natum ante omnia
saecula,
Deum de Deo, lumen de lumine,
Deum verum de Deo vero.
Genitum, non factum,
consubstantialem Patri:
per quem omnia facta sunt.
Qui propter nos homines
et propter nostram salutem
descendit de coelis.
Et incarnatus est de
Spiritu Sancto,
ex Maria Virgine: et
homo factus est.
Crucifixus etiam pro nobis
sub Pontio Pilato; passus
et sepultus est.
Et resurrexit tertia die
secundum Scripturas
Et ascendit in coelum,
sedet ad dexteram Patris.
Et iterum venturus est
cum gloria judicare vivos et
mortuos:
cujus regni non erit finis.
Et in Spiritum Sanctum,
Dominum et vivificantem:
qui ex Patre Filioque procedit,
Qui cum Patre et Filio simul
adoratur
et conglorificatur:

I believe in one God,
the Father almighty,
maker of heaven and earth,
and of all things visible and
invisible.
And in one Lord, Jesus
Christ,
the only begotten son of God.
And born of the Father before
all ages,
God of God, light of light,
true God of true God.
Begotten, not made,
of one substance with the Father:
by whom all things were made.
Who for us humans
and for our salvation
came down from heaven.
And was incarnate by the
Holy Ghost
of the Virgin Mary: and was
made man.
He was also crucified for us
under Pontius Pilate; he died
and was buried.
And he arose on the third day
according to the scriptures
and ascended into heaven,
and sits at the right hand of God the Father.
And he shall come again
with glory to judge the living and
the dead,
and his kingdom shall have no end.
And [I believe] in the Holy Spirit,
the Lord and giver of life,
who proceeds from the Father and the Son,
who like the Father and the Son is
adored
and glorified:

qui locutus est per Prophetas.	who spoke through the Prophets.
Et unam sanctam catholicam et apostolicam Ecclesiam,	And [I believe] in one holy catholic and apostolic church,
Confiteor unum baptisma	I confess one baptism
in remissionem peccatorum,	for the forgiveness of sins,
Et exspecto resurrectionem mortuorum	and I look for the resurrection of the dead
Et vitam venturi saeculi. Amen.	and the life of the world to come. Amen.

Sanctus

Sanctus, Sanctus, Sanctus,	Holy, Holy, Holy,
Dominus Deus Sabaoth.	Lord God of Sabaoth.
Pleni sunt caeli et terra gloria tua.	The heavens and earth are full of your glory.
Osanna in excelsis.	Hosanna in the highest.
Benedictus qui venit in nomine Domini.	Blessed is the one who comes in the name of the Lord.
Osanna in excelsis.	Hosanna in the highest.

Agnus Dei

Agnus Dei,	Lamb of God,
qui tollis peccata mundi,	who takes away the sins of the world,
miserere nobis.	have mercy on us.
Agnus Dei,	Lamb of God,
qui tollis peccata mundi,	who takes away the sins of the world,
miserere nobis.	have mercy on us.
Agnus Dei,	Lamb of God,
qui tollis peccata mundi,	who takes away the sins of the world,
dona nobis pacem.	grant us peace.

MASS IN C MINOR, K. 427/417A (*unfinished*)

About my moral commitment, yes, that's absolutely right;—it flowed out of my pen not unintentionally—I truly made that promise in my heart and really hope to keep it.—When I made it, my wife was still single— but the promise was easy to make because I was determined to marry her as soon as she recovered her health.—Time and circumstances have delayed our trip, as you yourself know;—but as proof that I really made that promise I have the score of half a mass lying here in hopes of getting finished.

(Letter to his father dated January 4, 1783)

This is all we know about Mozart's reasons for composing his monumental Mass in C Minor. The work was not commissioned, was performed only once in his lifetime—during the Salzburg visit alluded to here—and was never finished. Three years later, its two opening movements formed the basis for his cantata *Davidde penitente,* but that was for a nonliturgical, albeit Lenten occasion, and the words were not those of the Catholic Mass. Among his sacred works, this Mass looms as the largest in conception and easily the most flamboyant in style; yet its origins are far from clear.

While stating emphatically that he composed the work for personal reasons, the letter doesn't say what those reasons were. The "promise" bore some relation to Wolfgang and Constanze's upcoming visit to Salzburg (a city he hated), and his father was hounding him for repeatedly postponing that—hence Wolfgang's defensiveness ("Time and circumstances have delayed our trip, as you yourself know"). But to tease out more clarity than this would require access to letters we don't have. Most of what Leopold or anyone else sent him during his decade in Vienna is lost, as you may remember; of the scores of letters from his father, only one survives, perhaps by accident.

Examining this one isolated paragraph, it appears that he first had the idea for the Mass during Constanze's illness shortly before they were married in August 1782. That was when he "truly made that promise"—but to do what, exactly? To write a Mass celebrating her recovery; or to take her to Salzburg and introduce her to Leopold and Nannerl, presenting them with a new Mass to honor the occasion? Both, perhaps? There is still a third possibility. By the time he wrote this letter, Constanze was several months pregnant with their first child: Raimund Leopold would be born the following June and Mozart was ecstatic about it. Whatever the reasons behind this Mass, the fact that they were personal probably explains why he received no commission or remuneration—even though composing such an enormous work pro bono was egregiously impractical for a man whose music had to support himself, his wife, and, soon, their son.

Entrusting their baby to a nurse's care, the young couple arrived in Salzburg at the end of July. In his suitcase Mozart brought with him, in fact, only "half a Mass," the two movements already finished before he wrote that letter: the Kyrie and Gloria. Once in Salzburg, he worked on the first half of the Credo and the Sanctus. Some of the Mass's movements are not complete in copies that have come down to us, but a number of scholars dating back to 1901 have reconstructed them. Mozart never wrote the second half of the Credo or any of the Agnus Dei, though he later sketched ideas for the latter.

The Mass in C Minor was performed in Salzburg on Sunday, October 26, 1783, as Nannerl recorded in her diary entry for that day:

To Mass in St. Peter's, where my brother's Mass was performed. All the court musicians were there.

St. Peter's was (and is) a Benedictine abbey, some distance away from the cathedral, the seat of Archbishop Colloredo. Nannerl's statement that "all" the court's (i.e., the cathedral's) musicians came over to St. Peter's is astonishing. Granted, they were essential: the abbey had ten singers (five boys, five men) and ten instrumentalists. But if the court musicians were all at the abbey, who performed at the cathedral?

Equally unanswerable is the question of how Mozart's Mass could have been performed incomplete. The feast day of the abbey's second patron saint (the first being, of course, Saint Peter), Amand of Worms, was October 26. When this fell on a weekday, the Credo could be omitted; but in 1783 it was a Sunday, requiring musical substitutions for the Credo's second half and for the Agnus Dei. These might have been supplied from earlier works by Mozart or from works of other composers; the simplest solution would have been plainchant. We may never know what was done. Archival records in St. Peter's are silent about that day, and the Mass was never mentioned again in the (surviving) Mozart family correspondence.

This was the first such work Mozart had written since his Mass in C Major, K. 317 ("Coronation") (1779), and it is utterly unlike its predecessor. In fact, it violates every one of the regulations for sacred music promulgated by Emperor Joseph II (whose Enlightenment ideals and reform-minded government Mozart deeply admired) and, following the emperor's lead, Archbishop Colloredo (whom Mozart despised).

Although Mozart adhered more or less to these regulations in his "Coronation" Mass (there is a soprano aria, but a fairly short one), even managing to bring in the whole work in well under thirty minutes, for this new Mass he defied them all. Why did Colloredo allow it to go forward? Although as a Benedictine abbey St. Peter's was theoretically outside his jurisdiction, Colloredo held power over it as well; but he chose not to intercede, perhaps in the fanciful hope that such restraint might lure Mozart back into his service.

The C-minor Mass is exceptionally long—nearly equal, if complete, to Bach's Mass in B Minor or Beethoven's *Missa solemnis*. All three are considered liturgically unusable for this reason. Yet Mozart's rule-breaking went much further still, embracing every aspect of this work.

The orchestra is the largest he employed in any sacred composition, making those court musicians essential. The overall sonority is thicker and brassier than you may be accustomed to in his music because three trombones are added to horns and trumpets in pairs. Salzburg church music had traditionally reinforced the chorus's alto, tenor, and bass sections with trombones; but here they yield a total of seven brass parts. The absence of clarinets, a widely popular new instrument, is also surprising. By 1783 Mozart was writing regularly for them in orchestral works; later, for the virtuosic Anton Stadler, he composed the Clarinet Quintet, K. 581, and the Clarinet Concerto, K. 622. Salzburg, however, had no clarinets, which is presumably why there are none in this Mass.

During his five months in Mannheim in 1777 and 1778, the twenty-one-year-old composer had been thrilled by its superb orchestra, particularly its quartet of principal woodwind players. These musicians inspired him to incorporate soloistic wind parts into his own music—first in *Idomeneo* (1781), which in fact was written for that orchestra, and later in many other works including this Mass.

"Every Sunday at 12," Mozart wrote to Leopold in April 1782, "I go to Baron van Swieten's—and there nothing is played but Handel and Bach." Van Swieten, mentioned earlier in this book in connection with Mozart's visit to Leipzig in 1789 (see page 137), was a diplomat, a sophisticated musical amateur, and Joseph II's imperial librarian. He had previously served in Berlin as the Habsburg Monarchy's ambassador to Frederick the Great, where he acquired a taste for the music of Handel, Bach, and one of Bach's sons, Carl Philipp Emanuel Bach. Week by week, Mozart fell in love with this by then old-fashioned music. The first major work to demonstrate its impact is the Mass in C Minor, which is saturated from beginning to end with Handelian and Bachian counterpoint. Van Swieten later commissioned Mozart to update several of Handel's works to bring them in line with late eighteenth-century style. Best known today, from fairly frequent performances and recordings, is the Handel-Mozart *Messiah*, a marvelous blend of two interwoven musical styles.

A final violation of church-music regulations in the C-minor Mass is its extensive use of vocal soloists: soprano I and soprano II (each performing an aria in addition to their duet together), tenor (for a trio with the sopranos), and bass (for a quartet). We know that one of the sopranos was Constanze Mozart, as Nannerl records in her diary for Thursday, October 23:

> [Attended the] rehearsal of my brother's Mass, in which my sister-in-law sings the solos.

Like Bach's B-minor Mass and Beethoven's *Missa solemnis*, the Mass in C Minor is written "cantata style," which means that it divides the text of the Mass into brief segments, each of them provided with distinctive musical treatment. The result is an ever-changing musical tapestry—homophonic then polyphonic, solo then choral, minor then major, exuberant then mournful—as Mozart's music responds vividly and often phrase by phrase to words he had known by heart since boyhood.

The Kyrie opens with somber, plaintive, minor-key pleas for God's mercy before yielding to major keys for Soprano I's more confident prayer to the Son. This radiant "Christe eleison" bears such a resemblance to vocal exercises Mozart composed for Constanze the previous summer that it seems certain he wrote the first soprano part for her. Soprano II was probably one of Salzburg's two castratos, both of whom were close friends of the Mozart family and well regarded professional colleagues.

The Gloria, divided into seven sections, alternates dramatically—unsettlingly—between joy and sorrow. Following the chorus's jubilant opening, the "Laudamus" is a lightly scored, carefree operatic aria in old-fashioned ABA format. As always in his music, whether for soloists or for chorus, Mozart places melismas (vocal runs) with great care to highlight a single, important word: here, *glorificamus*. From this joyful aria, we are plunged first into the darkly driving rhythms of the "Gratias agimus tibi" and then into the "Domine Deus," a sunny duet for the two sopranos, and from that into a towering double chorus (i.e., sung by two four-part choirs), the "Qui tollis." Its intense, double-dotted rhythms, known to Mozart from both Handel's *Messiah* and French choral music, are joined to a repeating bass figure somehow reminiscent of music Mozart may also have known: the "Crucifixus" from Bach's Mass in B Minor. Bringing together these powerful, bygone gestures is of course no mere display of Mozart's compositional brilliance; its purpose is to portray graphically, almost physically, the scourging of Jesus before his crucifixion. The "Quoniam tu solus," a bright, contrapuntal trio for two sopranos and tenor, leads to the Gloria's triumphant, double-fugue conclusion, "Cum sancto spiritu." (A double fugue is a fugue with two "subjects"—musical themes—rather than one.)

The Sanctus is also a double chorus, though homophonic—a rarity in this Mass—as Mozart proclaims Isaiah's ancient invocation in solemn, brass-thick chords. The two settings of "Osanna in excelsis," surrounding the solo quartet's "Benedictus," are again polyphonic.

The Mass's most extended musical treatment is of "Et incarnatus est," the words with which Mozart's setting of the Credo ends. Recounting the miraculous birth of the Christ child, this aria for Soprano I is cast in what became, during his decade in Vienna, perhaps the composer's most distinctive idiom: the pastoral. This, too, had numerous models in Handel and Bach, among them "Come Unto Him" and the "Pastoral Symphony" (Pifa) in Messiah, an oratorio he knew intimately. He also draws again on his Mannheim experiences, calling for a woodwind trio of flute, oboe, and bassoon—here alluding to traditional pastoral instruments—to welcome the soprano's entrance with garlands of florid runs that seem to put us in mind of birds in paradise. The soloist—who most assuredly was Constanze—joins their song as soon as she arrives at the word Mozart emphasizes quite exorbitantly: *factus* ("made" or, in this case, "born"). The gentle 6/8 rhythms of a siciliana, an age-old type of Italian dance, here become a mother's lullaby. There seems no question that this aria, at once poignant and exultant, celebrates both the safe delivery of the Mozarts' baby boy and the birth of God's son.[40]

But there is a tragic ending to this story. Departing for Vienna the morning after the performance, Wolfgang and Constanze arrived home only to discover that Raimund Leopold had died of an intestinal infection. Apparently they had not been notified of this before.

■ MASS IN C MINOR, K. 427/417A (*unfinished*)
(Premiere: Salzburg, 26 October 1783)
For two sopranos, tenor, and bass; double chorus; flute, 2 oboes, 2 bassoons, 2 horns, 2 trumpets, 3 trombones, timpani, organ, and strings

Kyrie[41]
Kyrie eleison.	Lord, have mercy on us.

Soprano I:
Christe eleison.	Christ, have mercy on us.

Kyrie eleison.	Lord, have mercy on us.

Gloria
Gloria in excelsis Deo.	Glory to God in the highest.
Et in terra pax hominibus	And on earth, peace to people of
bonae voluntatis.	good will.

Soprano II:
Laudamus te. Benedicimus te.	We praise you. We bless you.
Adoramus te. Glorificamus te.	We adore you. We glorify you.
Gratias agimus tibi propter	We give thanks to you for
magnam gloriam tuam.	your great glory.

Sopranos I, II:
Domine Deus, Rex coelestis,	Lord God, heavenly King,
Deus Pater omnipotens,	God, the Father almighty,
Domine Fili unigenite, Jesu Christe,	Lord, the only-begotten Son, Jesus Christ,

---

40. Paul Corneilson describes this aria in similar terms while reaching different conclusions in his article, "Papa Mozart," in the *Newsletter of the Mozart Society of America: Special Edition on Mozart's 250th Birthday* (January 27, 2006), 4–5.
41. Portions of this Mass's text that Mozart did not set are in italics.

Domine Deus, Agnus Dei,
Filius Patris.

Lord God, Lamb of God, Son
of the Father.

Qui tollis peccata mundi,
miserere nobis.
Qui tollis peccata mundi,
suscipe deprecationem nostram.
Qui sedes ad dexteram Patris,
miserere nobis.

You who take away the sins of the world,
have mercy on us.
You who take away the sins of the world,
receive our prayer.
You who sit at the right hand of the Father,
have mercy on us.

Sopranos I and II, Tenor:
Quoniam tu solus sanctus.
tu solus Dominus,
tu solus altissimus,

For you alone are holy,
You alone are the Lord,
You alone are most high,

Jesu Christe,
cum Sancto Spiritu in gloria
Dei Patris. Amen.

Jesus Christ,
with the Holy Spirit in the glory of
God the Father. Amen.

Credo
Credo in unum Deum,
Patrem omnipotentem,
factorem coeli et terrae,
visibilium omnium et invisibilium.
Et in unum Dominum
Jesum Christum,

I believe in one God,
the Father almighty,
maker of heaven and earth,
and of all things visible and invisible.
And in one Lord,
Jesus Christ,

Filium Dei unigenitum.
Et ex Patre natum ante
omnia saecula,
Deum de Deo, lumen de lumine,
Deum verum de Deo vero.
Genitum, non factum,
consubstantialem Patri:
per quem omnia facta sunt.
Qui propter nos homines
et propter nostram salutem
descendit de coelis.

the only begotten son of God.
And born of the Father before
all ages,
God of God, light of light,
true God of true God.
Begotten, not made,
of one substance with the Father:
by whom all things were made.
Who for us humans
and for our salvation
came down from heaven.

Soprano I:
Et incarnatus est de Spiritu Sancto,
ex Maria Virgine: et homo factus est.

And was incarnate by the Holy Ghost
of the Virgin Mary: and was made man.

Crucifixus etiam pro nobis
sub Pontio Pilato; passus et
sepultus est.
Et resurrexit tertia die
secundum Scripturas
Et ascendit in coelum,
sedet ad dexteram Patris.

He was also crucified for us under
Pontius Pilate; he died and
was buried.
And he arose on the third day
according to the scriptures
and ascended into heaven,
and sits at the right hand of God the Father.

Et iterum venturus est	*And he shall come again*
cum gloria judicare vivos	*with glory to judge the living*
et mortuos:	*and the dead,*
cujus regni non erit finis.	*and his kingdom shall have no end.*
Et in Spiritum Sanctum,	*And [I believe] in the Holy Spirit,*
Dominum et vivificantem:	*the Lord and giver of life,*
qui ex Patre Filioque procedit,	*who proceeds from the Father and the Son,*
Qui cum Patre et	*who like the Father and the*
Filio simul adoratur	*Son is adored*
et conglorificatur:	*and glorified:*
qui locutus est per Prophetas.	*who spoke through the Prophets.*
Et unam sanctam catholicam et	*And [I believe] in one holy catholic and*
apostolicam Ecclesiam,	*apostolic church,*
Confiteor unum baptisma	*I confess one baptism*
in remissionem peccatorum,	*for the forgiveness of sins,*
Et exspecto resurrectionem	*and I look for the resurrection*
mortuorum	*of the dead*
Et vitam venturi saeculi. Amen.	*and the life of the world to come. Amen.*

Sanctus

Sanctus, Sanctus, Sanctus,	Holy, Holy, Holy,
Dominus Deus Sabaoth.	Lord God of Sabaoth.
Pleni sunt caeli et terra gloria tua.	The heavens and earth are full of your glory.
Osanna in excelsis.	Hosanna in the highest.

Sopranos I and II, Tenor, Bass:

Benedictus qui venit	Blessed is the one who comes
in nomine Domini.	in the name of the Lord.
Osanna in excelsis.	Hosanna in the highest.

Agnus Dei

Agnus Dei,	*Lamb of God,*
qui tollis peccata mundi,	*who takes away the sins of the world,*
miserere nobis.	*have mercy on us.*
Agnus Dei,	*Lamb of God,*
qui tollis peccata mundi,	*who takes away the sins of the world,*
dona nobis pacem.	*grant us peace.*

MOZART AND FREEMASONRY

Inducted into the Order of Freemasons on December 14, 1784, Mozart remained an active, committed Mason for the rest of his life—composing and conducting music for lodge meetings pro bono, contributing to his lodge's charities, and donating to the Masons proceeds from the music he wrote for them. It was on his recommendation that Joseph Haydn and Leopold Mozart joined the order. Leopold, initiated during his visit to Wolfgang and Constanze in April 1785, rose quickly to the rank of master Mason, as did his son.

Since Freemasonry was so clearly an outgrowth of the Enlightenment, it's no surprise to find among its adherents virtually every leading Enlightenment figure both in Europe and across the Atlantic in the American colonies: Goethe and Wieland in Germany; Rousseau and Voltaire in France; and George Washington, James Madison, Paul Revere, John Hancock, and Benjamin Franklin in what was to become the United States. In Josephine Vienna there were so many that wherever Mozart went—to a coffeehouse, a rehearsal, a concert, or a service in St. Stephen's Cathedral (members of the clergy were sometimes also Masons)—he found himself "virtually surrounded" by Brothers in the Craft.[42] Obviously, then, this was no mere fringe activity, but an intellectual, social, and philosophical movement that inspired the active involvement of a great many of the eighteenth century's most creative minds.

Freemasons were major architects of the American Revolution, planning its acts of protest, drafting its documents, and commanding the armies that brought it to victory. A Boston tavern where revolutionary ideas and tactics were fomented was also the site of Masonic lodge meetings. The chief authors of the Declaration of Independence, the Constitution, and the Bill of Rights were Masons, as were around 40 percent of the officers who served under General Washington. Both the Prussian officer von Steuben, who traveled from Prussia to help train Continental troops, and the Marquis de Lafayette, who was with Washington at Valley Forge and Yorktown, were Masons. In walking around the nation's capitol in Washington, you find Masonic symbols on nearly every corner, the largest and most visible being the Washington monument, a Masonic obelisk. It is no exaggeration to say that the Craft's ideals of egalitarianism, religious toleration, openness to other cultures, and freedom of thought—ideals Masonry shared with the Enlightenment—are engrained in the very foundations of American democracy.

Freemasonry traces its roots to the medieval guilds—to those skilled artisans, the stonemasons who built the great Gothic cathedrals. Toward the end of the Middle Ages, some guilds began accepting "speculative" masons, people who didn't actually build buildings but supported the guilds spiritually and financially. As time went on, such "speculative" masons began forming their own organizations, which eventually gave rise to modern Freemasonry. The first Grand Lodge was formed in England in 1717. From there the movement spread rapidly to other European countries, where, however, they very often did not find the door open to them.

Because the Order originated in England—a Protestant country

---

42. Braunbehrens, *Mozart in Vienna*, 241.

and worse, one governed by a parliamentary monarchy—Masonry was prohibited nearly everywhere else, since most other countries were not only Catholic but also ruled by absolute monarchs. Although Freemasonry was accused of being antimonarchical, Masons denied this, claiming they had no political agenda. In France, they were subjected to continual police harassment and forced to operate underground. Papal pronouncements against the Order, welcomed in Catholic Spain, had less effect in Catholic Vienna. Why? Surprisingly, Empress Maria Theresa's husband, Francis Stephen, was a Mason himself—though despite this, she did ban the Order in 1764. But in 1765, her son Joseph II became coregent with his mother, and he paid little attention to Rome's proclamations on any subject.

At first, Joseph allowed Freemasonry to exist and even expand, without censorship or interference, though he stopped short of publicly endorsing it. He appears to have admired its principles and probably hoped that, in return for a hands-off policy, its members might support his reformist agenda. For the most part, this worked. But as the years wore on and revolutionary fervor began to build, not only in France but, shockingly, in his own empire as well—his beloved Viennese were now accusing *him* of tyranny—Joseph finally had enough. In December 1785 he promulgated the Freemasonry Act, whose provisions, while not nearly as drastic as Rome would have liked, were threatening enough to send members fleeing from their lodges. Membership in the city collapsed from eight hundred to around two hundred. But the worst was yet to come: when his brother Leopold II succeeded him in 1790, the Craft was placed under constant surveillance, and after him, Francis II shut it down completely. Throughout most of Joseph's reign, however—which coincided with Mozart's decade in Vienna—Masonry was a central fact of Viennese intellectual, political, and social life.

What was it that made Masonry appear so dangerous to Rome and to Europe's rulers, most of whom were, like Joseph, "Enlightened"? First and foremost, lodges were governed democratically—a new and radical notion. Class structure was undermined: all brothers were equal—no one was master, no one servant. In Masonry, for the first time in any organization of the modern world, elected representatives drew up documents they called *constitutions*. Previously, this word referred solely to the physical makeup (the "constitution") of a person's body. Now it acquired its secondary meaning, one we take for granted today, as the setting forth of an organization's aims, policies, goals, and internal structure. Such documents were viewed by rulers as treasonable—as attacks on their "divine right" to create and enforce the laws of their realms.

But what did the Craft look like when viewed through the eyes of Masons?

Freemasons sought—and seek today—to mold themselves into moral and spiritual "temples" modeled on the biblical Temple of Solomon. They acknowledge the existence of a Supreme Being, though Masonry itself is not a religious movement. Indeed, members are urged to remain active in their own religious institutions, and discussions of religion are forbidden at lodge meetings. Nor may business be transacted or any sort of business contact initiated.

There are three "degrees" of membership: entered apprentice, fellow craft, and master Mason. Mozart was rapidly promoted to the highest degree.

The "three great principles" of Freemasonry are brotherly love, charity, and truth. Although none of this sounds threatening today, suspicion has followed the Masons from their founding nearly three hundred years ago right down to the present. Granted, there were many different types of lodges in the eighteenth century—even a few that welcomed women! Some were more politically aggressive than others, some more secretive, some more active in social welfare or charity.

What was the nature of Mozart's relationship to Freemasonry? Viennese Masonry differed in two key respects from practices elsewhere. First, its most influential lodge violated a cardinal Masonic principal by actively fostering political and social reforms. Second, some lodges were associated with esoteric spiritual movements, such as Rosicrucianism.[43]

Vienna's largest and most distinguished lodge was also the most overtly political. Its master was the eminent scientist Ignaz von Born, Vienna's most distinguished intellectual, who was a friend of Leopold Mozart and an admirer of Leopold's son. Born's lodge, True Concord (Zur wahren Eintracht), was known all over Europe as a hotbed of progressive ideas. But although Mozart often visited True Concord, he elected to join a smaller lodge with a younger and less aristocratic membership. Called "Beneficence" (Zur Wohltätigkeit), it was politically progressive as well, but more strongly identified with spiritual and charitable goals. It was one of the few to survive Joseph II's Freemasonry Act of 1785. Mozart himself was among the small number of well-known figures in Vienna who never wavered in their support of the Order—a stance requiring considerable courage on his part.

Music that Mozart composed for lodge meetings, a significant genre in his

43. Rosicrucianism, much older than Freemasonry, was a mystical brotherhood whose members believed that they possessed secret wisdom handed down from ancient sources. Their symbol was a rose on a cross.

oeuvre, includes cantatas, hymns, and chamber (small-ensemble) music. There is also his *Singspiel The Magic Flute* (1791), whose plot is loosely suggestive of a Masonic initiation rite—in which, however, not only the hero is initiated, but the heroine as well, something that would have been impossible almost anywhere. The role of the High Priest Sarastro may have been modeled on Ignaz von Born. Born died during the composition of *The Magic Flute,* and it is speculated that Mozart and his librettist Emanuel Schikaneder paid homage to his memory by portraying him as the High Priest.

A fact not widely known is that Mozart and his good friend and fellow Mason, Anton Stadler, for whom he wrote the Clarinet Concerto and the Clarinet Quintet, sketched ideas for a new Masonic lodge. Their plans do not survive—destroyed in 1790, probably, to avoid discovery after Leopold II clamped down on Masonry, inflicting punishments up to and including imprisonment. The new lodge was to be called "the Grotto." In Vienna, initiations were often conducted in grottoes, a popular feature of English gardens, and one of Europe's most spectacular grottoes was on the country estate of Count Cobenzl, Joseph II's vice chancellor, a deeply committed Mason, and a patron of Mozart. (A view of Cobenzl's estate is pictured on page 124.)

Finally, an important question to ask is whether Masonry served as a substitute religion for Mozart. This is hard to pin down, though it seems doubtful; nothing in his letters suggests any conflict between the two.

A Masonic initiation. Some believe that the figure seated on the extreme right is Mozart.

Freemasonry offered full expression to his idealism and his desire to be accepted as an equal. He coveted the friendships he formed there. And as an exceptionally, at times recklessly generous man, he responded to its ideals of brotherly love and charitable giving. But Catholicism was his religion and he practiced it. Most likely, both were essential to him.

In April 1787, Leopold Mozart was seriously ill, though his son didn't know that. In the letter below, after chatting about miscellaneous things for many lines—in his customary way—the composer suddenly gives expression to a fundamental article of Masonic belief, that life is only a pathway to death, "the true and ultimate purpose of our life." Both he and his father would have affirmed this.

LETTER TO HIS FATHER IN APRIL 1787

Vienna, April 4, 1787

Mon très cher Père![44]

It really distresses me that because of Madame Storace's stupidity my letter did not come into your hands.[45] —I wrote you, among other things, that I hoped you had received my last letter, but since you make no mention of it at all—it was my second letter from Prague—I don't know what to think; it is quite possible that one of Count Thun's servants thought it a nice idea to stick the postage money into his pocket. I would rather pay double postage than to know my letters are in the wrong hands. During Lent Ramm and the 2 Fischers came here—the bass and the oboist from London. If Fischer played no better when we knew him in Holland than he plays now, he certainly does not deserve his fame.—*But that is between us.*—I was too young then to be in a position to judge—I only remember that I liked him extraordinarily well, as did the whole world;—but this is quite natural when you consider that taste has changed enormously since then.—He plays according to an old school.—But no!—In a word, he plays like a miserable student. Young André, who studied with Fiala, *plays* a thousand times better—and then [Fischer's] concertos—of his own composition—every ritornello lasts a quarter of an hour—then the hero appears, lifts up one leaden foot after another, and bangs them down on the floor one after the other.—His tone is utterly nasal—and his sustained notes are like a tremolant on the organ; would you have imagined such a picture?—and it's nothing but the truth—but a truth I tell only *you.*—This minute I heard news that depresses me greatly—all the more so because I gathered from your last letter that you were, thank

---

44. "My dearest father" was Mozart's customary salutation to Leopold, always in French.
45. The Madame Storace Mozart refers to is not his friend, the soprano Nancy Storace, but her mother.

God, quite well;—but now I hear that you are really sick! I really don't need to tell you how I long to have a reassuring report from you yourself; and I certainly hope for it—though I have made it a habit to imagine the worst in all things—because death, properly understood, is the true and ultimate purpose of our life, I have over the last several years come to know this true, best friend of humankind so well that its image not only holds nothing terrifying for me anymore, but much that is soothing and consoling! And I thank my God that he has blessed me with the opportunity—you understand me—to come to perceive death as the *key* to our true happiness. I never lie down in bed without thinking that perhaps, as young as I am, I will not see the next day—and yet no one of all those who know me can say that I am moody or depressed in company—and for this happiness I thank my Creator every day and sincerely wish the same for all my fellow human beings.—I already wrote you my thoughts about this in the letter that Madame Storace packed with her luggage; these thoughts were occasioned by the sad death of my dearest and best friend, Count von Hatzfeld. He was just 31—like me—but I—I do not grieve for *him,* only for myself and for everyone who knew him as well as I did.—I hope and wish that, as I write this, you are feeling better; but if against all expectations you are not better, I ask you by . . . . . . [46] do not keep it from me, but write me the plain truth or have someone else write it to me, so I can be in your arms as quickly as humanly possible; I beseech you by all that's—sacred to us. However, I hope to receive a reassuring letter from you soon, and it is in this consoling hope that I, together with my wife and Carl [Thomas], kiss your hands 1,000 times and remain forever

your most obedient son
W. A. Mozart

Mozart's father died on May 28, 1787.

THE MAGIC FLUTE, K. 620 (*DIE ZAUBERFLÖTE*)
(Premiere: Vienna, September 30, 1791)
In July 1791 Mozart was working simultaneously on two different kinds of opera for two different cities—one for Prague, the other for Vienna—both with due dates in September. *La clemenza di Tito,* an opera seria, was commissioned for the coronation festivities for Emperor Leopold II, brother of the deceased Joseph II. *Tito* did not do well at the box office at first. However, it quickly grew quite popular and remained so for several

---

46. The ellipses are Mozart's own, and are unexplained.

decades before falling out of favor for well over a century, finally returning to the stage in the 1990s. *The Magic Flute* (*Die Zauberflöte*), written in the popular operatic genre known as *Singspiel*, was a success from the start, with more than twenty performances during its first month and over two hundred by 1800. It was Beethoven's favorite Mozart opera and Goethe planned a sequel to it; but it has long been the subject of widely varying interpretations.

What people disagree about is the most basic of questions: what is this opera about? Some productions play it as a comedy; others invest lavishly in its special effects; still others highlight its elements of fantasy, magic, and fairy tale, as Swedish director Ingmar Bergman did in his 1975 film version of the opera. *The Magic Flute* is all of the above—a comedy, a fantasy, a magic opera, and a fairy tale—and it is, moreover, laden from beginning to end with spectacular stage effects. Yet linking all these elements together is one central action: a journey toward enlightenment. Not the rational, cerebral Enlightenment of Immanuel Kant or the French *philosophes*, but inner, spiritual enlightenment: wisdom.

Singspiels, as you remember from *The Abduction from the Seraglio,* were comic or sentimental plays interspersed with lighthearted pop- or folk-style songs, all in the audience's own language, German. Unlike opera, dialogue was spoken rather than sung.[47] This, of course, lent itself to improvised ad libs, new ones every night, like live TV today. *Singspiels'* loosely hung plots were a mixture of sitcom-level comedy and rescue drama, often set in some exotic or imaginary locale. Vocal demands were relatively slight, since *Singspiels* were generally performed by actors rather than by operatically trained singers.

In 1778, as mentioned earlier, Emperor Joseph II had the noble idea of showcasing *Singspiel* at his Court Theater, the Burgtheater. Not only would this be much less expensive than opera, but surely, he thought, his German-speaking subjects would prefer spoken dialogue, simple plots, and lighthearted songs, all in German, to the pomp and high-wire vocalism of opera. He couldn't have been more wrong—they wanted full-dress opera in Italian.[48] Only one *Singspiel* filled the house: Mozart's *The Abduction from the Seraglio* (*Die Entführung aus dem Serail,* 1782), which not only made cash registers sing but brought its young composer to Vienna's attention.

---

47. Although *The Magic Flute* is a *Singspiel*, writers including this one commonly refer to it as an opera as well, as *Singspiels* are a type of opera.

48. The situation is very much the same today, with American opera audiences unaccountably yet overwhelmingly opposed to opera in English. Composers, on the other hand, have consistently approved, even urged, translation of their works into an audience's own language.

The venue for *The Magic Flute*, however, was the Freihaus-Theater auf der Wieden, a very different sort of house, just outside the city walls, which specialized in *Singspiel*, magic and fantasy operas, spoken comedies, and other light forms of entertainment. Mozart had known its manager, the experienced actor, singer, and director Emanuel Schikaneder, for over a decade. They had met in Salzburg, where Schikaneder's acting troupe was in residence for the season. He had played the title role in *Hamlet*, the first Shakespeare play Mozart ever saw and one that made a powerful impression on him.

In 1789 Schikaneder became manager of the Freihaus-Theater, and less than two years later he and Mozart collaborated on *The Magic Flute*. Schikaneder would serve as its producer, primary librettist, and second male lead. His theater was handsomely equipped for whatever opera or *Singspiel* required in the way of elaborate scenery, splendid costumes, and stage machinery, all of which would come in handy on this occasion.

As the action begins, we could be anywhere, anytime. The characters bear exotic names and seem a heterogeneous group, although as the story unfolds, they separate into two opposing realms, one ruled by the Queen of Night, the other by Sarastro, high priest of some sort of religious order.[49] There are also two parallel plots. The most important concerns Tamino, a Javanese prince,[50] who seeks to rescue Pamina, daughter of the Queen of Night, from Sarastro, a man the Queen describes as evil; she promises that if Tamino succeeds, he will win Pamina as his bride. A secondary, comic plot is about Papageno, a simple-minded birdcatcher sent along as Tamino's servant on his dangerous journey.[51] Tamino and Pamina, united after many adventures and trials, are rewarded with induction into Sarastro's priestly order. Papageno finds his female counterpart, Papagena, though he doesn't make it into the order because he fails the trials—a matter of no consequence to him, because all he wants is food, drink, and a wife. The Queen and her entourage are banished into eternal night just before the triumphant closing scene.

This plot—disregarding a few subplots, omitted here—is riddled with inconsistencies. At first, the Queen of Night is supposedly good and Sarastro evil; then we discover that he is noble, wise, and compassionate, which means it must be the Queen who is evil. Tamino, in a pivotal scene, agrees to undergo trials for admission into Sarastro's order; only after that

---

49. While the usual translation is "Queen of the Night," "Queen of Night" seems closer to the German *Königen der Nacht*.
50. Sometimes one sees "Japanese," but Javanese, which is correct, may have been chosen because no one knew where Java was.
51. The name Papageno derives from the German word for parrot, *Papagei*.

does he win Pamina. In fact, she leads him through the trials after almost committing suicide because his vow of silence had forbidden him to speak to her. At the end, they are initiated—both of them—and the Queen of Night is out of the picture entirely.

Many critics have simply given up trying to straighten this out, instead pointing to the libretto's sources. These are not only multiple but uncommonly complex: ancient and modern; Middle Eastern and European; fairy tales; medieval romances; Egyptian and Masonic rituals; a magic opera. How could the result be anything other than multi-layered and confusing? Yet there is a way to make sense of *The Magic Flute* if we approach it, not as pairs of opposites (light/dark, good/evil), with everyone being assigned to one or the other extreme, but as a progression from darkness toward light—from raw instinct and emotion to the wisdom born of spiritual enlightenment.

A Masonic motto is *lux ex tenebris,* "light out of darkness." Darkness, to Masons, signifies ignorance and untamed emotion, which lead to evil. The same understanding can be found in the Bible and in ancient Egyptian, Greek, and Roman religions. To dramatize it, Masonic initiations take place at night and with candidates' heads covered at the outset. *The Magic Flute* opens in darkness presided over by the Queen of Night. She and the characters in her domain—even Tamino as long as he is there—act purely on instinct. This does not make them evil, merely uninitiated and therefore ignorant. Sarastro's priestly realm is both orderly and sunlit—for the opera's final scene, "the whole stage is transformed into a sun." He and his priests act calmly, with foresight and compassion. Tamino's journey, shared in its climactic moments with Pamina, takes him from the darkness of ignorance to the light of wisdom; thus the opera dramatizes, in broad outlines, something like a Masonic rite of initiation. One very remarkable fact is Pamina's acceptance into the order. No Viennese lodge would have permitted that, but Schikaneder and Mozart quite evidently supported the idea.

The stage directions further underscore the ritual movement from dark to light. The Queen of Night's landscape is dark and unkempt, "a rocky area, overgrown here and there with trees," while we find Sarastro and his priests in "a palm grove," "a splendid garden," or "a pleasant garden with roses." There is particular emphasis on gardens.

As in *The Marriage of Figaro* and *Don Giovanni,* gardens in *The Magic Flute* are associated with serenity, quiet reflection, and wisdom. As mentioned earlier, during Joseph II's reign the Habsburg capital was sprinkled with examples of the new English garden, where instead of rigid geometry and bizarre topiaries, as in French gardens such as Versailles, one encountered meandering paths, undulating meadows, and plants and trees allowed to grow naturally. English gardens were also specifically identified with Freemasonry. Nearly all the builders of English gardens in both England and Vienna were Masons. Mozart and Schikaneder's association of spiritual enlightenment with open, inviting gardens bathed in sunlight, and ignorance with a dark, cluttered landscape, was directly and unmistakably Masonic, and members of the Craft would have immediately grasped that. This and other connections between *The Magic Flute* and Masonry seemed so obvious that Craft members in North Germany were outraged at the public unveiling of mysteries meant to be kept secret.

From the first notes of the Overture—a threefold, heraldic chord that we hear again later in the opera—*The Magic Flute* is obviously unlike anything Mozart or anyone else had written before. The sound itself is immediately striking and unusual. The standard orchestra of Mozart's time, which we have heard in work after work, was composed of these instruments:

2 flutes; occasionally, as here, a piccolo
2 oboes
2 clarinets (by 1791 these were standard)
2 bassoons
2 horns
2 trumpets, for festive or ceremonial works
timpani
strings (violins, violas, cellos, basses)

But what we hear now is mellower and more solemn, a sound suggestive of church music. Adding to this special sonority is the occasional, quite particularized use of basset horns and trombones, the two of them employed only whenever the threefold chord is sounded and in scenes involving Sarastro or his priests. Mozart had used basset horns—deeper, darker versions of the clarinet—as early as 1781, for his Serenade for Thirteen Instruments, K. 361/370a. But after he heard them at a lodge meeting in 1785 he included them in numerous Masonic compositions, and they may have begun to evoke that world for him. Trombones, associated with church music and, in opera, with the divine or supernatural, are employed only for the heraldic chords or in scenes with Sarastro, his priests, or the Three Boys. In similar fashion, trombones in *Don Giovanni* accompany the statue of the Commendatore (there are no basset horns in that opera). Viewed in this larger Mozartian context, the manner in which these instruments are used in *The Magic Flute* seems to suggest something more serious than a magic opera or a fairy tale.[52]

We hear other unusual sounds in this opera as well. Papageno accompanies his self-introductory aria in Act I on a panpipe, a simple folk instrument. Later he is given a glockenspiel ("silver bells" in the libretto), also a folk instrument. Tamino, an aristocrat, is given a magic flute to guard him from harm; flutes were pastoral instruments and associated with nobility. He plays it three times: when he is threatened by wild animals, when he is alone and frightened during the trials, and when, at the climax of his trials, Pamina leads him through the perils of fire and water.[53] As she explains to him, that flute, made by her father, possesses special power.

Even more so than *Don Giovanni*, *The Magic Flute* requires spectacular stage effects. The trick is to make them not just visually impressive but dramatically convincing and essential to the story. Here are major examples:

- The opera begins as Tamino is being chased by a monstrous serpent or dragon, a creature that must be genuinely frightening, not silly.
- The Queen of Night enters from a vast dark space behind the stage, severing a mountain into two parts, to the sounds of thunder and lightning.
- A group of wild animals becomes tame at the sound of Tamino's magic flute.
- The Three Boys (not trousers roles!),[54] who serve as spiritual guides, fly across the stage in a hot-air balloon large enough to contain themselves and a table set for dinner, proffered to the hungry Papageno (Tamino declines to eat during the trials). This astonishing scene was inspired by Jean-Pierre-François Blanchard's balloon flight in Vienna on July 6, 1791, seen by thousands and mentioned in Mozart's letter that day to Constanze.[55]
- Papagena, first presented to Papageno as an eighty-year-old hag,

---

52. David J. Buch argues that *The Magic Flute* is a fairy-tale opera with a few Masonic allusions in its libretto. See his "*Die Zauberflöte*, Masonic Opera, and Other *Fairy Tales*," Acta Musicologica 76 (2004): 193–219.

53. The number three is of symbolic significance in Freemasonry as in other contexts, for example, Christianity.

54. The role of the adolescent Cherubino in *The Marriage of Figaro* is intended to be sung "in trousers" by a woman (see pages 147 and 152). The "boys" here, however, are meant to be sung by boys with unbroken voices.

55. Blanchard also once took mail from England to France in his balloon, and on another occasion flew from Philadelphia to New Jersey, witnessed by President George Washington.

is transformed before his eyes into a beautiful eighteen-year-old dressed just like him, in a costume made of bird feathers.
- Tamino and Pamina's trials require them to walk through a rushing waterfall, then a stage engulfed in fire.

Vocal music in *The Magic Flute* embraces so many distinct, even opposing styles and forms that it seems impossible that they exist in the same opera. Papageno (the role was taken by Schikaneder) introduces himself in the opening scene with an imitation pop- or folksong, the simplest kind of music imaginable, perfect for this charmingly brainless character. A couple of minutes later, his mouth padlocked for lying, he can only snort "hm, hm, hm" as his contribution to the exquisite quintet led by Tamino and the Three Ladies, servants of the Queen of Night, until the Ladies free him. The Queen of Night is vocally not a character from *Singspiel* at all: her style is that of high-serious opera, rather like Donna Elvira in *Don Giovanni*. A frightened mother desperate to reclaim her daughter, she is often lampooned as a wicked, hysterical woman, as she is in *Amadeus*. Mozart, who gave Pamina's mournful Act II aria similar gestures as her mother's aria in Act I—and the same key—obviously took the Queen more seriously, and he entrusted this music of extraordinary vocal and dramatic difficulty to his talented sister-in-law, Josepha Weber Hofer.

Other strikingly unusual vocal styles include the show-stopping duet of Papageno and Papagena in Act II (beginning with the words—no kidding—"Pa-pa-pa"). Throughout the opera we are treated to aphorisms, many of them sung in what sounds to Americans like barbershop harmony—homespun truths such as, "If all liars had padlocks on their mouths, there would be love and brotherhood instead of hate, lying, and nasty rumors," or "Any man who can feel love has a good heart," or "When virtue and justice strew fame's path, then the earth is a kingdom of heaven, and mortals are like gods."[56] There are also solemn choral hymns in the same style Mozart chose for his Masonic cantatas; to us, they sound like church music, as indeed they are meant to. All the music in Sarastro's realm, in fact, is hymnlike, straightforward, and unadorned—a metaphor for his priesthood's serene, prayerful calm.

Before Tamino's final two trials, Two Men in Armor instruct him as follows:[57]

---

56. It was also customary to post aphorisms, including famous moral admonitions, in English gardens.
57. The two men are "in armor," not "armed," as the phrase is sometimes mistranslated. They aren't carrying weapons; there are no weapons in *The Magic Flute*.

Whoever walks this road so full of burdens
will be purified through fire, water, air, and earth;
if he can overcome the terror of death,
he will ascend from earth to heaven.

"Whoever can overcome the terror of death will ascend to heaven." Mozart expressed a similar thought in the letter he sent to his father four years earlier. A key article of Masonic faith, these words came to inspire what is undoubtedly the opera's most astonishing departure from the musical style of either opera or *Singspiel.* The two men sing a Lutheran chorale (hymn), "Ach Gott, vom Himmel sieh darein" ("Oh God, Look Down from Heaven"), an octave apart, surrounded above and below by counterpoint in the style of J. S. Bach. Bach's church music, not only Protestant but almost all of it in German rather than Latin, was probably unknown in Catholic Vienna. Mozart, who had immersed himself deeply in Bach's music at Baron van Swieten's and again in 1789 during his visit to Leipzig, chose to mimic that style of sacred music for these all-important words. Had Viennese church authorities recognized what he had done, there might have been trouble.

What should our answer be to the fundamental question about *The Magic Flute* posed at the outset? Should we think of it as a comedy, a fantasy, a fairy tale, a magic opera—or a mixture of all four, plus some amazing special effects? What the composer's own intentions might have been can be gleaned from his letter to Constanze on October 8–9, 1791, describing events during the previous night's performance:

[Name deleted] had a box today.— [Name or names again deleted] showed very clearly how much they liked *everything*, but he, the know-it-all, showed himself such a complete *Bavarian* that I couldn't stay, or I'd have had to call him an ass;—unfortunately, I was still there as the 2nd act [in Sarastro's realm] began, thus during a solemn scene.—He laughed at everything; at first I was patient enough to try and draw his attention to some of the speeches, but—he just laughed at everything;—now it was too much for me—I called him *Papageno* and left—but I don't think the fathead understood me. —So I went into another box . . . and stayed there to the end.

Scenes from *The Magic Flute*

Queen of Night (recitative and aria): "O zittre nicht . . . Zum Leiden bin ich auserkoren"

Tamino, the Three Ladies, and Papageno (quintet):
"Hm! Hm! Hm!"
Papageno and Papagena (duet): "Pa-Pa-Pa"

■ QUEEN OF NIGHT (RECITATIVE AND ARIA): "O ZITTRE NICHT . . . ZUM LEIDEN BIN ICH AUSERKOREN"

Soprano, 2 oboes, 2 bassoons, 2 horns, strings

Early in Act I, the Three Ladies, emissaries from the Queen of Night, show Tamino a picture of her beautiful daughter, Pamina. He falls in love immediately. Suddenly we hear thunder and lightning, a vast mountain divides in two, and the Queen on her star-filled throne emerges, heralded by orchestral crescendos of a majestic yet tension-building motif. She addresses the startled, awestruck Tamino in an accompanied recitative that segues into an aria.

[*Accompanied recitative*]	[*Accompanied recitative*]
O zittre nicht, mein lieber Sohn!	Don't tremble, my dear son!
Du bist unschuldig, weise, fromm;	You are innocent, wise, devout;
ein Jüngling so wie du vermag am Besten	a young man like you can best
dies tiefbetrübte	comfort this deeply troubled
Mutterherz zu trösten.	mother's heart.
[*Aria*]	[*Aria*]
Zum Leiden bin ich auserkoren,	I have been chosen for sorrow,
denn meine Tochter fehlet mir;	for my daughter is missing;
durch sie ging all mein Glück verloren.	because of that I lost all happiness.
Ein Bösewicht entfloh mit ihr.	A villain fled away with her.
Noch seh' ich ihr Zittern	Even now I see her trembling
mit bangem Erschüttern,	with fearful terror,
ihr ängstliches Beben,	her anxious shaking,
ihr schüchternes Streben.	her frightened struggling.
Ich mußte sie mir rauben sehen.	I had to watch her robbed from me.
"Ach, helft!" war alles, was sie sprach.	"Oh, help!" was all she said.
Allein vergebens war ihr Flehen,	But her cries were fruitless
denn meine Hilfe war zu schwach.	because my help was too weak.
Du wirst sie zu befreien gehen,	You will go to free her,
Du wirst der Tochter Retter sein;	you will be my daughter's rescuer;
und werd' ich dich als Sieger sehen,	and when I see you victorious,
so sei sie dann auf ewig Dein.	she will then be yours forever.

Accompanied recitatives occur only occasionally in opera and are generally reserved for principal characters at dramatic turning points. That this is the only such recitative in *The Magic Flute* tells us how important the moment is. For the audience in the Freihaus-Theater perhaps more than for us today, the Queen's opera seria style, beginning with its formidable orchestral introduction, was a shock—this was not typical *Singspiel* fare.

Up to this moment in Act I, we've had panic (the dragon), flirtation (the Three Ladies), a naive country bumpkin (Papageno), and a romantic lover (Tamino to Pamina's picture). What next, stylistically? All we can be sure of at this point is that the variety will keep coming; but with the Queen, we are suddenly elevated to a whole new level, deeply serious—even tragic.

The Queen's accompanied recitative, made tensely uncertain by the same throbbing, offbeat bass heard in its introduction, is not at all like her explosive entrance. Tamino probably expects something terrifying, but like her accompaniment, her voice is hesitant and almost fearful, the arc of her short phrases suggestive of sighs: Don't be afraid of me; I need your help, and you are just the sort of innocent, sensitive young man I've been looking for.

The aria, marked *larghetto* ("somewhat slow"), opens in triple meter and a minor key, evoking mournful, back-and-forth rocking: the gestures of a grieving mother. "I was born to a life of suffering," she mourns. Until she reaches the word *villain,* the Queen's melodies are softly sighing. Then her anger erupts as she recounts, in brief, jagged phrases, how Pamina was stolen from her and she could do nothing to stop it.

For its final section, beginning with the words "You will go to free her" ("Du wirst sie befreien gehen"), the aria shifts into fast, major-key, rhythmically pulsating commands. The first three words—"You, you, you!" ("Du, Du, Du!")—seem to point her finger threateningly at the young prince. The aria's climax is reached with her final line, "then she will be yours forever" ("so sei sie dann auf ewig Dein"), a series of melismas (long melodic cascades set to a single syllable of text) on the word *then* ("dann"), the last culminating in a dauntingly high note—making it clear that *only* then will Tamino win her.

As mentioned earlier, the Queen of Night is often characterized as vindictive, hysterical, indeed evil. But ask a mother whose child has been kidnapped how she feels, and you might hear something close to the volatile emotions of this recitative and aria: gratitude for a would-be helper; deep sorrow at her tragic loss; fury at the instigator; a bold challenge to rescue, and the promise of a huge reward. In Act II, when Tamino's trial of silence forbids him to speak to Pamina but she doesn't know the reason, she sings an aria of indescribable despair. It is in the same key as this aria and employs vocal gestures almost identical to those of this aria's opening section. Since Pamina is identified with wisdom and the good, her mother, whose music bears such resemblance to her own, is surely not to be viewed as evil.

■ TAMINO, THE THREE LADIES, AND PAPAGENO (QUINTET): "HM! HM! HM!"

Tenor, soprano, mezzo-soprano, contralto, baritone; 2 oboes, 2 clarinets,
2 bassoons, 2 horns, strings

Immediately following the departure of the Queen of Night, Tamino vows to take up the Queen's challenge, then walks away. Papageno waylays him, gesturing for help to rid himself of the padlock the Three Ladies have put on his mouth to punish him for lying (he bragged that he had slain the dragon that threatened Tamino; actually, the Ladies took care of it).

PAPAGENO
Hm! hm! hm! hm! hm! hm! hm!

PAPAGENO
Hm! hm! hm! hm! hm! hm! hm!

TAMINO
Der Arme kann von Strafe sagen,
denn seine Sprache ist dahin.

TAMINO
The poor guy can talk of punishment
because his speech is gone.

PAPAGENO
Hm! hm! hm! hm! hm! hm! hm!

PAPAGENO
Hm! hm! hm! hm! hm! hm! hm!

TAMINO
Ich kann nichts tun, als Dich
beklagen,
weil ich zu schwach zu helfen bin.

TAMINO
All I can do is feel sorry for
you—
there's no way I can help you.

PAPAGENO
Hm! hm! hm! hm! hm! hm! hm!

PAPAGENO
Hm! hm! hm! hm! hm! hm! hm!

TAMINO
Ich kann nichts tun, als Dich
beklagen,
weil ich zu schwach zu helfen bin.

TAMINO
All I can do is feel sorry for
you—
there's no way I can help you.

ERSTE DAME
Die Königin begnadigt Dich,
(Nimmt ihm das Schloß vom Munde)
erläßt die Strafe Dir durch mich.

FIRST LADY
The Queen pardons you,
(Removes the lock from his mouth)
lets me free you from punishment.

PAPAGENO
Nun plaudert Papageno wieder.

PAPAGENO
Now Papageno talks again.

ZWEITE DAME
Ja, plaudre! Lüge nur nicht weiter.

SECOND LADY
Yes, talk! Don't lie anymore.

PAPAGENO
Ich lüge nimmermehr. Nein, nein!

PAPAGENO
I'll never lie again. No, no!

DIE DAMEN
Dies Schloß soll Deine Warnung sein!

THE THREE LADIES
Let this lock be your warning!

PAPAGENO
Dies Schloß soll meine
Warnung sein!

PAPAGENO
This lock will be my
warning!

ALLE
Bekämen doch die Lügner alle
ein solches Schloß vor ihren Mund,
statt Haß, Verleumdung, schwarzer
Galle
bestünden Lieb' und Bruderbund.

EVERYBODY
If all liars were given
such locks on their mouths,
in place of hate, lying, and
rancor
there would be love and brotherhood.

ERSTE DAME
(gibt Tamino eine goldene Flöte)
O Prinz, nimm dies Geschenk
von mir!
Dies sendet uns're Fürstin Dir.
Die Zauberflöte wird Dich
schützen,
im größten Unglück unterstützen.

FIRST LADY
(gives Tamino a golden flute)
O prince, accept this gift
from me!
Our Queen sends it to you.
This magic flute will protect
you,
helping you in direst misfortune.

DIE DAMEN
Hiermit kannst Du
allmächtig handeln,
der Menschen Leidenschaft
verwandeln,
der Traurige wird freudig sein,
den Hagestolz nimmt Liebe ein.

THE THREE LADIES
With this you'll be
all-powerful
to transform human
passion.
A sad person will become joyful,
an old bachelor will fall in love.

ALLE
O so eine Flöte ist mehr
als Gold und Kronen wert,
denn durch sie wird Menschenglück
und Zufriedenheit vermehrt.

EVERYBODY
O, such a flute is
worth more than gold or crowns,
for through it, human happiness
and contentment will grow.

PAPAGENO
Nun, Ihr schönen Frauenzimmer,
darf ich—so empfehl' ich mich—

PAPAGENO
Now, you lovely ladies,
may I—may I excuse myself—

DIE DAMEN
Dich empfehlen kannst Du immer,
doch bestimmt die Fürstin Dich
mit dem Prinzen ohn' Verweilen
nach Sarastros Burg zu eilen.

THE THREE LADIES
You can excuse yourself anytime,
but now the Queen commands you
to hurry with the prince
to Sarastro's castle.

PAPAGENO
Nein, dafür bedank' ich mich!
Von Euch selbsten hörte ich,
daß er wie ein Tigertier!
Sicher ließ' ohn' alle Gnaden
mich Sarastro rupfen, braten,
setzte mich den Hunden für.

PAPAGENO
No, but thanks anyhow!
I heard from you yourselves
that he is like a tiger!
At the drop of a hat Sarastro
would have me plucked and roasted
and leave me for the dogs.

DIE DAMEN
Dich schützt der Prinz, trau'
ihm allein!
Dafür sollst Du sein Diener sein.

THE THREE LADIES
The prince will protect you;
trust him!
In return, you'll be his servant.

PAPAGENO
Daß doch der Prinz beim Teufel
wäre!
Mein Leben ist mir lieb,
am Ende schleicht, bei meiner Ehre,
er von mir wie ein Dieb.

PAPAGENO
Let the prince go to the
devil!
My life is dear to me;
in the end, by my honor, it will
creep up on me like a thief.

ERSTE DAME
(gibt ihm ein Kästchen mit einem
Glockspiele)

FIRST LADY
(gives him a box with a
glockenspiel)

Hier, nimm dies Kleinod, es ist Dein.

Here, take this treasure, it's yours.

PAPAGENO
Ei, ei! Was mag darinnen sein?

PAPAGENO
Wow! What's in it?

DIE DAMEN
Darinnen hörst Du Glöckchen tönen.

THE THREE LADIES
Inside you hear a glockenspiel.

PAPAGENO
Werd' ich sie auch wohl
spielen können?

PAPAGENO
Okay if I play it?

DIE DAMEN
O ganz gewiß! Ja, ja, gewiß!

THE THREE LADIES
Absolutely, yes, absolutely!

ALLE
Silberglöckchen, Zauberflöten
sind zu Eurem/unserm Schutz
von Nöten.
Lebet wohl! Wir wollen gehen.
Lebet wohl! Auf Wiedersehen!

EVERYBODY
Glockenspiel and magic flute
are yours/ours for times
of need.
Farewell! We have to go.
Farewell! Until we meet again!

TAMINO
Doch schöne Damen, saget an . . .

TAMINO
But lovely ladies, tell us . . .

PAPAGENO
Wo man die Burg wohl finden kann?
BEIDE
Wo man die Burg wohl finden kann?

PAPAGENO
Where is the castle?
TAMINO, PAPAGENO
Where is the castle?

DIE DAMEN
Drei Knäbchen, jung, schön,
hold und weise,
umschweben Euch auf Eurer Reise.
Sie werden Eure Führer sein;
folgt ihrem Rate ganz allein.

THE THREE LADIES
Three little boys, young,
handsome, noble, and wise,
will hover around you on your journey.
They will be your guides;
follow only their advice.

TAMINO, PAPAGENO
Drei Knäbchen, jung, schön,
hold und weise,
umschweben uns auf unsrer Reise.

TAMINO, PAPAGENO
Three little boys, young,
handsome, noble, and wise,
will hover around us on our journey.

DIE DAMEN
Sie werden Eure Führer sein;
folgt ihrem Rate ganz allein.

THE THREE LADIES
They will be your guides;
follow only their advice.

ALLE
So lebet wohl! Wir wollen gehen.
Lebt wohl, lebt wohl!
Auf Wiedersehen!

EVERYBODY
So farewell! We have to go.
Good-bye, good-bye!
Till we meet again!

Yet another startling shift takes us, with only two spoken sentences from Tamino as transition, from the Queen of Night's fiery outcry down to the bottom of the social and musical ladder: Papageno's inarticulate *Hm-hm-hms*, accompanied by a bleating bassoon. He seems naively unaware that he is nevertheless supplying rhythmic and harmonic foundation for Tamino's more melodious though verbally unhelpful replies; as a twosome, they make nice music together.

The First Lady croons that Papageno is now free—if he promises to stop lying—and the whole quintet proclaims the moral in short, snippy phrases sounding like a group of schoolmarms: if liars had their mouths locked shut, we'd have no more slander and hate in the world, only love and brotherhood. But sweetening those snippets are the strings' da-da-da-da-DUMs and above everyone, a teasing oboe.

What is evolving here is a Mozartian action ensemble, as characters express their individual thoughts and come together for moments of agreement. The liquescent musical texture flows with seeming effortlessness from one action to the next.

Next comes the presentation of the magic flute to Tamino. Mozart does not italicize the fact by treating us to a flute solo in the orchestra; in fact, there is no flute anywhere in this scene. Instead, we hear brief flutelike garnishes from the violins and, when all five voices come together for "Such a flute is worth more than gold or crowns" ("O so eine Flöte ist mehr als Gold und Kronen wert"), the singers are instructed to almost whisper their words (*sotto voce*), the better to savor the woodwinds' sugary chords and gently descending scales in the violins.

Papageno, thinking we're done now, starts to leave. Not so fast, answer the Ladies; you're going on this rescue mission with Tamino. Are you kidding me? That tiger Sarastro will tear me up and feed me to his dogs. This last thought returns him to repetitive, simple-minded rhythms like those with which he opened this scene. The First Lady calms him down with his own gift: a glockenspiel (which makes bell-like sounds, a little like a toy piano). He is delighted. Once more, all five voices come together, and with instrumental accompaniment rather similar to that used to celebrate Tamino's flute. They sing good-bye to each other longingly, then remember to ask: Where is Sarastro's castle anyway?

The answer is not geographic; instead, we are told about The Three Boys, who will be mirror images, in Sarastro's realm, of the Queen's Three Ladies. The Three Ladies' description of them as the men's spiritual guides, to be trusted absolutely, is more deliciously harmonious than anything else in Act I—a foretaste of Act II's serenely consonant music for Sarastro, his priests—and the Three Boys.

■ PAPAGENO AND PAPAGENA (DUET): "PA-PA-PA"
Baritone, soprano, 2 flutes, 2 oboes, 2 bassoons, 2 horns, strings
This duet always brings down the house. Schikaneder, who played Papageno, no doubt had a ball with it—after all, he wrote the words. Two scenes earlier, Pamina had led Tamino, playing his magic flute, through the trials of fire and water. Following that exalted moment, we are hurtled back into comedy in what has become the opera's pattern. Papageno, believing he has lost Papagena forever, threatens suicide but is saved by the Three Boys. As they walk back toward their flying machine, they stop to say, "Papageno, look!" And there she is. The two are so dumbfounded they can't even say each other's name.

PAPAGENO	PAPAGENO
Pa-Pa-Pa-Pa-Pa-Pa-Papagena!	Pa-Pa-Pa-Pa-Pa-Pa-Papagena!

PAPAGENA
Pa-Pa-Pa-Pa-Pa-Pa-Papageno!

PAPAGENA
Pa-Pa-Pa-Pa-Pa-Pa-Papageno!

PAPAGENO
Bist Du mir nun ganz gegeben?

PAPAGENO
Are you really mine now?

PAPAGENA
Nun bin ich Dir ganz gegeben!

PAPAGENA
I'm really yours now!

PAPAGENO
Nun, so sei mein liebes Weibchen!

PAPAGENO
Now, be my dear little wife!

PAPAGENA
Nun, so sei mein Herzenstäubchen!

PAPAGENA
Now, be my little turtledove!

BEIDE
Welche Freude wird das sein,
wenn die Götter uns bedanken,
unsrer Liebe Kinder schenken,
so liebe kleine Kinderlein!

BOTH
What joy that will be,
if the gods grant
to gift our love with kids,
such dear little kids!

PAPAGENO
Erst einen kleinen Papageno!

PAPAGENO
First, a little Papageno!

PAPAGENA
Dann eine kleine Papagena!

PAPAGENA
Then a little Papagena!

PAPAGENO
Dann wieder einen Papageno!

PAPAGENO
Then another Papageno!

PAPAGENA
Dann wieder eine Papagena!

PAPAGENA
Then another Papagena!

BEIDE
Papageno! Papagena!
Papageno! Papagena!
Es ist das Höchste der Gefühle,
wenn viele, viele Papageno,
Papagena
der Eltern Segen werden sein.

BOTH
Papageno! Papagena!
Papageno! Papagena!
It will be the greatest possible feeling
if many, many Papagenos and
Papagenas
come to bless their parents.

Who else but Mozart would think of setting *pa-pa-pa* to the music of a lovers' duet? Here, though, unlike the Act I quintet with its *hm-hm-hm*, the syllables don't function as foundation for somebody else's song, but lead first to woodpecker chattering (*papapapapapapapa*) and then to genuine melody and sunny vocal exchanges. Mozart's music transports us to an enchanted, childlike world. "Are you really mine; yes, I'm really yours" ("Bist Du mir nun ganz gegeben? Nun bin ich Dir ganz gegeben"). He writes in the instruction *ritardando* (slow down!) so that these innocent lovebirds will linger over hopes for their future children ("Kinderlein . . . Kinderlein, so liebe Kinderlein") before roaring into the duet's show-stopping climax over the competition they can already imagine: what shall we have first, Papagenos or Papagenas? How fast can you say *papapapapapapapapa*?

REQUIEM, K. 626 (*unfinished*)

Mozart was a happy man during the late summer and fall of 1791, albeit a very busy one—racing to fulfill a stack of commissions including *La clemenza di Tito* and, three weeks after that, *The Magic Flute*. *Flute* was a hit, but with his desk still piled high with work, he had no time to savor it. Plunging ahead, he finished the Clarinet Concerto, K. 622, for Anton Stadler in October, and on November 17 conducted a new cantata for his Masonic lodge, *Laut verkünde unsre Freude* ("Loudly Proclaim Our Joy"), K. 623. This was his last appearance in public. He died at 12:55 a.m. on December 5.

After his death, one major work lay on his desk unfinished. The previous July, Count Franz Wallsegg, through an anonymous emissary, had agreed to pay Mozart quite generously to write a Requiem, half of the fee to be paid in advance, the other half upon completion. Mystery and confusion continue to swirl around this commission and its possible relationship to the composer's death. Scholarship has long since cleared up most of it, though a few questions remain. One is quite basic: Why did the count approach Mozart for this in the first place?

The fact is that Mozart was not known in Vienna as a composer of sacred music. No one had commissioned him to write a major work for the church during his ten years there. The unfinished Mass in C Minor, K. 427/417a, composed in 1782/83, was written for Salzburg and probably never heard in Vienna—although Mozart did use some of its movements, set to different, nonliturgical words, in *Davidde penitente*, K. 469 (1785). But for this important commission, why didn't Wallsegg seek out someone more closely associated with sacred music? Mozart had, in fact, begun to work on ideas for church compositions around the year 1788, asking Nannerl to send him certain sacred works by Salzburg composers so that he could study them—toward what end, we don't know. But there were no requests that he write such music that we're aware of, and no public performances.

What we do know is that the count intended to have the Requiem performed annually in memory of his twenty-year-old wife, who had died suddenly in February 1791. Mozart undoubtedly knew the count and probably the young countess as well. Wallsegg often invited musicians to perform at his country home; he also owned the townhouse in Vienna where Michael Puchberg, Mozart's friend, Masonic brother, and sometime creditor lived. Wallsegg liked to hire composers to write music that he would then pass off as his own, paying them well and probably fully aware that his little subterfuge was not quite a secret. Wallsegg's emissary to Mozart was later described—accurately—as a "tall, thin man, dressed all in gray." Nineteenth-century writers made him also "mysterious" and "gaunt-looking." But there was no mystery; it was Franz Anton Leitgeb, an employee of the count who was tall, thin, and, because of his Turkish descent, dark-skinned.

A Requiem—the genre takes its name from its opening word (*Requiem aeternam dona eis, Domine* ["Grant them eternal rest, O Lord"])—served for centuries as the Catholic Mass for the Dead. Its words include many of those used in all Masses (Kyrie, Sanctus, Agnus Dei), omitting the Gloria and Credo and adding the Requiem aeternam, Sequence, Offertory, and Communio. Until this text, along with its liturgy and theology, was radically altered by the Vatican Council's reforms in the 1960s, it formed the basis for settings by composers including Berlioz, Verdi, Fauré, and Mozart. Brahms's *German Requiem* is different: a Protestant, Brahms selected texts from Luther's Bible. Benjamin Britten, in his *War Requiem* (1962), commissioned for the rededication of Coventry Cathedral after its near-total destruction in World War II, juxtaposed the Catholic text (although Britten was also not a Catholic) with searingly graphic antiwar poems by the most famous poet killed in World War I, Wilfred Owen.

Setting to work on the Requiem in October, Mozart sorely missed Constanze, who was in Baden recuperating from a painful and potentially serious leg infection. His letters to her are affectionate and full of high spirits. How could he be depressed? *The Magic Flute* was a triumph. Trips to England and Russia were still a possibility. Guaranteed pensions were in the offing from Hungary and Amsterdam. Within a few months or possibly a year or two, he expected to be named music director of St. Stephen's Cathedral with a salary of two thousand gulden.

According to legend, however, throughout most of September Mozart was ill, melancholy, and preoccupied with thoughts of his impending death. His letters plainly refute this; nor is there any evidence of serious ill health before November. His sudden illness in mid-November 1791 and his death three weeks later are discussed in detail in the following chapter. For most of that time he was so ill that it would have been impossible for him to compose or, at the end, even to hold a pen.

Before he died, Mozart was able to complete only the Requiem aeternam, much of the Kyrie, and portions of the Sequence. For some of the remaining sections he left sketches or drafts in varying states of completion; for the concluding movements, nothing. Yet despite the fact that only a fraction of the Requiem was written by Mozart himself, it is numbered today among his most beloved and most frequently performed works.

At his death, the Requiem looked like this:

Requiem aeternam:	complete
Kyrie:	vocal parts complete; bass line with figures (to indicate how the harmony should be filled out); orchestral parts sketched in here and there
Sequence:	same as the Kyrie, through measure 8 ("Judicandus homo reus") of the "Lacrimosa," the final stanza of the Sequence
Offertory:	same as the Kyrie and Sequence
Sanctus:	not composed; vocal parts possibly sketched, but lost
Benedictus:	not composed; vocal parts possibly sketched, but lost
Osanna:	not composed; vocal parts possibly sketched, but lost
Agnus Dei:	not composed; vocal parts possibly sketched, but lost
Communio:	repeats the music of the Requiem aeternam and Kyrie: was this Mozart's plan?

The Kyrie and nearly all of the Sequence were in good enough shape to be finished by someone else. However, the Sequence's last stanza, the "Lacrimosa," ended abruptly after eight measures and for this reason was long thought to have been the last music he composed. But Alan Tyson and Christoph Wolff argue that he was probably so sure how the rest of the "Lacrimosa" would go that he simply didn't bother to write it down, hurrying on instead to draft two of the Sequence's more complex sections, the "Domine Jesu" and the "Hostias."[58] It was then, they believe, that he had to stop. The autograph manuscript shows no signs of haste or fatigue. Right to the end, it seems, Mozart had no idea that he was dying.

After his death, Constanze, faced with the task of supporting herself and their two young children, needed the other half of that fee from Count Wallsegg. She asked three composers to bring the Requiem to completion, but they all had trouble following in Mozart's footsteps. Ultimately, the

---

58. Christoph Wolff, *Mozart's Requiem: Historical and Analytical Studies, Documents, Score* (Berkeley: University of California Press, 1994), 29–32.

responsibility fell to Mozart's assistant, Franz Xaver Süssmayr. Laboring under what must have been indescribable emotional pressure, he completed the work in February 1792, thereby rescuing Constanze, an act of generosity rarely if ever acknowledged by Mozart scholars. Thanks to him, the count received the manuscript in due course and paid Constanze the promised sum.

There is harsh criticism of Süssmayr's work, however: errors of harmony abound, and his musical ideas proved no match for Mozart's. Nevertheless, many conductors prefer his version to any that have followed it. Süssmayr worked closely with Mozart for a period of years, was with him at the end, and surely had a good sense, if anyone did, of the composer's overall plan for the work. While Süssmayr's orchestral music for the Sanctus and Benedictus is disappointing, the vocal parts seem stronger, and his Agnus Dei is quite fine. Did Mozart perhaps leave sketches for some of these sections? For the Communio ("Lux aeterna" and "Cum sanctis tuis"), Süssmayr repeated music from the "Te decet hymnus" section of the Requiem aeternam and the following Kyrie. Either Mozart told him to do this, or Süssmayr, pressed for time, did so out of desperation.

The style of the Requiem is without parallel elsewhere in Mozart's works. Its closest analogues are found, surprisingly, not in his other church music (most of which was written before he moved to Vienna), but in *The Magic Flute* and his Masonic choral music. The Requiem's sonority bears a strong resemblance to that of the priestly scenes in Act II of *The Magic Flute*: two basset horns, two bassoons, two trumpets, three trombones, timpani, and strings. But the Requiem is darker still, because there are no upper woodwinds—no flutes, oboes, or clarinets—and no horns; the highest woodwinds are the basset horns. The result is mahogany: deeply solemn, yet warm.

Mozart sets the Requiem's ancient words "cantata style," as he had done in his unfinished Mass in C Minor, K. 427/417a, subdividing each movement into short clusters and setting each of them individually. Much of the writing stands at one extreme or the other: either richly contrapuntal or hymnlike in its simplicity. The contrast with the C-Minor Mass could not be sharper: here there are no arias, with one exception discussed below. Nearly all the nonchoral moments feature, not individual singers, but the whole vocal quartet, whose music is lyrical, gentle, and unadorned.

The musical highpoints of the Requiem are choral. The influence of Bach is everywhere apparent—for example, in the masterful double fugue juxtaposing an ominous "Kyrie eleison" with a light-winged "Christe eleison." Mozart borrowed the melody for the "Kyrie eleison" from the chorus "And with his stripes we are healed" in Handel's *Messiah*, a work he had revised on a commission from Baron van Swieten in 1789.

The Sequence offered composers rich opportunities for choral illustration, and Mozart employs his theatrical brilliance to bring them startlingly to life. The Sequence's stanzas, each composed of three rhymed lines, seem to portray a penitent sinner confronting the wrath, power, goodness, and healing mercy of God. In dramatizing this vast emotional span, Mozart allots two-thirds of the poem (twelve stanzas) to the calming music of the solo quartet, with only six stanzas given to the chorus; yet those six are quite overwhelming. Beginning with the driving, minor-key "Dies irae" ("Day of Wrath"), we move to the monumental "Rex tremendae" ("King of awful majesty"); then, after an emotional respite of seven stanzas by the quartet, to the fiery "Confutatis maledictis" ("When the sinners have been confounded") set against the angelic "Voca me cum benedictis" ("Call me with the blessed"), coming at last to the (incomplete) minor-key pastoral lament, the "Lacrimosa" ("Tearful will be that day").

The third stanza of the Sequence provides the Requiem with its one very brief aria: "Tuba mirum" ("A trumpet, spreading a wondrous sound through the graves of all lands, will drive mankind before the throne"). Mozart sets this as a dialogue between baritone and solo trombone. Why trombone? Whereas English Bibles translate the Latin word *tuba* as "trumpet," in the German Bible it is "trombone." Neither of these is an accurate rendering of *tuba*, St. Jerome's fifth-century guess at the meaning of the Greek word for shofar or ram's horn—the instrument played today, as it was in Mozart's time, on Rosh Hashanah and Yom Kippur. As you will hear, however, trombones are heard not only during the "Tuba mirum" but also throughout much of the Requiem. They signify, as they do in *Don Giovanni* and *The Magic Flute*, the presence of the divine.

Early writers on Mozart were unanimous in believing that the Requiem marked a new direction in his work, away from opera and instrumental music toward a thoroughgoing reform of church music. The new style, as they envisioned it, would banish operatic display and blend ancient (i.e., Renaissance and baroque) polyphony with modern, symphonic ideas of form. Were these writers on to something? Had Mozart truly embarked on a fundamental rethinking of his style? There is, in fact, evidence that he had, in particular the Requiem itself, with its sharp departures from his earlier music. At all events, we are mistaken if we think of this as a late work. To him, it was simply the next work—the next commission. He could not have known that it would be his last and that he would not live to finish it.

Requiem, K. 626, the unfinished "Lacrimosa"

■ REQUIEM, K. 626 (*unfinished*)

For soprano, alto, tenor, and bass soloists; chorus; 2 basset horns, 2 bassoons, 2 trumpets, 3 trombones, timpani, organ, and strings[59]

Requiem
Requiem aeternam dona eis, Domine,
et lux perpetua luceat eis.

Requiem
Grant them eternal rest, O Lord,
and may perpetual light shine on them.

Soprano
Te decet hymnus, Deus, in Sion,
et tibi reddetur votum
in Jerusalem.

Soprano
You, O God, are praised in Sion,
and to you shall the vow be performed
in Jerusalem.

Chorus
Exaudi orationem meam,
ad te omnis caro veniet.

Chorus
Hear my prayer,
to you shall all flesh come.

---

59. Since Mozart completed the orchestration for only the first movement (Requiem aeternam) and left only sketches or, for some movements, no music at all, the instruments listed here are partly conjectural. See the discussion of this issue that precedes this text.

Requiem aeternam dona eis, Domine, et lux perpetua luceat eis.	Grant them eternal rest, O Lord, and may perpetual light shine on them.

Kyrie
Kyrie eleison.
Christe eleison.
Kyrie eleison.

Kyrie
Lord, have mercy upon us.
Christ, have mercy upon us.
Lord, have mercy upon us.

Sequentia
Dies irae, dies illa
Solvet saeclum in favilla,
Teste David cum Sibylla.

Sequence
Day of wrath, that day
Will dissolve the earth in ashes
As David and the Sibyl bear witness.

Quantus tremor est futurus
Quando judex est venturus
Cuncta stricte discussurus.

What dread there will be
When the judge shall come
To judge all things strictly.

Baritone
Tuba mirum spargens sonum
Per sepulcra regionum
Coget omnes ante thronum.

Baritone
A trumpet, spreading a wondrous sound
Through the graves of all lands,
Will drive mankind before the throne.

Tenor
Mors stupebit et natura
Cum resurget creatura
Judicanti responsura.

Tenor
Death and Nature shall be astonished
When all creation rises again
To answer to the Judge.

Liber scriptus proferetur
In quo totum continetur,
Unde mundus judicetur.

A book, written in, will be brought forth
In which is contained everything that is,
Out of which the world shall be judged.

Alto
Judex ergo cum sedebit
Quidquid latet apparebit,
Nil inultum remanebit.

Alto
When therefore the Judge takes His seat
Whatever is hidden will reveal itself.
Nothing will remain unavenged.

Soprano
Quid sum miser tunc dicturus,
Quem patronum rogaturus,
Cum vix justus sit securus?

Soprano
What then shall I say, wretch that I am,
What advocate entreat to speak for me,
When even the righteous may hardly
be secure?

Chorus
Rex tremendae majestatis,
Qui salvandos salvas gratis,
Salve me, fons pietatis.

Chorus
King of awful majesty,
Who freely saves the redeemed,
Save me, O fount of goodness.

Solo Quartet
Recordare, Jesu pie,

Solo Quartet
Remember, blessed Jesus,

Quod sum causa tuae viae.	That I am the cause of your pilgrimage.
Ne me perdas illa die.	Do not forsake me on that day.
Quaerens me sedisti lassus,	Seeking me, you sat down weary;
Redemisti crucem passus,	You redeemed me, suffering death on the cross;
Tantus labor non sit cassus.	Let not such toil be in vain.
Juste judex ultionis	Just and avenging Judge,
Donum fac remissionis	Grant forgiveness
Ante diem rationis.	Before the day of reckoning.
Ingemisco tamquam reus.	I groan like a guilty man.
Culpa rubet vultus meus.	Guilt reddens my face.
Supplicanti parce, Deus.	Spare this suppliant, O God.
Qui Mariam absolvisti	You who forgave Mary Magdalene
Et latronem exaudisti,	And hearkened to the thief,
Mihi quoque spem dedisti.	To me also have You given hope.
Preces meae non sunt dignae,	My prayers are not worthy,
Sed tu bonus fac benigne,	But You in your merciful goodness grant
Ne perenni cremer igne.	That I do not burn in everlasting fire.
Inter oves locum praesta,	Place me among your sheep
Et ab haedis me sequestra,	And separate me from the goats,
Statuens in parte dextra.	Setting me on your right hand.

Chorus	*Chorus*
Confutatis maledictis	When the sinners have been confounded
Flammis acribus addictis,	And given over to the bitter flames,
Voca me cum benedictis.	Call me with the blessed.
Oro supplex et acclinis.	I pray in supplication on my knees.
Cor contritum quasi cinis,	My heart contrite as the dust,
Gere curam mei finis.	Safeguard my fate.

Lacrimosa dies illa	Tearful will be that day
Qua resurget ex favilla	When from the dust shall rise
Judicandus homo reus.	Guilty man to be judged.
Huic ergo parce, Deus.	Therefore spare him, O God.
Pie Jesu Domine,	Merciful Jesus, Lord,
dona eis requiem.	Grant them rest.

Offertorium

Domine, Jesu Christe, rex gloriae,	Lord Jesus Christ, king of glory,
libera animas omnium fidelium	deliver the souls of all the faithful
defunctorum	departed
de poenis inferni, et de profundis lacu:	from the pains of hell and from the bottomless pit;
libera eas de ore leonis;	deliver them from the lion's mouth,

Offertory

ne absorbeat eas tartarus,
ne cadant in obscurum,

neither let them fall into darkness
nor the pit,

Solo Quartet
sed signifer sanctus Michael
repraesentet eas in lucem sanctam

Solo Quartet
but let St. Michael, your standard-bearer,
lead them into the holy light

Chorus
quam olim Abrahae promisisti
et semini ejus.

Chorus
which you long ago promised to Abraham
and all his seed.

Hostias et preces tibi, Domine,
laudis offerimus;
tu suscipe pro animabus illis,
quarum hodie memoriam facimus:
fac eas, Domine, de morte transire
ad vitam,
quam olim Abrahae promisisti
et semini ejus.

Prayer and praise, O Lord, we
offer unto you;
receive it for those souls
whom today we commemorate;
allow them, O Lord, to cross from death
into life
as you promised Abraham
and all his seed.

Sanctus
Sanctus, Sanctus, Sanctus,
Dominus Deus Sabaoth.
Pleni sunt caeli et terra
gloria tua.
Hosanna in excelsis.

Sanctus
Holy, Holy, Holy,
Lord God of Sabaoth.
The heavens and the earth are full of
your glory.
Hosanna in the highest.

Solo Quartet
Benedictus qui venit
in nomine Domini.

Solo Quartet
Blessed is he who comes
in the name of the Lord.

Chorus
Hosanna in excelsis.

Chorus
Hosanna in the highest.

Agnus Dei
Agnus Dei,
qui tollis peccata mundi,
miserere nobis.
Agnus Dei,
qui tollis peccata mundi,
dona nobis pacem.

Agnus Dei
Lamb of God,
who takes away the sins of the world,
have mercy upon us.
Lamb of God,
who takes away the sins of the world,
grant us peace.

Communio
Soprano
Lux aeterna luceat eis, Domine,
cum sanctis tuis in aeternum,
quia pius est.

Communio
Soprano
May eternal light shine upon them, O Lord,
with your saints forever,
because you are merciful.

Chorus
Lux aeterna luceat eis, Domine,

Chorus
May eternal light shine upon them, O Lord,

cum sanctis tuis in aeternum,	with your saints forever,
quia pius est.	because you are merciful.
Requiem aeternam dona eis, Domine,	Grant them eternal rest, O Lord,
et lux perpetua luceat eis	and may perpetual light shine upon them
cum sanctis tuis in aeternum,	with your saints forever,
quia pius est.	because you are merciful.

"Gravesite" monument. Erected in Vienna's St. Marx Cemetery in 1891, a century after the composer's death, this monument does not mark his gravesite, since we do not know where that is.

7

THE FINAL YEAR, DEATH, AND BURIAL

1791

March — Mozart performs his recently completed Piano Concerto in B-flat Major, K. 595, at a concert in Vienna.

April — Performance of an aria and one of his symphonies (perhaps one of the final three?) at a benefit concert for musicians' widows and orphans.

He petitions the Vienna city council to name him *Kapellmeister* at St. Stephen's Cathedral, because the present *Kapellmeister* is ill and quite old. Mozart is appointed his assistant, but without salary.

Early summer — Constanze, pregnant, is at Baden, where Mozart often visits her. He writes *Ave verum corpus*, K. 618, for the choirmaster there, as a gift.

July — Franz Xaver Wolfgang Mozart is born.

Mozart sends cheerful, funny letters to Constanze (no replies survive).

Money doesn't seem to be an issue.

Schikaneder commissions *The Magic Flute*.

The Requiem is commissioned.

Prague commissions *La clemenza di Tito* for its coronation celebrations for the new emperor, Leopold II (brother of Joseph II).

August — Mozart arrives in Prague with Constanze on August 25 to finish writing *La clemenza di Tito* and see to its premiere.

	He seems to have suffered some brief illness around this time.
September	Mozart sees a performance of *Don Giovanni* in Prague on September 2.
	La clemenza di Tito premieres on September 6.
	He races back to Vienna to finish *The Magic Flute* for its premiere on September 30.
October	He takes his son Carl Thomas, his mother-in-law, Frau Weber, and Salieri to a performance of *The Magic Flute*.
	He teases Schikaneder (playing the role of Papageno) by misplaying the glockenspiel accompaniment to his Act I aria.
	He writes the Clarinet Concerto, K. 622 for his friend Anton Stadler.
	His letters to Constanze are full of energy and high spirits.
November	On November 17, Mozart conducts a new cantata for his Masonic lodge at one of its meetings. This is his last completed work and his final public appearance.
	Suddenly very ill, he takes to his bed on November 20.
December	On December 3, he feels better.
	On the evening of December 4, he takes a sharp turn for the worse. Dr. Closset is summoned. He bleeds Mozart and applies cold compresses to combat his high fever. The composer falls into a coma and dies at 12:55 a.m. on December 5.

WHAT DID HE DIE OF?

More than 150 theories have been put forward over the past two centuries in an attempt to explain Mozart's death. Most of them are little more than hunches. Some are patently absurd, such as the notion that he was poisoned by Salieri, Freemasons, or some jealous rival. A few years ago an article in a highly respected medical journal cited a letter from Mozart about some pork cutlets he was about to consume one night in October 1791. Might he have died of trichinosis, the writer wondered?

Yet we also have serious, knowledgeable, scientifically plausible diagnoses. These presuppose a thorough knowledge of Mozart's medical history, an analysis of his symptoms at the time of his fatal illness, a careful study of the reports submitted by his doctors, and—crucially—an understanding of eighteenth-century medical practice. As you might suspect, only a handful of those who have written about Mozart's death meet these standards.[1]

Mozart's terminal illness began suddenly on November 20, 1791, with edema (swelling) in his hands and feet, which later spread throughout his body, rendering him nearly immobile and causing him great pain. The swelling was accompanied by high fever, body rash, sweating, and projectile vomiting. These symptoms all point to acute rheumatic fever.

Mozart had suffered multiple episodes of rheumatic fever as a child, along with a variety of respiratory ailments, some of which were serious. He also contracted scarlet fever; smallpox, which left him pockmarked for life; typhoid fever; and on at least two occasions, acute infectious polyarthritis. In 1784 he came down with severe colic that lasted several days, and in 1786 he was again very ill for a brief time.

What triggered the onset of his fatal illness in November 1791? One likely cause was sheer exhaustion from a grueling schedule that had begun the previous summer, when he received three major commissions nearly simultaneously: the Requiem, *La clemenza di Tito*, and *The Magic Flute*. For much of this frantically busy time Constanze was away in Baden on orders from her doctor, who feared that a severe infection in her leg might develop into gangrene. During the late fall, an epidemic of infectious disease swept through Vienna, taking the lives of hundreds of people. It has recently been proposed that this was a streptococcal infection, that Mozart may have succumbed to it, and that this then led to acute kidney failure and death.[2] Whether it was one or all of these factors—or something else altogether—we do not know.

The doctors who treated him during his final illness were highly esteemed physicians following accepted medical practice of that time. This included bleeding Mozart daily—perhaps twice a day—and administering emetics, which must have been nearly unbearable for someone whose body was wracked with pain in every joint. When his fever suddenly spiked on the evening of December 4, he was bled yet again and cold compresses

---

1. I am indebted to Bruce Cooper Clarke for sharing with me the fruits of his comprehensive study of this topic and for steering me away from errors I would otherwise have committed. Clarke believes that the definitive discussion of this topic is Anton Neumayr, *Music and Medicine* (Bloomington, IN: Medi-Ed Press, 1994), 1:167–218, especially 188, 205. Dr. Neumayr is a Viennese physician, a pianist, and an expert on eighteenth-century medical terminology and practice. My brief summary of Mozart's symptoms and the causes of his death is largely based upon Dr. Neumayr's findings.

2. Richard H. C. Zegers, Andreas Weigl, and Andrew Steptoe, "The Death of Wolfgang Amadeus Mozart: An Epidemiologic Perspective," *Annals of Internal Medicine* 151 (2009): 274–78.

were applied to bring down his temperature. Instead, he went into shock, then coma, from which he never awoke. The underlying cause of death appears to have been acute rheumatic fever complicated by polyarthritis. The immediate causes were the enormous loss of blood over a two-week period and the shock of cold compresses suddenly placed on his feverish body. He died at 12:55 a.m. on December 5, 1791.

BURIAL

The funeral service and burial of Wolfgang Amadè Mozart took place in accordance with decrees handed down by Emperor Joseph II that were still in force in 1791, even though Joseph had died in 1790 and his brother, Leopold II, was now emperor.[3] Joseph's policies—which most Viennese found loathsome—vastly simplified church services, minimized distinctions between rich and poor, guaranteed even the poorest of citizens a decent burial, and protected the city against possible infections from people who had died of contagious diseases.

For example, wealthier families were not only no longer permitted to stage lengthy, ostentatious funeral ceremonies, but were charged twice the amount that average families paid, while the poor were charged nothing. Mozart, as we know, was by no means poor; however, it appears that all or most of his burial expenses were paid by the Baron van Swieten. There were three levels of fees. Mozart's was third class—which did not mean low class or pauper, as legend would have it, but rather what an average family could afford. Although this was far below the level to which his father had aspired, it corresponded to what Viennese society (including the Baron van Swieten) deemed suitable for a court employee—which is what Mozart was.

There would have been a cortege from the Mozarts' apartment on Rauhensteingasse (a short block from St. Stephen's Cathedral), with a crucifer (a person carrying a cross), lantern-bearers, and two pallbearers. In a chapel of the cathedral, a service was conducted during which the priest blessed the casket. Since no burials took place sooner than forty-eight hours after death—to avoid the potential tragedy of someone's being buried alive—the casket was kept inside the cathedral until the next day, when it was taken by a hearse drawn by two horses to St. Marx Cemetery, a distance of perhaps two miles. All bodies were interred outside the city limits to guard against infection. The chapel service probably took place on

---

3. For most of the information in this section I am again grateful to Bruce Cooper Clarke (1991 BBC radio interview, kindly furnished by Mr. Clarke), and particularly to Walter Brauneis, "Exequies for Mozart: A New Documentary Finding Concerning the Requiem Mass Held for W. A. Mozart in St. Michael's Church in Vienna on 10 December 1791," trans. Bruce Cooper Clarke, accessible at AproposMozart.com.

December 6, followed by burial the next day.

Mozart's body was laid to rest in what was called a "common individual grave." This meant that it was buried in the ground rather than in a vault, and that the location was not purchased as private property. Such graves, part of a third-class burial, were generally dug up and reused every ten years or so. It is impossible to know today just where his remains might have been laid.

Possibly there was a gravestone, though it has not survived. A Viennese newspaper on December 31 printed what might have served as its inscription:

MOZART: AN INSCRIPTION FOR HIS GRAVE
Who rests here, as a child swelled the world's wonders
With the strings of his lyre; as a man, he surpassed
Orpheus himself.
Go hence! And pray earnestly for his soul.[4]

We don't know who was present at Mozart's obsequies. Constanze, Carl Thomas, and the five-month-old Franz Xaver Wolfgang may have stayed home. In addition to close friends, Masonic brothers, private students, patrons, and musical colleagues, those in attendance would presumably have included Constanze's sisters, Sophie, Josepha, and Aloysia (the last two both celebrated singers in Vienna), with their respective husbands; the Baron van Swieten; Mozart's assistant, Franz Xaver Süssmayr; his two live-in students, Franz Jacob Freystädtler and Otto Hatwig; and, evidence suggests, Court Composer Antonio Salieri.

As cited in the list of events below, several of Mozart's friends, led by fellow Freemason Emanuel Schikaneder (also the producer, librettist, and star of *The Magic Flute*), arranged for a funeral Mass to be said on December 10 in St. Michael's Church, near the Hofburg. Vocal soloists, choristers, and instrumentalists who had known and loved the composer and his music performed the completed portions of his unfinished Requiem during the service. There is no record that they charged any fee.

AFTER DECEMBER 5, 1791

December 7   Notice of Mozart's death appears in a Vienna newspaper; the anonymous writer speculates that the composer was poisoned.

December 10   Emanuel Schikaneder and others arrange for a funeral Mass

---

4. Translation of the original Latin inscription by Bruce Cooper Clarke. The author initialed his epitaph "K," which may point to Leopold Kozeluch, a well-known Czech composer then working in Vienna.

in St. Michael's Church near the Hofburg, during which they perform the completed portions of Mozart's Requiem. Schikaneder also gives a benefit performance of *The Magic Flute* to raise money for Constanze and the children. Baron van Swieten promises to look after the kids.

Mozart's Masonic lodge holds a memorial service, at which a touching eulogy is read.

December 11   Constanze petitions Leopold II for a pension (Mozart never got around to joining the Musicians' Society, which would have entitled her to apply for a pension from them) and permission to stage benefit performances of his music; both requests are granted.

December 15   A huge memorial service is held in Prague, with music by a 120-member chorus and full orchestra, conducted by Mozart's friend, soprano Josepha Duschek.

February 1792   Süssmayr finishes the Requiem and Constanze gives it to Count Wallsegg, who pays her the remaining one-half of the fee.

1798   Breitkopf and Härtel, now Mozart's publisher, presents his "complete works," which in 1803 number 225 compositions— chiefly instrumental music, especially for piano and for string quartet; two of his Masses; the Requiem; and several operas, including *Don Giovanni*, which is soon to become all the rage in the *Singspiel* version by Friedrich Rochlitz.

1862   First edition of Köchel's catalog of Mozart's works.

8

AMADEUS

Stage Play: Peter Shaffer, 1979
Screenplay: Peter Shaffer, 1984
Music Director: Sir Neville Marriner
Director: Milos Forman

BACKGROUND AND CONTEXT OF THE FILM

Knowing all that you now know about Mozart, you are uniquely prepared to view this influential, brilliant, frustrating film and decide for yourself what sort of image of the composer it projects.

The movie—which differs in many respects from the play—was chiefly filmed in Prague and Kremsier before the Iron Curtain came down in 1989; a few scenes were shot in Vienna. *Amadeus* takes place during the decade Mozart lived in Vienna and consists largely of flashbacks narrated by Court Composer Antonio Salieri, who did, in fact, admire Mozart's music, particularly *The Magic Flute* (a few scenes of which you see toward the end of the movie). Salieri, a married man with eight children, is here depicted as celibate, a malevolent conniver, and a musical numbskull: a mythological hat trick! Late in life he suffered episodes of insanity, during one of which he claimed to have poisoned Mozart. Although he denied this as soon as he came to his senses, it was too late. Aleksandr Pushkin had already turned the idea into a play (*Mozart and Salieri*), on which Rimsky-Korsakov later based an opera with the same title, and from which, much later, Peter Shaffer created his play and subsequently the screenplay for this movie.

ISSUES TO THINK ABOUT WHILE VIEWING *AMADEUS*

We see "Mozart" through the eyes of "Salieri," which suggests that we are not meant to regard this portrayal as unbiased or historically accurate. But it is easy to forget this crucial factor as the film progresses.

Nearly all the major characters in the film are costumed in attire identical to that in which they were painted in eighteenth-century portraits. For example, compare the clothing Joseph II wears in most scenes of the movie to those pictured on page 42. Actually, this was his battlefield uniform.

Two musical excerpts, each heard five times, dominate the film: the "statue music" from the Act II finale of *Don Giovanni* and "Contessa, perdono," from the end of *The Marriage of Figaro*, where the Count begs the Countess's forgiveness and she grants it. We first hear the "statue music" at the movie's outset, in darkness, as Salieri's voice screams, "Mozart! Forgive me!" Its second appearance accompanies the threatening, intimidating arrival of Leopold Mozart on the stairway of the Mozarts' apartment. He is dressed all in black, and his son, stricken with fear at first, quickly smiles in welcome. Subsequent uses of this theme identify it with an authoritarian, judgmental father; later, with Salieri once again; finally, with a wrathful God demanding repentance from a willful sinner.

"Contessa, perdono" is the opposing symbol, of grace-filled, undeserved forgiveness. We first hear it as Mozart composes *The Marriage of Figaro* while mindlessly pushing a billiard ball so that it comes back to the starting point. A few minutes later we hear this music again, as Mozart retreats to his billiard room as his father and Constanze argue heatedly outside. Both "Contessa, perdono" and the "statue music" are so carefully, thematically placed in the movie that they quite obviously represent contrasting sides of Mozart's character, analogous to Salieri's repeated description of him as divinely gifted yet morally obscene.

These two instances are not the only examples of the soundtrack's immense significance. The music we hear throughout *Amadeus,* far from being mere background music, constitutes a second, parallel film of its own, which too few viewers seem to realize. You, however, are now in a position to recognize this and to follow it scene by scene. Here is a detailed blow-by-blow.

MUSIC ON THE *AMADEUS* SOUNDTRACK
Giovanni Battista Pergolesi (1710–1736), *Stabat mater* (during Salieri's childhood)

Works by Mozart, not necessarily in this order (titles in **boldface** denote music discussed in this book):

Serenade for Thirteen Instruments, K. 361/370a, 3rd movement
The Abduction from the Seraglio, finale
Symphony in G Minor, K. 183/173dB, 1st movement
Symphony in A major, K. 201, 1st movement

Zaide (Singspiel), K. 344/336b
Concerto for Flute and Harp, K. 299
Adagio for Glass Harmonica, K. 617
Eine kleine Nachtmusik, K. 525
German Dances, K. 509
Sinfonia concertante, K. 364/320d, 1st movement
Concerto for Two Pianos, K. 365/316a, finale
Mass in C Minor, K. 427/417a, "Kyrie eleison"
Piano Concerto in E-flat, K. 482, finale
Piano Concerto in D minor, K. 466, 2nd movement
The Marriage of Figaro, **K. 492** (especially "Contessa, perdono")
Don Giovanni, **K. 527** (especially the "statue music")
The Magic Flute, **K. 620**
Requiem, K. 626 (Requiem aeternam; "Dies irae"; "Lacrimosa")

Only works discussed in this book are cited in the following timings.

Approximate Timings

00'00"	We hear the *Don Giovanni* "statue" music as Salieri screams, "Mozart! I confess, I killed you!"; then, as the credits roll and Salieri, having slit his throat, is carried on a stretcher through a dark night over snow, the "Little" Symphony in G Minor, K. 183/173dB.
04'00"	The film's next six minutes are devoted to Salieri: his interview with the priest in the asylum, his childhood, his father's death.
10'21"	Mozart is introduced as a blindfolded child playing keyboard. Salieri's childhood is contrasted with Mozart's.
16'18"	Constanze and Mozart play games under a piano as Salieri peeks.
20'00"	Mozart, hearing his Serenade for Thirteen Instruments, K. 361/370a, leaves Constanze abruptly to conduct it.
21'00"	Mozart meets Joseph II.
27'00"	Joseph II plays Salieri's march; Mozart redoes it; discussion of *The Abduction from the Seraglio.*
38'00"	Catarina Cavalieri with Salieri; she sings "Martern aller Arten"

from *The Abduction*; the scene shifts to that opera's finale.

45'20"	Mrs. Weber and Constanze are introduced to Joseph II onstage.
47'20"	Leopold grovels to Colloredo; we hear the Kyrie from the C-minor Mass as background to the wedding of Constanze and Mozart.
52'00"	Constanze Mozart appeals to Salieri, who marvels at Mozart's music.
59'00"	We hear the *Don Giovanni* statue music for the second time, as Leopold swoops down the stairs of Mozart's apartment house.
1 00'00"	They find Constanze asleep.
1 03'00"	Everybody goes to a masked ball; it is presumably Carnival time.
1 08'44"	Mozart is seen composing for the first time (*The Marriage of Figaro*) while fiddling with a billiard ball as we hear the Count's plea for forgiveness, "Contessa, perdono," for the first time.
1 11'54"	Mozart returns to the billiard room and we hear "Contessa, perdono" again as Leopold says, "He parties all night." Salieri enters the apartment as Mozart goes to the Augarten to perform the Piano Concerto in E-flat Major, K. 482.
1 15'00"	Salieri asks the maid, "Where does he work?"
1 16'00"	"Contessa, perdono" is heard a third time, as Salieri enters the billiard room and sees the *Figaro* score.
1 16'47"	Mozart defends the opera to Joseph II—"I hate politics," opera seria is boring, its characters "shit marble"; he explains the opening Figaro-Susanna duet, then we see it in rehearsal.
1 24'30"	The end of Act III of *Figaro* is rehearsed with and without the ballet music.
1 30'17"	The finale of Act IV is staged: we hear "Contessa, perdono" a fourth time.
1 32'02"	Joseph II yawns.
1 37'17"	Constanze: "These gentlemen are from Salzburg . . . your father is dead."

1 37'31"	The *Don Giovanni* statue music is heard a third time as we see a portrait of Leopold on the wall. Cut to *Don Giovanni* performance at the entrance of the statue; then we hear Salieri say this is Mozart's "darkest opera" and the statue is Leopold "raised from the dead." The opera (performed without its final scene) comes to an end; weak applause.
1 43'00"	The soundtrack segues to the Piano Concerto in D Minor, K. 466.
1 44'00"	As Mozart composes, he drinks wine straight from the bottle.
1 44'48"	The *Don Giovanni* statue music is heard a fourth time as Salieri, disguised as the "mysterious stranger," arrives at Mozart's apartment.
1 46'03"	We hear the opening music of the Requiem.
1 48'57"	Constanze, Mozart, and little Carl Thomas at the Theater auf der Wieden (run by Schikaneder). They watch takeoffs of Mozart's *Don Giovanni* and *The Abduction*; the audience sings along at favorite passages.
1 52'25"	"Contessa, perdono" (fifth time) performed to close this vaudeville show—sung straight, *not* parodied as *Don Giovanni* was.
1 55'10"	Constanze and Mozart in bed; "Dies irae" ("Day of wrath") from the Requiem.
1 55'30"	A knock at door—is it the masked stranger again?—no, just Schikaneder.
1 56'00"	Schikaneder calls *The Magic Flute* a "vaudeville" (Mozart does, too, later).
1 59'20"	We hear the slow introduction to *The Magic Flute* overture, as the maid reports back to Salieri—
1 59'40"	and as Mozart, disheveled, looks in on Constanze and their son sleeping.
2 00'50"	Mozart thumbs his nose at his father's portrait and dances to the fast second section of *The Magic Flute* overture.
2 01'08"	The *Don Giovanni* statue music is heard for the fifth time as

Salieri (masked) is at the door again.

2 02′50″	Mozart tells Constanze that composing the Requiem is killing him.
2 03′50″	As they talk, or rather don't talk, the soundtrack plays the "Rex tremendae" ("King of awful majesty") from the Requiem.
2 04′00″	Constanze falls asleep; Mozart goes partying at Schikaneder's, where everybody is playing and singing excerpts from *The Magic Flute*.
2 06′00″	Mrs. Weber is transformed into that opera's Queen of Night (who therefore is seen to be a hysterical woman).
2 08′51″	Mozart looks ill as he conducts a performance of the opera.
2 09′00″	Schikaneder as Papageno (in a reproduction of the actual costume Schikaneder wore in 1791); Mozart collapses; Salieri takes him home.
2 16′50″	Mozart dictates the Requiem's "Confutatis maledictis" to Salieri.
2 25′00″	Constanze returns from Baden with Carl Thomas.
2 28′40″	Mozart dies. We hear the Requiem's "Lacrimosa" ("There will be tears on that day") as his casket is taken away for burial. For the final scene, the film returns to the asylum and Salieri.

EXCERPTS OF LETTERS FROM
THE CHILDHOOD TOURS, 1762–1773

Before reading these letters, it may be useful to consult the map of Europe on page 37, "A Mozart Chronology," and "Childhood and Youth, 1756–1773." [1]
The excerpts included here are taken from the following letters:

From Trip 2 (1762–1763)
Vienna—Leopold Mozart's letters to Lorenz Hagenauer
(beginning on page 250)

From Trip 3 (1763–1766)
Paris—Leopold's letters to Lorenz Hagenauer and
one to Frau Hagenauer (beginning on page 256)
London—Leopold Mozart to Lorenz Hagenauer
(beginning on page 261)
The Hague—Leopold Mozart to Lorenz Hagenauer
(beginning on page 267)

From Trip 4 (1769–1770)
First Italian tour—Leopold Mozart to Frau Mozart (beginning
on page 270)

Leopold covers a lot of ground in these letters, detailing his efforts to arrange, put on, and reap a profit from concerts in city after city and country after country. Along the way, he offers a course in eighteenth-century European life on a host of topics:

- Medicine, home remedies such as black powder, and good and bad doctors

---

1. Translations by R. E. W.

- Religion, religious ceremonies, and clergymen at all levels up to and including the pope
- Political machinations at courts (including Salzburg's)
- Poverty, abuse, and the miserable lives of peasants
- The price of food, lodging, carriages, clothing, jewelry—and postage[2]
- The obnoxious pomposity of some aristocrats
- The surprising generosity and kindness of some royalty

Musically, these trips provided the children with an ongoing and deeply enriching experience. Imagine: in town after town and court after court, including the eighteenth century's most magnificent courts—Versailles, London, Vienna (and for Wolfgang, Rome as well)—they heard the most up-to-date music performed by Europe's most celebrated composers, singers, and instrumentalists. Not only did they meet leading musicians; they performed alongside them—these young children from Salzburg—in the palatial salons of European heads of state.

VIENNA
OCTOBER–JANUARY 1763

Linz [on the way to Vienna]
October 3, 1762

[To Lorenz Hagenauer in Salzburg]
    . . . Now, something of a description of our journey. . . . We are very well looked after [by] two women who keep their inn [or rooming house: *Wirtschaft*] going after the death of their parents and who love my children so much that they do everything in their power for them. My children, by the way, amaze everybody. . . . Up to now we are well, though I have a pinch of gout here and there from time to time. The children are happy and act everywhere as if they were at home. The boy is as intimate with everybody, especially officials, as if he had known them all his life. I enclose my bank draft for this month. Please get it cashed; the tax on it must be paid. Take half of it for the rent I owe you, and I ask your wife, to whom we convey our special regards, to arrange for 4 Masses to be said on our behalf as soon as possible. . . . You are all in good health, I hope? That is our heartfelt wish. We shall write you soon from Vienna. Perhaps we will have news before then, but as of now we know nothing. . . .

---

2. To save paper and thus postage, Leopold crowds as much information as he can into the smallest possible space, rarely dividing letters into paragraphs.

Vienna
October 16, 1762

[To Lorenz Hagenauer]

We left Linz at 4:30 in the afternoon on the Feast of St. Francis, on the so-called ordinary boat, and arrived in Mauthausen at 7:30 that same day, in total darkness. At noon the next day we came to Ybbs, where 2 Franciscans and a Benedictine monk, who were also on the boat, said Mass, during which our Woferl scampered over the organ keys, playing so well that the Franciscans, who were sitting with guests for lunch, left their meal along with their guests, ran into the choir loft, and nearly died with surprise. . . . [O]n Wednesday at 3 we arrived in Vienna, where at 5 we ate lunch and dinner at the same time. On the trip we had constant rain and a lot of wind. Wolfgangerl had already caught a cold in Linz but in spite of our disorderly life—getting up early, eating and drinking irregularly, plus the wind and rain—he is healthy, thank God. . . . We have been here 8 days but still don't know where the sun comes up in Vienna, because up to now it has done nothing but rain and with the constant wind, also snowed a little. . . . One thing I have to mention especially is that we got through [customs] really fast. For that, Herr Woferl is responsible, for he made intimate friends with the customs officer right away— showed him his clavichord,[3] invited him to visit us, and played him a minuet on his little violin—and with that, we were passed right through. . . . [A]ll the ladies are in love with my boy. We are already being talked about everywhere, and when I was alone at the opera on the 10th I heard Archduke Leopold [one of Empress Maria Theresa's sons, who became emperor in 1790] say a lot of things to another box—that there was a boy in Vienna who played the harpsichord so excellently, etc. At 11 that same night I received the command to go to Schönbrunn[4] on the 12th. . . . Everyone is amazed, especially by the boy, and I have yet to hear anyone who doesn't say it is incomprehensible. . . . [W]e have been welcomed by Their Majesties with such extraordinary graciousness that when I tell people [back home in Salzburg] about it they will take it for a fable. Wolferl [*sic*] jumped up onto the empress's lap, put his arms around her neck, and kissed her warmly. In short, we were there from 3 to 6 o'clock and the emperor himself [Francis I] came out of the next room to fetch me to hear [young Archduke Ferdinand] play the violin. On the 15th the empress had her paymaster deliver two sets of clothes, one for the boy and one for the girl.[5] As soon as the command comes, they must appear at court and the paymaster will pick them up. Today at 2:30 they have to go to the two youngest archdukes, at 4 to Count Palfi, the Hungarian chancellor. . . . Yesterday we were at Count Kaunitz's and the day before yesterday at Countess Kinsky's and later at Count von Ulfeld's. We are already booked for the next 2 days. Please tell everybody that we are healthy and happy, praise God. I send greetings and am your old

Mozart.

---

3. A clavichord was a small, delicate-sounding keyboard instrument.
4. The empress's summer palace outside the city, where she preferred to live year-round.
5. For pictures of the Mozart children in these outfits, see page 26.

Vienna

October 19, 1762

[To Lorenz Hagenauer]

Early today I was summoned to the paymaster, who received me with the greatest courtesy. His Majesty wanted to ask if I couldn't stay here a little longer. I said I was most humbly at His Majesty's disposal. The paymaster then paid me 100 ducats and said His Majesty would call us again soon. If I may speculate—as I always do—I expect that we will probably not come home before Advent [the month leading up to Christmas], but before then I will ask [the Salzburg archbishop] for an extension [of my leave of absence]. Even if I could get away from here in two or three weeks, I have to travel slowly because of the children, so that they can rest several days now and then and not get sick. . . . If I can find a good carriage at a decent price I am determined to buy one, to give my children more comfort. Today we were at the French ambassador's. Tomorrow we're invited to Count Harrach's from 4 to 6, but I don't know what for. . . . Everywhere we go, we are picked up in a carriage by a servant and then brought back home. From 6 or 6:30 we are to perform for six ducats at a big concert given by a certain rich nobleman, where Vienna's finest virtuosos will perform. Noblemen send us invitations 4, 5, 6, or 8 days in advance in order not to miss us. The chief postmaster, Count Paar, has already engaged us for next Monday. Woferl gets enough carriage driving, at least twice a day. Once we drove at 2:30 to a place where we stayed until 3:45; there, Count Hardegg had us picked up in his carriage and drove at a full gallop to a lady's house where we stayed till 5:30. From there, Count Kaunitz had us picked up and we were at his house until almost 9. I can hardly write, because my [quill] pen and ink are both wretched and I have to steal the time to write. I have absolutely no news to write because here the war is little talked about,[6] as if there weren't one. Never in my life have I heard so little news, or known as little, as during the 4 or 5 weeks I have been away from Salzburg. I would like to hear some news from you, at least I hope you will report some to me. Is His Princely Grace home yet?[7] I hope he is well. . . . Do you know where I am living? I live on Fierberggassl, not far from the High Bridge, on the second floor of the carpenter's house. The room is 1,000 feet long and one foot wide. You laugh? But in fact, it is not funny for us when we walk on each other's corns. It is even less funny when my boy throws me and the girl throws my wife out of our miserable beds, or when they kick a few of our ribs every night. Each of our beds is 4 1/2 feet wide, and this amazing palace is divided by a wall into 2 parts, one for each of these big beds. Patience! We are in Vienna. My wife would very much like to have her lined fur here, but we think it would cost too much to send by the mail coach, and it might get damaged on the way. It is in the chest in the little room, but since

---

6. The Seven Years' War, 1756–1763, known in America as the French and Indian War.
7. Archbishop Schrattenbach, Prince-Archbishop of Salzburg until 1772.

I think I will have a new one made for her in Salzburg and let her wear the old one for ordinary occasions, it would be better to buy something for her here, where there is so much choice. Would you like to know what Woferl's suit of clothes looks like?[8] It is made of the finest lilac-colored cloth; the vest is moiré,[9] the same shade as the coat, and both coat and vest are bordered in wide gold braid. It was made for Prince Maximilian. Nannerl's dress was the court dress of a princess. It is made of white brocaded taffeta, with all sorts of trimming. It is a pity that you can't make anything but a petticoat out of it, but it has a little bodice, too. My sheet of paper is now full and the time is gone. Greetings to everybody in the Salzburg world.

Vienna
October 30, 1762

[To Lorenz Hagenauer]

. . . I almost thought for 14 days in a row that we were far too happy. God has sent us a small cross. . . . On the 21ˢᵗ at seven o'clock in the evening we were again at the empress's. . . . [O]ur *Woferl*, though, was not quite right as he usually is, and before we drove there and also as he was going to bed, he complained a good deal about his backside and his feet. When he was in bed, I examined the places where he said he had pain and found several flecks as big as a kreuzer [a coin] that were very red and somewhat swollen, and painful to the touch. But they were only on both shinbones, both elbows, and a few on his backside, but very few. He had a fever and we gave him a black powder[10] and margrave powder.[11] He slept fitfully. The next day, Friday, we repeated the powders morning and evening and found that the spots had spread; they were larger but there weren't more of them. We had to send messages to all the nobles where we had engagements for the next 8 days, canceling each one, day after day. We continued to give margrave powders and on Sunday he began to sweat, as we hoped, for up to then his fever had been drier. I met the physician of the Countess von Sinzendorf, who herself was not here, and told him the situation. He came with me at once. He liked what we had done and said it was a kind of scarlet fever rash. . . . Praise God, he is now so well that we hope he will get out of bed the day after tomorrow, his name day,[12] and stand up for the first time. At the same time he has just cut a molar, which caused his left cheek to swell. The nobles not only graciously asked every day about the boy's condition, but urged the doctor to take good care of him, so that Dr. Bernhard (that is his name) could not possibly have done more. Meanwhile, this affair has cost me *at least fifty ducats*. But

---

8. Leopold is referring again to the hand-me-down outfits the empress gave the children.
9. A kind of silk, with a wavy pattern in it.
10. "Black powder" seems to have been almost a universal remedy, used for a wide variety of ailments.
11. Named after its inventor, Andreas Sigismund Marggraf.
12. Your name day, as opposed to your birthday, honors the saint after whom you were named.

I thank God endlessly that it has turned out so well, for these scarlet fever spots are a fashionable complaint for children here, but dangerous, and I hope that Woferl is now immunized, for the change of air was the main cause.... Please give my most respectful greeting to your wife and tell her that I must worry her again and ask her to be so kind as to arrange for three Masses to be said in Loreto at the [Church of the Holy Child] and three Masses in Bergl at St. Francisco de Paola.[13] I shall repay everything with thanks....

I beg you to do everything possible to find out what His Grace [Archbishop Schrattenbach] will eventually do and what hope I have for the post of *Vize-Kapellmeister*.[14] I don't ask without a reason. You are my friend. Who knows what I should do? If only I knew how it will finally turn out, for one thing is certain: I now find myself in circumstances which would allow me to earn my bread here as well. I still prefer Salzburg to all other possibilities. But no one must hold me back. I ask you again; for otherwise I myself don't know what I may let others persuade me to do.

Vienna
November 6, 1762

[To Lorenz Hagenauer]

...I have received all your kind letters in due course. How grateful I am for your many efforts! ... From my last letter you will have perceived what danger my Woferl was in and how anxious I was for him. Praise God! All is well again. Yesterday we paid our good Dr. Bernhard with a concert. He invited a number of good friends and sent his carriage to pick us up.... I have been addressed as *Kapellmeister* of Salzburg since my arrival, and the emperor himself, when he wanted to take me in to hear one of his children play the violin, came out and called, "Where is the *Kapellmeister* of Salzburg?" Recently, I have deliberately left off [the title], for people might have thought it an invention [which it was]. There are opportunities almost every day when I have to contradict such statements, for it is far from me to be full of lies and bragging. Now you understand me. I trust to your friendship.

Vienna
November 24, 1762

[To Lorenz Hagenauer]

... [H]ere the nobility are afraid of pock-marks and all kinds of rash; the result is that my boy's illness has set us back about four weeks; for although since his recovery we have taken in twenty-one ducats, this is a mere trifle, since we barely manage every day on one ducat, and daily there are additional expenses;

13. Churches near Salzburg which the Mozarts frequently attended. The church in Loreto was in a convent; San Francisco de Paula was a pilgrimage site.
14. Leopold received this appointment four months later, in February 1763.

except for this we are in good spirits. The lady-in-waiting, Countess Theresa von Lodron, recently conferred a great honor on us: she gave us a box at the play (which is difficult to get) and honored my Woferl with shoe-buckles that have little gold plates and look like solid gold. On [November 19] we saw the gala-table. The nobility bestowed exceptional honors and kindnesses on us. It is enough to say that Her Majesty the empress called me away from the table to ask if my boy was now quite well. . . . When shall we be home? By Christmas or the New Year?

Vienna

December 10, 1762

[To Lorenz Hagenauer]

. . . I wrote to His Grace[15] and also to our Father Confessor and both letters were composed in the way my best friends suggested. I also added a lengthy apology for not being able to return to Salzburg at the prescribed time. To put it briefly, I cannot get home before Christmas or the New Year. . . . It is a good thing that we are not at home now! We are afraid of smallpox, and it may find its way up to us.[16] . . . Meanwhile give my worthy and holy Father Confessor my most humble greetings and tell him that if by staying away I were to lose the favor of His Grace [Archbishop Schrattenbach], I am ready at his first wink to leave by mail coach[17] for Salzburg. Right now there are still many things to keep us here at least a month; just think, Count Durazzo, music director at this court, has not yet been able to arrange for us to play at his *accademia* or public concert. If we agreed to do so, we could stay on until Lent or Easter and draw a lot of money every week. You will think that Vienna makes everybody a fool. Yes, in fact, when I compare Salzburg with Vienna in certain respects, I soon become confused. Well, if God keeps us healthy, I hope to wish you a Happy New Year from my carriage. . . . I am your honest friend

Mozart.

Vienna

December 29, 1762

[To Lorenz Hagenauer]

Homo proponit, Deus disponit.[18] On the 26th [I meant to] leave Vienna in order to reach Salzburg on New Year's Eve. But on the 19th I had an unusually bad toothache . . . in the whole row of my upper front teeth, which are perfectly good and otherwise healthy. All through the night my whole face swelled up and the

---

15. Archbishop Schrattenbach of Salzburg.
16. That is, to Salzburg.
17. Not a first-class means of travel. Leopold is pouring it on to emphasize his financial prudence to his creditor, Herr Hagenauer.
18. "Man proposes, God disposes"—i.e., human beings think up plans and ideas, but God either allows them to happen, or doesn't.

next day I looked like a trumpeting angel, so much so that Lieutenant Winckler (the court drummer's brother), who came to visit us, did not recognize me. . . . I had to console myself with the thought that in any case we were held up by the unusually cold weather, for . . . the only way they could get the post-bags across the Danube was with small boats and the postilion on a field-horse.

. . . I said good-bye. . . . That day our journey was not very comfortable, for though the road was frozen hard, it was indescribably bumpy and full of deep ruts and ridges. . . . Now I am most certainly leaving here on Friday morning and with God's help will reach Linz on Sunday, and on the Vigil of the Epiphany, [January] 5, 1763, I hope to see you. . . . I am burning with excitement to tell you a lot of things. . . .

My wife and children send their greetings. If you could get the room heated for a few days. . . . Only a little is necessary, in the front stove.

Paris
December 1763–April 1764

Paris
December 8, 1763

[To Lorenz Hagenauer]
Monsieur mon trés [*sic*; should be *très*] cher Ami!
. . . On November 10 we arrived at the townhouse of Count van Eyck in Paris,[19] luckily found the count and countess at home, and they received us most warmly and provided us with a room where we are comfortable and happy. We have the countess's harpsichord in our room, because she has no need for it; it is a good one and, like ours, has 2 manuals.[20] . . . Perhaps you would like to know how I like Paris? If I were to tell you this in complete detail, neither a cow's hide nor a rhinoceros's skin would be big enough. Buy yourself for forty-five kreuzers Johann Peter Willebrandt's . . . *Historical Reports and Practical Observations on Trips, etc. to Frankfurt and Leipzig 1761*. It will give you much pleasure. . . .

Paris
February 1, 1764

[To Frau Hagenauer]
Madame,
One must not always write to men, but must sometimes remember the fair and devout sex. Whether the women in Paris are pretty, I really can't tell you

---

19. Van Eyck, Bavarian ambassador to the French court and a relative of the chamberlain to Archbishop Schrattenbach in Salzburg, invited the Mozarts to stay with him during their visit to Paris.
20. A manual is a keyboard. Some harpsichords, like organs, had two of them.

because they are painted so unnaturally, like Berchtesgarten dolls,[21] that even a naturally beautiful woman wearing this detestable makeup is unbearable to the eyes of an honest German. As for piety, I can assure you that it takes no effort to search out the miracles achieved by French women saints; the greatest of them were performed by those who were neither virgins nor wives nor widows, and these miracles were all performed by living bodies. Later on we shall speak more clearly on this subject. But really it is extremely difficult to tell who is the lady of the house here; each person lives as he likes and, if God is not especially gracious, the same thing is going to happen to France that happened to the ex-Persian Empire. . . . [T]he most important and certainly to you the most pleasant piece of information I can give you is that, praise God, we are all well. . . . Everything here, even more so than at other courts, goes at a snail's pace, so . . . one must be patient. If the recognition we get equals the pleasure my children have given this court, it ought to turn out very well. It is worth noting that it is not the custom here to kiss the hand of royal persons or . . . even to speak to them *au Passage,* as they say . . . which means, when they walk through the gallery and the royal apartments on their way to church. . . . On the contrary, one stands up straight, without the slightest movement, and in this position watches the king and his family go by. You can easily imagine how impressed and amazed these French people . . . must have been when the king's daughters . . . stopped when they saw my children, came up to them, and not only allowed them to kiss their hands but kissed *their* hands innumerable times. . . . But what appeared most extraordinary to these people was that . . . on the evening of New Year's Day, not only was it necessary to make way for us to go up to the royal table, but my Herr Wolfgangus had the honor to stand next to the queen, to talk constantly to her, entertain her, and kiss her hands repeatedly, as she fed him from the table. The queen speaks as good German as we do, and since the king doesn't know any, she translated everything that our heroic Wolfgang said. . . . You can hardly expect me to describe Versailles to you. . . . I heard good and bad music there. Everything sung by individual voices and which is supposed to resemble an aria was empty, frozen, and wretched—French; but the choruses are good and even very good. . . . The king's Mass takes place at 1 o'clock unless he goes hunting, in which case it is at 10, and the queen's at 12:30. . . . In Versailles . . . for every carriage ride, one has to pay twelve *sous.* So you see that, on many days, for the weather was always bad, we had to have at least 2 if not 3 sedan-chairs [a small carriage, with room for one person, carried rather than pulled by horses], [which] cost one laubthaler and sometimes more. . . . If you now add 4 new black suits, you will not be surprised if our visit to Versailles comes to 26 or 27 louis d'or. Now we will see what comes to us from the court. . . . My Master Wolfgang . . . has received from Madame la Contesse de Tessé a gold

---

21. A town near Salzburg famous for its painted figurines.

snuffbox and a gold watch, valuable on account of its smallness, the size of which
I trace here:

Nannerl has been given an uncommonly beautiful, heavy, solid-gold toothpick
case. From another lady, Wolfgang received a traveling writing-case in silver and
Nannerl an unusually fine tortoiseshell snuffbox, inlaid with gold. . . . [We have
also received] . . . a host of trifles that I do not value very highly, such as sword-
bands, ribbons, and armlets, flowers for caps for Nannerl . . . and so forth. . . . I can
assure you that you do not need a telescope to see everywhere the evil results of
the last war.[22] The French insist on continuing their appearances of splendor to the
highest degree and consequently only [large-scale, government-sponsored farmers]
are rich, while the nobles are deep in debt. The greatest wealth belongs to about
100 people, a few big bankers and large-scale farmers; and finally, most money goes
to Lucretias [i.e., creditors], who do not stab themselves [i.e., who make out well
at everyone else's expense]. That you see remarkably beautiful and precious things
here, you can imagine; but you also see astonishing follies. In winter, the women
wear not only clothes trimmed with fur, but also collars or ties of fur, and instead
of flowers, all sorts of fur in their hair and fur armlets and so forth; but the most
ridiculous is a kind of sword-band in fashion here, bound round and round with
fine fur—that's a smart idea, so the sword won't freeze. . . . You will not soon find
any other city filled with so many miserable and mutilated people. You spend barely
a minute in a church, or walk along a few streets, before you meet someone blind
or lame or limping, or some half-putrefied beggar, or find someone lying on the
street whose hand was eaten away by pigs when he was a child, or someone else
who, while his foster father and family were working in the fields, fell into the fire
and had half an arm burned away. . . . Now I am going to jump from the ugly to
the charming and moreover to someone who has charmed a king. You surely want
to know what Madame Pompadour[23] looks like, don't you? She must have been
beautiful, because she is still pretty. She is a tall and imposing person, fat or rather
well-covered, but very well proportioned, blond, and . . . in her eyes [you see] a
resemblance to Her Majesty the empress [Maria Theresa]. She exudes dignity and
an exceptional intelligence. Her apartments at Versailles are like a paradise, looking
out on the gardens. In Paris, she has a most splendid house in the Faubourg St.

---

22. The Seven Years' War, which had ended in 1763.
23. The Marquise de Pompadour (1721–1764), Louis XV's mistress, was also said to have
political influence. She was famous, or notorious, for both.

Honoré, all newly rebuilt. In the room where the harpsichord is (which is all gilt and most artistically lacquered and painted) is her life-size portrait, and beside it, a portrait of the king. . . . Now for something else! Here there is a constant war between Italian and French music.[24] The whole of French music is not worth a [penny]. But now they are starting to make radical changes . . . in 10 to 15 years [the current] French taste will, I hope, have completely disappeared. . . . At present, four sonatas of M. Wolfgang Mozart are being engraved. Picture to yourself the furor they will make in the world when people read on the title-page that they were composed by a 7-year-old child, and when the doubters undertake to test him, which has already happened,[25] imagine when someone asks him to write down a minuet or something, and then immediately and without touching the harpsichord, he writes in the bass part and, if asked, a 2nd violin part. . . . I can tell you, dearest Frau Hagenauer, that every day God performs fresh miracles through this child. By the time we reach home, if God wills it, he will be ready to perform court service. He accompanies in public concerts. He even, when accompanying arias, transposes *a prima vista*[26]—and everywhere Italian and French works are put before him, which he plays at sight. My little girl plays the most difficult works [given to her]. . . .

Paris

February 22, 1764

[To Lorenz Hagenauer]

. . . My dear Wolfgang suddenly got a sore throat and a cold, so that on the 16th, the morning when it started, he got such an inflammation in his throat that he was in danger of choking. . . . The phlegm that he couldn't cough up fell back into his stomach, so I took him out of bed quickly and led him back and forth around the room. The phlegm came free right away. He also had a very high fever. . . . After four days he got up and is now well again. As a precaution I wrote by local post to our friend the German Doctor Herrnschwand, who is the doctor for the Swiss Guards. But he did not have to come more than twice. Then I gave the boy a small dose of Vienna laxative water; now, praise God, he is well. My little girl, too, is suffering from a cold, but has no fever. . . . Within three or, at most, four weeks important things will happen, if God wills. We have planted well; now we hope for a good harvest. You have to take things as they come. I would have at least twelve more *louis d'or* if my children had not had to stay at home for a few days. I thank God that they are better.—Do you know what people here always want?—They want to

---

24. Such musical wars persisted in Paris. Another raged in 1778 when Wolfgang Mozart was there; see page 108f.
25. Both in Paris and London, Wolfgang was tested to see if he was the real thing. He passed easily.
26. To transpose is to play a piece in a different key than the one in which it was written; *a prima vista* means "at first sight," i.e., immediately, without prior study or rehearsal.

persuade me to let my boy be inoculated with smallpox. After I clearly explained my resistance to this, they left me in peace. Here inoculation is the fashion....[27] But for my part, I leave it to the grace of God. It depends on His divine grace whether He wishes to keep this prodigy of nature in the world into which he has placed it, or to take it to Himself. I shall certainly watch over it so well that it makes no difference whether we are in Salzburg or in any other part of the world. But that is what makes traveling expensive. . . .

Paris

April 1, 1764

[To Lorenz Hagenauer]

. . . We are all well and we thank God endlessly. And now I can tell you with pleasure that I hope in a few days to hand over to the bankers Turton et Baur 200 louis d'or, to be entrusted to safe hands and then to be sent off to Salzburg. . . . [A]t the concert on March 10 I took in 112 louis d'or. But 50 to 60 louis d'or are not to be disdained either and, if it is more, you stick it into your bag. Not a kreuzer is paid at the entrance, but whoever has no ticket is not let in, no matter who it is. My friends sell the tickets 8 days beforehand, each one for a laubthaler or a federthaler, 4 of which make one louis d'or; and they collect the money. But most of the tickets are given to ladies in blocks of 12 and 24, who sell them easily, because out of politeness nobody can refuse them. . . . I request that a Mass be said for us every day for eight days, April 12, 13, 14, 15, 16, 17, 18, and 19. You can divide them up as you like, in whatever church or before whatever altar, as long as 4 are said at Loreto at the Holy Child and 4 at an altar of Our Lady. . . . But please, these 8 days from the 12th to the 19th inclusively. But if this letter does not arrive until after April 12, though I think it will arrive before that, please see that the Masses are begun right away, the next day. . . .

But now you must know who this man is, this great friend of mine, who does everything for me, this M. Grimm.[28] He is secretary to the Duc d'Orléans, a learned man, and a great friend of humanity. All my other letters and recommendations came to nothing, even those from the French ambassador in Vienna, the Imperial ambassador in Paris, and all the letters of introduction from our minister in Brussels, Count Cobenzl, Prince Conti, the Duchesse d'Aiguilon, etc., etc., and all the others, of whom I could write down a whole litany Only M. Grimm, to whom I had a letter from a Frankfurt merchant's wife, has done everything. He brought our matter to the court [Versailles]; he arranged for the first concert, and

---

27. The vaccine against smallpox, discovered by Jenner, did not appear until 1796. Leopold is talking about injecting healthy people with smallpox from affected persons, the most recent effort against the disease.

28. Baron Friedrich Melchior Grimm, whose help proved invaluable in Paris and also during Wolfgang's job-hunting trip to Paris in 1778. See Grimm in "Important People in Mozart's Life."

he himself paid me 80 louis d'or, that is, he took care of 320 tickets; he also paid for the lighting, as more than 60 large table candles were burnt. Now this Grimm has secured permission for the first concert and is now arranging for the second, for which over 100 tickets have already been sold. See what a man can do who is intelligent and has a good heart. He is from Regensburg, but has been in Paris for over 15 years and knows how to launch everything on the right road, so that it is bound to turn out the way he wants. . . . My children send their greetings to all, as does my wife. M. de Mechel, a copper-engraver, is working frantically to engrave our portraits, which M. de Carmontelle (an amateur) has painted extremely well. Wolfgang is playing the harpsichord, I am standing behind his chair playing the violin, and Nannerl is leaning on the harpsichord with one arm, while in the other hand she is holding music, as if she were singing.[29]

LONDON
APRIL 1764–SUMMER 1765

London
April 25, 1764

[To Lorenz Hagenauer]

Praise God, we have come safely over the [English Channel], though not without [vomiting], . . . it overtook me more than anyone else. But it saved money [not to take] medicine for it, and, thank God, we are all well. Whoever has too much money should just undertake a journey from Paris to London; that will certainly lighten his purse. . . . As soon as you arrive at Dover, it is even worse; and when you get off the boat, you see yourself surrounded by 30 to 40 people all saying they are your servant and who want to grab your baggage away from your own servants to carry it to the inn, and then you have to pay them whatever they demand.

. . . It looks to me as if everyone in London is wearing costumes; and what would you think about how my wife and my little girl look in English hats and I and big Wolfgang in English suits? My next letter will tell you more. We greet you.

Mozart.

London
May 28, 1764

[To Lorenz Hagenauer]

Monsieur!

You know that the farther away a thing is, the smaller it looks to the eye. So it is with my letters. My handwriting gets smaller the farther I am from Salzburg. If we sailed over to America, it would probably become totally illegible. For a simple letter without an envelope, the cost from here to Germany is a shilling, plus another

---

29. For this portrait, see page 25.

shilling for the envelope, so that a letter with an envelope you have to pay two shillings. A guinea is 21 shillings and is equal to the louis d'or, for in Dover the banker Miné, to whom I had been recommended in Paris, gave me 12 guineas for 12 louis d'or, since French money is not accepted here. You can easily figure out what a shilling is worth. Our most gracious Frau Hagenauer suggested in her letter to me in Paris, "Perhaps [you'll] even [go to] England and Holland?" Going to England was only half-decided when I left Salzburg, but since the whole world, including people in Paris, urged us to go to London, I had to decide to do it; and now by the help of God we are there. But we shall not go to Holland, of that I can assure everyone.[30] . . . On April 27 we were from 6 to 9 with the king and queen[31] in the queen's palace in St. James's Park. . . . Thus on the fifth day after our arrival we were already at court. Their present to us was only 24 guineas, which we received immediately on leaving the king's room, but the graciousness with which His Majesty the king as well as Her Majesty the queen received us was indescribable. In short, their easy and friendly manner made it impossible to think of them as the king and queen of England. At all courts up to the present we have been received with extraordinary courtesy, but what we have experienced here exceeds all the others: 8 days later we went walking in St. James's Park. The king came driving through with the queen, and although we had on different clothes [from those we had worn at court], they recognized us right away and not only greeted us, but the king opened the window, leaned his head out, and smilingly greeted us with waves, especially our Master Wolfgang. . . . I can report nothing more, except that on May 19 we were again with the king and queen from 6 to 10 in the evening, when the only other people present were the two princes. . . . When we left the room we were again handed 24 guineas; if this happens every three or four weeks, we can endure it. . . . [S]ince the 4th is the king's birthday and therefore many of the nobility will come into town from the country,[32] we must dare to profit from this moment to make ourselves known. Each person pays half a guinea and, if it were wintertime, I could certainly count on 600 people, that is, 300 guineas. . . . It will go well, if with God's help we keep healthy and if God only keeps our unconquerable Wolfgang healthy. . . . [W]hat he knew when we left Salzburg is just a shadow of what he knows now. It exceeds all imagining. . . . There is not a day that he doesn't talk at least 30 times about Salzburg and his and our friends and patrons. He now always

---

30. But they did go to Holland; see his letters from The Hague (beginning on page 267).
31. King George III (later famous as the British monarch during the American Revolution, 1775–1783) and Queen Charlotte. Both were pretty good musicians.
32. In London as in Vienna, members of the aristocracy generally spent the summer months at their country houses. This created a problem for touring musicians, who had no way to get out to these estates (assuming they could wangle an invitation) but had to centralize their efforts in the cities, where the courts were. The happy coincidence of the king's birthday on June 4 meant that for a day or so before and after that, the Mozarts had access to a lot of nobility.

has an opera in his head that he wants to perform in Salzburg with nothing but young people. . . .

London
June 8, 1764

[To Lorenz Hagenauer]
Monsieur!

With the greatest pleasure in the world I received your letter of May 21 on June 6. This letter had a favorable wind over the ocean. I am infinitely happy that my first letter reached you safely and I hope that the second, which I sent off on the 28th, has arrived in the meantime. . . . I have had another shock, namely, taking in 100 guineas in three hours. Happily, it is now over. I have already written that everyone is now out of town. June 5 was the only day we could try [to hold a concert], because the 4th was the king's birthday. . . . There were only 8 days, or 2 or 3 days really, when we could distribute the tickets, because hardly anyone was in town. But . . . to everyone's amazement there were no more than a few hundred present, but they were the top people in all of London; not only all the ambassadors, but the first families of England, and the pleasure was universal. I cannot say whether a profit of 100 guineas will remain, since I have not yet received the money [from various people], and the expenses are astonishingly high. But it will certainly not be less than 90 [guineas]. . . . The hall without lighting or music stands, etc. costs 5 guineas; for each harpsichord, of which I had to have 2 on account of the concerto for two harpsichords, a half guinea. . . . The first violin [gets] 3 guineas, and so on; and all who play the solos and concertos 3, 4, and 5 guineas. . . . Well, God be praised, this undertaking is over. . . . [M]y little girl is one of the most skillful players in Europe, although she is only 12 years old, and . . . my boy in this his 8th year of age knows what one would expect from a man of 40; whoever does not see and hear it cannot believe it. You yourself and all our Salzburg friends know nothing about it, for the situation is now utterly different.

I must close, for the post is going, and I am your most obedient servant.

Mozart.

P.S. My wife and I, Nannerl, and our all-powerful Wolfgangus send greetings to you, your whole household and all Salzburg.

London
August 3, 1764

[To Lorenz Hagenauer]
Monsieur,

Do not be frightened! But just prepare your heart to hear one of the saddest events. Perhaps you will have already noticed in my handwriting what condition I find myself in now. Almighty God has visited me with a sudden and severe illness that I am too weak to describe. Well! I have been [given an enema], purged, and because of a severe inflammation in my throat, also bled. Now that is all over and the doctors have declared that I have no fever and should eat, but I am like a child. My stomach has no desire for anything and I am so weak that I can hardly think sensibly. . . .

London
August 9, 1764

[To Lorenz Hagenauer]

I congratulate you on your name day! I intended to write to you right after I received your welcome letter; but I was much too weak. I am now in a spot outside the city, where I was carried in a sedan-chair, to improve my appetite and regain my strength from the good air. It has one of the most beautiful views in the world. Wherever I look, I see nothing but gardens and, beyond them, the finest castles; and the house where I am living also has a lovely garden.

It is up to the grace of God whether He will preserve my life. His most holy will be done.

Chelsea near London
September 13, 1764

[To Lorenz Hagenauer]
Monsieur,

. . . My wife and children send their greetings. My wife has much to do now because of my illness, and many worries, as you can easily imagine, and in Chelsea, at first we had our food brought to us from an eating-house; but since it was poor, my wife began to do our cooking herself and we are now so well that when we return to town next week we shall continue to do our own housekeeping. Perhaps too my wife, who has become very thin, will get a little fatter. . . . By the way, I shall doubtless spend at least the whole winter here and make thousands of gulden, if God wills, as you will have already figured out for yourself. I am now in a place where no one from the Salzburg court has ever yet dared to go and where perhaps no one will go in the future. . . Both in Salzburg and in London, we are in His hands. He knows my good intentions. Now come a few months when I shall have enough to do to bring the nobility over to my side, which will cost me a lot of galloping around and hard effort, but if I reach my goal, I shall have a fine fish or a good catch of guineas.

London
November 27, 1764

[To Lorenz Hagenauer]
Monsieur!

Do not be surprised that I am answering you somewhat late; I have more to do than some people would imagine, although the nobility are not in town and Parliament, contrary to custom, will not assemble until January 10 next year, and therefore guineas are not yet flying about, and I am still living out of my purse. Yet it will soon be time for me to fill it up again, for from the beginning of July until now I have spent over 170 guineas. In addition, I have the heavy expense of having 6 [piano] sonatas [K.10, 11, 12, 13, 14, 15] by Herr Wolfgang engraved and printed, which are being dedicated to the queen of England (at her own request)....

London

February 8, 1765

[To Lorenz Hagenauer]

Monsieur,

... On the evening of the 15th we will perform a concert[33] that will probably bring me about 150 guineas. Whether—and what I make after that, I cannot know. The king, by postponing Parliament (which usually assembles 2 months earlier), has dealt a heavy blow to all arts and sciences. The explanation for this would take too long....

Nobody is making much money this winter except Manzuoli[34] and a few others at the opera. Manzuoli receives 1500 pounds sterling for this winter and the money has to be guaranteed in Italy, because the previous impresario ... went bankrupt last year; [unless they had given him this guarantee] Manzuoli would not have come to London. In addition to this, he is giving a benefit, that is, an evening recital for himself,[35] so that this winter he will draw more than 20,000 German gulden. He is the only person they have had to pay decently in order to restore the opera.... I am writing this letter, which will soon be followed by another, simply in order not to miss the opportunity of sending a few sonatas [Wolfgang's K. 6–9] to Augsburg and Nuremberg.... Please have this announced in our local newspapers, ... that the little composer wants to let his fellow townsmen each have a copy [at a low price] to encourage the youth of Salzburg to apply themselves industriously to music.... Oh, how much I have to do. The symphonies at the concert will all be by Wolfgang Mozart.[36] I must copy them myself, unless I want to pay 1 shilling

---

33. By "we" Mozart means his children. In some letters he speaks of "my" concert, but it was always theirs. He did not perform with them on any occasion during these tours, as far as we know.

34. A famous male soprano, i.e., castrato. Through most of the eighteenth century, castratos were celebrated and paid like today's rock stars. They went out of fashion during the course of Mozart's lifetime, though he composed numerous works for them.

35. Which means that the profits would be his. Benefit concerts were common. Mozart put on benefits like this for himself in Vienna; he also wrote music pro bono for friends to perform at their benefit concerts.

36. Leopold arranged for the ads to say that Wolfgang was eight years old; actually, he was nine.

for each sheet.—Copying music is profitable here. Estlinger [one of the Mozarts' Salzburg copyists] would laugh. I congratulate him . . . Addio.

London
March 19, 1765

[To Lorenz Hagenauer]
Monsieur!

. . . My concert[37] of the 15ᵗʰ . . . was not performed until the 21ˢᵗ, and on account of many [other] entertainments (which make one weary) [attendance] was not as strong as I hoped; nevertheless I took in about 130 guineas, and since the expenses amounted to over 27 guineas, I did not made much more than 100 guineas. I know, however, what was missing, and why people didn't treat us more generously, although since our arrival in London we have made a few 100 guineas—I did not accept a proposal that was made to me. But how useful is it to say much about something about which I have made up my mind deliberately, after mature consideration and several sleepless nights, and which is now done with, as I will not bring up my children in such a dangerous place (where the majority of the inhabitants have no religion at all and where one only has evil examples before one's eyes). You would be amazed if you saw the way children are brought up here; not to mention other matters connected with religion. . . . Now I must ask you to reply to this letter as soon as possible; since it may happen that I leave London at the beginning of May, I must have an answer *by the end of April* . . . The queen has given our Wolfgango [*sic*] a present of 50 guineas for the dedication of the sonatas. . . . Please ask our dear friend Spitzeder to forgive me for never answering his very nice letters. He is so reasonable, he knows what a man has to do who is keeping his whole family in a city where, even with the strictest economy, it costs 300 pounds sterling a year, and where in addition he ought to be saving some . . .

London
April 18, 1765

[To Lorenz Hagenauer]
Monsieur!

I was pleased to get your letter. Everything you have done was well done. I have no more news to write you. . . . As for my departure, I have nothing to write, and any reasonable person must realize that it is not fun. It takes time to get us away from here, getting all our baggage in order—the sight of it makes me sweat— just think! When you live a whole year in one place—why, we have made this our home—it requires even more preparation than when we left Salzburg. . . .

---

37. "My concert" means "the one I arranged," not one Leopold himself played in.

London
July 9, 1765

[To Lorenz Hagenauer]

Monsieur!

No doubt you all think we swam over the sea a long time ago, but it is not yet possible; we are still in London, and once we leave, we cannot return to England in 3 days. . . .

I ask that as soon as you read this letter you arrange for *6 Holy Masses* to be said, *2 at the Holy Child at Loreto, 2 in the parish,* and 2 at Maria-Plain. These should prepare our way over the sea. . . . I thought when I left Paris that I had asked my friend M. Grimm to send you a number of the portrait engravings,[38] but since I never heard anything about it, I inquired recently from him and he replied that I had never said anything about it. I therefore wrote him to send you a large supply, so you'll know, if something arrives, what it is. Please present a copy to our most gracious lord.[39] These copper engravings were done when the boy was 7 and the little girl 11, immediately after our arrival in Paris. . . . [I]n Paris, each one sells for 24 sous. . . .

The Hague
September 1765–Winter 1766

The Hague
November 5, 1765

[To Lorenz Hagenauer]

Yes, yes! Most certainly! *Homo proponit, Deus disponit.* I have a sure proof of this. Man cannot escape his fate. I had to come to Holland against my inclination; and though I have not lost my poor daughter, I have seen her lying nearly at the point of death. Yet who urged us to come to Holland more than my daughter? She had the greatest longing to go where her fate was driving her. You remember that in my first letter from here I told you that my daughter had caught a cold on September 12, the second day after our arrival. At first it appeared to be of no significance and even seemed to be getting better, so she was never in bed. But on the evening of the 26th she suddenly started to shiver and asked to go to bed. After the shivering came a fever, and I saw that her throat was inflamed. The following day she was no better, and I sent for a doctor. To cut a long story short, at 4 o'clock in the evening on the 28th she was bled; and although her pulse improved somewhat, there was still a little fever. . . . The doctor himself gave up hope. My poor child sensed the danger herself, feeling how weak she was. I prepared her

---

38. Also mentioned earlier, in Leopold's letter from Paris dated April 1, 1764; for the portrait, see page 25.

39. Archbishop Schrattenbach.

to resign herself to God's will, and not only did she receive Holy Communion but the priest found her in such a serious condition that he gave her the Holy Sacrament of Extreme Unction,[40] for she was often so weak that she could hardly utter what she wanted to say. Whoever could have listened to the conversations which we 3—my wife, myself, and my daughter—had on several evenings, when we convinced her of the vanity of this world and the happy death of children, would not have heard it without damp eyes. Meanwhile little Wolfgangl [*sic*] in the next room was amusing himself with his music. On October 21, when we had the Holy Sacrament given to her at 5, I arranged for a consultation at half past one. . . . [This doctor] showed at once that he understood the case better. First, he took the child's hand and felt her pulse. He put on his glasses and examined her eyes, her tongue, and her whole face, then he perceived the *statum morbi*.[41] This was the first time that I had special reason to be thankful for my knowledge of the Latin language. If I had not known Latin, Herr Professor would have been informed quite differently. For once the doctor was already convinced by his conscience that he had made a big mistake, he had, of course, to explain and describe the *statum morbi* in a way that justified the remedies he had used. But whenever he spoke a lie, I contradicted him, as I had already when he talked of lesions, boils, pockmarks on the lung (or whatever he christened them). In particular he said that she had pain and could not lie on both sides, which was absolutely not true and which I contradicted every time, because she never had felt any pain and could lie and sleep on both sides. . . . Whether asleep or awake, she was never herself and talked in her sleep, now in English, now in French, and now in German; and since she had a lot of material in her head from our travels, we had to laugh in the midst of our sorrow. This was something that brought Wolfgangerl out of the sadness he felt for his sister. . . . Now it depends on whether God's grace will allow her to recover her strength or whether some other accident befalls that will send her into eternity. We have always left it to the Divine Will and even before we left Salzburg we prayed to God earnestly either to prevent or to bless our intended journey. If my daughter dies, she will die happy. If God gives her the gift of life, then we pray to Him to grant her such an innocent death as she would have now. I hope for the latter, for on that Sunday when she was very ill, I read the Gospel for that day: *Domine, descende.* "Come, Lord! before my daughter dies." And this Sunday it was, "Your daughter was sleeping; your faith has helped you." You will find it if you look it up in the Gospel.—But you can easily imagine how we are living now, and how my whole plan is upside down. We could not and would not entrust our child to foreigners. As a result for a long time my wife did not gone to bed until 6 [a.m.], when I got up and looked after my daughter until noon; then

---

40. Administered when one is thought to be at the point of death.
41. The "state of the illness."

my wife and I divided the time from nighttime until midday, each of us sleeping 5 or 6 hours. And how long will it be before my daughter, should she recover, is well enough to travel?— . . . [I]f God gives her the gift of life, I cannot expose her wantonly to the obvious danger of losing her life through an untimely journey. It is easy to understand that I have derived no advantage, but the greatest loss from this accident, and I think that one can only wonder (if one considers it well) how I am able to withstand these tours. For France, England, and Holland are not countries where one talks about pieces of twelve and pennies, but only about louis d'or, guineas, ducats, and *reitters*. . . . My present expenses are absolutely awful, for here one must pay for everything. . . . Basta! [Italian for "Enough!"] After all, what is money! If only I come away with my family healthy again!

Please arrange for *a Mass* to be said for my daughter *at Maria-Plain, one at the Holy Child at Loreto, one in honor of St. Walpurgis,*[42] and *2 at Passau at the Mariahilfberg.* . . .

The Hague
December 12, 1765

[To Lorenz Hagenauer]

So that I can relieve you of all worry right at the beginning, I tell you that, God be praised, we are all alive.—Yes, I can almost say we are all healthy. For dear Wolfgangerl has, through the help of God, survived his horrible battle and is on the way to recovery. My daughter was scarcely a week out of bed and had just begun to walk across the bedroom floor by herself, when on November 15 Wolfgangerl was overcome by an illness which in four weeks left him in such a miserable condition that he is not only absolutely unrecognizable, but has nothing left but his tender skin and his little bones, and for the last 5 days has been carried daily from his bed to a chair; yesterday and today, however, we led him a few times across the room so that gradually he can learn to move his feet again and stand up by himself. You want to know what was wrong with him? God knows! I am tired of describing illnesses to you. It began with a fever. We had no more black powder, so we gave him as usual 3 doses of margrave powder one after the other, but to no effect. . . . Our night watches went back to their old routine as during my daughter's illness. It is thus the great grace of God that we, and especially my wife, could withstand all this. But patience! What God sends, one must accept. Now I can do nothing but wait for the time when the Almighty will give my Wolfgang enough strength to enable us to undertake such an important journey at such a season of the year. Expense must not be considered. The devil take the money, if one only gets off with one's skin! . . .

---

42. Nannerl was named after this saint: her full name was Maria Anna Walpurga Ignatia Mozart.

Italy
First Italian Journey (of three),
December 1769–March 1771
(Frau Mozart and Nannerl remained at home)

During this first Italian trip, Wolfgang began appending postcripts to his father's letters and occasionally writing a few letters himself. His contributions are omitted here, but you can enjoy idiomatic translations of them in Robert Spaethling, Mozart's Letters, Mozart's Life, *pages 5–42. Leopold's letters now become somewhat different in both tone and content because he is writing to his wife rather than to his creditor (and friend), Lorenz Hagenauer.*

[Innsbruck, Austria]

I think it is December 17, 1769; I haven't got a current calendar anymore.
[To Frau Mozart]

His Excellency Count Spaur . . . not only . . . sent his servant at once, with his compliments, to inform me that his carriage would pick us up at 2 on Saturday to drive us to his house, but together with his wife received me graciously and offered to place his carriage at our disposal, an offer I accepted. Early Sunday morning I received a note from him inviting us to a concert at 5. . . . Wolfgang was given a very beautiful concerto, which he played at sight. As usual we were received with all respect and were brought home later by Count Spaur himself. In short, we are utterly pleased. Tomorrow I mean to pack my things, which will be done all the quicker because I did not unpack much; and on Tuesday, God willing, I think we will leave. . . . I hope you are all well. I will write again from Bozen [a town on the border between Austria and Italy]. You must keep all our letters.[43] . . .

Mzt

Verona [Italy]
January 7, 1770

[To Frau Mozart]

. . . It is not necessary to write about how Wolfgang has brought honor to himself. . . . In the afternoon we went to the organ of the principal church [in the town of Rovereto], and although only 6 or 8 of the leading people knew we were coming, we found all Rovereto gathered in the church and some strong fellows went in front of us to clear a path for us to the choir, where it took several minutes to reach the organ, as everyone wanted to get close to us . . . [W]e went to lunch only at 3. After lunch we drove to the church of St. Thomaso to play on the church's two organs; and although this decision was made during lunch and although only

---

43. One of several such urgings to his wife, as also earlier to Lorenz Hagenuer; Leopold planned to base his future book about his son on these letters.

a few tickets had been sent . . . such a throng of people had gathered that we hardly had room to get out of the coach. The crush was so great that we were forced to go through the monastery, where in a moment so many people rushed up to us that we would not have been able to find room if the Fathers, who were already waiting for us at the portals, had not taken us in with them; when it was over, the throng was even larger, for everyone wanted to see the little organist. As soon as we were in our carriage, I directed that we be driven home, where I locked the door and began to write this letter. But I had to force myself away, otherwise they would not have left us in peace long enough for me to write you . . . [T]he day after tomorrow we shall pack and on Wednesday morning, with God's help, travel to Mantua which, although it is near, is almost a winter day's journey because of the dirty road. . . . Farewell, I am your old

MZT.

Mantua
January 11, 1770

[To Frau Mozart]

We arrived here yesterday evening and an hour later went to the opera, at 6. We are, praise God, well. Wolfgangerl looks as if he had been through a [battlefield] campaign: a little red-brown especially around the nose and mouth because of the air and the open fire. For example, the way His Majesty the emperor looks. My beauty has not suffered much yet, or I would be in despair. I have nothing to write you from here yet. . . . Tomorrow we are invited to lunch at Count Francesco Eugenio d'Arco's; then I shall be able to write more. Meanwhile I must tell you something about Verona. We have seen the [ancient Roman] amphitheater and the Geological Museum; you can read about these in Keyssler's *Reisebeschreibungen*, and I will bring back a book on the antiquities of Verona. . . . It would make the letters too heavy and expensive if I included the newspaper pages that have been written about Wolfgang in Mantua and other places. I enclose one, in which there are two mistakes; it says "the present *Kapellmeister*" and "not yet *thirteen years old*," instead of fourteen.[44] But you know how it goes: newspaper writers write how it strikes them, and whatever strikes them . . .

Good-bye. I am your old

MZT.

All possible greetings to all our good friends. I cannot write to anybody, for I am plagued. Nothing but dressing and undressing, packing and unpacking, and besides that, no warm room, frozen like a dog, everything I touch is ice. And if you could see the doors and locks in the rooms! Like prisons! . . .

---

44. Might Leopold himself have given out such erroneous information?

Milan

January 26, 1770

[To Frau Mozart]

... We reached Milan at noon on the 23rd. ... You complain that you have had no word from me for three weeks, but I wrote to you from Verona and from Mantua. You ought to have received my first from Verona, which I mailed on January 7. The second cannot be in Salzburg yet, for I only mailed it *in Mantua on the 15th.*[45] ... I wish you had seen the place where the concert took place, called the Teatrino della Accademia Filarmonica.[46] In all my life I have never seen anything more beautiful of this kind; and since *I hope that you will carefully collect all our letters,* I will describe it to you later. It is not a theater, but is built like opera houses, with boxes. ... The crowds of people,—the shouting, clapping, yelling, and bravo after bravo—in short, the whole clamor and admiration the listeners show, I cannot adequately describe to you. ... I can assure you that everywhere I have found the dearest people and in every place we have found special people who have been with us up to the last moment before our departure and have done everything in their power to make our visit pleasant. ... You need to know, however, that neither [our concerts in Mantua nor those in Verona] were performed for money; everybody goes in free. In Verona, it is only the nobility who arrange these concerts; but in Mantua the nobles, the military, and the upper classes attend them together, because they are subsidized by Her Majesty the empress.[47] ... [E]ven if you ... hardly ever eat at home, supper, room, firewood, etc. are all so expensive that after 9 to 11 days in an inn you seldom get away for less than 6 ducats. I often thank my God that I left you and Nannerl at home. First, you would not have been able to stand the cold. Second, it would have cost us an exorbitant amount of money, and [Wolfgang and I] would not have been so free to live the way we do; for here we are staying at the Augustinian monastery of San Marco,[48] not that we do so free, no! We can live comfortably and safely and we are near His Excellency Count Firmian. We have three large guest rooms: in the first room we have a fire, we eat and give audiences; in the second I sleep and we have put our trunk there; in the third Wolfgang sleeps and our other small luggage is there. We each sleep on four good mattresses and every night the bed is warmed, so that Wolfgang, when he goes to bed, is always happy. We have a[n Augustinian] brother, Brother Alfonso, at our service and we are well cared for. But I cannot

---

45. There were continual problems with mail taking too long or never arriving. Leopold's concern, of course, is twofold: first, aware that the Salzburg court's censor is perusing all these letters, he counts on their contents being whispered into the archbishop's ear and all around Salzburg, increasing his bragging rights; second, he plans on using these letters in the planned biography of his son.

46. The Accademia filarmonica, presided over by Padre Martini, is to become an important feather in Wolfgang Mozart's cap; read on, and also note the caption under the illustration on page 67.

47. Maria Theresa. The Habsburgs also controlled northern sections of Italy.

48. Where, presumably, women were not allowed.

tell you how long we shall stay here. His Excellency the count is suffering from a cold, and wanted to give a concert in his house and invite the Duke of Modena. So I have not been able to deliver the other letters [of introduction], because this concert must take place first. I think it will happen next Tuesday or Wednesday, for His Excellency is already feeling better. I wrote you that Wolfgang had gotten red hands and a red face from the cold and the open fires. He is well again now. Madame Sartoretti in Mantua gave him a pomade to rub on his hands at night, and in 3 days it was better; now he looks as he did before. Otherwise, praise God, we have always been well; and the change of air only gave Wolfgang a dry cough, which went away a long time ago. . . .

I am your old faithful

L.Mzt

We kiss you both a thousand times.

Milan

February 3, 1770

[To Frau Mozart]

. . . I have nothing to say except that, praise God, we are well . . . that yesterday we were at the dress rehearsal of the new opera *Cesare in Egitto;*[49] that the opera is very good and that we saw and spoke to [the composer,] Maestro Piccinni . . . ; that for the last 14 days the weather has been most beautiful; that every day Wolfgang rejoices in his well-warmed mattress-beds; that he cannot write to you because he is composing 2 Latin motets for 2 young castratos, one of whom is 15 and the other 16 and both of whom begged him and, since they are comrades of his and sing beautifully, he could not deny them anything; that it is very distressing to me to see and hear these boys and to know that I cannot take them back to Salzburg; that I expect we shall stay longer in Milan than I had imagined; that His Excellency Count Firmian has not yet completely recovered from his cold; that during the last few days I have again found something in the newspapers about how the people of Bozolo literally waylaid us, . . . that Wolfgang and I kiss you and Nannerl 1000 times, and that I am forever your

upright husband

Mozart

Have our two guns been cleaned?[50] Is Nannerl playing the piano industriously?

---

49. *[Julius] Caesar in Egypt.* The composer, Piccinni, whose music became one side of the Piccinni-Gluck debate in Paris in the mid-1770s, is discussed in the Paris section of "In Search of Employment."
50. A reference to the family's favorite pastime, air-gun shooting; see "Childhood and Youth, 1756–1773."

Milan

February 17, 1770

[To Frau Mozart]

. . . We are, praise God, both well! That the winter is not so dangerous in Italy as the summer, I can well believe; only we hope that God will take care of us. . . . Wolfgang will not ruin his health by eating and drinking. You know how he controls himself; and I can assure you that I have never seen him so attentive to his health as he is in this country. Whatever does not seem right to him he leaves on his plate, and on some days he eats very little, yet he is fat and cheerful and happy all day long.[51] . . . [I]n the evening we are driving in masks[52] to the opera and after the opera there will be a ball. . . . Next Friday there will be a concert for the general public; then we shall see [what money we can make]. There will not be much profit in Italy; the only pleasure is that there is greater curiosity and insight here and the Italians recognize what Wolfgang [is capable of]. Otherwise one must be "paid" with admiration and a bravo, but I must tell you that everywhere we have been received with nothing but the greatest courtesy and that on all occasions we have been taken to meet the high nobility.

Milan

March 13, 1770

[To Frau Mozart]

. . . For the concert yesterday at Count Firmian's house, Wolfgang had to compose 3 arias . . . and I was forced to copy the violin parts myself and then have them duplicated to keep them from being stolen.[53] Over 150 members of the leading nobility were present, among whom the most important were the duke, the princess, and the cardinal. Now it's decided that we will leave Milan, with God's help, on Thursday, that is, the day after tomorrow, though we will not reach Parma until Saturday morning. You can easily imagine that I have an amazing amount to do, all the more since, because of our long stay, the whole trunk was unpacked. . . . Wolfgang has been asked to write the first opera for next Christmas.[54] If this happens, you can be happy because then we will get home sooner than otherwise, for we have enough to do to get to Rome for Passion Week.[55] . . . I kiss you and Nannerl 1,000 times and I am your old

Mzt.

---

51. To be fat was considered a good thing; thinness, so valued today, signified poor health.
52. To a Carnival (i.e., pre-Lenten) party.
53. A real possibility!
54. An enormous coup for a fourteen-year-old, this was his first important opera: *Mitridate, rè di Ponto,* an opera seria.
55. Passion Week is the week before Holy Week, which ends with Easter Sunday.

Bologna
March 27, 1770

[To Frau Mozart]

...There was a concert yesterday at Count Pallavicini's, to which His Eminence the cardinal and the leading nobles were invited. . . . [A]s soon as [the Count] heard that I intended to be in Rome during Holy Week, he said at once that he would try the next day to arrange not only to hear this extraordinary young virtuoso himself, but to grant the same pleasure to the leading nobles of the city. All the circumstances, how, for instance, we were picked up in His Excellency's carriage and waited upon, I won't touch upon, only that about 150 members of the leading nobility were there. The famous Padre Martini[56] was also invited and, though he otherwise never goes to concerts, he came to this one, and this concert began at 7:30 and lasted until 11:30 because the nobles didn't want to interrupt it. . . . What pleases me especially is that we are uncommonly popular and that Wolfgang is admired here even more than in all the other cities in Italy, because [Bologna] is the center and home of many maestros, artists, and learned people. Here, too, Wolfgang has been most thoroughly tested and has increased his reputation throughout Italy, because Padre Martini is the idol of the Italians, speaks of Wolfgang with great admiration, and administered the tests himself. . . . We have been to the Instituto [museum] and seen the fine statues. . . . Everything I have seen here surpasses the British Museum; for here are not only rarities of nature *but everything is science,* preserved like a dictionary, in beautiful rooms and in clean and orderly fashion. In short, you would be amazed. I will say nothing about churches, paintings, beautiful architecture, and furnishings in various palaces, for I am so sleepy I can hardly write, as it is after 1, Wolfgang has been snoring a long time already, and I am falling asleep as I write. . . . I kiss you and Nannerl 1,000 times. My greetings to all Salzburg. I am your faithful and sleepy husband

Mzt.

Florence
April 3, 1770

[To Frau Mozart]

On the evening of March 30 we arrived safely in Florence; on the 31st we spent the whole day indoors and Wolfgang stayed in bed until lunch, having caught a slight cold from the rain and strong wind we drove through over the mountain. I had him take tea and violet juice and he sweated a little. On April 1 at 10 we drove to Count von Rosenberg,[57] who received us immediately although more than 50

---

56. Padre Martini, an expert in the intricacies of counterpoint, was respected throughout Europe. He took kindly to Wolfgang, tested him, and facilitated his appointment to the Accademia filarmonica.

57. Count Orsini-Rosenberg, then stationed in Tuscany, was later director of court theaters at Vienna and as such became a key figure in Mozart's life. (The count is also portrayed in *Amadeus.*)

people were in the antechamber, because we brought a letter from Count Firmian and he already had a report on us from Count Kaunitz, who arrived in Florence the day before we did and is staying with Count Rosenberg. . . . Count Rosenberg at once sent . . . a message to introduce us to the grand duke. . . . We heard the sermon and Mass in the chapel and after the service we had an audience. The grand duke was uncommonly gracious and asked at once about Nannerl. He said that his wife was very eager to hear Wolfgang, and he spoke with us for a good quarter of an hour. Yesterday evening, the 2nd, we were picked up and driven to the castle outside the city and stayed there until after 10. Everything went off as usual, and admiration was all the greater as the music director is the greatest expert in counterpoint in Italy, and he laid the most difficult fugues[58] before Wolfgang and the most difficult themes, which Wolfgang played through and worked out like someone eating a piece of bread. Nardini, [a celebrated] violinist, accompanied him. . . .

Rome
April 14, 1770

[To Frau Mozart]

. . . For 5 days we had to travel from Florence to Rome in the most horrible rain and cold wind. . . . [W]e went on Wednesday and Thursday in beautiful weather to St. Peter's and the Sistine Chapel to hear the Miserere[59] during the Mass, and on our way home were overtaken by such a torrential downpour that our coats had never been so baptized. But I will not give you a long description of that dreadful journey. Picture to yourself a mostly uncultivated country and the most horrible inns, filthy, with nothing to eat but, with luck, here and there eggs and broccoli, and they sometimes made a fuss on fast-days about giving us the eggs. . . . When we arrived here on the 11th, we went to St. Peter's after lunch and then to Mass; on the 12th we were present at [Holy Week services], and when the pope was serving the poor at the altar we were so close to them that we were standing next to him. This was all the more amazing since we had to pass through two doors guarded by Swiss guards in armor and push our way through many 100s of people. . . . [B]ut our good clothes, the German language, and my customary freedom of manner, with which I told my servant to order the Swiss guards in German to make way for us, soon helped us through. They took Wolfgang for a German cavalier, others, for a prince. . . . I myself was thought to be his tutor. . . . You have perhaps often heard of the famous Miserere in Rome, which is so highly esteemed that the performers in the chapel are forbidden on pain of excommunication to carry off a single part of it, to copy it, or to give it to anyone. *But we have it.* Wolfgang has written it down, and we would have sent it to Salzburg in this letter if it were not necessary for us to

---

58. See "fugue" in the glossary.
59. A famous composition by the late Renaissance composer Gregorio Allegri. It is still sung today.

be there to perform it. . . . Moreover, as it is one of the secrets of Rome, we do not want it to fall into other hands.

. . . You cannot imagine how conceited the clergy are here. . . . I am looking forward to tomorrow, when we shall walk past all these proud men and leave them in ignorance of who we are. . . . On Monday we shall begin to deliver our twenty letters of introduction. Although I am glad that you two did not travel with us, I am sorry that you are not seeing all these Italian cities, especially Rome. It is useless, indeed impossible, to give a brief description of it. . . . [T]oday and yesterday I have been a bit of a patient, for I have taken three digestive powders; but, praise God, I feel well. Wolfgang is also fine and sends you a contredanse.[60] He would like [the Salzburg dance master] to make up steps for it . . . It would be by far the best idea to have it danced by five couples. The first couple should begin the first solo, the second dance the second couple, and so on. . . . Pray earnestly to our loving God for our health. We shall certainly do our share, for I can assure you that we take all possible care and that Wolfgang pays as much attention to his health as if he were the most grownup person. May God keep you both likewise in good health. . . . I am your old

MZT

Wolfgang and I kiss you and Nannerl 1,000 times.

Rome
April 21, 1770

[To Frau Mozart]

Your letters of the 2nd and the 6th are, I assume, in reply to my two letters from Bologna. Meanwhile you will already have in hand one from Florence and my first from Rome, in which I hurriedly described the bad weather and the difficult journey we had, but forgot to mention that we arrived at noon under thunder and lightning and that the weather a good hour away from Rome received us with crackling and flashes and so accompanied us to Rome, as one greets grand lords with the firing of great artillery. Up to now the weather has been rainy and today is the first day we can see one or two places safely. We have met an astonishing number of Englishmen here . . . and with them and some other Englishmen we walked a few hours this morning in the garden of the Villa Medici. . . . [T]he deeper we go in Italy, the greater is the amazement. Wolfgang does not stand still with his knowledge, but grows from day to day, so that the greatest connoisseurs and masters cannot find adequate words to express their admiration. . . . In Florence we found a young Englishman[61] who is a pupil of the celebrated violinist Nardini. This boy, who plays *wonderfully* and who is the same age and size as Wolfgang, came to the house of the learned poet Signora

---

60. A popular type of dance in either duple or triple meter.
61. His name was Thomas Linley, and he was a prodigy like Wolfgang Mozart. Linley drowned when he was twenty-two.

Corilla.... The 2 boys performed one after the other the whole evening, constantly embracing each other. On the next day the little Englishman, an absolutely dear boy, brought his violin to us and played the whole afternoon, Wolfgang accompanying him on his violin. The next day ... these two boys again played the whole afternoon, not like boys, but like men! Little Tommaso accompanied us home and cried the bitterest tears because we were leaving the next day. But when he heard that we weren't scheduled to leave until noon, he came to us at 9 in the morning and with many hugs gave Wolfgang a poem.... Then he accompanied our carriage to the city gate. I wish you had seen this scene....

Rome
April 28, 1770

[To Frau Mozart]

... On May 12, with God's help, we will leave for Naples, where we have already reserved lodging. The roads to Naples have been very unsafe for the last 14 days and a merchant was beaten to death; but police and the bloodthirsty papal soldiers were immediately sent from Rome and we hear that there was already a battle in which 5 policemen and 3 robbers were killed, 4 robbers were arrested, and the rest scattered. But they have now come closer to the borders of Naples; and if it is true that they have killed a courier from Naples on his way to Spain, every effort will be made to clear the roads. I will not leave here until I know it is safe, and in a [stagecoach] one is in a large group.

... Wolfgang is in good health, praise God, except for a slight toothache, as usual on one side of his face.

We kiss you and Nannerl 1,000 times and I am your old

MZT.

Naples
May 26, 1770

[To Frau Mozart]

This is the third letter I am writing you from Naples. The situation of this city pleases me more and more every day, and Naples itself is on the whole not ugly; if the people were only not so godless and certain people not so dumb.... And the superstition!—This is so deeply rooted that I can say with certainty that total heresy is now spread everywhere.... I will explain this to you later. I hope to bring back copper engravings of the views and rare sights of Naples, such as I already have of Rome. We are both well, God be praised. The tailor is working on 2 suits.... Mine is ... dark red moiré, lined with sky-blue taffeta and has silver buttons. Wolfgang's is of apple-green moiré, with silver buttons and lined with rose-colored taffeta. On Monday there will be a concert, which the Countess von Kaunitz, the Imperial ambassador's wife, Lady Hamilton, Princess Belmonte . . . [etc.] are organizing and which will probably bring us at least 150 zecchini. We certainly need money, for if we leave, we will have a long trip with no chance to take in anything; if we stay, we will have to survive for 5 months. It is true that here we should always be able to earn enough for our necessities, but I am still determined to leave in 3 weeks. We hope to be introduced to the king and queen [of Naples] next week. . . .

Farewell to you and Nannerl. We kiss you both and I am your old

Mzt

Naples

May 29, 1770

[To Frau Mozart]

I am probably writing far too often now, and you will be surprised to see a letter from me every post-day! But this is a precaution, in case some letter never arrives. We are rather far from each other, and it takes a letter 14 days to get from Salzburg to Naples. This is my fourth letter from Naples. I still intend to leave Naples on the 16th of next month, if there is no obstacle to that. Yesterday we gave our concert, which was a success. The court returns to town tomorrow, the 30th, to celebrate the king's name day with an opera and other festivities. . . .

Naples

June 5, 1770

[To Frau Mozart]

. . . You will be frustrated that I don't send you more details about our earnings. I don't do it because in Salzburg one sees only the income and doesn't think about the expenses, and there are very, very few people who know what travel costs. It will be enough for me to tell you that, praise God, we lack nothing that is necessary for us to continue our journey in honorable fashion. . . .

Naples

June 9, 1770

[To Frau Mozart]

. . . In a certain sense it is a pity that we cannot stay here longer, for during the summer there are many pleasant things to see and there is a constant variety of fruits, vegetables, and flowers from week to week. The situation of the town, its fruitfulness, the liveliness of the people, the rare sights, etc. and a hundred beautiful things make me sad to leave. But the filth, the crowds of beggars, the dreadful people—yes, the godless people—the poor bringing up of children, the incredible boisterousness even in church, make it possible to leave behind what is good quite calmly. I will bring back not only all the rare sights in several beautiful copper engravings, but I have received from Herr Meurikofer a fine collection of lava from Vesuvius, not the lava that everyone can get very easily, but choice pieces with a description of the minerals each of them contains, which are rare and not easy to get. If God permits us to return in good health, you will see beautiful things. . . . Keep well, both of you. We kiss you both 1,000 times and I am your old

Mozart

. . . Next week we will visit Vesuvius and the 2 buried cities[62] where entire ancient rooms are being excavated. . . .

Rome
June 27, 1770

[To Frau Mozart]

We arrived in Rome yesterday at 8 p.m., making *in 27 hours* with the mail coach the same trip that took us 4 and a half days with the carriage. But we really flew. . . . I thought it better to travel by ourselves, since one often does not find many horses at the post-stages, so one has the honor of sitting and waiting half a day for the coach. . . . So we left Naples by ourselves and I let it be thought that I was the steward of the Imperial ambassador, because stewards of such people are held in high esteem in these parts. This not only made our journey safe, but I got good horses, fast service, and in Rome I did not have to go to the Customs Office for the usual examination, because at the gate I was bowed deeply to and allowed to drive home directly, and I was so pleased that I threw a few paoli [a form of currency] in their faces. Since we had slept for only 2 out of the 27 hours of our trip and eaten only 4 cold roast chickens and a piece of bread in the carriage, you can easily imagine how hungry, thirsty, and sleepy we were. Our good [hostess] . . . gave us some nice boiled rice and we ate nothing but two lightly boiled eggs each, etc. As soon as we got to our bedroom, Wolfgang sat down on a chair and at once began snoring and sleeping so soundly that I completely undressed him and put him to bed without his showing the least sign of waking up; indeed he went on snoring, although now and then I had to lift him up and put him down again and finally drag him to bed sound asleep. When he woke up after 9 the next morning, he did not know where he was or how he had gotten to bed. He had lain in the same place almost the whole night. God be praised, we are well. . . .

Rome
June 30, 1770

[To Frau Mozart]

. . . You ask if Wolfgang has begun his opera? There has been no thought of it. You will have to ask when we have reached Milan on November 1. So far we know

---

62. Herculaneum and Pompeii.

neither the singers nor the libretto, though we do know who the *primo uomo*[63] and the tenor are. . . . You ask if we played before the king of Naples. Nothing less! We got only the stock compliments the queen made us wherever she saw us. She can do nothing, and what sort of a subject the king is, is perhaps wiser for me to tell you than to write you. . . . I have been forced either to stay indoors or to limp around very slowly, so I have not yet been able to pay my respects to princes and cardinals. I omitted mentioning the cause in my first letter, but as it is now looks better I will report my unfortunate accident. You know that 2 horses and a postilion[64] are equal to 3 beasts. During the last stage to Rome the postilion whipped the horse that was between the shafts and thus keeping the coach on track. The horse reared, caught in the sand and dirt—which was more than half a foot deep—and fell heavily on one side, pulling the front side of the coach down with him, because there were only two wheels. I held Wolfgang back with one hand so that he wouldn't be thrown out, but the plunge forward pulled my right foot toward the middle bar of the falling dashboard so violently that I gashed half the shinbone of my right leg about a finger wide. . . . On the second day the injury looked rather dangerous, because my foot was very swollen, and I stayed in bed most of yesterday and today. But today, as I write this, it is much better and the wound, which is very long, looks good; there is less pus and I have no pain. I brought nothing but the white ointment and have used nothing else. Maybe this accident had to happen, since otherwise you would have packed the ointment for nothing. . . . You must not worry, for with God's help, it will heal. . . .

Rome
July 4, 1770

[To Frau Mozart]

I have nothing to write you except that, praise God, my foot is well. On the other hand I have a little rheumatism in my left shoulder. . . . Just now a servant of Count Pallavicini came to tell us we are to have lunch with His Eminence tomorrow, and Friday we are dining with His Excellency the Tuscan ambassador. . . . Tomorrow we expect to hear a piece of news which, if it is true, will fill both of you with amazement. Cardinal Pallavicini is said *to have been commanded by the pope to present Wolfgang with the cross and diploma of [the Order of the Golden Spur].*[65] . . .

Rome
July 7, 1770

[To Frau Mozart]

. . . What I wrote recently about the cross of an order is correct. . . . It is the same order Gluck has and is worded as follows: [*translation of the Latin:* We create

63. Leading male singer, which in Italian opera seria meant a castrato.
64. A rider on horseback who rides alongside the horses that pull the carriage.
65. For a portrait of the young Mozart wearing this order, see page 67.

you a Knight of the Golden Spur].[66] Wolfgang must wear a beautiful gold cross, which he has received, and you can imagine how I laugh when I hear everybody calling him "Signor Cavaliere" now. . . . Tomorrow we have an audience with the pope. . . .

Bologna

August 25, 1770

[To Frau Mozart]

. . . [Wolfgang's clothes are now] too small for him. . . . But you shouldn't imagine him so tall, only that his limbs are bigger and stronger. He now has no singing voice at all—it is completely gone; he has neither low notes nor high notes, not five pure tones. This is something that really annoys him, because he can't sing his own music. . . . [Wolfgang was fourteen.]

---

66. Christoph Willibald Gluck was one of Europe's most esteemed composers during this period. His music formed one half of Paris's Piccinni-Gluck debate in the 1770s.

IMPORTANT PEOPLE IN MOZART'S LIFE

Arco, Count Carl Joseph Felix (1743–1830) was chamberlain to Archbishop Colloredo and a longtime friend of Leopold Mozart. He tried to give Wolfgang Mozart some good advice in the spring of 1781, warning him that Vienna had lots of fickle music lovers and was perhaps not the utopia Mozart imagined it to be. In spite of this, the composer had a blowout argument with Colloredo and later said that Arco pushed him "out the door with a kick on my ass." Mozart was now unemployed or, expressed more positively, a freelancer. This is exactly what he wanted, but his financial situation remained precarious until his success with *The Abduction from the Seraglio* a year later.

Bach, Johann Christian (1735–1782) was the youngest son of J. S. Bach. After his father's death in 1750 he moved first to Berlin, then to Italy, and finally to London, where he lived for the rest of his life. The child prodigy Wolfgang Mozart became friendly with Bach during his London visit of 1764–1765, admired his music, and soon began to imitate it in youthful works of his own. When Bach died, in 1782, Mozart expressed his sorrow in a letter to his father. When you see the name "Bach" in the Mozart letters, it's nearly always J. C. Bach who is meant.

"Bäsle, the" [Maria Anna Thekla Mozart] (1758–1841). This was Mozart's cousin in Augsburg. They were about the same age, had the same ribald sense of humor, and may or may not have engaged in sexual exploration in September 1777, when Mozart and his mother visited Augsburg on their way to Mannheim and Paris. For some erotic, funny letters—including drawings and poems and some scatological puns—see his letters to her during that fall. Hers to him do not survive.

Cannabich, a family of musicians active at Mannheim, later Munich. Christian Cannabich (1731–1798) was a fine violinist and composer. By 1774 he was director of instrumental music at the Mannheim court, and in 1778 he moved with that court to Munich. He and his wife were warmly hospitable to Mozart and his mother during their stay in Mannheim in 1777–1778. Mozart respected Cannabich's musicianship and enjoyed his colleagueship. The Cannabichs' talented daughter Rosa became Mozart's pupil, and he composed a piano sonata (K. 309/284a) for her.

Cavalieri, Catarina (1755–1801), the Italian name she took upon herself to further her career; she was born Franziska Helena Kavalier in Vienna. She was trained as a soprano by Salieri and became his mistress. She made her debut in 1775, and from 1778 on was engaged at the Burgtheater. Mozart greatly admired her singing but not her acting. She premiered the role of Constanze in *The Abduction from the Seraglio*, sang Donna Elvira in the first Viennese performance of *Don Giovanni* (1788), and portrayed the Countess in the 1789 revival of *The Marriage of Figaro*.

Duschek, Franz Xaver (1731–1799), was a pianist, teacher, and composer in Prague. In 1776 he married his pupil Josepha (1754–1824), a fine soprano, and the next year the couple became Mozart's friends. It was at their villa near Prague that Mozart finished *Don Giovanni*, and for Josepha he wrote the concert aria "Bella mia fiamma," K. 528, in 1787.

Épinay, Louise-Florence-Petronille Tardieu d'Esclavelles, Madame d'; *see under* Grimm, Baron Friedrich Melchior von.

Grimm, Baron Friedrich Melchior von (1723–1807), diplomat and man of letters, was secretary to Count Friese of Saxony and later to the Duke of Orléans in Paris, where he was Mozart's most influential champion in 1763–1764, 1765, and 1778. The child Mozart's prodigious gifts were glowingly reported in Grimm's *Correspondence littéraire*, a newsletter he compiled with friends among the Encyclopedists—including his friend and intellectual colleague Madame d'Épinay—and mailed twice a month to European monarchs and aristocrats. In July 1778, after the death of Mozart's mother, Wolfgang lodged with Grimm and Mme. d'Épinay during what became a highly significant intellectual period for the young composer. However, towards the end he complained to his father that "Grimm may be able to help *children*, but not grown-ups." Grimm practically threw him out, and Mozart left Paris in September 1778.

Hagenauer, Lorenz (1712–1792). Landlord, creditor, and friend of Leopold Mozart, to whom a great many of Leopold's letters were addressed during the childhood tours.

Haydn, Joseph (1732–1809). This is the famous Haydn, whom Mozart deeply admired and loved, calling him "Papa" in the most respectful terms. The two met in the 1780s in Vienna and saw each other fairly frequently after that. Mozart dedicated six string quartets to him, known as his "Haydn" Quartets; he said that it had cost him tremendous effort trying to match the achievements of his beloved older friend. Haydn told Leopold Mozart, during Leopold's visit to Vienna in 1785, that his son was "the greatest composer I know, either personally or by name." In Salzburg, Haydn's younger brother Michael (see below) was composer at the cathedral. Usually when Mozart mentions Haydn he means Michael—though in later years, he meant Joseph.

Haydn, Michael (1737–1806) was, like his more celebrated brother Joseph (see above), a chorister at St. Stephen's Cathedral in Vienna as a boy. In 1763 he became *Konzertmeister* to the Archbishop of Salzburg, where he was a colleague of Leopold Mozart; in 1781 he took over from Wolfgang Mozart (when Mozart moved to Vienna) the post of cathedral organist as well. Michael Haydn was reputed to be an alcoholic, who for that reason sometimes failed to produce compositions required by the archbishop. Mozart filled in for him once or twice by supplying the missing works.

Holzbauer, Ignaz (1711–1783) was named *Kapellmeister* at Mannheim in 1753. There he wrote symphonies, chamber music, and operas, one of which, *Günther von Schwarzburg* (1776), was important in the revival of German opera and excited the twenty-one-year-old Mozart, who saw it in Mannheim in 1777.

Lange, Aloysia Weber (ca. 1760 or 1761–1839) was the second daughter of Fridolin Weber and a gifted soprano. Mozart met her in Mannheim in 1777, wrote several arias for her, and fell in love with her. The following year, she jilted him, later marrying the actor, singer, and portrait painter Joseph Lange. Both Langes enjoyed successful careers in Vienna. In 1782 Mozart married Aloysia's sister Constanze. The Mozarts and Langes became good friends in Vienna. Aloysia sang Donna Anna in the Viennese premiere of *Don Giovanni* in 1788, and Joseph's unfinished portrait of the composer is on this book's cover.

Lange, Joseph (1751–1831): *see under* Lange, Aloysia Weber.

Lichnowsky, Count Carl Alois (1761–1814), lawyer, amateur musician, Freemason (he belonged to Mozart's lodge), and patron of Mozart who accompanied the composer on a trip to various cities in 1789, but who in November 1791, one month before Mozart's death, sued him for more than 1,400 gulden. The case was not known to Mozart researchers until

1991; how it was resolved, if it ever was, is still unknown. Lichnowsky was the son-in-law of Mozart's friend and patroness Countess Thun.

Linley, Thomas (1756–1778) was, like Mozart, a child prodigy, and the two fourteen-year-olds met and became friends in Italy in 1770. Linley later had a promising career as a violinist and composer in England until he drowned in a boating accident when he was twenty-two.

Martini, Padre Giovanni Battista (1706–1784) was a Franciscan monk and *maestro di cappella* at the church of San Francesco in Bologna. He composed voluminously, was a gifted and highly respected teacher, amassed a huge library and portrait collection (including a painting of Mozart), published an unfinished history of music, and left an enormous and important correspondence. Mozart studied with him during his visit to Bologna in 1770, and in September 1776 sent him a copy of one of his sacred works, *Misericordias Domini*, K. 222/205a, with a letter saying, "I never cease to grieve that I am far away from that one person in the world whom I love, revere, and esteem most of all...." Padre Martini was Mozart's most crucial teacher other than his father. He also enabled the young composer, at fourteen, to become a member of the esteemed Accademia filarmonica.

Puchberg, Johann Michael (1741–1822) was manager of a textiles firm in Vienna, a Freemason, and a close friend of Mozart. He lived in a building owned by Count Wallsegg and between 1787 and 1791 lent Mozart a lot of money. He made no claim to it after Mozart's death (Mozart may have repaid at least some of it). Mozart's letters to him asking for money are the most poignant in his correspondence.

Raaff, Anton (1714–1797), was a celebrated tenor who was well into his sixties and vocally past his prime when Mozart met him at Mannheim in 1777, though he was a distinguished man and of great help to the composer in various ways. For example, he may have been instrumental in helping get the commission to write *Idomeneo* in 1780—which enabled the composer to get out of Salzburg that fall, and, as it turned out, Mozart never had to go back.

Ramm, Friedrich (1744–1811) was a fabulous oboist in the court orchestra at Mannheim and a close companion of Mozart there. He joined Mozart and Wendling in Paris in 1778 and was to have played in the canceled performance of a sinfonia concertante that has not survived (this was a woodwind composition, not the Sinfonia Concertante in E-flat Major for violin and viola, K. 364/320d).

Salieri, Antonio (1750–1825) was a celebrated Italian composer and, during Mozart's years in Vienna, music director of the court opera.

Salieri was also a leading composer in Paris, for whose theaters he wrote successful operas. If you've seen *Amadeus,* the "Salieri" you find there is a cartoon figure. The real Salieri was respected throughout Europe and the teacher not only of Beethoven, Schubert, and Liszt, but also of Mozart's son Franz Xaver Wolfgang.

Stadler, Anton (1753–1812) and his brother Johann (1755–1804) were both excellent performers on clarinet and its lower relative, the basset horn. Anton was known particularly for his playing in the clarinet's lower register and devised a downward extension of his instrument to emphasize that. It was for this modified clarinet that Mozart wrote his Clarinet Quintet, K. 581, and his Clarinet Concerto, K. 622. The Stadlers were also Freemasons, and Anton and Mozart hoped to open a new lodge.

Stein, Johann Andreas (1788–1792) was a well-known manufacturer of fortepianos in Augsburg. The piano was rapidly replacing the harpsichord, and piano makers sought advice from traveling players such as Mozart. Stein met the Mozart family in 1763, when Leopold bought a practice piano from him. In 1777, Mozart praised Stein's pianos in letters to his father (October 14 and 17, 1777).

Storace, Nancy (1765–1817) was a gifted soprano who premiered the role of Susanna in *The Marriage of Figaro* (Vienna, 1786) and with her brother Stephen, a composer, was a close friend of Wolfgang and Constanze Mozart. Nancy Storace specialized in comic roles, where her acting ability and superior musicianship could shine; the fact that she was short, chubby, and had a relatively narrow vocal range kept her from the leading roles in opera seria. It is said that she lost her high notes as the result of a teenaged singing match with a castrato, during which she damaged her vocal cords. Perhaps Mozart's most endearing concert aria, "Ch'io mi scordi di te," K. 505, was written for her farewell concert in December 1786; the solo piano part with its affectionate melodic garlands was performed by Mozart himself.

Süssmayr, Franz Xaver (1766–1803) moved to Vienna in 1788, where he became Mozart's assistant, sort of an apprentice, during the composer's last few years. Süssmayr completed the Requiem after the composer's death. Franz Xaver was a very common name; still, in naming their youngest child (born in July 1791) Franz Xaver, the Mozarts may have had in mind Wolfgang's assistant.

Swieten, Baron Gottfried van (1733–1803), was a German diplomat, extremely devoted musical amateur, and patron of musicians, especially in Vienna. He idolized older music—notably that of Bach (J. S.)

and Handel—and beginning around 1782 began inviting musicians (among them Mozart) to his house every Sunday morning to play through music by these composers. Mozart was soon named musical supervisor and conductor, and van Swieten also commissioned him to update certain older works, for example, Handel's *Messiah*, a revision he completed in 1789. Performing this highly contrapuntal music week after week influenced Mozart's own style from 1782 on.

Weber, a family of musicians. The father, Fridolin, was a theater prompter and box-office attendant in Mannheim. The Webers had four daughters, including Aloysia (*see* Lange, Aloysia Weber) and Constanze, who married Mozart in 1782. Josepha Weber Hofer created the role of the Queen of Night in *The Magic Flute*.

Wendling, a family of musicians, colleagues, and friends of Mozart in Mannheim and later in Munich. Johann Baptist Wendling (1723–1797) was a very fine flutist in Mannheim. In 1777 Mozart helped him orchestrate one of his flute concertos, and the following year Wendling was to have been a soloist in the canceled performance of Mozart's woodwind sinfonia concertante (now presumed lost; not to be confused with the Sinfonia Concertante in E-flat Major for violin and viola, K. 364/320d). In 1752 Wendling married the singer Dorothea Spurni, for whom Mozart wrote the part of Ilia in *Idomeneo*.

BUILDING A PORTFOLIO
OF RECORDINGS

For listeners eager to explore Mozart's entire oeuvre, the recording industry offers two choices. During the Mozart Year 1991, the composer's complete works—180 discs in all, with detailed liner notes, full commentary, and multilingual librettos—came out under the Philips label in a series of boxed sets, with a combined price tag of three thousand dollars. A version of this complete edition, albeit with shortened liner notes and less deluxe packaging, can now be purchased online for around $300, with individual sets (e.g., the middle-period Italian operas, the string quartets, the piano sonatas) going for $40–$50. These individual sets can also be downloaded. Meanwhile, during the Mozart Year 2006, serious competition arose from a small Dutch label: Brilliant Classics began offering a single boxed set of 170 discs featuring period-instrument performances (most performances in the Philips set employ modern instruments) for around $135, with individual sets also available—all, however, with minimal commentary and no librettos.

Those wishing to start with a much smaller portfolio might begin with the CDs cited in analyses of compositions in this book. These, however, are all recordings of instrumental works, where exact timings are needed to clarify formal diagrams; in the case of vocal and choral works, analytical comments are keyed to words, rendering specific timings unnecessary. The CDs listed below—many of them also available in MP3 format—comprise both alternatives to those used in this book's diagrams of instrumental works and suggestions for operas, sacred compositions, and those few instrumental works discussed but not diagrammed in the book. Performances are on eighteenth-century instruments except where otherwise noted. Timings will vary, as no two performances are ever the same. Works are listed in K number order.

Divertimento K.131

Orpheus Chamber Orchestra [modern instruments; plays without a conductor]. *Mozart: "Eine kleine Nachtmusik," Divertimenti.* Deutsche Grammophon 419192.

Symphony in G Minor, K. 183/173dB; Symphony in D Major, K. 297 ("Paris"); and Symphony in C Major, K. 551 ("Jupiter")

Amsterdam Baroque Orchestra; Ton Koopman, conductor. *Mozart: Symphonies Nos. 25, 31 ("Paris"), and 41 ("Jupiter").* Apex 0927490452.

Concerto in G Major for Violin and Orchestra, K. 216, and Sinfonia Concertante in E-flat Major for Violin, Viola, and Orchestra, K. 364/320d

Gidon Kremer, [modern] violin; Kim Kashkashian, [modern] viola; Vienna Philharmonic Orchestra; Nikolaus Harnoncourt, conductor. *Mozart: The Five Violin Concertos and The Sinfonia Concertante, K. 364/320d.* Deutsche Grammophon 453043 (two discs).

Variations for Piano on "Ah vous dirais-je, maman," K. 265/300e

Ronald Brautigam (fortepiano). *Mozart: Complete Solo Piano Music,* Vol. 7. BIS 894.

Sonata for Piano in A Minor, K. 310

Ronald Brautigam, fortepiano. *Mozart: The Complete Piano Sonatas,* Vol. 3. BIS 837.
András Schiff, [modern] piano. *Mozart: Piano Sonatas,* Vol. 2. Decca 417571.

Mass in C Major, K. 317 ("Coronation")

Catherine Wyn-Rogers, Barbara Bonney, sopranos; Jamie MacDougall, tenor; Stephen Gadd, baritone; English Concert Choir; English Concert; Trevor Pinnock, conductor. *Mozart: "Coronation" Mass; "Vesperae solennes de confessore," K. 339; "Exsultate jubilate," K. 165/158a.* Archiv Production (Deutsche Grammophon) 445353.

Serenade in B-flat Major for Thirteen Instruments, K. 361/370a

Consortium Classicum. *Mozart: Serenades/Divertimenti.* EMI Classics Double Forte 69392 (two discs).

Mass in C Minor, K. 427/417a
Sylvia McNair, Diana Montague, sopranos; Anthony Rolfe Johnson, tenor; Cornelius Hauptmann, baritone; Monteverdi Choir; English Baroque Soloists; John Eliot Gardiner, conductor. Philips 420210.

String Quartet in C Major, K. 465 ("Dissonance")
Emerson String Quartet [modern instruments]. *Mozart: "Hunt" Quartet [K. 458] and "Dissonance" Quartet [K.465]; Haydn: "Emperor" Quartet [Op. 76, No. 3].* Deutsche Grammophon 427657.

Concerto in E-flat Major for Piano and Orchestra, K. 482, and Concerto in C Minor for Piano and Orchestra, K. 491
Murray Perahia, [modern] piano; English Chamber Orchestra; Murray Perahia, conductor. *Mozart: Piano Concertos Nos. 22 [K.482] and 24 [K. 491].* CBS 42242.

The Marriage of Figaro, **K. 492**
Christiane Oelze (Susanna), Hubert Claessens (Figaro), Patrizia Biccire (Countess), Monica Groop (Cherubino), Werner van Mechelen (Count); La Petite Bande; Namur Chamber Choir; Sigiswald Kuijken, conductor. Brilliant Classics 93966.

Symphony in D Major, K. 504 ("Prague")
Academy of St. Martin in the Fields [modern instruments]; Sir Neville Marriner, conductor. *Mozart: The Last Five Symphonies* [K. 504 ("Prague"), K. 425 ("Linz"), and the "last three": K. 543, K. 550, and K. 551 ("Jupiter")]. Philips Duo Catalog 438332.

Don Giovanni, **K.527**
Håkan Hagegård (Don Giovanni), Arleen Augér (Donna Anna), Kristinn Sigmundsson (Leporello), Nico van der Meel (Don Ottavio), Della Jones (Donna Elvira), Gilles Cachemaille (Commendatore), Bryn Terfel (Masetto), Barbara Bonney (Zerlina); Drottningholm Court Theatre Orchestra; Drottningholm Court Theatre Chorus; Arnold Östman, conductor. Decca 470059.

Quintet in A Major for [Basset] Clarinet and Strings, K. 581
Eric Hoeprich, basset clarinet, with the Aston Magna String Quartet. *Mozart Quintets.* Harmonia Mundi 3957059.

The Magic Flute, K. 620

Michael Schade (Tamino), Christiane Oelze (Pamina), Gerald Finley (Papageno), Harry Peeters (Sarastro), Cyndia Sieden (Queen of the Night); Monteverdi Choir; English Baroque Soloists; John Eliot Gardiner, conductor. Archiv Production (Deutsche Grammophon) 449166.

Requiem, K. 626 (as completed by Süssmayr)

Nathalie Stutzmann, soprano; Anna Maria Panzarella, mezzo-soprano; Christoph Prégardien, tenor; Nathan Berg, baritone; Chorus and Orchestra of Les Arts Florissants; William Christie, conductor. Erato 10697.

WHAT SHOULD I LISTEN TO NEXT?

Serenades, Divertimentos, Etc.

K. 250 the "Haffner" (most of it was later turned into the "Haffner" Symphony, K. 385)

K. 320 the "Posthorn" Serenade

K. 522 *A Musical Joke*

K. 525 *Eine kleine Nachtmusik*

String Quartets and Quintets

K. 387, 421, 428, 458, and **464** string quartets—the rest of the "Haydn Quartets"

K. 516 Quintet in G Minor

Symphonies

K. 201 in A Major

K. 319 in B-flat Major

K. 385 in D Major ("Haffner") (derived from the "Haffner" Serenade, K. 250)

K. 543 in E-flat (the first of the "final three" written in 1788)

K. 550 in G Minor (the second of the "final three")

Piano Concertos

K. 175 (he took this with him on the Mannheim-Paris trip, and played it numerous times)

K. 271 (his breakthrough concerto and one of his most innovative works in any genre)

K. 365 (for two pianos)

K. 466 (Beethoven's favorite, along with K. 491)

K. 488 (with a poignantly lovely slow movement)

K. 503

Woodwind Concertos

K. 191 for bassoon

K. 412, 417, 447, and **495** for [natural] horn

K. 622 for clarinet (actually, for basset clarinet, an invention of Anton Stadler's)

Small-Ensemble Music

K. 478 Piano Quartet in G Minor

K. 493 Piano Quartet in E-flat Major

K. 498 Trio in E-flat Major for Clarinet, Viola, and Piano ("Kegelstatt")

Piano Music

K. 330/300h Sonata in C Major

K. 331/300i Sonata in A Major (ending with the famous "Rondo alla turca")

K. 457 Sonata in C Minor

K. 533 Sonata in F Major

K. 545 Sonata in C Major, "for beginners"

K. 475 Fantasia in C minor

Church Music

K. 165/158a *Exsultate, jubilate* (motet for soprano [originally, castrato] and orchestra)

K. 339 *Vesperae solennes de confessore*

K. 618 *Ave verum corpus*

Masonic Music

K. 471 *Die Mauerfreude,* cantata

K. 477 Masonic Funeral Music

K. 623 Masonic Cantata, *Laut verkünde unsre Freude* (which Mozart conducted at his last performance)

Operas

K. 366 *Idomeneo*

K. 384 *Die Entführung aus dem Serail* (The Abduction from the Seraglio)

K. 588 *Così fan tutte* (That's How Women Act)

NOTES FOR MUSICAL BEGINNERS

A PRIMER OF BASIC TERMS AND CONCEPTS

Mozart: An Introduction encourages you to listen to music thoughtfully—consciously and deliberately. This does not require that you be able to read music; but if you would like to acquire that skill, you can find interactive resources on the Web. The goal of these notes is simply to introduce key terms and concepts, which are also defined in the glossary.

Here are four ways to describe a musical sound:

1. By its location in audible space—its *pitch*
2. By its speed and patterns of accent—its *meter, rhythm,* and *tempo*
3. By how loud or soft it is—its *dynamics*
4. By its unique quality or character—its *tone color* or *timbre*

1. Pitch

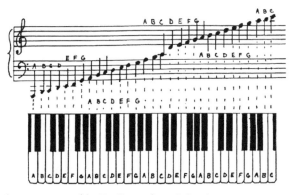

Notes have letter names (A, B, C, etc.) and further terms to specify exactly which *pitch*— which particular A, B, or C—you're referring to. Look at the keyboard, above. *Higher* pitches are those that move to the right ("up" the keyboard), *lower* pitches, to the left. Any D sounds higher than the C on its left. The famous Middle C is the C nearest the middle of the keyboard.

Clefs and Registers

If you follow the tracer lines from the notes on the keyboard to the notes directly above, you'll see that the lines converge at middle C. To its left are the notes of the *bass clef,* indicated by the bass clef logo, or sign, at the extreme left. To its right (i.e., moving higher in pitch) are the notes of the *treble clef,* with its clef sign at the extreme (top) left.

Treble instruments and voices perform in the upper *register*—violins, trumpets, flutes, oboes, clarinets, women, children—and men singing *falsetto* (by using their "head" voice, as does, say, Mandy Patinkin).

Bass-register notes are for men (singing in their regular, "chest" voice), cellos and double basses, bassoons, and bass-register brass instruments including the lowest, the tuba.

Half-Steps

Now look at the keyboard's pattern of *white notes* and *black notes.* Black notes are grouped in twos and threes. There are two places where no black notes appear: between every B and C and every E and F.

From E to F, from B to C, and from a white note to its adjacent
black note = one *half-step.* In addition,
From G to the black note either to its right or to its left
= one half-step.
From C to the white note to its left or the black note on its right
= one half-step.

Whole Steps

From C to the D on its right = two half-steps = a *whole step.*
From B to the black note on the right of C = two half-steps
= a *whole step.*

Sharps and Flats

A note that is one half-step higher than the note next to it is called a *sharp.* The black note to the right of C is C-sharp. A pitch one half-step lower is called a *flat.* The black note to the left of A is A-flat.

However: while the black note to the right of C is (in its relation to C) C-sharp (it *raises* C by a half-step), the same note in its relation to D is D-flat (it *lowers* D by a half-step.) So what you see on the keyboard can sometimes be called by different names, depending upon its function.

ACCIDENTALS

Sharps and flats are called *accidentals*. (We're skipping a third sign called the *natural*.) A sharp is written as a symbol similar to a superscript number sign: C$^\sharp$. Or you can simply write "C-sharp." A flat is written as a symbol similar to a superscript "b": A$^\flat$. Or you can simply write "A-flat."

SCALES: MAJOR AND MINOR

There are two kinds of scales you encounter most of the time: *major* and *minor*. A major scale is composed of eight successive notes, inclusively, such as from C to C:

C	D	E	F	G	A	B	C
1	2	3	4	5	6	7	8

Looking at the keyboard, you see that this scale is composed of whole-steps, except between steps 3 and 4, and between 7 and 8, which are half-steps:

1	2	3	4	5	6	7	8
		½				½	

The major scale built on C is the model for all major scales. This means that you can build a major scale starting on any note as long as you maintain the same pattern used here: whole-steps everywhere except for half-steps between 3 and 4, and between 7 and 8.

Starting on a note other than C will mean using one or more accidentals. If you start on G, you will need to sharp the F to form the half-step from 7 to 8:

G	A	B	C	D	E	F$^\sharp$	G
1	2	3	4	5	6	7	8
		½				½	

You can also start on a black note (or on any note at all). Beginning on E-flat:

E$^\flat$	F	G	A$^\flat$	B$^\flat$	C	D	E$^\flat$
1	2	3	4	5	6	7	8
		½				½	

Minor scale: There are several kinds of these. Most useful is the *harmonic minor scale.* This is composed of whole-steps except between 2 and 3, 5 and 6, and 7 and 8.

1	2	3	4	5	6	7	8
	½			½		½	

Because of its half-steps in such un-major-key locations, the harmonic minor has a very different feel from the major scale. (Not only that, but you'll observe that this scale requires a huge leap of 1 1/2 steps between 6 and 7 because 7 is "sharped"—raised by a half step.)

If you are not sure that you can hear the difference between minor and major, try this. Sing the first three notes of "The Star-Spangled Banner" ("Oh-oh say"). The notes go down a major scale from step 5 to step 3 to step 1. Sing them again; now, sing up the scale: 1-2-3-4-5. If you sing step 3 a half-step *lower* (making the scale minor), it sounds wrong because "The Star-Spangled Banner" is written in a major key. If you can hear this difference, you're in good shape. Practice it until it becomes aural habit.

A harmonic minor scale beginning on C looks like this:

C	D	E♭	F	G	A♭	B	C
	½			½		½	

INTERVALS

A musical interval is the distance between two notes, inclusively. From C up to E is a *third;* from C up to G is a *fifth;* from C to the next C, an *octave* (= 8 notes).

CHORDS

A *chord* is a group of notes *derived from a scale* and *played simultaneously.* The notes—there must be at least three of them—employ alternate steps in the scale, such as

C–E–G = a C-major chord, with C as its root, or tonic.
C–E♭–G = a C-minor chord, with C as its root, or tonic.

KEYS

A *key* consists of all the notes in a particular scale, plus the chords that can be built using each scale step as a *root.* The key of C major = the seven notes of its scale (omit the second C, because it duplicates the first), plus the chords built on each successive note of the scale:

	G	A	B	C	D	E	F
	E	F	G	A	B	C	D
Roots:	C	D	E	F	G	A	B

Relative Minor and Relative Major Keys

Every major key has a *related minor key,* and vice versa. Keys are related if they require the same accidentals to form their respective scales. This cluster of required accidentals—say, two flats or three sharps—is a particular key's *key signature.* Minor and major keys with identical key signatures are "relatives" of each other.

G major requires one sharp. The minor key that requires one sharp (and only one) is E minor. This makes E minor the *relative minor* of G major, and G major the *relative major* of E minor. The significance of this relationship is twofold: it's easy to *modulate* between the two keys—that is, to change from one to the other—and they "relate" to one another as sunshine (major) relates to clouds (minor).

2. Duration

Duration is described in three ways: as *meter, rhythm,* and *tempo.*

Meter

Meter is the "beat"—the one-two-three, and so on, of a conductor's baton. Meter is notated in *measures* (also called *bars*), separated into equal-size units by vertical bar lines. Basically, meter can be *duple* (occurring in groups of two beats, or multiples of two, such as four or eight), *triple* (in groups of three beats), or *compound* (in groups whose total number of beats is divisible by three, such as six, nine, or twelve. Often, however, compound meter can also be perceived as duple: six and twelve are also divisible by two).

Dance music is often in triple or compound meter. Marches need to be duple, because we have but two feet. An aria (song), concerto movement, or movement of a symphony can jump suddenly from one meter to another. Listen for this—there's always a very good reason for it, of course, and the unexpected switch can be exciting.

Note values

Duple Meters	Triple Meters
○ whole note	○. (= ○ + ◽)
◽ half note	◽. (= ◽ + ◽)
♩ quarter note	♩. (= ♩ + ♪)
♪ eighth note	♪. (= ♪ + ♪)
♬ sixteenth note	♬. (= ♬ + ♬)
thirty-second note	(= +)

♫ = ♪♪   ♫ = ♪♪ (etc.)

RHYTHM

Rhythm refers to the patterns of accent (bebop—beboppitybop) played or sung against, yet in synch with a steady, unrelenting beat—which is the meter. If you tap out a duple meter—say, 1-2-3-4, 1-2-3-4, and so on, always exactly the same, no faster, no slower—you're providing the beat. Now, with the other hand (or foot, or pencil), be a jazz drummer: tap out *irregular* patterns *against* that unvarying beat, without violating its boundaries. That's rhythm, and rhythm is the soul of music. Your other hand is, relatively speaking, a clock.

TEMPO

Tempo means rate of speed—how fast or slow the conductor's beat is. The conventional terminology is Italian, and it's all related to how we walk:

largo	lento	adagio	andante	moderato	allegro	presto	prestissimo
very slow walking pace			moderate walking pace		quick	very quick pace	

3. DYNAMICS

Dynamics refers to *volume*—how loud or soft the music is. The degrees of volume are conventionally defined by Italian words. Here are the most frequently used terms, with the softest to the left and the loudest to the right. Below each term is its customary abbreviation:

pianissimo	piano	mezzo piano	mezzo forte	forte	fortissimo
(pp)	(p)	(mp)	(mf)	(f)	(ff)
← ———— softer ———————————— louder —————————— →					

To *increase* the volume gradually, composers write the word *crescendo* (Italian, "increasing," abbreviation: *cresc.*) at the appropriate point in the music. To *decrease* the volume, they write *decrescendo* (Italian, "decreasing," abbreviation: *decresc.*) or *diminuendo* (Italian, "diminishing," abbreviation: *dim.*).

4. TIMBRE OR TONE COLOR

Timbre (French; pronounced "tamber") or *tone color* (the two terms are used interchangeably) is the characteristic quality or personality of a tone—the special sound of a cat meowing, a bird warbling, a saxophone crooning, a tuba bellowing. Every instrument in the orchestra possesses its own unique tone color. People's voices do, too. Notice how quickly you recognize a friend's voice over the phone? That's timbre.

GLOSSARY OF MUSICAL TERMS

action ensemble

A group of solo singers, one singer to a part, each not only performing his or her music but at the same time acting and interacting with others in the ensemble. Perfected by Mozart and Lorenzo da Ponte in *The Marriage of Figaro* and used in all subsequent Mozart operas.

adagio

Very slow tempo. *See also* **tempo.**

allegretto

Not quite as fast as **allegro.**

allegro

The word means "gay"—by extension, fast.

andante

Moderate tempo; a strolling walk. *See also* **tempo.**

andantino

A bit slower than **andante.**

arco

"Arc"—i.e., bow. Tells a string player to play with the bow rather than to pluck the string (the word for plucking is **pizzicato**).

aria

"Air"—i.e., a song—a formal, structured song in a format such as ABA, ABAB, etc.

arpeggio

Arpa means harp, so an **arpeggio** is a **chord** played harp-style: one note at a time, either upward or downward.

baritone

Male voice range between tenor (e.g., Pavarotti) and bass (the lowest male voice; fairly rare).

bass

The lowest male voice. Note the spelling: no e as in baseball.

beat

What the conductor "beats": one, two, three, four. "One" is the downbeat, the strongest beat. **Beat** is more or less synonymous with **meter**—the fundamental, underlying rhythmic pulse; this is what you move your feet to when you dance. *See* **meter** in Notes for Musical Beginners.

cadence

A melodic or harmonic series of events leading to a sense that a melody or a larger section of the music is coming to an end. When you sing Amen, you're singing a cadence.

cadenza

A showy passage by a soloist (vocal or instrumental) at a key point in a piece, just before the end. Normally, there is no orchestral accompaniment—the soloist gets to shine alone.

cantabile

"Singingly." Play this as if you were singing it—i.e., smoothly.

chamber music

Music for a group of instruments, intended (in Mozart's day) to be played indoors in a "chamber" rather than in a church or an opera house. **Symphonies** and **concertos** were considered chamber music then—until orchestras grew larger. Today, the term refers to small ensembles only.

chord

Simultaneous playing of three or more pitches related to a given key or scale. **Chord:** notes played at the same time. **Melody:** notes played one after the other. *See* **chord** in Notes for Musical Beginners.

chromatic

The word means "colored." A normal scale (do–re–mi, etc.) is **diatonic.** If you play a "wrong" note—one that doesn't belong to that scale—you're playing a **chromatic** note. This is not a mistake, but a means to greater intensity of expression. Generally, such notes are half-steps (accidentals)—G-sharp, say, instead of G. A **chromatic scale** consists entirely of half-steps.

clavier

Eighteenth-century generic term for keyboard instruments, particularly the early piano (**fortepiano**) or the **harpsichord,** which the fortepiano replaced during the second half of the century.

coda

The word means "tail." The coda occurs at the end of a piece or a movement.

concerto

Orchestral composition for one or more soloists (usually, one) and orchestra. Generally has three movements: fast, slow, fast. The first movement is usually in **concerto first-movement form.** *See* below. Examples include the Violin Concerto in G Major, K. 216; Piano Concerto in C Minor, K. 491; Piano Concerto in E-flat Major, K. 482; and Sinfonia concertante, K. 364/320d.

concerto first-movement form

The musical design evolved, chiefly by Mozart, for the first movement of concertos. It combined elements of the older [Baroque] concerto format (alternating sections for orchestra with sections for the soloist) with **sonata form,** the design preferred by composers of Mozart's era.

contrapuntal

Adjective form of **counterpoint.** Note that the noun's u drops out for the adjective.

counterpoint

Roughly synonymous with **polyphony.** Two or more melodies played *simultaneously*; this is not a melody with an accompaniment (you plus guitar chords), but two or more melodies (you and your guitar, or you, a guitar, and a friend, singing or playing concurrently two or three different *tunes*). Counterpoint creates dramatic tension; it is also beautiful. No other art but music can express several different ideas at the same time without risking chaos.

coup d'archet

French for "stroke of the [stringed-instrument] bow." This was a fashionable musical gesture in Mannheim and Paris during the late 1770s, which Mozart used to great effect in the opening movement of his "Paris" Symphony, K. 297/300a. It requires all the strings—or all the violins—to play the same notes together, rushing very fast up the scale.

crescendo

The word means "increasing." A gradual increase in volume. *See* **crescendo** in Notes for Musical Beginners.

dance form
The form (i.e., musical design) used for any sort of dance, e.g., the **minuet.**

decrescendo
The word means "decreasing." A gradual decrease in volume. *See* **decrescendo** in Notes for Musical Beginners.

dynamics
The controlling of volume—i.e., of loud (*forte*) and soft (*piano*). *See* **dynamics** in Notes for Musical Beginners.

ensemble
A vocal or instrumental group in which there is only one singer (or player) to a part—as opposed to a chorus (of many singers performing each part) or an orchestra. *See also* **action ensemble.**

fugue
A lengthy and complex form of imitative **polyphony** (imitative **counterpoint**) in which a composition, or a portion of a composition, is devoted to polyphonic imitation of a single melody (called a *subject* rather than a *theme*). In Mozart's day, fugues were chiefly associated with church music, particularly by composers of a bygone day, such as Handel or J. S. Bach. A **double fugue** is a fugue employing not just one, but two melodies in imitation.

galant
French word used internationally in the eighteenth century, always in French, to denote light, simple, airy, easy-listening music designed for amateur playing and/or listening. Divertimentos have a lot of **galant** music. The second theme (**B**) in the opening movement of the "Little" G-minor Symphony, K. 183/173dB is **galant** in style—in contrast to its agitated Sturm und Drang first theme (**A**).

genre
A category of composition. Symphonies, concertos, operas, piano sonatas are all **genres.**

gesture
Not really a musical term, though musicians use it as if it were. Hearing music as a series of **gestures** can be both enriching and clarifying. As you listen, think of whether a particular section or subsection of a piece seems to embody or express the **gesture(s)** of a dance (a minuet perhaps, and if so, what kind—gentle, frolicsome, thrashing?), a march, a love song, a sigh (**sospiro**), throwing down the gauntlet to incite a duel, strolling through a garden, etc. This is not making the music tell a story, but simply noticing that particular rhythms, harmony, and melody—sometimes also the choice of instruments—can choreograph, suggest, or evoke certain human gestures. Mozart's music does this constantly, so always listen for it. Wye J. Allanbrook's excellent book on this topic is listed in the annotated bibliography. *See also* **pastoral,** which is one type of gesture.

grazioso
The word means "gracefully."

harmony
A sequence of **chords** that creates the underlying musical structure of a composition.

harpsichord
The **keyboard** instrument of choice until it was replaced by the **fortepiano** during the late eighteenth century. Mozart played the harpsichord and clavichord as a child, but grew up with the fortepiano as it gradually gained prominence, a process in which he played a significant role.

homophony
One of music's two main textures. Consists of a line of melody plus its

underlying accompaniment. Songs are generally **homophonic.** The other type of texture is **polyphony (counterpoint).**

imitation

The copycatting of a melody (tune) in other parts of a composition; repeating it note for note (either exactly or more or less), generally beginning on a different pitch (note) each time. Example with identical pitches each time: "Row, row your boat." **Imitation** creates **polyphony.** *See* **counterpoint** and **polyphony.**

improvise

To perform music (vocal or instrumental) spontaneously, without looking at any music or with only rudimentary cues of some kind. Jazz musicians do this. In the eighteenth century improvisation was commonplace—expected of all musicians. The **cadenza** in a concerto movement was improvised. Improvisation, however, was (and is today) performed within a given formal framework; otherwise the other players in the ensemble or orchestra won't know when to come in.

interval

The distance between two musical notes, inclusively. From C up to G is a fifth; from C to the next C (either up or down), an octave. *See* **interval** in Notes for Musical Beginners.

key

Two meanings. First, a piano or clarinet or oboe has keys. Second, the notes of a scale plus the chords built on each note make up a given **key.** C major = C, D, E, F, G, A, B plus the chords built atop each of these notes. *See* **key** in Notes for Musical Beginners and **tonality** in this glossary.

larghetto

Not quite as slow as **largo,** maybe with a little lilt to it.

largo

Very slow tempo. *See also* **tempo.**

legato

The word means "connected" or "tied together." To play or sing **legato** is to play or sing very smoothly, with little or no discernible break from one note to the next. The opposite of **staccato.**

lento

Extremely slow tempo. *See also* **tempo.**

libretto

The words—the script—of an opera, *Singspiel,* cantata, oratorio, etc.

major

A key is either **major** or **minor.** A **major** scale has half-steps between steps 3 and 4 and 7 and 8 (between *mi* and *fa* and *ti* and *do*). There are several different **minor** scales; most useful in this book is the "harmonic" minor, which has half-steps between steps 2 and 3, 5 and 6, and 7 and 8. *See* **major scale** and **minor scale** in Notes for Musical Beginners.

ma non troppo

"But not too much." The marking "Adagio **ma non troppo**" means "slow, but not too slow."

melisma

A long run of notes—ten, fifteen, even more—set to a single syllable of text to intensify the meaning or emotional strength of a particular word. Adjective: **melismatic.** By contrast, providing each syllable with just one note (more or less) of music means to set them **syllabically.**

meter

The underlying, fundamental pulse of a piece is indicated by its **meter.** This corresponds to the **beat** you feel in your feet when you dance and which you observe in the up and down motions of a conductor's baton. **Meter** is generally in groups of two (duple meter), three (triple meter), or multiples of these—four, six, etc. Meters divisible by three are **compound meters**—for example, six, nine, or twelve. *See* **meter** in Notes for Musical Beginners.

mezzo-soprano

A woman's vocal range between soprano (the highest voice) and contralto (the lowest). **Mezzo** means "middle." **Mezzos** (as they are called) have voices of slightly heavier quality than sopranos.

minor

See **major.**

minuet

See **dance form.**

moderato

"Moderate" tempo: an easy walking gait. *See* **tempo** in Notes for Musical Beginners.

modulate, modulation

Literally, to change "modes," from minor mode to major mode; but the terms are routinely used to describe any change of key.

motif, motive

The opening of Beethoven's Fifth Symphony—*da-da-da-dum*—is a **motif,** out of which Beethoven molds a much longer theme. A **motif** is the kernel or seed of a theme.

movement

A large, (usually) self-contained section of a piece. For example, symphonies generally comprise four **movements.** On a CD, these are four different tracks.

mute

A device to soften the sound of an instrument; it also alters its tone. The Italian direction to the musician is to play **con sordino.**

octave

Eight notes inclusively up or down from a given note: C up (or down) to the next C.

orchestration

A composer's selective assigning of the orchestra's instruments, using each to its maximum effectiveness. Deciding, for example, to have a flute play this passage and an oboe that one, followed, say, by a passage for **tutti** (the whole orchestra).

ornament

One or more notes added as decoration to a single pitch. Example: a **trill** (alternating quickly between two pitches).

pastoral

Commonly used as both noun and adjective. The root of the word is **pastor,** "shepherd." The pastoral world isn't on any map except the one in your heart. It's a utopia—in Judeo-Christian terms, a Garden of Eden or the Kingdom of Heaven; in pagan terms, Arcadia. We dream of it and somehow seem to remember it. The sun always shines, the grass is green, there's no work, suffering, war, or death; we play, loll on the grass, sing and make merry. No one is servant or master; all are equal. There are evocations of it in Genesis and in the pastoral poetry of Greek and Roman antiquity and the Renaissance. The **pastoral** in music dates from Renaissance madrigals. There is both happy, innocent (major-key, up-tempo) pastoral and melancholy, mournful (minor-key, slower tempo) pastoral. Musically, the pastoral of *both* types features some or all of these characteristics:

- languid tempo (*andante, allegretto, larghetto*); not too slow
- very simple harmonies
- no counterpoint
- simple, often circular-sounding melody

• often a drone (a low, sustained note in the bass) to simulate a village bagpipe

Employing some or most of these **gestures** conveys innocence, simplicity, and peace. The **pastoral** acquired special importance in Mozart's music during his Viennese years (1781–1791).

pedal point
Technique borrowed from organ playing, where "pedal" notes are played by the feet. In orchestral music, a **pedal point** (usually in the bass register) sustains a single note for a long time against dissonant-sounding harmonies above. The harmonies resolve toward the note played in the pedal.

pizzicato
Plucked rather than bowed; a term used in stringed-instrument playing.

poco
The word means "little" or "a bit." **Poco adagio** means "a bit slow." **Poco a poco** means "bit by bit."

polyphony
Same as **counterpoint.**

presto
Very fast tempo. *See* **tempo** in Notes for Musical Beginners.

recitative
"Speaking" style, rather than singing. Recitatives are found in all types of dramatic music—opera, oratorio, cantata. There were several kinds of recitative in the eighteenth century. **Recitativo semplice** (simple recitative; sometimes called **secco,** "dry"), used for narration or conversation, is the least melodic and has a very spare accompaniment, a keyboard instrument plus some bass-register instrument such as bassoon or cello (note: *bass*-register: *not* a violin, flute,

trumpet, etc.). **Recitativo accompagnato** or **stromentato** (accompanied or orchestral recitative) is used for more emotional scenes, is more melodic, and employs more instruments, perhaps the whole orchestra. *See also* **aria.**

ritornello
An orchestral refrain—orchestral music that recurs throughout a composition to provide structural unity. Used, for instance, to describe the instrumental introduction and interludes of an aria. **Ritorno** is Italian for "return"; a **ritornello** is a brief return.

rondo
A form employing the regular return of a main **rondo** theme (called either R or A) in alternation with other, non-**rondo** sections called "episodes." Example: ABACA (or RERER). *See* the finale of Mozart's Violin Concerto in G major, K. 216, for a diagram of **rondo form.**

rondò aria
A two-section aria, the first section (ABA) slow, the second (CC) fast. In a rondò aria a singer showcased the ability to excel at both slow, expressive melodies and quick, ornamented runs. Mozart wrote very few such arias, always for a principal character at a dramatic turning point; e.g., the Countess's "Dove sono" in Act III of *The Marriage of Figaro* and Donna Anna's "Non mi dir" in Act II of *Don Giovanni.* The vocal rondò should not be confused with the instrumental **rondo.**

rubato
The word means "robbed." **Tempo rubato** refers to the practice of temporarily slowing down the juicy part of a melody (on a piano, this is usually played by the right hand). What Mozart was careful to avoid was allowing

that to slow down the left hand as well. The left hand (the accompaniment) must keep its beat steady while the right hand holds back a little bit to give its melody more espressivo. In vocal music, the singer is the "right hand" and the accompanying instrument or instruments the "left hand."

scordatura

Tuning a stringed instrument in an unusual manner in order to achieve a special sound. Mozart asks the violist to do this in the Sinfonia concertante in E-flat major for violin and viola, K. 364/320d, so that the naturally dusky-sounding viola won't be upstaged by the brighter-sounding violin.

scrittura

Italian word for a contract to compose an opera, usually for the following season.

secular music

Music is either **sacred** (intended for performance in a religious service) or **secular** (for "the world," i.e., nonreligious).

sentimental, sentimentality

A concept that originated in England with Laurence Sterne's novels *Tristram Shandy* (1760) and *A Sentimental Journey* (1768). Sterne defined the word, *not* as gooey overemoting (which it has come to mean today), but as a delicate, finely tuned sense of compassion and empathy that is innate in all of us, but must be nurtured and developed. A purely **rational** person might say, when passing a beggar on a street corner, "The government will take care of that," or "He'll just spend it all on whiskey." A **sentimental** person will stop, engage the beggar in conversation, hear his or her story, and offer to help. Although the Count in *The Marriage of Figaro*

regards himself as the only rational person in the house (demonstrating either that he isn't very rational or that reason isn't all one needs), the Countess responds **sentimentally** to his plea for forgiveness at the end of Act IV. An example of a **sentimental** aria (it's also a **pastoral** lament) is Barbarina's "L'hò perduta" in Act IV, Scene 1. Mozart also wrote a lot of instrumental music in this style, e.g., the Adagio of the Serenade for Thirteen Instruments, K. 361/370a. The German word for **sentimental** is *empfindsam.*

Singspiel

A **genre** that evolved during Mozart's lifetime: opera with spoken dialogue rather than **recitatives,** and in German. Mozart's *The Abduction from the Seraglio* and *The Magic Flute* are *Singspiels.*

sonata form

The most significant and widely used musical design from ca. 1750 through much of the twentieth century and beyond. It evolved ca. 1740–1760, pioneered by various composers, firmly established by Joseph Haydn in his symphonies and string quartets, then adopted by all European composers.

sordino

To play an instrument *con sordino* is to play with a mute. *See* **mute.**

sospiro

"Sigh." A musical **gesture** mimicking a human sigh by employing two descending notes followed by a rest, then two more descending notes, and so on. A poignant example occurs in the instrumental accompaniment in the "Lacrimosa" of Mozart's Requiem.

staccato

Opposite of **legato.** To play a piece with each note detached from the next, rather than connected, as in **legato.**

syllabic

In contrast to a **melismatic** setting of music to words, in a **syllabic** setting there is one syllable per note, more or less. *See* **melisma.**

tempo

The speed of the **beat.** Terms such as **allegro, presto,** and **andante** are indications of **tempo.** *See* **tempo** in Notes for Musical Beginners.

tempo rubato

See **rubato.**

texture

The weaving together of musical lines in a piece. *See* **homophony** and **polyphony.**

theme

A melodic, rhythmic, or harmonic idea of chief importance in a composition. A theme normally comprises subsections, in analogy to a sentence or paragraph. Themes are almost always repeated, to establish their importance.

theme and variations

See **variation form.**

timbre

The distinctive quality of a sound that makes it recognizable—the sound of a flute vs. that of a trumpet. Your aunt's voice vs. your significant other's. *See* **timbre (tone color)** in Notes for Musical Beginners.

tonality

See **key.** These two terms are nearly synonymous, but **tonality** refers not only to a given **key** (say, C major) but also to its family of closely related keys (including G major, F major, A minor). The whole package forms the **tonality** of C major.

tone color

See **timbre.**

trill

A type of musical **ornament.** The extremely rapid alternation of two adjacent notes, such as C–B–C–B–C–B–C–B . . .

tutti

The word means "all, everybody." Refers to the whole orchestra as opposed to an instrumental soloist or soloists; or, in choral music, to the chorus and/or orchestra as opposed to the vocal soloists.

unison

The word means "one sound." Everybody playing and/or singing the same pitch (note).

variation form

Consists of a **theme** (generally comprising two short sections, each repeated: **aabb**) followed by any number of **variations** on that theme. Each variation is expected to (and usually does) follow the format of the theme itself (**aabb**). Mozart's Piano Variations, K. 265/300e; the second movement of the Piano Concerto in E-flat Major, K. 482; and the final movements of the Piano Concerto in C minor, K. 491, and the Clarinet Quintet, K. 581, are examples.

vibrato

The word means "vibrated." Rapid fluctuation of pitch to create a more resonating, expressive tone. On stringed instruments, this is accomplished by moving the appropriate finger of the left hand back-and-forth on the string, causing the string to vibrate.

virtuoso

An exceptionally skilled and brilliant performer whose abilities far exceed those of someone very talented, even if that person has been well trained.

SELECT ANNOTATED BIBLIOGRAPHY

Mozart Web Sites
Web sites for classical music, which are often maintained by amateurs, tend to be unreliable. You can trust the information you find at these three sites:

www.AproposMozart.com. A cornucopia of articles related to Mozart, collected and posted by Bruce Cooper Clarke, whose name appears in numerous footnotes in this book. Many of the articles have been translated by Clarke.

www.GroveMusic.com. Online version of *The New Grove II* (see below), a comprehensive musical encyclopedia that also contains articles headed "Mozart," "Opera," "Symphony," "Fortepiano," "Salzburg," and so on, as well as articles about particular compositions (*Don Giovanni*, "Jupiter" Symphony, etc.).

www.MozartSocietyofAmerica.org. The Web site of the Mozart Society of America includes links to all important Mozart Web sites, recent editions of the society's newsletter, and announcements of interest to Mozart aficionados both amateur and professional.

General Reference Works
The New Grove Dictionary of Music and Musicians. London: Macmillan, 1980. (20 vols.) A comprehensive encyclopedia covering musical topics from A to Z, with extended articles on each member of the Mozart family. Each essay includes a list of compositions (where applicable) and a bibliography.

The New Grove Dictionary of Music and Musicians. New York: Grove's Dictionaries, 2001. (29 vols.), 2nd ed. Often informally called *New Grove II*, this is an expanded and updated version of the *New Grove Dictionary*, with more emphasis than its predecessor on world music, rock, blues, country, and pop. It is often useful to compare entries here with those in the first edition. This second edition is also available online (to subscribers; most academic institutions belong), as noted above under GroveMusic.com above.

The New Harvard Dictionary of Music, ed. Don Michael Randel. Cambridge, MA:

Belknap Press, 1999. Contains brief definitions of all important musical terms; includes shorthand histories of terms such as *symphony, opera,* and *orchestra.*

The Norton-Grove Concise Encyclopedia of Music, ed. Stanley Sadie. New York: W. W. Norton, 1988. A handy one-volume dictionary/encyclopedia.

INDIVIDUAL TITLES
Except for the collected edition of Mozart letters in the original German, this section includes only books, written in English.

Allanbrook, Wye Jamison. *Rhythmic Gesture in Mozart: Le nozze di Figaro & Don Giovanni.* Chicago & London: University of Chicago Press, 1983. The path-breaking book on Mozart's music as "gesture," with scene-by-scene analysis of these two operas.

Anderson, Emily, ed. and trans. *The Letters of Mozart and His Family.* 2 vols. New York: W. W. Norton, 1985. This 1937 translation of many (not all) of the family letters is still very valuable, containing far more letters than either Spaethling or Eisen-Spencer.

Bauer, Wilhelm A., Otto Erich Deutsch, and Joseph Heinz Eibl, eds. *Mozart Briefe und Aufzeichnungen.* Kassel: Gesamtausgabe, hrsg. von der Internationalen Stiftung Mozarteum Salzburg. 7 vols., 1962–1975. The letters of Mozart and his family in German, with original spellings and punctuation.

Branscombe, Peter. *W. A. Mozart: Die Zauberflöte* [The Magic Flute]. Cambridge: Cambridge University Press, 1991. One of the Cambridge Handbooks, a series of volumes on individual operas edited by an expert on that particular opera and containing essays on a variety of topics including libretto, musical style, first performances, and so on.

Braunbehrens, Volkmar. *Mozart in Vienna, 1781–1791.* Trans. Timothy Bell. New York: Grove Weidenfeld, 1990. Indispensable and richly detailed, but the English version is still out of print.

Cairns, David. *Mozart and His Operas.* Berkeley: University of California Press, 2006. A very fine book, elegantly written, rich with insights, musical analyses, and historical research.

Carter, Tim. *W. A. Mozart: Le nozze di Figaro.* Cambridge: Cambridge University Press, 1987. One of the Cambridge Handbooks, a series of volumes on individual operas edited by an expert on that particular opera and containing essays on a variety of topics including libretto, musical style, first performances, and so on.

Clarke, Bruce Cooper. *The Annotated Schlichtegroll: Wolfgang Mozart's Obituary, with Critical, Historical, and Explanatory Notes.* St. Anton a. d. Jessnitz, Austria: [private publication], 1997. A detailed, line-by-line analysis of this first biography/obituary of the composer.

Da Ponte, Lorenzo. *Memoirs of Lorenzo da Ponte.* Trans. Elisabeth Abbott, ed. Arthur Livingston. Philadelphia and London: J. B. Lippincott, 1929. A wonderful and richly informative read, though da Ponte often rearranges facts to make his story more colorful.

Deutsch, Otto Erich. *Mozart: A Documentary Biography.* Trans. Eric Blom, Peter Branscombe, and Jeremy Noble. 2nd ed. Stanford: Stanford University Press, 1966. An indispensable collection of reviews, quotations from the diaries of contemporaries, letters, and so on, arranged chronologically. Supplemented and updated by Cliff Eisen's 1991 publication listed below.

Einstein, Alfred. *Mozart: His Character, His Work.* New York & London: Oxford University Press, 1945. A breakthrough biography by the world's top Mozart scholar at that time, this book is now seriously out of date though still very useful when supplemented with more recent studies. Einstein, a refugee from Hitler's Germany, wrote the book without any notes because he had left them behind in Europe, so there are no footnotes.

Eisen, Cliff. *New Mozart Documents: A Supplement to Otto Erich Deutsch's Documentary Biography.* Stanford, CA: Stanford University Press, 1991. Additions to Deutsch's compilation of decades earlier (see above).

Eisen, Cliff, and Simon P. Keefe, eds. *The Cambridge Mozart Encyclopedia.* Cambridge: Cambridge University Press, 2006. An extensive collection of Mozart-related articles by various authors on topics ranging from "Salzburg," "Freemasonry," "Köchel," and "Vienna" to "symphonies," "chamber music," and "concertos."

Eisen, Cliff, and Stanley Sadie. *The New Grove Mozart.* New York: Palgrave, 2002. A revision and updating of Sadie's *The New Grove Mozart* published in 1983 (see below), this is a separately bound edition of Eisen and Sadie's entry for Mozart in the 2001 *New Grove Dictionary of Music and Musicians.*

Eisen, Cliff, ed., and Stephen Spencer, trans. *Wolfgang Amadeus Mozart: A Life in Letters.* London: Penguin Books, 2006. English translations of 600 letters, with emphasis on those by Leopold Mozart, which in Anderson's translation were sometimes abbreviated. Helpful footnotes. Includes a chronology, list of important people, and a listing of Mozart's compositions.

Glover, Jane. *Mozart's Women: His Family, His Friends, His Music.* London: Macmillan, 2005. An engagingly written, lively biography by an outstanding conductor of Mozart's music.

Halliwell, Ruth. *The Mozart Family: Four Lives in a Social Context.* New York: Oxford University Press, 1998. A sociological study of the conflicting issues and agendas of members of the Mozart family.

Heartz, Daniel. *Mozart's Operas.* Berkeley: University of California Press, 1990. An excellent collection of essays on various aspects of several Mozart operas.

Hunter, Mary. *Mozart's Operas: A Companion.* New Haven, CT: Yale University Press, 2008. A thorough treatment of *all* the operas, not just the famous ones.

Keefe, Simon P., ed. *The Cambridge Companion to Mozart.* Cambridge: Cambridge University Press, 2003. Articles by various scholars on topics ranging from "Mozart in Salzburg" to "The Keyboard Music," "Mozart's German Operas," and "Mozart and the Twentieth Century."

Kerman, Joseph. *Opera as Drama.* 2nd ed. Berkeley: University of California Press, 1988. Includes an excellent chapter on Mozart's operas.

Knepler, Georg. *Wolfgang Amadé Mozart.* Trans. J. Bradford Robinson. London and New York: Cambridge University Press, 1994. Knepler wrote this book mostly without the benefit of scholarship unavailable to East Germans until long after the collapse of the Berlin Wall in 1989. See especially the chapter called "A Turning Point," Knepler's interpretation of Mozart's journey to Mannheim and Paris.

Küster, Konrad. *Mozart: A Musical Biography.* Trans. Mary Whittall. New York: Oxford University Press, 1996. Musical, biographical, and cultural studies of key individual compositions, arranged in chronological order to form "a musical biography."

Landon, H. C. Robbins. *Mozart and Vienna.* New York: Schirmer Books, 1991. A highly readable survey of Mozart's experiences in Vienna as both child and adult; includes Pezzl's "Sketches."

Landon, H. C. Robbins, ed. *The Mozart Compendium.* New York: Schirmer Books, 1990. Similar to Zaslaw and Cowdery's *The Compleat Mozart* (see below), but more detailed.

Levin, Robert D. *Who Wrote the Mozart Four-Wind Concertante?* Stuyvesant, NY: Pendragon Press, 1988. Levin's detailed study of the missing K. 297b.

Morris, James T., ed. *On Mozart.* Cambridge: Cambridge University Press, 1994. Articles by a variety of experts on topics such as "How extraordinary was Mozart?" "On the economics of musical composition in Mozart's Vienna," and "Mozart as a working stiff."

Neumayr, Anton. *Music and Medicine.* Bloomington, IN: Medi-Ed Press, 1994.

Pianist, physician, and student of the medical practices of centuries ago, Neumayr is the major resource behind this book's section called "What Did He Die Of?"

Rice, John A. *Mozart on the Stage.* Cambridge: Cambridge University Press, 2009. Topical exploration of aspects related to Mozart's operas—composition, theater management, singers, staging, fees, commissions, and much else besides.

Rushton, Julian. *Mozart.* Oxford: Oxford University Press, 2006. A full life-and-works in 250 pages, therefore briskly paced; best read after you know a good deal about Mozart and his music and have had a course in elementary music theory.

Rushton, Julian. *W. A. Mozart: Don Giovanni.* Cambridge: Cambridge University Press, 1981. One of the Cambridge Handbooks, a series of volumes on individual operas edited by an expert on that particular opera and containing essays on a variety of topics including libretto, musical style, first performances, and so on.

Sadie, Stanley. *Mozart: The Early Years, 1756–1781.* New York: W.W. Norton, 2006. A 600-page life-and-works up to Mozart's move to Vienna. You need a general familiarity with Mozart and his music and some knowledge of musical terminology to read through this easily.

Sadie, Stanley. *The Mozart Symphonies.* London: Ariel, 1986. A comprehensive study of Mozart's symphonies.

Sadie, Stanley. *The New Grove Mozart.* New York: W. W. Norton, 1983. A separately bound edition of Sadie's article on Mozart for the 1978 *New Grove Dictionary of Music and Musicians.*

Sisman, Elaine R. *Mozart: The "Jupiter" Symphony.* Cambridge: Cambridge University Press, 1993. A brilliant, thorough, lucid study and analysis of Mozart's last symphony.

Solomon, Maynard. *Mozart: A Life.* New York: HarperCollins, 1995. Densely packed with information, some of it speculative, with insightful musical analyses; employs a Freudian approach.

Spaethling, Robert, ed. and trans. *Mozart's Letters, Mozart's Life.* New York: W. W. Norton, 2000. An idiomatic translation of 275 letters written by Mozart; none by others.

Stafford, William. *The Mozart Myths: A Critical Reassessment.* Stanford: Stanford University Press, 1991. A much-needed, thorough study of many of the myths.

Till, Nicholas. *Mozart and the Enlightenment: Truth, Virtue and Beauty in Mozart's Operas.* New York: W. W. Norton, 1992. Enlightenment themes in Mozart's operas.

Wolff, Christoph. *Mozart's Requiem: Historical and Analytical Studies, Documents, Score.* Berkeley: University of California Press, 1994. Thorough, clear, painstaking study of all aspects of this unfinished composition. Includes a facsimile of the manuscript.

Zaslaw, Neal, ed. *The Classical Era: From the 1740s to the End of the 18th Century.* Englewood Cliffs, NJ: Prentice-Hall, 1989. Essays include "Music and Society in the Classical Era," by Neal Zaslaw; "Maria Theresa's Vienna," by Bruce Alan Brown; "Vienna under Joseph II and Leopold II," by John A. Rice; and "The Mannheim Court," by Eugene K. Wolf.

Zaslaw, Neal. *Mozart's Symphonies: Content, Performance Practice, Reception.* Oxford and New York: Oxford University Press, 1989. A comprehensive treatment of Mozart's symphonies, one by one and in groups.

Zaslaw, Neal, and William Cowdery, eds. *The Compleat Mozart: A Guide to the Musical Works of Wolfgang Amadeus Mozart.* New York: W. W. Norton, 1990. Comparable to Landon's *Mozart Compendium* (see above), though more concise.

INDEX

Persons identified in "Important People in Mozart's Life" are not listed here as well unless their names appear in the body of the book. For individuals named "Mozart," familial relationships to Wolfgang Amadè Mozart are given in parentheses.